THE LOST SISTERHOOD

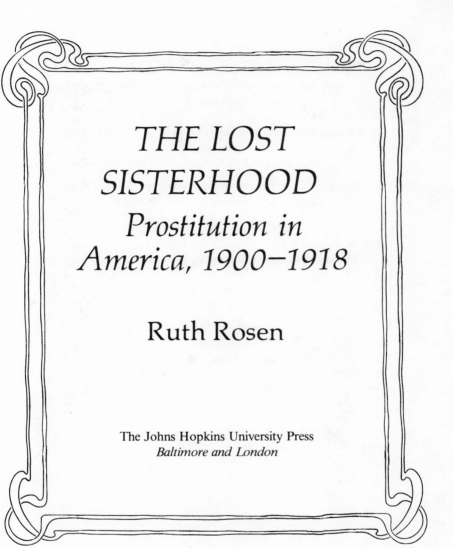

THE LOST
SISTERHOOD

Prostitution in
America, 1900–1918

Ruth Rosen

The Johns Hopkins University Press
Baltimore and London

This book has been brought to publication with the
generous assistance of the Andrew F. Mellon
Foundation.

The Johns Hopkins University Press, Baltimore, Maryland 21218
The Johns Hopkins Press Ltd., London

Library of Congress Cataloging in Publication Data

Rosen, Ruth.
The lost sisterhood.

Bibliography: p. 211
Includes index.
1. Prostitution—United States.   I. Title.
HQ144.R76   1982   306.7′4′0973   81–23678
ISBN 0–8018–2664–0   AACR2

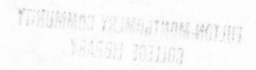

In Memory of My Mother

CONTENTS

ACKNOWLEDGMENTS

Throughout the many years that it took to complete this book, many people and institutions provided generous assistance, advice, and support that I would like to publicly acknowledge.

Research for this study was supported in part by a predoctoral training fellowship from the Social Science Research Council, a Humanities Fellowship from the Rockefeller Foundation, and a Junior Faculty Fellowship and numerous faculty research grants from the University of California at Davis.

My earliest intellectual debt is to those individuals who, by raising education to an art, inspired and encouraged me to pursue my intellectual concerns wherever they led. They are Loren Baritz, Natalie Davis, Arlie Hochschild, Pauline Bart, Reggie Zelnik, and Larry Levine.

I would also like to thank the following friends and colleagues who read all or part of the manuscript and offered critical suggestions and sound advice during various stages of the project: Cynthia Brantley, Carl Degler, Milton Cantor, David Brody, Rose Glickman, Larry Levine, David Pivar, Mary Ryan, Carroll Smith-Rosenberg, Kitty Sklar, Judy Walkowitz, Ron Walters, Miriam Wells, and Martha Vicinus.

Many people offered significant intellectual contributions during conversations, which took place in cafes, at the university swimming pool, in the early morning hours at conventions, on casual strolls, and on rugged hikes through the California mountains. I am deeply grateful to Nat Huggins, Mike Rogin, Carroll Smith-Rosenberg, Joan Levinson, Susan Griffin, Kathy Barry, and Gerda Lerner for their help in formulating and refining many of the ideas and insights that appear throughout this book.

Let me also thank the Berkeley Women's Faculty Research Seminar, whose sustained criticism and support vastly improved my conceptualization of this subject.

I am especially indebted to Beth Magnus, whose contribution to this book is invaluable. In addition to typing the manuscript and providing exceptional research assistance, she edited several versions of the manuscript and repeatedly discovered lapses in my thought and judgment. Naturally, neither she nor others who have contributed to this book should be held responsible for errors that yet remain.

I would also like to thank Henry Tom, social sciences editor, and Miriam Tillman, copy editor, at The Johns Hopkins University Press for seeing the book through the many stages of production with the highest degree of professional competence and with personal compassion.

I am especially grateful to certain individuals whose love and friendship played a critical role in supporting me during difficult years of research and writing. My father, from my earliest years, has repeatedly demonstrated his belief in "his daughter, the professor." Mary Bolton, Carol Groneman, Jack Litewka, Valerie Miner, Karen Paige, Jim Pitman, Zack Powell, Steve Walch, Blanch Walch, and my entire family gave of themselves in special and remembered ways. Joan Levinson and Alice Quateman provided the kind of intellectual inspiration and unflagging friendship that few people are privileged to know in their lifetime. To both of them, I want to express my deep gratitude, appreciation, and love.

Finally, this book could not have been written outside of the sisterhood of feminist poets, writers, scholars, and activists with whom I have shared my most stimulating and exciting hours over the last decade. Without them, this book might never have been written, for they provided the friendship, intellectual companionship, and constant encouragement necessary to ask new questions of age-old problems.

INTRODUCTION

Prostitution has been tolerated throughout much of Western history, but because of its "unspeakable," stigmatized, and clandestine nature, it has been largely unrecorded. Occasionally, during periods of intense religious, social, or economic change, the uneasy truce between society and prostitution has been
broken by outbursts of social indignation, providing historians with some evidence about the lives of usually invisible people. Such was the case in the United
States at the turn of the century.

The American Progressive Era, 1900–18, was the setting for one of Western
society's most zealous and best-recorded campaigns against prostitution. What
earlier Victorians had discreetly regarded as a "necessary evil," turn-of-the-
century Americans came to view as the "Social Evil," a moral problem and a
national menace. As one might expect, the controversy created a deluge of committee reports, surveys, studies, and official public records. These documents
recorded the indignation of reformers and, to a lesser extent, the perspective of
the prostitutes themselves.

The Progressive Era was a period of dramatic contradictions and conflicting
trends. Progressive middle-class reformers' attempts to restore free enterprise
through "trust busting" coincided with the large-scale consolidation of modern
American corporate capitalism; extreme labor unrest coincided with the consolidation of business and management power. Society publicly acknowledged the
plight of impoverished urban dwellers, while reacting to each new wave of immigration with xenophobia and racism. Attempts to "Americanize" and uplift the
poor clashed with immigrant groups' more radical class-based politics. Immigrants developed complex political, social, and economic networks on the basis
of ethnic solidarity; reformers accused them of municipal corruption and "boss-
ism." An urban working-class culture, in which liquor and the saloon played an
important part, grew alongside a campaign to legislate Prohibition.

Family life was changing rapidly as well. Working-class women were joining
the labor force in large numbers, and middle-class women were challenging the
Victorian definition of a separate women's sphere by creating a national network
of clubs to initiate social reforms and agitate for women's rights. Victorian ideals
of gentility were being increasingly questioned. At the same time, social conservatives mourned the loss of the "traditional family," upheld the values they associated with American rural life, and sought to restore women to their proper
place.

The diverse activities and movements of the Progressive Era represented

Americans' search for social order at a time when the nation was reeling from social and economic changes brought about by unprecedented rapid industrialization, urbanization, and immigration. During this period Americans first attempted to employ the state for diverse and competing goals: to legislate morality; to protect the consolidation of business and political interests; and to regulate and rationalize an increasingly industrialized and pluralistic nation. It is within this context that the national campaign against prostitution adds yet another dimension to our understanding of these complicated years.

Early twentieth-century Americans were not the first to campaign publicly against prostitution. Moral reformers in the 1830s and social purity crusaders in the late nineteenth century had preceded them. Nevertheless, the early twentieth century represents a watershed in the history of American prostitution. Horrified by the large-scale commercialization and rationalization of prostitution by third-party agents (property owners, politicians, police, procurers, doctors, cabdrivers, and liquor interests, to name but a few), reformers succeeded by 1918 in enlisting the state to close down the previously tolerated red-light districts in most American cities.

This, of course, did not mean that prostitution disappeared from American life; it simply assumed new forms and was forced underground. Because of the trade's new criminal status, its entire subculture radically changed. The relative security of public brothels became increasingly replaced by the riskier, but less visible, act of streetwalking. New forms of prostitution, such as massage parlors and call girls, developed to thwart police detection and "protect" the prostitute from the law. Control of prostitution shifted from madams and prostitutes themselves to pimps and organized crime syndicates. Like the independent artisan who had become a salaried worker, the prostitute would rarely work henceforth as a free agent. In addition, she faced increased brutality, not only from the police, but also from her new "employers."

Such is the historical narrative that frames this study—the activities and consequences of one generation's unsuccessful attempt to abolish prostitution in the United States. This book is not intended as a study of a reform movement, however. Rather, it is about how gender and class affected the lives and attitudes of the men and women who had an important stake in the issue of prostitution during the first decades of this century. As Judith Walkowitz's superb study on *Prostitution and Victorian Society* has demonstrated, the subject of prostitution tends to illuminate a society's social structure and cultural values. It can function as a kind of microscopic lens through which we gain a detailed magnification of a society's organization of class and gender: the power arrangements between men and women; women's economic and social status; the prevailing sexual ideology; the underlying class relations that govern different groups' access to political and economic resources; the ways in which female erotic and procreative sexuality are channeled into specific institutional arrangements; and the cross-class alliances and antagonisms between reformers and prostitutes.

The Progressive Era, then, offers a unique opportunity to make a series of inquiries into prostitution and the culture and society of early twentieth-century America. To set the stage for this investigation, the study begins with a survey of the growth of urban prostitution and explores the first public reactions to this phenomenon. Next, I examine the actual public policy that Progressive reformers created, how the attempt to abolish prostitution failed, and why it worsened the lives of prostitutes.

The remainder of the book examines prostitution as both a cultural symbol and a social institution that women used as a means of survival. Writing history from "above"—from the perspective of reformers who attempted to eradicate prostitution—would offer a fascinating, but class-biased and one-sided, picture of prostitution. Similarly, adopting the perspective of those who actually practiced the trade would provide an extremely provocative ethnohistorical study, but one that would ignore prostitution's important relation to the dominant culture. In short, it seemed necessary to explore both perspectives in order to achieve a broad understanding of how Americans of different classes and different sexes experienced and viewed prostitution.

To middle-class reformers, prostitution became a cultural symbol of the birth of a modern industrial culture in which the cold, impersonal values of the marketplace could invade the most private areas of people's lives. Engaged in a symbolic public discourse, reformers discussed prostitution in terms that reflected their acute anxieties about other unresolved ills and problems of the day: the unrestricted immigration, the rate of venereal disease, the anonymity of the city, the evils of liquor, the growth of a working-class urban culture, and, most important of all, the changing role of women in society. As women from all classes increasingly entered the public arena, either through their participation in the labor force or through their involvement in middle-class social reform movements, they implicitly challenged the nineteenth-century doctrine of separate male and female spheres. Moreover, their entry into public life blurred the tidy distinctions between "public" women and respectable wives and mothers. In so doing, these women symbolically threatened the traditional patriarchal values of the dominant group of reformers.

Not all reformers viewed prostitution in the same way. Although both men and women participated in the repressive campaign to suppress prostitution, women reformers and feminists provided another perspective and analysis of prostitution which frequently differed from that of the larger civic campaign. For many women, prostitution represented the quintessential symbol of the sexual and economic exploitation of women in a patriarchal society. In challenging the sexual double standard, women entered the public sphere to proclaim their right to protect the purity of their private sphere in the home. For them, the eradication of prostitution presaged the elevation of the status of all women. Unfortunately, women reformers did not foresee the consequences of the public policy they supported. Moreover, the cross-class alliances that they occasionally forged with prostitutes were frequently undermined by class and ethnic prejudices that prevented women from making a united stand on the issue of prostitution.

To those who lived in the red-light district or practiced prostitution, in contrast, prostitution was neither a symbol of social disorder nor a symbol of female economic and sexual exploitation. Rather, it was simply a form of work: an obvious means of economic survival which occasionally even offered some small degree of upward mobility.

The world of the prostitute was quite complex. Within the red-light district an entire subculture flourished, with its own values, class structure, political economy, folk culture, and social relations. Yet even though the life of the prostitute and that of the reformer seemed worlds apart, both were influenced by the increasing rationalization and commercialization of society. Moreover, a close examination of the underside of American society reveals certain values that governed the dominant culture as well.

The book ends with an investigation into the causes of prostitution and the lives of the women and girls who worked as prostitutes. Some forced prostitution did exist. An inquiry into white slavery, on which reformers typically blamed most of prostitution, not only provides a study in cultural hysteria, but also constitutes an important and neglected chapter in the history of women. Although its incidence during the Progressive Era was highly exaggerated, white slavery does play a part in the story of prostitution.

The vast majority of women, however, entered prostitution more or less voluntarily, viewing the trade as an "easier" and more lucrative means of survival than the other kinds of jobs open to them. Although in general sexual and economic exploitation may be considered the preconditions of prostitution, a complicated web of particular economic, social, and family difficulties led individual working-class women to choose prostitution as a survival strategy. Here, then, is the story of the prostitute: how she explained her past, perceived her work, and regarded her future.

Although some reformers called prostitutes the "lost sisterhood," the women did not in fact accept this view of themselves. They were not "lost" within their own communities, where they played an integral and highly visible role in shaping the character of many urban neighborhoods. Nor did prostitutes generally view themselves as morally "lost," as pathological or fallen victims of sinister forces. Their life was grim and frequently degrading, but prostitutes were actors in history who understood that they made choices, even when those choices were severely constrained by painful social relations, demoralizing economic circumstances, and limited alternatives.

Nevertheless, these women have become lost to history and do, therefore, constitute a "lost sisterhood" of the American past. As we delve into the personal histories of the women who chose to work as prostitutes, I hope that readers may gain a new comprehension of the obstacles and deprivations that the vast majority of poor women, not only prostitutes, have experienced in the American past.

Prostitution has only recently captured historians' attention. Previously, both historians and society viewed the "oldest profession" as a permanent and unchanging aspect of the human condition. Like many other aspects of women's history, however, the history of prostitution is characterized by gradual change within a context of continuity. Contrary to popular belief, moreover, prostitution has not served the same function in all societies. The meaning and practice of prostitution has ranged from that of a sacred fertility ritual (in ancient Babylonia, Cyprus, Phoenicia, and India) to its more familiar role as a form of commercialized vice in modern complex societies.

Prostitution was also neglected as a topic because it concerned the most devalued female members of society. Until recently, historians neglected the lives of such ordinary people (including the vast majority of women), preferring to concentrate on the high drama provided by powerful elites. In the context of the "new social history," however, the study of prostitution contributes to our knowledge of the lives and subcultures of historically "invisible" groups such as working-class and immigrant women; in doing so, it offers new insights into the dominant culture as well.

In pursuing my own research on prostitution, I have been especially concerned with the historiographical issues raised in the literature on women's history, sexuality, and the family. As a result I have stressed, in addition to the importance of class, the significance of gender—the social and cultural identity given each sex— in shaping each person's historical experience. The concept of gender has further led, in the literature on women's history, to a working formulation of a "gender system": the way in which a society prescribes the behavior and identities of women and men. A gender system determines which sex controls economic resources, who defines the values and division of labor between the sexes, and how female sexuality in both its erotic and its procreative aspects is organized in a society. A gender system exists alongside a class system, strongly shaping each individual's psychosexual reality. Like a class system, a gender system is not a static phenomenon: gender continually interacts dialectically with economic conditions to produce new institutional sexual arrangements and norms.

A study that addresses the lives of both reformers and prostitutes required a wide variety of sources as well as a flexible and complex methodology. At first the task seemed formidable. As members of an "inarticulate" subculture who left few personal records of their own, prostitutes have been excluded from most traditional histories, mentioned only in footnotes as the "ladies of the night" with whom famous men consorted. On occasion, they made brief appearances as colorful characters in anecdotal literature or as shadowy figures lurking in the background of institutional histories of antivice organizations.

Further investigation, however, uncovered a considerable body of primary sources. Like all historical records, these sources present problems, and the historian must tread carefully, using judgment based on extensive exposure to the period's attitudes, biases, and source materials. Census records, for example, are notoriously poor indices of the actual extent and location of prostitution. Vice commission reports, which document the efforts of antivice campaigners, are self-serving records that mirror reformers' attitudes. It is surprising to discover, however, that they can also be an important source of information on prostitutes themselves. This is because reformers' conclusions, based on preconceived notions about women and prostitution, were frequently at variance with the data they had collected. The historian who uses social workers' or missionaries' written records encounters similar problems and can similarly obtain reliable information through careful decoding and translating.

The few prostitutes' memoirs in existence present another problem, similar to that of slave narratives. Most, in my opinion, were written by reformers, just as slave narratives were largely written by zealous abolitionists. Yet some of these memoirs, like slave narratives, are indeed based on fact and afford the historian a glimpse into the life of a particular woman and the milieu in which she lived. As in all historical research, we can only learn the difficulties and dangers associated with the use of specific sources and then bravely and cautiously use what the past has left us.

This study has also required a broad range of historical, sociological, and anthropological approaches. My intent at all times has been to allow the questions and available sources, rather than methodological concerns, to shape the material at hand. I have therefore tried to incorporate the strengths of several historical approaches. Much of the "new social history" has greatly increased our understanding of the past through detailed studies of a particular social group or community; more traditional cultural history has richly illuminated the meaning of society's efforts to respond to social conflict and cultural crisis. Neither social nor traditional approaches, however, seemed sufficient to encompass the meaning of prostitution as both cultural symbol and lived history.

Because the Progressive campaign addressed itself almost exclusively to the problems of prostitution in an emerging urban and industrial culture, this study has done likewise. The subject of prostitution on the Western frontier and in the relatively unindustrialized South has not been considered here. Moreover, I have chosen the strategy of studying prostitution within a national, rather than a local, context for specific reasons. The goals of this study are not to illuminate the specific labor, ethnic, demographic, or political situation in one city, but rather to understand how reformers all over the country regarded the Social Evil and what kinds of options poor women perceived in their lives. Neither reformers' views nor women's options varied substantially from city to city. A comparison of reports from forty-eight separate urban vice commissions across the country presents a fairly uniform picture. All the commissions raised very similar questions about prostitution and all offered nearly identical solutions—the eradication of the Social Evil from the American urban landscape. The data they collected, moreover, transcended regional differences to provide a fairly consistent and predictable demographic profile of both reformers and prostitutes.

Today, prostitution is again receiving widespread attention in the United States as a social problem, a feminist issue, and a question of official policy. Increasingly, Americans are asking whether the legal solution of the Progressive Era, namely the prohibition of prostitution, is still relevant to contemporary society.

This public debate has forced me to sharpen my own views on the issue. Readers have a justifiable curiosity to know how an author, after years of research, has come to regard such a controversial subject, for it does necessarily influence the questions one asks and the perspectives one adopts. Some contemporary feminists, like their Progressive counterparts, regard prostitution as the quintessential exploitation of women in a patriarchal society. Other feminists and some prostitutes have romanticized prostitution as an occupation that frees women from family oppression or economic subservience. Most Americans probably regard prostitution as a public nuisance and view prostitutes as social deviants.

Drawing from my own knowledge of women's past, I regard prostitution neither as the worst form of exploitation women have ever suffered, nor as a noble or liberating occupation, but rather as a dangerous and degrading occupation that, given the limited and unattractive alternatives, has enabled thousands of women to escape even worse danger and deprivation. When I look closely at the life stories of poor women during the early years of this century, I am struck again and again by most prostitutes' view of their work as "easier" and less oppressive than other survival strategies they might have chosen. The statement that prostitution offered certain opportunities and advantages for some women, however, should not be interpreted as a positive or romanticized assessment of the life of a prostitute. Instead, it should be read as an indictment of the limited range of opportunities that early twentieth-century women faced in their daily struggle for economic, social, and psychological well-being. Denied access to social and economic power because of their gender and class status, poor women made their choices from a position of socially structured powerlessness. All too often, a woman had to choose from an array of dehumanizing alternatives: to sell her body in a loveless marriage contracted solely for economic protection; to sell her body for starvation wages as an unskilled worker; or to sell her body as a "sporting woman." Whatever the choice, some form of prostitution was likely to be involved.

Ruth Rosen

THE LOST SISTERHOOD

CHAPTER 1

FROM NECESSARY TO SOCIAL EVIL

Never before had Americans exhibited such widespread concern over prostitution. National in scope, urgent in tone, the antivice campaign that emerged between 1900 and 1918 became an offensive campaign waged against an internal domestic enemy: the Social Evil. Although the battle grew out of sporadic skirmishes of the previous century and employed weapons left behind by earlier reformers, a new and dramatic goal had been set: to eradicate prostitution across the American urban landscape. Two and a half centuries after the creation of a sanctified community in the wilderness, Americans lamented the loss of their national innocence.

Prostitution had not always seemed such an urgent problem. During the colonial period, religious leaders worried more about adultery or fornication than about scattered cases of prostitution. Calvinists had certainly inherited a harsh judgment of women in the "oldest profession"; but demographic and economic factors, along with religious sanctions, had mitigated against the growth of a professional class of prostitutes. The shortage of women and the acute need for domestic labor in the colonies helped guarantee most women the economic security and protection of family and community life. In the southern colonies as well, religious and demographic factors helped ensure an absence of professional prostitutes. To provide wives for colonial bachelors, the British sent shiploads of young women to Virginia. Here, too, women found easy access to marriage and family life.[1]

Despite the absence of widespread commercialized vice, prostitution was not unknown in the colonies. In public fights, the epithet *whore* was used as a form of insult. In some cases, the term *prostitution* referred merely to illicit sexual behavior. A white woman who engaged in sexual relations with a black man, or an Indian woman who admitted having relations with a white man, was called a prostitute. In other cases, the term referred to women who bartered sexual favors for food or goods, a form of exchange typical of preindustrial societies. Prosti-

1

tution, however, was a personal, not a commercial vice; a temporary state of sin, rather than a permanent occupation or status.[2]

The legal and systematic sexual exploitation of female indentured servants and black female slaves constituted one form of forced prostitution. Female slaves and indentured workers encountered not only forced labor but also the sexual exploitation of their owners. Forced to submit to masters' sexual demands, both groups of women gave birth to children sired by their masters. The law underscored their total lack of rights: a pregnant indentured servant earned a lengthened period of servitude, and the slave saw her offspring become the property of her rapist. Such forced prostitution, however, was a form of sexual slavery and differed from the commercial sale of sex.[3]

It was not long before the colonies began to encounter visible evidence of commercial prostitution. In his diary, Cotton Mather recorded: "There has been this last Week, a remarkable Instance of the divine Judgments on an infamous Harlott. There are more of her Tribe, and of their bewitched Followers, in the Neighbourhood."[4] Although most church records discussed only fornication or adultery, two seventeenth-century cases suggest that prostitution was not as rare as written evidence would indicate. One case involved a twelve-year-old boy who received admonishment for going to a brothel; the other, the excommunication of a woman who was a prostitute.[5]

By the late seventeenth century, local clergy had begun complaining about "lewd" and "licentious" women who roamed the streets. In New Amsterdam, Boston, and Philadelphia, prostitutes openly plied their trade, prompting legislation in 1699 that made "nightwalking" an offense. The first law against brothels, passed in 1672, indicated the troubling appearance of "bawdy" houses. By the middle of the eighteenth century, towns and cities were recording with dismay the increased visibility of "nightwalkers" and brothels.[6] Benjamin Franklin remembered seeing women "who by throwing their head to the right or left of everyone who passed by them, came out with no other design than to revive the spirit of love in Disappointed Bachelors and expose themselves to sale at the highest bidder."[7] During the revolutionary war, large numbers of camp followers posed strategic and sanitary problems for an all-male army.[8] Prostitution had become a permanent feature of American life.

The gradual growth of prostitution was integrally yoked to parallel changes in women's lives and in the family. As the deeply religious and agrarian colonies grew into an increasingly secular and commercialized nation, profound social and economic changes in family life increased the prostitute population. As self-sufficient farms turned to the production and transportation of cash crops, market relations intruded upon the family's traditional religious and patriarchal values in new and unexpected ways. Men bartered less and instead received cash for their agricultural labor. As early manufacturing transferred some of women's work outside the home, women's vital partnership in a traditional domestic economy began to diminish.

Such early commercialization affected women and their families in different ways. In the middle and upper classes, women found their domestic labor reduced, their status diminished, and their sphere narrowed. Many of these women now bought the household items that they had formerly produced. In an attempt to widen their sphere, some of these women would later initiate the social reform and women's rights movements of the nineteenth century.

In poorer families, women joined their children and husbands as wage earners, contributing to a single and precarious family economy. Young rural women, whose labor was no longer needed in a home transformed by a market economy, began entering the labor force as domestics or workers in early manufacturing centers.[9]

As servants or milliners, poor single girls and women encountered a different world outside the family. Both wage discrimination and sexual exploitation shaped their working experiences. At best, most female employment offered subsistence wages. In addition, young women faced new sexual difficulties in their encounters with men. The sexual exploitation of domestic servants was a common occurrence. Seduction and false promises of marriage frequently resulted in premarital sexual activity, which had been practiced in rural areas. Far from the family and community, however, the rules were different. When such relations resulted in pregnancy, neither the family nor the community was present to ensure the traditional enforcement of a proper marriage.[10] Such abandoned women then faced the shame of returning home with an illegitimate child; the bleak prospect of trying to support a child on subsistence wages; an attempted abortion; or survival through prostitution.

In the second half of the nineteenth century, rapid industrialization accelerated and intensified these changes in family life and contributed to the steady increase in prostitution. Most poor families had ceased to function as self-sufficient economic units. Instead, they survived through the combined wages of individual family members. Drawn from poor native-born American families and successive waves of immigrant populations, unmarried women entered the industrial ranks or found work as domestic servants. As they left the social and economic protection of their families to encounter sexual exploitation and low wages, they became part of the potential supply of new prostitutes. Sometimes, they were unable to find any employment other than prostitution. Richard Evans, in his study of German prostitution, has convincingly argued that prostitution probably reaches its greatest heights during the second wave of industrialization, when heavy industry excludes women from participation in the labor force. It is with the growth of the tertiary clerical and service sector that women find greater opportunities for employment and that prostitution consequently declines.[11] Therefore it is likely, though no statistics are available, that the peak of women's engagement in prostitution took place between 1850 and 1900 rather than during the early years of the twentieth century, when, ironically, it assumed the status of a major social problem.

The demand for prostitutes was also increasing during the second half of the nineteenth century. Westernization, the transportation revolution, and growing militarization created all-male populations that could support large numbers of prostitutes.[12] In the rapidly developing cities, prostitutes increasingly became attached to the saloons and vice districts that working men frequented.

The majority of American families, of course, began to feel the effects of commercialization and industrialization only during the late nineteenth and early twentieth century. Nevertheless, as a result of these dramatic changes, women's traditional economic role and men's patriarchal authority in the family were being challenged and transformed. First in cities on the northeastern seaboard, but eventually across the nation, families came to face similar challenges to their structure and values. For women in the working classes, it was a question of when, not if, they would enter the marketplace unprotected by their families and by traditional social restraints. Prostitution was an inevitable result of the transformation of the family in the nineteenth century.

Before the Progressive Era, Americans condemned prostitution but did not classify it as a criminal offense. Social disapproval of prostitution was expressed through sporadic and unofficial harassment. In the eighteenth and early nineteenth centuries, this harassment was carried out mainly by segments of the laboring community. The gangs and rowdy clubs that acted as a kind of informal police in most cities punished prostitution as they punished other violations of community standards, by mob attacks. These unorganized, spontaneous, and violent outbursts, called "whorehouse riots," were a common occurrence in urban areas. As early as 1734, crowds demolished several houses of prostitution in Boston. Again, in 1793, 1799, 1823, and 1825, indignant neighbors and prostitutes battled in the streets of Boston's poor neighborhoods. In 1825, two thousand rioters tore up brothels and fought police in Lenox, Pennsylvania. In the same year, three riots in Portland, Maine, failed to close down a neighborhood's brothels. By the end of the third battle, one person had been killed and many wounded. In 1857, indignant Chicago citizens—joined by the mayor—burned down an entire row of brothels, then self-righteously proclaimed that they had restored order to their community.[13]

By the mid-nineteenth century, the task of harassing prostitutes had been taken over by the professional police departments just then being formed in major cities. Prostitutes, madams, and procurers could be arrested, at the discretion of police, on charges of "lewdness," vagrancy, or keeping a "disorderly house." The general effect and intent of this policy was to hide prostitution from view. In "respectable" neighborhoods, prostitution existed only in the most discreet high-class houses catering to a wealthy clientele. There, immunity from raids could be bought by madams' silence about their patrons or by payment of "fines" to the police. All other prostitution was deliberately limited to urban slums, where genteel society could ignore its existence. The professionalization of the police helped to create the red-light districts that sprang up in many American cities during the second half of the nineteenth century. In these areas, houses of prostitution were quietly allowed to carry out their business, except when they failed to pay off local police or when the political climate demanded a raid to demonstrate elected officials' implacable hostility to vice. When arrested, prostitutes generally received fines rather than jail sentences.[14]

The Victorian policy of quiet toleration suggests underlying attitudes toward prostitution that were quite different from the public expressions of condemnation. A few isolated individuals expressed these attitudes in words. For example, one 1892 newspaper editorial explained:

> Like gambling, it [prostitution] is ineradicable, yet—if handled properly, it can be curtailed. Against houses of illfame, the *Mascot* makes no crusade, so long as they are not located in respectable neighborhoods, for they are a necessary evil. The subject is a delicate one to handle, but it must be admitted that such places are necessary in ministering to the passions of men who otherwise would be tempted to seduce young ladies of their acquaintance.[15]

The 1916 Bridgeport, Connecticut, Vice Report summarized this characteristically Victorian attitude: "Vice is one of the weaknesses of men; it cannot be extirpated; if repressed unduly at one point, it will break out more violently and bafflingly elsewhere; a segregated district is really a protection to the morality of the womanhood of the city, for without it rape would be common and clandestine immorality would increase."[16]

These passages reflect beliefs about male and female sexuality that were prevalent in America during the nineteenth century. Victorians described the male sex drive as strong, passionate, and potentially destructive. They sought to control it because they believed that if excessively indulged, it could weaken and damage mind and body. The female sex drive, in contrast, was in most cases thought to be weak or nonexistent. As one widely read medical book on sex declared, "The majority of women are not very much troubled with sexual feelings of any kind. What men are habitually, women are only exceptionally."[17] If men were not to unleash their passions on "young ladies of their acquaintance" or wives too delicate and asexual to cope with their sexual demands, they had to exert heroic self-control; if they failed in these efforts, they could still protect women in their own milieu by going to prostitutes.[18] The prostitute thus functioned as the "protector of the home," a doctrine best articulated by William Edward Hartpole Lecky, who argued in his history of European morals that the prostitute was "ultimately the most efficient guardian of virtue. But for her, the unchallenged purity of countless happy homes would be polluted. . . . On that one degraded and ignoble form are concentrated the passions that might have filled the world with shame."[19]

The prostitute could be the focus of "passions that might have filled the world with shame," servicing men's sexual needs as other women could not, because a great gulf separated her nature from that of other women. Other women were pure; she was depraved. Through loss of premarital virginity or betrayal of conjugal fidelity she had fallen from virtue. Her reputation, once lost, was irredeemable. Having broken the cardinal rule of feminine conduct, she became capable of any crime. "No one without experience," explained a prison chaplain, "can tell the obduracy of the female heart when hardened and lost in sin. As woman falls from a higher point of perfection so she sinks to a profounder depth of misery than man."[20] Women were thus madonnas or magdalens, Marys or Eves, angels or whores. As one male speaker in 1837 asserted, "in the female character, there is no midregion; it must exist in spotless innocence or else in hopeless vice."[21]

The belief that a virtuous woman could so easily become sexually depraved indicates an underlying male ambivalence about women's alleged asexuality. Medical and religious authorities of the period urged the most elaborate precautions to shield women from sexual stimuli lest they become corrupted. Furthermore, despite the asexuality of "normal" women, doctors reported many cases of women whose overly passionate inclinations had to be "cured" by sexual surgery. Conveniently, the large numbers of lower-class and immigrant women in prostitution could be explained by these women's alleged tendencies to be less moral, more animalistic, and less sheltered by upbringing and education from corrupting influences. Lower-class women were thus especially fitted for an occupation that deflected men's sex drives from upper-class women.[22] In the South, white slave owners similarly argued that the forced prostitution of black female slaves, both on plantations and in brothels, constituted a necessary evil in that it provided an outlet for male sexual drives that would otherwise pollute white womanhood; and in California, certain whites argued that Chinese prostitutes protected white womanhood. The "protection" of nonwhite women was not considered.[23]

Victorian attitudes about prostitution were thus intricately bound up with class, gender, and racial systems. Although prostitutes were prevailingly characterized as outcasts with no place in society, in actuality they held an important place and served vital social functions.[24] Economically, prostitution was a source of income to the police, to procurers, madams, doctors, politicians, and liquor interests. Politically, it upheld gender and class divisions. The singling out of a caste of degraded women served as an object lesson and a threat to other women. The specter of the whore was always before them as a reminder of what they might become or how they might be treated if they failed to live up to the angel image or lived outside of male protection. For men, prostitution upheld the double standard, the polarized images of women as angelic or monstrous, but in neither case fully human, and the ideology that women existed to serve men. The association of prostitution with lower-class, immigrant, and nonwhite populations served to divide women from one another. It also justified the low ranking of these populations in the social hierarchy. The visible association of brothels with lower-class neighborhoods and customers, which made it seem as if lower-class men had recourse to prostitutes whereas upper-class men did not, and the association of sexual indulgence with weakened health and ambition, provided one rationalization for poverty, unemployment, and disease among the poor.

Although the general attitude toward prostitution during the nineteenth century was one of tacit acceptance, two waves of antiprostitution reform prefigured the crusade of the Progressive Era. These earlier reformers, like the reformers of the Progressive Era, were disturbed not simply by prostitution itself, but by the social order into which it was so thoroughly integrated. Whether they looked forward to a social order free from male domination and the commercial exploitation of women, or backward to an idealized vision of traditional rural life based on religious values, they were profoundly dissatisfied with the present.

The first wave of antiprostitution reform began in 1832, when the New York Magdalen Society, led by a young divinity student named John McDowall, issued its first annual report. Fueled by the evangelical zeal of the Second Great Awakening, a series of religious revivals that swept the Northeast in the 1830s, members pledged themselves to the task of purifying American society by exhorting obedience to the seventh commandment and exposing the extent of vice. In a city-wide survey that prefigured later reformers' attempts to document the extent of vice and their inclination to exaggerate it, the Magdalen Society dramatically reported that at least ten thousand prostitutes blighted the city. This statistic, they added, caused the "blood to chill within the veins; and each particular hair to stand erect, like quills upon the fretted porcupine."[25] With a sensationalism that offended the established families of the city, they boldly exposed the names of gentlemen who had frequented New York's best brothels.

Although the society soon disbanded because of public opposition and lack of funds, its mission was continued by church-affiliated groups of upper- and middle-class women, who by 1834 had founded the New York Female Moral Reform Society and had purchased McDowall's newspaper, the *Advocate of Moral Reform*. By 1839, the society had become a national organization with 445 auxiliaries. At first, women reformers asked for male support. "The work belongs to men," wrote the *Advocate*'s editors, "and when they will come up and take the mighty labour off our hands, most gladly we will retire."[26] When men eventually formed their own Seventh Commandment Society, however, and suggested that the women's society become their auxiliary, the women refused, asserting that women had to take the lead in moral reform.

Women did in fact take the lead, and their predominance was reflected in the movement's two major goals: "rescuing" prostitutes and reforming the sexual conduct of men. As Barbara Berg points out in her study of women's voluntary associations during the antebellum period, male reformers tended to portray prostitutes as women "so totally bereft of shame, that they [were] . . . beyond the possibility of reform."[27] McDowall, like many other male antivice crusaders, believed that prostitutes' sufferings were "self-inflicted . . . the necessary result of voluntary vice," and depicted prostitutes as "malevolent, cruel, and revengeful" women who led innocent young men astray.[28] Women reformers, in contrast, tended to see prostitutes as victims of male misconduct. "It cannot be concealed," reported the Female Benevolent Society, "that the treachery of man, betraying the interests of . . . woman, is one of the principal causes which furnishes the victims of licentiousness. Few, very few . . . have sought their wretched calling." "Our mothers, our sisters, our daughters are sacrificed by the thousands every year on the altar of sin," declared the Boston Female Reform Society, "and who are the agents in this work of destruction? Why, our fathers, our brothers, and our sons."[29] Female reformers in such societies typically concentrated their attacks not on prostitutes, but on their male customers and on the male seducers and adulterers who had caused their fall. The aim of these reformers was to force men to live up to the ideals of sexual purity they had set for women. As Carroll Smith-Rosenberg, Mary Ryan, and Barbara Berg have argued, prostitution came to symbolize the injustices suffered by all women as a result of the sexual double standard. Reformers' tactics included publishing the names of brothel customers and other licentious men, urging women to ostracize such men, siding with prostitutes in murder and assault cases, invading or standing outside brothels to drive customers away, urging women to supervise the sexual education of their sons, and lobbying to make seduction a criminal offense.[30]

Female reformers' efforts to rescue prostitutes from their profession revealed ambivalent attitudes about the underlying causes of prostitution. On the one hand, attempts to distribute Bibles and tracts; hold prayer meetings in brothels, hospitals, and jails; and instruct prostitutes in morality and religion reflected the belief that women entered prostitution because they were morally ignorant or corrupt. This belief in turn reflected class and ethnic prejudices that could not easily be overcome. On the other hand, female reformers showed an incipient understanding of prostitution's economic causes in their efforts to open homes and refuges to prostitutes, teach them new trades, and find employment for them. Eventually, in the 1840s and 1850s, female moral reformers began to urge the opening of male occupations to women and to advocate higher wages and even unions for working women. Many of the reformers came to recognize the precariousness of their own social and economic position as women, and thus to articulate feelings of identification between themselves and prostitutes. The New York Female Benevolent Society, for instance, dedicated itself to assisting the "many sisters in the common tie of humanity, who are fallen—treated as outcasts"; and reformer Lydia Maria Child emphasized the similarities of all women, each within "a hair's breadth" of being the other.[31] In their publications, female reformers repeatedly challenged the socially upheld distinctions between madonnas and magdalens and declared their solidarity with all women. The *Advocate* served as a forum in which women could not only attack prostitution and the double standard but also condemn male abuses of authority and occasionally even question openly the very basis of that authority.[32]

The second wave of moral reform began in the 1870s as a response to a growing campaign to regulate prostitution. The "regulationists" or "reglementarians" wanted to have prostitutes registered by the state and placed under close surveillance by doctors and police. They advocated compulsory medical examinations of all prostitutes and compulsory hospitalization of those with venereal disease. The new antivice reformers, known variously as "social purity" advocates, "abolitionists," and "antireglementarians," fought attempts to regulate prostitution and sought instead to abolish it altogether through the reformation of the nation's morals. Their tactics and arguments were influenced by both earlier moral reformers and their regulationist opponents.[33]

Regulationists articulated the private belief of most nineteenth-century Americans that prostitution, though evil, was necessary to accommodate men and preserve the purity of the home. Unlike most Americans, however, they were willing to act on their belief by publicly admitting, and in a way sanctioning, prostitution's existence. They argued that prostitution was ineradicable and that, consequently, state regulation was the only practical means of controlling the social and medical problems that it presented. As one regulationist explained, "Prostitution is a crime against the state and it must therefore be regulated by law. It cannot be wholly eradicated, but the good of society demands it shall be regulated."[34]

The regulationist movement was led by medical authorities and police officials. Its composition was reflected by its reliance on medical and scientific evidence and its goals of social control and management. To support their claims, regulationists produced medical reports on the newly discovered dangers of venereal disease and surveys that established the scientific model for most future research on prostitution. One of the main works they cited was William Sanger's *History of Prostitution: Its Extent, Causes, and Effects throughout the World*, published in 1858. As a resident physician on Blackwell's Island in New York, Sanger had interviewed several thousand prostitutes for his study; he had drawn on numerous medical and historical sources as well. His data and conclusions on the persistence of prostitution throughout history, the extent of prostitution in the United States, and the connection between unregulated prostitution and epidemic venereal disease gave strong support to the regulationist position.[35]

Regulationists also tried to show that regulation was widely accepted throughout the world as the most "modern" solution to the problem of prostitution. They pointed to the resolution of the 1873 European medical congress in Vienna to have all attending nations sign an international agreement requiring medical examinations for prostitutes in licensed brothels. Vice needed to be brought into the open, argued regulationists, where it could be controlled "as it has been in Paris and other cities of Europe."[36] In support of their position, regulationists cited examples of state or municipal regulation of prostitution in Belgium, France, Austria, Hungary, Russia, Italy, Spain, Portugal, most of Germany and Scandinavia, and many cities of the Orient.

In their preoccupation with obtaining social control over prostitution, regulationists did not challenge the assumptions about gender and class that made prostitution a "necessary evil." Sanger's book supported growing xenophobic attitudes by underscoring that most prostitutes were recent immigrants. It also helped absolve employers of industrial exploitation by reporting that half of the prostitutes interviewed had formerly worked as domestics, and another quarter had entered prostitution straight from their parents' homes.[37] Regulationists, like most nineteenth-century Americans, laid the blame for prostitution on "debauchery of the degenerate . . . already past hope of redemption."[38] Despite their pioneering efforts to break the Victorian "conspiracy of silence," the regulationists were in many ways profoundly conservative in their assessment of prostitution.

As its "antireglementarian" label suggests, the second wave of antiprostitution reform in the last decades of the nineteenth century was first formed in opposition to the threat of regulation. Coalitions of groups espousing feminist, religious, and civil libertarian principles united to drive back regulationist efforts in cities across the country. In most areas, they succeeded. The first plans to regulate prostitution in New York state were defeated in 1867; repeated attempts there also met with failure. Later attempts in Chicago (1871), Pennsylvania (1874), and Cincinnati (1874) similarly failed.[39] In 1879, a loophole in a state law enabled the City Council of St. Louis to vote for official regulation of prostitution. The experiment was repeatedly attacked by reformers throughout its operation and was ended only four years later owing to the efforts of women's groups and a state legislature dominated by rural and religious interests.[40] In the following decades, Detroit, Minneapolis, San Francisco, and Douglas, Arizona, experimented briefly with the regulation of vice, but in general regulation failed to take hold in American cities. Regulationists' outspoken acknowledgment and acceptance of prostitution's continuing existence were offensive to the majority of Americans, most of whom were still unwilling even to discuss the problem. In addition, regulationist advocacy of state intervention in sexual matters went against the grain of American individualism.[41]

Ironically, many regulationist arguments and tactics backfired, contributing to the cause of those reformers who sought to abolish prostitution. Alarming facts from studies on the extent of vice or the dangers of venereal disease could be used even more effectively by antiprostitution reformers than by regulationists. The examples of regulation in Europe were another double-edged weapon. Reformers in St. Louis attacked regulation by decrying the institution of "Parisian values" at the expense of American "morals." Antireglementarians could appeal to nativistic prejudice by asserting that regulation of prostitution was tantamount to an acceptance of "polluted" European values, and that by accepting such systems Europeans had already compromised their morals in ways not fitting for Americans to emulate. Feminists in particular could describe regulation as "a measure essentially foreign in its aspects and a by-product of the old world opinions on the question of women's inferiority to man . . . the attenuated survival of the medieval opinion in foreign-born men and sons which permits the discrimination against the woman of loose morals in favor of the man who has less."[42] Further, antireglementarians could explain, as one writer did, that Americans, unlike Europeans, had a tradition of liberty that prevented them from accepting the "police state" required to administer regulation.[43] They could point to the example of the British Contagious Diseases Acts, passed in 1866 to protect sailors from venereal disease. The acts, which required the compulsory examination of any woman "believed to be a common prostitute" and the compulsory detainment for up to nine months of any prostitute found to be venereally infected, were fought bitterly by feminist groups on civil liberties grounds and were rescinded in 1886. The British experiment of regulation lent support to the antireglementarian argument that regulation was not only a threat to civil liberties but also practically unworkable. As might be expected, relatively few prostitutes had willingly registered themselves as public women, and most prostitution had continued to operate without state interference.[44]

By the 1880s and 1890s, once regulation no longer posed a significant threat, antiprostitution groups had developed broader objectives. Their "abolitionist" label reflected their new aim, not merely to abolish regulation, but to abolish prostitution entirely. The name "social purity" described a movement to reform the sexual mores of American society. Its goals encompassed not only the abolition of prostitution but also the censorship of pornography, reformation of prostitutes, sex education, prosecution of prostitutes' customers, and establishment of women's right to refuse to have marital sex.[45]

The social purity movement cannot be called entirely feminist. It included individuals of both sexes who opposed women's suffrage, employment, and higher education. Some social purity advocates, in the spirit of McDowall and other early male reformers, focused on depraved female sexuality as the source of pollution in American society and depicted the prostitute as a menace "to the chastity of our women and the sanctity of our home."[46]

Nevertheless, feminism and social purity were very much intertwined, with members of each movement supporting causes of the other. Female social purity reformers, like their predecessors in the 1830s and 1840s, seized on the issue of prostitution to express dissatisfaction with the sexual conventions by which their lives were governed and to attack, however covertly, male domination from a morally unassailable position. Like their predecessors, they condemned male sexual conduct and expressed feelings of identification with prostitutes. Clara Cleghorne Hoffman of the National Women's Christian Temperance Union (W.C.T.U.), for example, speaking out on social purity in 1888, declared that "in thousands of homes everything seems to be perfectly pure, perfectly moral . . . and yet . . . hundreds go forth from these homes to swell the ranks of recognized prostitution, while thousands more go forth into the ranks of legalized prostitution under the perfectly respectable mantle of marriage."[47] Female social purity advocates condemned men's "excessive" sex drive that led them to buy sex or force it on their wives without their consent. Like Belle Mix of the National Purity Association, they urged the "rebellion of woman against the lustful domination of man."[48] They declared that regulation represented "masculine thinking": the "ancient feeling of the social necessity of the prostitute class and the sexual subordination of women."[49] It was true that many men had previously believed that "the low demands of human nature required it; and for the presumed protection of virtuous women, there was permitted the public exploitation of their poorer sisters."[50] Now, however, the double standard would be replaced by a "single standard" of purity, to which men would and *could* conform.[51]

By the last decade of the nineteenth century, social purity and abolitionist groups had established several organizations through which to publicize their positions. In 1879, Aaron Powell, one of the most active purity reformers, began publishing the *American Bulletin*. In 1885, it became the *Philanthropist*, the official journal of the American social purity movement. By 1890, a network of municipal vigilance societies had been formed. The Watch and Ward Society of Boston, typical of urban watchdog groups, expended great energy scrutinizing Boston's sins and protecting the city's morals. The Florence Crittendon homes, founded after Charles Crittendon experienced a religious conversion in 1883, expanded over the next decade into a nationally chartered organization of homes for young "wayward" women.

The growing concern over white slavery in Europe and the United States created an international forum for the abolitionist position. Legalized prostitution, from the abolitionist perspective, had caused white slavery. Due to the constant demand for new and fresh young women for licensed houses, white slavers supposedly exported and imported young women in an international slave market. Whether or not regulated prostitution contributed to white slavery, such publicity gave American abolitionists serious ammunition for their campaign.

By the end of the century, American abolitionists could regard themselves as part of a national and international movement. Aggressive and outspoken, they had gained strong support from feminists, clergy, the National W.C.T.U., and other urban reformers, and had developed close ties with abolitionist groups in Great Britain and Europe. Gradually, a movement to abolish prostitution through a reformation of morals was transformed into the Progressive Era's drive to abolish prostitution through the intervention of the state.

As the Victorian Era gave way to the Progressive Era, moralistic and medical-scientific perspectives merged to influence antiprostitution reformers in significant ways. Although physicians had failed to institute regulation, they continued to influence the antivice crusade through their language and research. By publicizing studies on venereal disease, they had helped to break the conspiracy of silence surrounding prostitution and to alert the American public to dangers posed by uncontrolled infection. They were, in fact, largely responsible for associating prostitution with the ravages of venereal disease. Their dire warnings intensified reformers' sense of urgency and transformed a "necessary evil" into the Social Evil, an untenable problem requiring immediate and drastic action. Physicians' early advocacy of state intervention to solve the problem of prostitution served as a precedent for Progressive reformers.

By the turn of the century, reformers were showing an increasing tendency to state the problem of prostitution within a scientific framework rather than in the moral terms of their predecessors. Some reformers, influenced by the scientific community's interest in genetic and eugenic issues, adopted a hereditarian perspective. Their arguments became powerful weapons in the hands of those who wished to label and control the sexual behavior of the poor. Others, influenced by the rise of social science, emphasized the effects of environment and described prostitutes as "victims" of economic forces and social injustices. The early nineteenth-century preoccupation with saving the souls of individual prostitutes was replaced by a tendency to view prostitutes collectively.

Nevertheless, a profoundly moralistic perspective continued to dominate the Progressive crusade against prostitution. Like their predecessors, Progressives frequently viewed prostitution with moral repugnance and attacked it with religious fervor. Beneath the scientific language and statistics lay a strong legacy of moral self-righteousness. To many Progressives, prostitution remained a moral problem that symbolized the shaky state of the nation's soul.

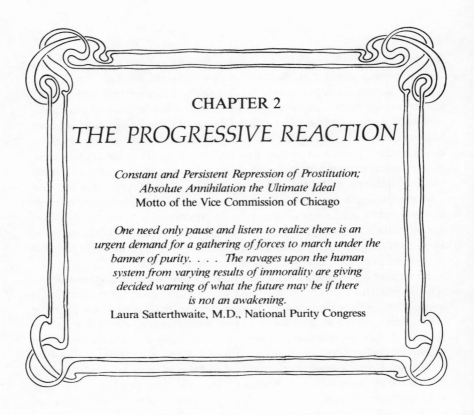

CHAPTER 2

THE PROGRESSIVE REACTION

Constant and Persistent Repression of Prostitution;
Absolute Annihilation the Ultimate Ideal
Motto of the Vice Commission of Chicago

One need only pause and listen to realize there is an
urgent demand for a gathering of forces to march under the
banner of purity. . . . The ravages upon the human
system from varying results of immorality are giving
decided warning of what the future may be if there
is not an awakening.
Laura Satterthwaite, M.D., National Purity Congress

By the turn of the century, the social purity movement, supported by medical warnings of a potential epidemic of venereal disease, had ignited a national outburst of civic righteousness. Over the next decade, scathing sermons, journalistic exposés, and municipal vice reports helped create and reach a national audience.

In 1890, social purity reformers, alarmed by what they perceived as an enormous increase in prostitution and venereal disease, called upon Congress to form a national crime commission to investigate the causes and extent of the Social Evil.[1] When Congress ignored their request, reformers decided to create their own municipal vice commissions. In 1900, the New York Committee of Fifteen, one of the earliest vice commissions, met to investigate prostitution in New York City. Two years later it published the results of its investigation in *The Social Evil*, the first of many published vice reports issued throughout the next decade.

The municipal vice report became an effective weapon in the hands of abolitionist Progressive reformers. Between 1910 and 1917, forty-three cities conducted formal investigations of prostitution.[2] Reflecting the contemporary passion for scientific statistical surveys, vice reports ostensibly presented an objective picture of the nature and extent of urban prostitution. In most cases, cities published at least a portion of their vice commission's report.

To gather hard-to-obtain data, the vice commissions—usually composed of civic and business leaders and clergy—hired underground investigators who interviewed thousands of prostitutes, probed political connections to vice and the economic workings of the commercialized vice market, and returned powerful ammunition to their employers. Such information could and would be used to oust political enemies from office. Like other Progressive reformers, vice fighters were gradually learning to translate their morality into political power.

Muckraking exposés in newspapers, films, sermons, and books heightened public curiosity, concern, and controversy over prostitution. In 1892, Dr. Charles Parkhurst, minister of the fashionable Presbyterian Church of New York, issued a scathing sermon on municipal protection of and connections with the vice market. When little action was taken by the police, Parkhurst followed the example set by the British reformer William Stead, who had personally entered the underworld of vice to prove his assertion that girls were bought and sold in England in the white slave market. After conducting his own investigation of prostitution in New York, Parkhurst similarly exposed the brutality and violence associated with the underground vice market.

The growing hysteria over white slavery greatly contributed to the momentum of the antivice movement. In 1909, the famous muckraking journalist George Kibbe Turner published his controversial exposé of the political connection between white slavery and Tammany Hall, titled "The Daughters of the Poor." A year later, a New York grand jury substantiated some aspects of the white slavery trade. Meanwhile, in 1907, Congress formally responded to reformers' concerns by appointing a commission to investigate "the importation of women for immoral purposes." After two years of sending investigators across the country to secure testimony from white slaves and procurers, the commission delivered its report to Congress. Significantly, the commission's findings gave credence to reformers' concerns. White slavery *did* exist. People *did* buy and sell women for the purpose of forcing them into prostitution.[3]

Public anxiety over white slavery and prostitution peaked during the years 1911–16. Reformers' campaigns to alert the nation linked prostitution to every imaginable form of individual and public corruption and portrayed American cities as steeped in every kind of iniquity: liquor, crime, and sexual vice. After a decade of publicity, millions of Americans—drawn from such diverse groups as women's clubs, settlement houses, welfare leagues, suffragist chapters, municipal civic leagues, social hygiene groups, penal reform organizations, juvenile protective leagues, refuge homes, immigrant protective leagues, legal aid societies, temperance groups, and commerce organizations—had become active participants in the antivice crusade.[4] Even corporate interests were involved. Two highly influential investigations of prostitution, George Kneeland's *Commercialized Prostitution in New York* (1913) and Abraham Flexner's *Prostitution in Europe* (1914), were sponsored by John D. Rockefeller through the Bureau of Social Hygiene.[5]

Reformers expounded widely differing theories on the causes and meaning of prostitution and its relation to social, political, and economic institutions; these theories were reflected in the kinds of reform that each group attempted. Many female reformers, for instance, agitated for minimum wage laws to protect working women and for more severe sanctions against men who bought and sold prostitutes' services. Social hygienists agitated for sex education; social purity reformers, for censorship; municipal reformers, for better urban recreational facilities and social services. Within this diverse coalition, the concerns most effectively legislated were those shared by the coalition's most powerful members. Measures to close red-light districts, keep close surveillance over prostitutes, and control venereal disease were in the interests of the crusade's powerful medical, judicial, business, and political leaders; broader concerns about the welfare of the prostitute, the status of women, the double standard of sexual morality, or industrial exploitation were not. Therefore, reformers with widely differing motivations and attitudes—feminists and antifeminists, liberals and conservatives, religious moral reformers and scientific social hygienists—ended up contributing to the same institutional results: increased state repression of the most visible evidence of commercialized vice, and increased state control over the lives of prostitutes.

As they gained public support, Progressive antivice crusaders sought definitive solutions to prostitution. They soon realized that most contemporary remedies, which they could observe in other countries, offended their own sense of morality. The regulation of vice, debated throughout the nineteenth century, continued to lose favor among civic leaders. Nevertheless, several cities experimented with regulation. In Minneapolis, the city's mayor enlisted two physicians to give weekly checkups to all prostitutes for five months during 1902. In exchange for a dollar, each woman was issued a "certificate of freedom from communicable diseases." Any infected woman received orders to cease her practice until cured. This system was soon abandoned when the "prevailing sentiment" of the population held that "the system of official medical inspection of inmates . . . was immoral, illegal, a dangerous assumption of power on the part of the city's executive, ineffective . . . conducive of official corruption and public demoralization, and, if persisted in, likely to bring great harm upon our city, in reputation abroad and conditions at home without any public benefit whatsoever."[6]

From March 1913 until May 1915, the city of San Francisco also attempted to regulate prostitution through the newly created Municipal Clinic for the Prevention of Venereal Disease. Proposed and supported by Dr. Julius Rosenstirn, the San Francisco clinic examined prostitutes every four days. If found infected, prostitutes were forbidden to practice and were given free treatment. If found healthy, they received certificates that guaranteed them immunity from police harassment. Unlike physicians enforcing regulation in other cities, Rosenstirn and his colleagues appear actually to have made substantial efforts to treat prostitutes with sensitivity and consideration.

The regulation of prostitution in San Francisco crystallized the national debate between those Progressive reformers who advocated the eradication or abolition of prostitution and those who fought for the efficient and rational control of venereal disease through regulation. Rosenstirn, an intelligent and articulate supporter of regulation, defended his clinic against abolitionist attacks with well-reasoned medical arguments. As a physician, Rosenstirn felt that medical experts now possessed the scientific knowledge and technical ability to regulate prostitution efficiently. Like his nineteenth-century predecessors, Rosenstirn viewed prostitution as a permanent and ineradicable feature of urban life. Regulation, he argued, would reduce the worst aspects of prostitution: namely, venereal disease, economic exploitation of prostitutes, and municipal graft.

Rosenstirn also strongly disagreed with those reformers who wanted to "moralize" the city through the attempted legal abolition of prostitution. Moral legislation, he explained, would not effectively solve social problems. Putting his faith in a managerial, rational, and efficient program of venereal disease control, Rosenstirn felt that it would "not suffice to close the brothels, to tear down the shelter of the prostitute, to hunt and imprison the street walker." The way to end prostitution was to change American institutions, not to legislate morality. Similar to many men of his generation, Rosenstirn placed his faith in society's ability to use expert knowledge and management to cope with social problems.[7]

Progressive abolitionists, in contrast, were unwilling to accept the presence of prostitution and wanted to moralize municipal affairs through legislation. They furthermore believed in the efficacy of laws to solve social problems and in the obligation of the government to act as a moral agent. From their perspective, San Francisco would ultimately be judged by the moral worthiness of its laws. If the city regulated prostitution, then it publicly identified itself with immorality.

Almost as soon as the clinic began, abolitionists began petitioning the mayor to end regulation. Interestingly, the business community had initially supported the clinic as a way of maintaining civic and social order. But when local social purity reformers, joined by abolitionists from all over the United States, threatened to boycott the upcoming Panama-Pacific International Exposition through a barrage of adverse national publicity, San Francisco's mayor and businessmen decided to protect the city's reputation and economic investment by closing the clinic.[8]

The power of abolitionists to threaten a city such as San Francisco testified to their national strength and organization. Regulation was no longer perceived as a viable solution to prostitution in the United States by the nonmedical population. As one reformer sarcastically noted, regulation was "likely to be as effectual as would be an attempt to stem the Niagara River with a lace pocket handkerchief."[9]

Nor was segregation a viable remedy. At least forty cities had denounced the nineteenth-century segregation of vice into circumscribed districts. As the Philadelphia Vice Commission explained, segregation was ineffective because "it segregates a small minority of the sexually vicious, it can never isolate disease, and promotes rather than reduces clandestine prostitution." They accused it of "lowering values of properties for reputable purposes, . . . forcing families of the poor into evil association, . . . raising crime to the dignity of a business, . . . promoting the double standard of morality, . . . [and] debauching police morals." Finally, segregation of vice rested on the assumption that prostitution was "a natural and ineradicable feature of society": a position against which Progressive reformers, trying to preserve a tradition of genteel morality, instinctively rebelled.[10]

Other solutions never emerged as serious possibilities during the Progressive Era. The decriminalization of prostitution was implicitly suggested by Brand Whitlock, a publicist and novelist who was also the ex-mayor of Toledo and minister to Belgium. "Why is it constantly necessary to do something *to* people?" he asked. "If we can't do something *for* them, when are we going to learn to let them alone? Or must this incessant interference, this meddling, this mauling and manhandling, go on in the world forever and ever?" When involuntary poverty ended, he concluded, Americans would no longer have to *do* something about prostitution.[11] Whitlock's views, however, were not supported by most of his contemporaries. The very idea of decriminalization—which views prostitution as a victimless crime that should not be regulated or legalized by law—countered the Progressive impulse to utilize the state to purify society.[12]

Reformers never seriously considered complete rehabilitation, either, the method later employed by the Russian, Chinese, and Cuban revolutionary governments. In these countries, prostitutes were forced into special institutions to learn new attitudes and skills with which to reenter society as productive workers. Such coercive state intervention reflects the socialist belief that the prostitute was the victim of class exploitation. Society, therefore, owed her *thorough* rehabilitation. Despite their emphasis on social and economic forces, however, many Progressive reformers still viewed prostitutes with moral repugnance and implicitly blamed them for their own fate. The idea of a society taking *full* responsibility for its deviants, moreover, found little enthusiasm in a nation just beginning to utilize the state to regulate economic and social life.

Nevertheless, Progressive reformers, unlike their American predecessors, *were* willing to use the state as a regulator of the nation's morals. By 1916, it appeared as though a national consensus had been reached. Although advocates of regulation and segregation continued to advance their positions, and although many Americans continued to believe privately that prostitution could not be eradicated, Progressive abolitionists had seemingly won the public's sympathy and support. "Absolute annihilation of the Social Evil" was declared a national goal synonymous with the preservation of a moral society. No halfway measures were to be countenanced. As the Portland, Maine, vice report pointed out, "The real question is whether the community shall hold up an uncompromising standard for purity, or a compromise standard for impurity." Between 1910 and 1915, at least thirty-five vice commission reports concluded that the presence of the Social Evil was "an intolerable fact of life."[13]

Although Progressive antivice crusaders aspired to enlist the government, in most cases the "state" referred to local government. On a national level, there was little that the federal government could do about prostitution except during war. To prevent the importation of women into the United States for the purposes of prostitution, federal officials tightened immigration regulations and procedures. The Mann Act, passed in 1910, aimed at preventing the transportation of women across state lines for "immoral purposes." Such federal intervention, however, left most intrastate and local prostitution untouched.

Much of the progressive campaign against prostitution, then, centered on state and municipal efforts to close down recognized vice districts. Reformers also relied upon penal and judicial reform and "preventive measures" to repress the Social Evil.[14] In each instance, a profoundly moralistic impulse shaped the direction of reform. Although nearly all reformers vowed to extricate the prostitute from commercialized vice, many of these reforms backfired and worsened prostitutes' condition.

In the area of penal reform, Progressives sought to end the fine system through which prostitutes had been punished in the courts. Such fines, they correctly argued, only forced women to engage in further prostitution in order to pay them. In its place, penal reformers advocated probation or "rehabilitation" in the newly created women's reformatories. In addition, they established special "morals," or night, courts to separate prostitutes from other criminals. The Domestic Relations Court in Philadelphia, the Morals Court in Chicago, and the Women's Court in New York were products of these new judicial systems.[15]

The growth of special courts, vice squads, social workers, and prisons to deal with prostitution paradoxically provided for the long-term institutionalization and bureaucratization of the Social Evil. By creating a separate, highly elaborate penal and judicial system to deal with female sexual deviance, reformers provided for the ultimate classification of prostitution as a crime. The creation of special morals courts, moreover, gave extra impetus to special morals, or vice, squads to entrap and imprison prostitutes.[16]

The widely applauded ideal of probation unfortunately benefited few prostitutes. Judges were strongly influenced by popular ideas about adolescence and a double standard of morality in dealing with young female offenders. For boys, adolescence was viewed as the period in which permanent character took shape. Their deviance was a short-term threat to society since their character could be changed through probation and parental restraint. For girls, however, the situation was different. Theoretically, a girl's morals were instilled in childhood and tested in adolescence. When a girl "sinned," many judges viewed her as a "soiled dove" who would probably not benefit from probation. Female crime seemed more "permanent"; girls, therefore, received probation less often than did boys.[17]

Court records indicate how little probation was actually used for girls. More frequently, judges sent young female sexual offenders—including prostitutes—to reformatories or to county workhouses. A sample of cases in a New York night court over a period of two weeks shows, for example, that of 262 women arraigned and sentenced, 104 were sent to a county workhouse, 7 sent to Bedford Reformatory, 64 discharged with a reprimand, 37 discharged for lack of evidence, and 16 placed on probation.[18] It is interesting to note, moreover, that most prostitutes, according to one well-known social worker, apparently preferred fines or sentences to probation. It seems that the prospect of enduring a probation officer's scrutiny for an extended period of time constituted greater punishment than imprisonment.[19]

Judges took a harsh view toward the sexual "offenses" of young adolescent females. The court lectured girls on chastity, probed their sex lives to ascertain the extent of their sin, and extolled the virtues of married women's purity. Many of the girls sent before the court were from racial and ethnic minorities. Reflecting society's exaggerated concern about the sexual activity of young, poor, adolescent females, the courts frequently manifested an interventionist, invasive, and punitive attitude toward female sexual offenders. In some cases, both daughter and mother were severely castigated for the sexual "irregularities" that had taken place. When young girls did not publicly repent—a form of civil confession—they received a reformatory sentence as punishment.[20]

Female adolescent "sex offenders" truly *offended* both the court's and society's definition of proper female sexual conduct. In one case, for example, a fifteen-year-old girl, Deborah Horwitz, was brought into court for staying out with boys and "flaunting" her sexual activities. Her probation officer, after ransacking her belongings, found a racy letter that the girl had written to a sailor, along with photos showing her with the top button of her blouse undone and her hat off. Deborah's mother helplessly tried to explain that she had many other children whom she had to feed and care for. Deborah, for her part, defiantly insisted that she had never coaxed or invited anyone's sexual attention. Nevertheless, she was committed to the state reformatory for girls.[21]

Like probation, the female reformatory rarely helped prostitutes and certainly did not eradicate prostitution. Although reformers applauded the rehabilitation offered at the few new "training farms," women's reformatories, and industrial schools, in fact only a few female reformatories existed. The first female reformatory had only just been established in Indiana in 1873, and other famous institutions were established only shortly thereafter, at Framington, Massachusetts, in 1877 and at Bedford Hills, New York, in 1901. As a result, the majority of cities had inadequate provisions for the custody of women prisoners. County workhouses or jailhouses, then, were most often used to house female criminals, including prostitutes.

In most cases, "rehabilitation" in reformatories meant practicing sewing, scrubbing, and cooking in preparation for work as a domestic servant—an occupation for which many prostitutes felt special contempt. Such work, moreover, was offered only to women under eighteen. Older women were presumably beyond redemption.[22] Even the best reformatories meant jail sentences, which merely prepared young women to return to the unskilled work "suitable" to their class and gender. In Portland, Oregon, and in California, for example, reformers tried to end the fine system by instituting rehabilitation at a "home" or training farm. These "training farms," however, offered no more training than jails did.[23] Even the famous Waverly House, founded in 1908, which was widely praised as a refuge for women on probation, offered only basket weaving, sewing, cooking, and gymnastics as "rehabilitation."[24]

Although ostensibly secular, reformatories reflected the deeply religious and evangelical spirit of the moral reform tradition. Concern for the "moral uplift" of the inmates pervaded the ideology of penal reform. Although no educational opportunities were offered, prison officials tried to instill proper middle-class feminine and domestic values. Like the small religious rescue home, reformatories operated on the belief that proper training in feminine domesticity was an essential precondition for redemption.

Religious values mixed with class expectations to provide an atmosphere in which prostitutes were to be redeemed. Jessie Hodder, superintendent of the Massachusetts Reformatory for Women during the early 1900s, freely explained how young female deviants needed to find redemption more than economic rehabilitation. "Sin," she argued, "is the cause of crime and conversion the cure; there should be industrial training, school work and medical care as assistants to the central purpose of religious conversion."[25] Most prostitutes received an indeterminate sentence and needed a letter of recommendation from the superintendent of the institution in order to be released. To gain such sponsorship, they had to prove themselves worthy of religious and middle-class approbation.[26]

In reformatories, prostitutes also found themselves subjected to eugenicists' mental tests and theories. After 1910, prostitutes became one of the first mass populations to be tested for hereditary and genetic defects. Courts, for example, began establishing clinics to determine whether or not female criminals were "feeble-minded." Although such tests were flawed by functional illiteracy and language barriers, many reformers began arguing that a major cause of prostitution was feeble-mindedness. By 1913, twelve states had laws that permitted the sterilization of criminals, idiots, the feeble-minded, imbeciles, syphilitics, moral and sexual perverts, epileptics, and rapists. Such legislation, like the reformatories and prisons in which prostitutes were housed, reflected a society that increasingly associated degeneracy with poverty and gradually sought means to control the sexual behavior of the poor.

A surprisingly high percentage of prostitutes were described as feeble-minded, and gradually the belief in feeble-mindedness as a cause of prostitution received widespread acceptance. The Massachusetts White Slave Commission found that only 154 out of 300 interviewed prostitutes could be described as "normal." The "mental defects" of the others, they asserted, "were so pronounced and evident as to warrant the legal commitment of each one as a feeble-minded person or as a defective delinquent." Other reformers and authorities found similar strains of "mental degeneracy" among prostitutes.[27] The superintendent of the State Reformatory for Women at Bedford, New York, declared that "of 2,000 common prostitutes of New York City, of whom we have data, we marked as normal, 49.13%; epileptic, 1.2%; insane, 2.4%; neurotic, 2.64%; feebleminded in varying degrees, 29.2%; or a total of 35.5% subnormal and 15.17% on whom we have not sufficient data."[28] The Illinois Training School for Women, the Massachusetts Reformatory for Women, and the Virginia Board of Charities and Corrections also reported a high incidence of feeble-minded prostitutes.[29]

What was feeble-mindedness? Maude Miner, the director of the Waverly House for Women in New York, noted that inherited strains of degeneracy appeared in 247 of 1,000 prostitutes' families as "some actively vicious element or clearly degenerate strain, drunkenness or prostitution." Describing the mental deficiency of a prostitute named Elsi, Miner pointed out that the girl's mental feeble-mindedness was unquestionably due to her inheritance from a tubercular mother and a drunken, immoral father who "came from a degenerate family of 'worthless alcoholics.' "[30] Another writer noted that two kinds of feeble-mindedness existed among prostitutes: those "whose sexual inclinations are abnormally strong or whose power of self control over natural impulses is abnormally weak" and those "who are passive, non-resistant, and will yield to anyone."[31] The Massachusetts investigation into white slavery further explained that "the well known immoral tendencies and suggestibility and social incapacity of the feebleminded cause them to drift naturally into prostitution. The feeble-minded need only opportunity to express their immoral tendencies."[32]

It appears, then, that feeble-mindedness had little to do with women's mental capacities; rather, the term instead "explained" both "inherited strains of degeneracy"—for which the prostitute could not really be blamed—and willful, immoral behavior. That many prostitutes expressed contempt for middle-class niceties and values was offered as strong evidence of their feeble-mindedness. The Massachusetts investigators, for example, revealingly concluded that

> the general moral insensibility, the boldness, egotism and vanity, the love of notoriety, the lack of shame or remorse, the absence of even a pretense of affection or sympathy for their children or for their parents, the desire for

immediate pleasure without regard for consequences, the lack of fore-
thought or anxiety about the future—all cardinal symptoms of feeble-
mindedness—were strikingly evident in every one of the 154 women.[33]

Rather than indicating mental deficiency, the label *feeble-minded* instead referred to prostitutes' refusal or failure to conform to middle-class values and
behavioral patterns. Using the scientific language of the day, reformers could
both excuse and blame prostitutes at the same time, thus expressing their deep
ambivalence about the nature of prostitution and female sexuality. If a woman
were described as feeble-minded, she could be classified as the *passive* victim of
inherited strains of degeneracy. Given their own class perspective toward female
sexuality, most reformers could not imagine that a woman would voluntarily
engage in illicit sexual behavior. Nevertheless, bold, aggressive, *active*, and de-
fiant prostitutes deeply offended reformers' sense of morality. In fact, feeble-
mindedness described inappropriate gender and class conduct. By labeling such
women feeble-minded, reformers could defend against, as well as condemn, poor
women's sexual aggressiveness, social boldness, impatience with delayed gratification, and disregard for the future. The term *feeble-minded*, then, became a way
of classifying aggressive female sexuality, as well as expressing the growing class
and cultural conflicts between penal reformers, eugenicists, and antivice crusaders and the target of their efforts, prostitutes and sexually "deviant" women.

As young female delinquents became exposed to the growing bureaucratization represented by these new institutions and penal reforms, their alienation
from family and community frequently increased. The consequences of reformers' efforts did not escape all of them. One active social worker in Massachusetts publicly decried the invasive and repressive nature of the new reforms.
Protection of young women, argued C. C. Carstens, was indeed the responsibility of the community. "But when we come to examine the procedure that our
communities have provided for her protection, we reach an almost equally baf-
fling problem." Basically, a young woman was subjected to weeks of humiliating
and degrading court examination. "She must convince the jury of the truth of her
statements and must be subjected to the most grilling cross-examination in open
court at the hands of the defendant's counsel." After such an experience, "does
anyone here feel sure that there remains to this young girl a shred of the modesty
which it is reasonable for us to assume was still left at the time that her wretched
experience was first revealed?"[34]

The consequences and effects of these newly created institutions on prostitutes
are even better described by the inmates themselves. Maimie Pinzer, a young
woman who corresponded with a prominent Bostonian lady, Fanny Quincy
Howe, between 1910 and 1922, has left us a unique description of her experience
as a young juvenile delinquent.[35] Born in 1885 of immigrant Polish-Russian
parents, Maimie Pinzer enjoyed a modest degree of comfort during her early
childhood in Philadelphia. At the age of thirteen, however, her life was irrevoca-

*Maimie Pinzer with her dog, Poke. Reprinted by permission
of the Schlesinger Library, Radcliffe College, Cambridge, Mass.*

bly transformed when her father was killed "by persons unknown." Without her
husband's income, Julia Pinzer, Maimie's mother, faced the formidable task of
providing for five children. As a result, Maimie was put to work in the house,
doing the "sort of work I despised, because I had never been taught how—and
too, because I loved school and books and the things that school meant." Unable
to attend school, without any money of her own, Maimie finally got a job as a
"saleslady" at a regular department store. Estranged from her mother, Maimie
sought emotional companionship and peer acceptance from the young men who
"to this day . . . come during the afternoon hours to make 'dates' for the eve."

In one of her letters to Mrs. Howe, Maimie recounted the experience that resulted in her imprisonment, probably around 1900. Her story offers an unusual and vivid portrayal of the transformation of sexual deviancy into a criminal act.

> Of course, the inevitable thing happened. Some young man took me to his room; and I stayed three or four days before I put in an appearance in the neighborhood of my home. As I neared our house, a man spoke to me by name and told me he was a "special officer" and that he had a warrant for my arrest. He took me to the Central Station, which is in the City Hall—the large building which is in the center of the city of Philadelphia.[36]

On the request of her mother, Maimie had been arrested as an incorrigible child. The conflict between daughter and mother had been brewing for a long time. Misunderstandings between a first generation immigrant mother and an assimilated daughter who sought to enjoy the normal sexual and social adventures of American adolescence had become frequent. On one occasion, Maimie, proud of her gleaming smile, had discovered American health aids with which to protect her teeth. Her mother, ignorant of American practices, became convinced that Maimie had purchased the tooth powder for lewd sexual practices and viciously attacked her daughter for presumed sexual perversions.

Although Maimie had not yet bartered sex for money, she soon learned how to exchange sexual favors for prison privileges. Her first night in jail was terrifying.

> Of course I was terribly frightened—but imagine my horror when I was placed in a cell! It was a horribly filthy, vile-smelling hole. I cried and begged they should send for my mother—and though they did, after awhile, she refused to come. It was nightime and there was no light; and I could hear the rats, which I feared more than death. I was terrified, and pleaded to be taken out of there. It was only after I permitted one of the men, who seemed to be in charge at the time, to take all sorts of liberties with me, that I was permitted to come out of the cell; and I sat up the rest of the night in the room where he, too, sat all night. The man was perhaps fifty, or even older.[37]

The next morning, Maimie was brought to a "hearing" at which both her mother and an uncle who "did me the first wrong, when I was a tiny girl, and any number of times since then" asked that she be sent away as an incorrigible child. Maimie felt outraged at her mother's betrayal as well as by the appearance of an uncle who had continually sexually molested her. A formal charge needed to be made to prove Maimie's criminality. "A further hearing was demanded for this. . . . I was then led away to the same cell, pleading to my mother, in shrieks, to take me home. . . . There was only a bench and an exposed toilet in the cell, and it was, as I thought, terrible."[38]

The process of being labeled a criminal and deviant continued as Maimie was led through the new juvenile justice system. Still a young adolescent, she experienced great terror before the impersonal and seemingly uncaring penal system.

At noon, there were footsteps and the jangling of keys and the cell was opened . . . I was labouring under the delusion that I was being taken home. I saw some men in line, and I was told to get behind the last one. Still, I had no suspicion of what was coming. The line moved, as did I. And oh! what a lot they were . . . they were the dregs and scum of the earth. I looked on them with alarm, and was dismayed that I had to walk with them, though I did not even guess at my destination. We filed down the stairs, and the line in front got outside; and as I was last, I saw them filing into a prison van—the kind called "Black Maria." They are usually painted quite dark, and resemble a closed bus with air- or peep-holes on top. It was just at noon; and there were thousands going thru the courtyard, enroute to their lunches. Quite a crowd had gathered to watch the prisoners; and as I saw that, I became so mortified that I could not move—though, due to the imprecations of the guard behind me, I really wanted to. Of course, little ceremony was wasted on me. I was fairly dragged to the van, and thrown in. When I recovered my sense, I found the wagon was moving. . . . The ride lasted perhaps an hour. Time can never efface my impressions thru that ride. . . . The ride was probably the worst of the whole harrowing experience.[39]

At Moyamensing Prison, Maimie found herself in a rather odd situation. Years ago, her father had donated a library of Yiddish books to the prison for Jewish prisoners. Now Maimie, his daughter, was one of its prisoners. A prison matron registered Maimie, brought her "some very coarse, rough looking clothes," and proceeded to hack off her hair. After one more day in prison, Maimie was once again returned to court and sentenced for a year at a Magdalen home, which, in Maimie's own words, was a "mild sort of reform school for girls who have gone astray."

At the reform school, Maimie, like most girls in similar institutions, received no education. "Though I was the youngest girl there by four years," she later wrote, "still, I taught the ones who had little or no schooling, during our school hours, I received absolutely no school training here whatever—except what I derived from teaching girls of seventeen and eighteen their alphabets and the simple sums." What she did learn, however, further estranged her from her family and prepared her for a life as a prostitute for the next few years.[40]

Maimie Pinzer's experiences may or may not accurately reflect the treatment accorded other female adolescents during the Progressive Era. In some cities, for example, a young girl might initially have been segregated from adult prisoners. Several aspects of Maimie's story, however, do highlight important trends of the period. First, both families and authorities increasingly relied on external institutions to cope with parent-child conflict and female adolescent sexual deviancy. Second, the process of labeling sexual deviants had been transformed by an impersonal and bureaucratized system of courts, social workers, and reformatories. Third, a double standard of sexual morality continued to influence the new agencies of sexual control so that Maimie, and not her male friend, received punishment for "sexual transgression." Finally, and most importantly, sexual "promiscuity"—especially among the poor—was increasingly being perceived and treated as criminal behavior.

As a result of these changes, women who transgressed middle-class conventional sexual norms—either for pleasure or for survival—faced the very real possibility of being labeled a criminal, receiving a prison sentence, and joining a social group of criminal outcasts. The experience, as Maimie's story testifies, could be traumatic. One young prostitute never forgot her imprisonment. "Every time she goes to sleep," her sister explained, "she sees the cell and the iron bars, and is almost afraid to open her eyes for fear she is still there."[41] As "sexual sinners" met a more hardened class of criminals, they soon assimilated the language and attitudes of a criminal subculture. As one prostitute later explained, "I was no bad girl when I got put away in the Home. Now I know everything bad. I lived with the vilest women, the down-and-out kind, who have taught me and lots of other girls more innocent than I, how to solicit the streets." The result was a more professionalized class of street-wise prostitutes.[42]

The net effect of reformatories, then, was to label young women as *both* sinners and criminals. Long jail sentences, which were commonly given to young females, served only to create a more hardened and sophisticated professional class of female criminals. Reformatories also tended to further interfere with or disrupt family authority and integrity. Since most reformatories had purposely been constructed in distant rural areas "to avoid the evils of the city," families found it difficult to visit their daughters, and inmates lost important family and legal assistance. Isolated in rural areas with other female criminals, without any real rehabilitation, inmates could only learn to perfect their "trade."[43]

Knowing the limitations of penal and criminal reform, many Progressive reformers also sought "preventive measures" that would keep women from entering prostitution in the first place. The measures they suggested reflected their diverse views on the causes of prostitution. Female reformers, many of whom emphasized the seduction and rape of young girls as a cause of prostitution, tried in some states to raise the age of consent ("the age at which no girl can legally consent to carnal relations with the other sex") to eighteen or twenty-one. This was an important consideration; in some states a man could rape a ten-year-old without threat of conviction.[44]

In addition, female reformers and some male reformers fought to achieve a minimum wage law. Through extensive inquiries into the wages and working conditions that women encountered, reformers across the nation had gradually, and sometimes reluctantly, conceded that women did not work for "pin money," but out of dire necessity. By the second decade of the twentieth century, moreover, a number of reformers were also willing to admit that subsistence wages forced young female workers into prostitution. Despite bitter resistance from employers of female workers, eight states enacted such minimum wage laws by 1913.[45]

Other reformers, such as Jane Addams, stressed the failure of cities to provide wholesome recreational activities for urban youth as a cause of prostitution. Young people, Addams strongly argued, needed amusement and diversion; it was the responsibility of urban reformers to make sure that America's youth could enjoy themselves in *carefully* supervised centers and parks.[46] While the establishment of public parks and recreational areas greatly enriched urban life, its effects on rates of prostitution were probably negligible.

Still other reformers focused on the moral degradation of America as leading to prostitution and tried to counter it through "moral uplift" campaigns. Movie houses, ice cream parlors, saloons, steamboat ferries, and dance halls—any recreation that took place outside the "safe" confines of the family—was severely condemned. Vice reformers further asked parents to censor their children's reading and demanded that authorities censor movies and books, supervise places of amusement, and establish morals commissions in every town and city.[47] Such commissions, like the New England Watch and Ward Society, the New York Committee of Fourteen, and the Los Angeles Morals Efficiency Committee, solicited vice information, reported it to the police, and agitated for vice reform.

In general, the effects of such moral reforms were social repression and social control of the laboring poor. James Rolph, mayor of San Francisco, a city whose legendary lively night life attracted reformers' wrath, challenged the "humanitarian" motives of moral reformers. The campaign against prostitution, he argued, had become harsh and particularly harmed prostitutes and poor people. "I reply to all the self-advertising pharisees and all who have been agitating so loudly to reform other people's morals—many who are calling for intolerant restriction would not be satisfied until they destroyed all the amusement and entertainment that have given San Francisco life and character. What will be done with all the women put out of work?"[48] Caught up in the campaign to end prostitution, few moral reformers bothered to answer his question.

Preventive measures, like judicial and penal reform, had limited effect on the spread of prostitution. In a society characterized by increased geographic mobility, moral persuasion was a relatively weak weapon. Reformers needed laws and they knew it. Unlike moral reform, legal statutes gave them the needed muscle to eradicate the most visible aspects of prostitution.

On a state level, where most of the legislation against prostitution took place, legislators circulated a series of model laws aimed at closing down all the red-light districts. Passed first in 1909 in Iowa, the red-light abatement act permitted any private citizen to file a complaint against a particular building used for prostitution. After the court issued a temporary vacate order to the owner, a hearing would be set to determine whether or not a particular building had in fact been used for "immoral purposes." If found guilty, the owner received a permanent injunction, with the building sealed under judicial supervision. In some states, such as New York, the abatement act also permitted fines levied against the owners of the building. In addition to the loss of rental income, legal fees and fines theoretically persuaded owners to keep their buildings free of prostitution. In practice, however, the abatement acts were more frequently used to warn owners of impending hearings. Landlords simply vacated offensive tenants and rarely lost much rental income.[49]

Not surprisingly, the agitation for the red-light abatement laws prompted considerable controversy. For one thing, such laws attempted to regulate the use of private property. Equally important, the abatement laws threatened landlords with the loss of enormous profits gained from charging madams higher than usual rents for the opportunity of conducting a brothel. In California, for example, real estate owners and businessmen canvassed the state against the red-light abatement act, arguing that such legislation would result in more serious crimes against decent women, would be used to blackmail real estate owners, or would simply scatter prostitutes all over the community.[50]

Reformers, however, had equally strong arguments. The so-called limited red-light district, they argued, had in fact spilled over into "decent" neighborhoods. Vice could not be contained. Reformers also appealed to a higher sense of civic morality. Once prostitution was abolished, they claimed, a new and more purified society would result. In the end, antivice reformers were better organized than their opponents. The national scope of the antiprostitution crusade meant that California moral reformers could provide private and public assurances from other city officials where such legislation had been passed. Waving letters from St. Louis or Seattle, local reformers could command a certain authority in such matters—and they did. By 1917, thirty-one states had adopted some form of the Iowa Abatement Act.[51]

Despite well-funded opposition, then, the red-light abatement acts became important weapons in the arsenal of legislation against prostitution.[52] Another attempt to prevent landlord exploitation of prostitution was passed in Portland, Oregon, in 1913. Called the Tin Plate Ordinance, it required a tin plate bearing the owner's name and home address on every building. The attempt to intimidate landlords who would not want to be publicly associated with prostitution was copied across the nation.

In addition to undermining real estate exploitation of prostitution, most states also passed a series of laws aimed at other third-party exploitation of prostitution. Procuring, pandering, pimping, keeping a "disorderly" house, and using saloons as assignation houses became illegal in most parts of the United States. Many states also passed laws prohibiting the sale of liquor at dance halls, as well as in the small booths and connecting rooms used for prostitution in saloons. A few states also passed "white slave" laws prohibiting the sale of women for "immoral purposes."[53]

The successful passage of such legislation heightened public expectations that prostitution would be abolished. In most cases, however, the chief of police responded to civic pressure simply by ordering the closing of the district. Police generally notified madams and prostitutes that the district would be closed. As prostitutes scattered from red-light districts, arrests of prostitutes skyrocketed across the nation. A majority of arrested women were sent to the county workhouse, the rest receiving fines, suspended sentences, or reformatory sentences.[54]

Unfortunately, reformers made few provisions for the thousands of prostitutes they forced out of the red-light districts in dozens of cities. The situation corresponded to the freeing of black slaves by the "older" abolitionists. Freed without the much heralded "forty acres and a mule" on which economic independence might have been forged, freedmen and freedwomen faced a "free," competitive, racist labor market as unskilled workers. Similarly, when the "new" abolitionists attempted to abolish vice from American cities, freed prostitutes faced a "free," sexist labor market as unskilled and stigmatized workers.

As a result of their "liberation" from the vice districts, prostitutes in fact faced a bleak future. True, in closing the brothels, reformers temporarily freed prostitutes from third-party exploitation by madams and landlords. Many of these people, however, had provided the shelter, support, and protection on which prostitutes depended. Police crackdowns also disrupted the subculture and friendship networks that had thrived for years in the vice districts. Now all members of the districts—not only prostitutes—had to find new locations or means of survival.

In most cases, thousands of prostitutes simply left town and went to another city where the local vice district remained open. Such a scatter syndrome was observed in a number of cities; prostitutes and police played a game of cat and mouse across the country. When Bridgeport, Connecticut, closed its vice district, prostitutes fled to New Haven, Connecticut, where the "houses were still open."[55] "Business is very poor, this week," one prostitute admitted to investigators from Hartford, "and I am afraid it will be worse. If things don't open up next month we are going to Pittsburgh, my friend and I, it is wide open there."[56]

After most major cities had closed their red-light districts, however, few areas remained "wide open." By 1916, the American Social Hygiene Association had published a list of forty-seven cities that had closed their vice districts.[57] In a very real sense, the campaign against prostitution *had* to become national; each city had to protect itself from refugee prostitutes by closing its own red-light district.

After the red-light district in Des Moines, Iowa, was closed, one reformer lamented that "there were a great many of them who left the city. It was not our prime idea to drive them out of the city, but our idea to drive them into decency."[58] Few prostitutes, however, were driven into "decency." For most, the closing of the red-light districts meant an immediate loss of shelter, friends, and income, accompanied by a desperate urgency to accommodate to the new criminal and legal sanctions against their trade. Finding "respectable work" was neither easy nor, in many cases, desirable. Needed references from families, friends, or former employers were frequently impossible to obtain. Untrained, many prostitutes had difficulty in acquiring skilled work. The wages earned as an unskilled domestic or factory worker, moreover, rarely compared with prostitutes' former incomes. Subsistence wages could not support a young woman unless she lived with her family—and few prostitutes felt they could return to their parents or families.

When the Washington, D.C., area decided to close its red-light district in 1914, a group of prostitutes, perhaps through the agency of some sympathetic reformers, wrote the following public letter complaining of their dilemma:

> Knowing that public opinion is against us, and that the passing of the Kenyon "Red Light" Bill is certain, we, the inmates of the underworld, want to know how the public expects to provide for us in the future?
>
> We do not want "homes." All we ask is that positions be provided for us. The majority will accept them. We must live somehow. We are human. With all the resorts in nearly all the large cities closed, it is useless for us to leave Washington.
>
> How many citizens will give employment to women of our class? Very few would be so liberal minded. They would consider us a detriment to their business. If we must reform, you who recommend these reformations, help us to lead a better life.
>
> In years past, it has been tried and as soon as previous reputations were discovered, our positions were made unbearable. Then, through necessity we had to return to the old life.[59]

Such public demands by prostitutes were probably quite rare in American newspapers. Nevertheless, the letter does reveal some of the consequences of the campaign to "abolish" prostitution. In their plans to end prostitution, most reformers neglected to consider the future of prostitutes in a "purified" society. Their attitudes are illustrated by an encounter between "Golden Rule" Jones, the ex-mayor of Toledo, and moral reformers. It seems that a committee of reformers called on Mayor Jones to demand that he obliterate the social evil in Toledo.

> "But what am I to do?" he inquired. "These women are here."
>
> "Have the police," they said, a new, simple and happy device suddenly occurring to them, "drive them out of town and close up their houses!" They sat and looked at him triumphantly.
>
> "But where shall I have the police drive them? Over to Detroit, or to Cleveland, or merely out into the country? They have to go *somewhere*, you know."
>
> It was a detail that had escaped them, and presently, with his great patience, and his great sincerity, he said to them:
>
> "I'll make you a proposition. You go and select two of the worst of these

women you can find, and I'll agree to take them into my home and provide
for them until they can find some other home and some other way of making a living. And then you, each of you, take one girl into your home, under
the same conditions, and together we'll try to find homes for the rest."
   They looked at him, then looked at each other, and seeing how utterly
hopeless this strange man was, they went away.[60]

   Some reformers, especially feminists, tried to find prostitutes other employment. Their efforts, however, were small-scale, "charitable" enterprises that
could in no way meet the needs of large numbers of women. In Washington,
D.C., for example, the attempts of the Florence Crittendon local to give jobs to
prostitutes backfired because the women rejected menial labor at subsistence
wages.[61]
   Some reformers' thinking seemed almost magical: if only prostitution were
legally prohibited, it would disappear. In many cases, however, it was simply a
question of priorities. When asked what they would do with prostitutes driven
from town, a member of the Louisville, Kentucky, Vice Commission responded,
"Why should a community hesitate or consider as to what will become of a few
women when the greater question, of the moral and physical health of the larger
body of the community and of the children that are yet to be born, is the problem
that actually confronts us?"[62] The problems of eradicating visible evidence of
prostitution and quelling the fear of the "Great Scourge" of venereal disease were
urgent and visible; the fate of poor women was not.
   What happened to prostitutes driven from American cities? Evidence concerning the long-range effects of their "liberation" from the districts is unsubstantial
and mostly nonexistent. In one study completed in Baltimore, investigators
found that of 256 prostitutes, 56 were not found; 43 returned to prostitution; 15
probably engaged in clandestine prostitution; 20 lived with men; 43 left town; 26
married; 15 became involved in some kind of business; 16 worked regularly; 7
died; and 5 lived with relatives. Although data of this kind probably raise more
questions than they answer, they do indicate that the majority of prostitutes
probably moved to new sections of Baltimore or other cities and engaged in new
forms of prostitution.[63]
   The new forms of prostitution that emerged had one specific goal: to avoid
police detection. Since brothels and parlor houses could no longer advertise their
wares, rooming houses, flats, hotels, and massage parlors became the predominant sites for prostitution. To avoid detection, madams and prostitutes who had
once catered to a wealthy clientele began to rely on the "call girl" system of
prostitution, in which customers call to see a particular prostitute. In this way,
connections could be made secretly without danger of police harassment.
   For the majority of poor women, however, the closing of the houses meant
increased streetwalking, which was immediately noticed in most American cities.
Without recognized districts or brothels, prostitutes could no longer receive customers in the semiprotected environment of a brothel or district. Instead, they

had to search for business in public places—hotels, restaurants, cabarets, or on the street.[64]

The search for customers made prostitutes extremely vulnerable to both customer and police harassment. The number of arrests for streetwalking quickly jumped during the years following the closing of the districts.[65] Given these conditions, it is not surprising that pimps began dominating the practice of prostitution. Warding off the dangers posed by both customers and police, providing legal assistance, offering a semblance of emotional support, pimps moved in to fill needs that madams and other prostitutes had previously met in brothels.[66]

In a sense, the control of prostitution changed hands. Despite third-party exploitation of prostitution in the vice districts, madams and prostitutes had wielded considerable power in their relations with customers. Now prostitutes became the easy targets of both pimps and organized crime. In both cases, the physical violence faced by prostitutes rapidly increased.

As one Chicago observer noted, "With the initiation of the period of suppression of commercialized vice, prostitution went underground." During the twenties and thirties, rings of privileged vice syndicates gained control over major aspects of urban prostitution. As the same observer commented, "If commercialized vice did not disappear with the passing of the segregated district, it is true that the difficulties of dealing with vice now that it was organized, entrenched and protected, were greatly increased. The vice lords and their syndicated resorts and their alliances with local politics, have been able to organize a resistance which the forces of reform have thus far not been able to successfully overcome."[67] Contrary to the glowing reports of the vice commissions—during and after the closing of the districts—vice did not disappear from American urban life; it merely assumed new forms.

Like penal reform and preventive measures, the closing of the red-light districts neither eradicated prostitution nor helped prostitutes. On the contrary, as Progressive reformers increasingly relied on the expanded force of the state to deal with the Social Evil, prostitutes became victims of repressive legislation. It was not until the entry of the United States into the first World War, however, that the antivice movement developed into a full-scale repressive movement against the prostitute.

America's entry into the war coincided with the national municipal movement to eradicate prostitution. In an atmosphere already charged by the fanatic enthusiasm to combat the Social Evil *and* a "war to end all wars," the exigencies of combat prompted quick federal action to ensure a healthy and fit armed services. As the army increased to five million men, federal authorities became concerned with experts' concern that half the army might be infected with gonorrhea. Prostitutes, as potential carriers of disease, soon became identified as a significant and dangerous internal domestic enemy.[68]

With surprising speed, federal agencies began assuming control over social hygiene and the regulation of prostitution. In 1916, in anticipation of America's entrance into the war, Congress authorized legislation that provided for cooperation between voluntary and governmental agencies. The Chamberlain-Kahn Act of 1917 created a Division of Venereal Diseases in 1917, and by 1918 President Wilson had created an Interdepartmental Board of Social Hygiene.

In large part, the federal campaign against venereal disease continued in directions already followed by Progressive vice crusaders. The government helped to close down red-light districts near military camps or cantonments. Preventive measures aimed at moral and physical prophylaxis of the military resulted in a number of new attempts to educate the population. Women's groups, under the aegis of the War Department Commission on Training Camp Activities, became deeply involved in the war effort. Katharine Davis, an early penal reformer, coordinated a campaign in which female physicians and orators spoke with large audiences across the nation. Women's groups showed such films as "Fit to Fight" and "The End of the Road" under the direction of E. H. Grifith.[69]

Most Americans appeared to support the government's efforts to "cleanse the nation." David Pivar, who has closely studied the government's battle with prostitution during World War I, explains:

> The enthusiasm to cleanse American morals became pandemic as the Federal government undertook this millenarian campaign. Civic organizations, health agencies, reform groups, religious denominations and prominent individuals flooded the government with telegrams and letters pledging support. Ministers even prepared "Health Sunday" sermons to familiarize their congregations with new ideals of sex education and legitimate the movement. The Progressives' dream of closing the saloon and brothel seemed close to realization. No "personal liberties" could be tolerated when the nation was threatened by alcoholism and venereal disease, characterized as "social murder" and "social suicide." Impurities of all sorts were the enemy.[70]

Yet it soon became apparent that something had changed. The tone of the federal campaign seemed different; social hygienists now dominated the effort to control prostitution.

As part of the voluntary social movement to control prostitution, social hygienists had cooperated with municipal reformers, purity reformers, and feminists throughout the Progressive Era. Unlike many of their counterparts, however, social hygienists focused primarily on the control of venereal disease, its medical prevention and treatment. Through the formation of social hygiene groups across the nation, the American Social Hygiene Association had successfully popularized the association of prostitution with the spread of disease.

Many social hygienists pressed for the dissemination of sexual knowledge and for laws that would make venereal disease reportable. After the Wasserman test became available in 1906, they further agitated for medical marriage certificates for both men and women. By 1921, twenty states had required the Wasserman test for a marriage license. Seeking to break the "conspiracy of silence" that had surrounded the subject of venereal disease, social hygienists also sought to institute sexual education into the public school curriculum. Although some of their measures were vehemently resisted by other reformers, social hygienists shared with their opponents an emphasis on a single standard of sexuality and chastity for both men and women and an exaggerated concern about the sexual practices of the poor.[71] Their perspective was amplified by the Progressive belief in the power of experts to wield new technological and political power wisely for the common good.

As the government increasingly relied on the advice and professional expertise of such social hygienists, the campaign against prostitution became more repressive. Concern for rational and efficient protection of the armed forces resulted, for example, in the development of the "American Plan." Under this new plan, the military could arrest any woman within five miles of a military cantonment. Under the new health laws, when women were arrested their civil rights were suspended. If found infected, a woman could be sentenced to a hospital or a "farm colony" until cured. By the end of the war, 15, 520 infected prostitutes had been imprisoned for an average stay of seventy days in "detention homes" and in reformatories for an average stay of 365 days. Most of the prostitutes never received the promised "rehabilitation" or medical hospitalization. Rather, the majority spent their sentences in jails, stockades, and county workhouses. Not surprisingly, no men were arrested under the American Plan, which was directed solely against women.[72]

Given the earlier strength of social purity and feminist reformers, one is surprised to find that little resistance met the implementation of the American Plan. In Europe, as well as in the United States, abolitionists tried to attack this newest form of state regulation. Like the Contagious Diseases Acts (1866–69) or the American regulation of prostitution in Manila after the accession of the Philippines in 1899, the American Plan was viewed by abolitionists as an infringement of women's civil rights, as a legitimization of the double standard, and as the perpetrator of continued vice.

Despite strong support from British and European abolitionists, however, opposition to the American Plan failed to have any serious impact on the federal government. Most of the organized women's movement was deeply committed to and involved in the war effort. Public disapproval of the plan, they soon found, was equated with lack of patriotism. Although the Interdepartmental Board of Social Hygiene always invited women to participate in its meetings, it solicited women who either shared or bowed to the social hygienist perspective. Inevitably, the acquiescent participation of nationally known women on the board served to undermine other women's opposition to the American Plan.

Nevertheless, it was individual feminists and female reformers who provided the most sustained opposition to the plan.[73]

At the end of the war, it was clear that the social hygiene movement had become divorced from the older abolitionist coalition and thoroughly integrated into government policy making. No longer members of an independent voluntary movement, social hygienists had emerged as the professional experts who would direct government policy on prostitution and venereal disease. "Social Hygienists," as Pivar explains, "would become instrumentalities of a new leadership of health officials whose earlier contacts with reform movements, including the women's movement, had been minimal and whose understanding of veneral disease was motivated by narrower and more limited concerns and interests than reformers."[74]

Gone were earlier concerns for the prostitute, her exploiters, and the causes of her "downfall." Gone was the belief in the potential transformation of sexual morality into a single standard for men and women. Gone was the feminist exhortation to fight patriarchal exploitation of all women. In their place stood the social hygienists: more powerful, better organized, and now federally legitimated as the professional experts on prostitution and venereal disease control. When the war ended, the prostitute fared no better; an intensification of efforts to formalize legislation against prostitution and venereal disease spread across the country. Voluntary clinics for prostitutes, like those advocated in England, were rejected in favor of continued repression of the Social Evil.[75]

By the end of the war, America's longest and noisiest debate over prostitution had ended. The legal and medical foundation for controlling prostitution and venereal disease had been laid; the state apparatus for enforcing new legislation had been erected. Before 1917, most laws had been directed at commercialized vice, rather than at the prostitute herself: women had been arrested for vagrancy or for disturbing the peace. By the end of the war, however, the law had recognized a class of prostitutes who would constitute a social group of criminal outcasts.[76]

Although repressive measures against the prostitute had intensified during the war, the American Plan and other social hygiene efforts represented merely a tactical departure from the larger Progressive campaign against prostitution: like other Progressive measures, the American Plan sought to cope with the problem of prostitution through repressive legislation that directly affected the prostitute, but not the customer.

As American reformers increasingly turned to the state to legislate morality, the shrill voice of religious intolerance for "evil" became transformed by social experts into repressive laws against prostitution. Although the impulse remained highly moralistic, the means of achieving change became increasingly bureaucratized. The effort to preserve an older morality and the uncompromising moralism of the religious reform movement found modern legislative translation in the punishment of the prostitute for society's Social Evil. Now the state, rather than the clergy or the community, became instrumental in labeling and ostracizing society's deviants; yet the state, unlike religious moral reformers, offered little hope of redemption. In the end, the moral indignation of the abolitionist was joined by the managerial, efficient, medical perspective of the social hygienist to create an atmosphere in which the prostitute became a scapegoat and a symbol of society's ills.

In the war against the Social Evil, the welfare of the prostitute had been largely ignored. The long battle against commercialized vice—initiated by early reformers to protect the exploited prostitute—had been transformed by a new generation of professional experts into repressive laws directed at the prostitute. Offended by visible evidence of vice, Progressive abolitionists had attempted to banish prostitution from sight. Without significant changes in the class or gender system, however, the abolition of prostitution translated into the immediate unemployment and impoverishment of prostitutes and the long-term institutionalization of criminalized prostitution.[77]

Driven underground, prostitution became integrated into the underworld of crime. Like the prohibition of liquor, the criminalization of prostitution became a self-fulfilling prophecy. Like the birth control movement—which also began with the aim of elevating women's status—the antiprostitution movement resulted in the professional and official victimization of poor women.[78]

Against the urge to repress the Social Evil, the prostitute remained relatively helpless to protect herself. As poor women, prostitutes suffered doubly from gender and class discrimination. Despite all rhetoric to the contrary, the prostitute remained a moral pariah: an unfortunate casualty in the war against prostitution.

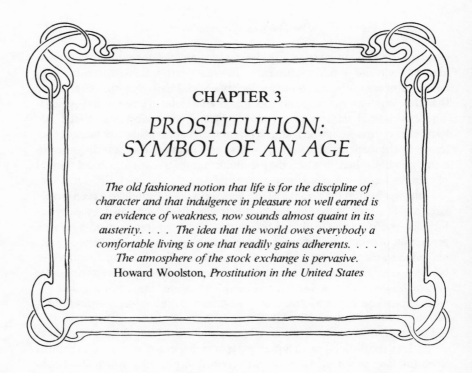

CHAPTER 3

PROSTITUTION: SYMBOL OF AN AGE

The old fashioned notion that life is for the discipline of character and that indulgence in pleasure not well earned is an evidence of weakness, now sounds almost quaint in its austerity. . . . The idea that the world owes everybody a comfortable living is one that readily gains adherents. . . . The atmosphere of the stock exchange is pervasive.
Howard Woolston, *Prostitution in the United States*

Public response to prostitution in the early decades of the twentieth century was marked by an unprecedented hysteria and panic. Reformers represented the Social Evil as a moral contagion: an "infectious disease" and a "curse, which is more blasting than any plague or epidemic."[1] Venereal disease was wholly identified with prostitution and feared with an intensity disproportionate to its probable incidence. Both were described as invading enemies. "You doubtless think you are safe," the Reverend John P. Peters told his congregation in an ominous sermon on prostitution. "Don't be too sure. It's getting close, it's creeping up to you. Within a week word has come to me of things you wouldn't like me to tell you about here that are very close to you."[2] Urging the populace to guard its collective health, one federal official warned that

> if this country were threatened with an invasion by a foreign foe or with destruction by internal enemies, the fact that they were large and powerful and that the nation was in deadly peril, would serve not to cause us to lie supinely and hopelessly while our country was being overwhelmed and our women and girls butchered and ravished, but the very enormity of the danger should only serve to arouse us as true Americans to the greater and intense patriotism and activity; and so it must be in the presence of this monstrous danger to our social institution, our altar, and our home.[3]

Viewing this furor over prostitution with a mixture of astonishment and amusement, Emma Goldman wondered why Americans had suddenly become so concerned about the Social Evil. "How is it," she asked, "that an institution, known almost to every child, should have been discovered so suddenly? How is it that this evil, known to all sociologists, should now be made such an important issue?"[4]

In fact, Goldman's cynical view of the antiprostitution crusade raises significant questions. For nearly a century, moral reformers had been trying to alert the public about prostitution. Yet it was not until the Progressive Era that the struggle against prostitution became a national campaign against an evil of terrifying dimensions. Why did prostitution suddenly assume such significance?

Some reformers might have replied that venereal disease and prostitution had substantially increased by the turn of the century. Whether this is true, however, remains unclear. Statistics on vice are notoriously unreliable. Most American cities never registered prostitutes, and it is impossible to estimate the vast number of "occasional" prostitutes who were never arrested, hospitalized for disease, or made notorious by scandal. Census, arrest, and hospitalization records and statistics offered by moral reformers reveal merely that social concern about prostitution had increased.[5] Widespread alarm about venereal disease may indicate not an epidemic but the public's heightened awareness and magnified fears of venereal disease's signs and consequences.

Some studies on prostitution have indicated a possible association between rates of urbanization and rates of prostitution.[6] Certainly, the population of most major American cities increased enormously between 1890 and 1900. For example, while the population of the United States increased 20 percent during this period, the population of New York City skyrocketed 126.8 percent.[7] A relationship between prostitution and urbanization, however, cannot be generalized to all historical situations.

If, as Richard Evans has argued, rates of prostitution peak during the second wave of industrialization (when heavy industry excludes women from the labor force) and decline with the growth of the tertiary clerical and service sector (when women find greater opportunities for employment), prostitution was probably in decline by the early years of the twentieth century.[8] The important *and* reliable fact, however, is that most Americans *perceived* enormous increases in both venereal disease and prostitution and *thought* that both had reached epidemic proportions—which is "as telling to the cultural historian as its actual incidence."[9] In considering deviant behavior, it is wise to remember that it is not the prevalence of deviance which triggers social reform, but rather what deviance symbolizes. "Deviance," as Howard Becker reminds us, "is not a quality that lies in behavior itself, but in the interaction between those who commit an act and those who respond to it."[10] What is deviant during one period of history may receive public toleration in another, and prostitution appears to be particularly susceptible to cycles of public toleration and persecution.

Changes in attitudes toward prostitution around the turn of the century coincided with several important transformations in American society. As a result of
the rapid commercialization, urbanization, and industrialization of the recent
past, Americans in the Progressive Era found themselves in a bewildering new
world. Many of them felt threatened by the influx of immigrant populations, the
migrations of blacks to the North, the changes in family and class structure, the
new roles for women, the challenges to Victorian morality, the glorification of
market values, and the breakdown of community life in the rapidly expanding
cities.[11] Their speeches and writings frequently contrast the impersonality, anonymity, social mobility, and immorality of the city to the innocence, intimacy,
neighborliness, social stability, and "morality" of the small town in a mytholo-
gized rural past. This kind of social conservatism was a common theme in the
reports of the vice commissions, business and medical organizations, and major
newspapers and journals that expressed the dominant voice of the antiprostitution movement. The publications of these groups reflected the concerns of the
primarily male and middle-class reformers who controlled them. Mark Connelly
points out that the Vice Commission of Chicago, which in 1911 produced the
influential report *The Social Evil in Chicago*, was

> the voice of specific, powerful, and established groups in Chicago. . . .
> Twenty-five of the twenty-nine individuals represented, essentially, five ma-
> jor groups: organized religion (three Roman Catholic, two Jewish, three
> Protestant); the legal profession (one U.S. district attorney, two judges, one
> lawyer); the Chicago medical community (four physicians, one social hy-
> gienist); academics (one college president, three professors); and the Chi-
> cago business community, including the president of Sears Roebuck. Two
> of the commissioners were women.[12]

For such reformers, the topic of prostitution was a focus for expressing discontent and anxiety about changes that were corrupting and invading traditional
American society, undermining "the old morality, the life of purity, thrift, sobri-
ety, the family tie."[13] Prostitution was a major context in which these changes
were discussed and deplored. In this sense, prostitution became a powerful symbol of the forces, only dimly understood, that were transforming the social order.
    Many reformers, for example, argued that prostitution was flourishing be-
cause urban conditions made it difficult to maintain the social restraints charac-
teristic of the small "bucolic community," where the "main external check upon a
man's conduct, the opinion of his neighbor, had been such a powerful influence."[14] Ignoring the existence of close-knit immigrant neighborhoods, New
York reformers categorically stated that "one has no neighbors. No man knows
the doings of even his close friends; few men care what the secret life of their
friends may be."[15] Katherine Davis, a well-known penal reformer and writer
concerned with prostitution, similarly argued that "in the past, the small size and
cultural homogeneity of communities tended to create agreement on the rules

and facilitate face-to-face surveillance of behavior and enforcement of the norms."[16]

Another common theme in discussions of prostitution was discontent with the shift from a producer orientation to a consumer orientation, emphasizing the accumulation and display of luxuries and the pursuit of expensive pleasures. One vice fighter recalled that "in olden times, when our people lived in villages, boating and fishing, outdoor games and rambles in the summer time, skating and coasting in the winter, the church sociable or the simple village entertainment had furnished the necessary recreation for young people."[17] The Louisville (Kentucky) Vice Commission nostalgically reminded their readers that long ago

> the *chief occupation was the business of living*, the hours of labor were exceedingly long; men worked from sunrise to sundown; coming home weary after a day of toil; they were not as prone to social recreation as they are in this day and time. However, with the development of twentieth century inventions, the commercialization of almost every phase of human life, has fundamentally changed.[18]

This "commercialization of almost every phase of human life" was seen as encouraging "prostitution" of all kinds, including the sale of one's moral values for money and status. As one writer explained, "Everything now has its price. This is the day of the dollar. Money talks. Even virtue has its market. Men barter their brains for good incomes; women trade their hospitality for social position; candidates for public office modify their principles in view of preferment. Sell out is common."[19] Another claimed that "the extravagance born of resource—has so corrupted every portion of our national life that the moral tone of the nation is no longer what it once was, but has reached a depth so low as to be shocking to ourselves."[20]

Prostitution in the most literal sense was considered to be encouraged by the new cultural emphasis on material acquisition and commercialized leisure. Many reformers saw the prostitute as a woman whose desire for "luxury," "excitement," and "finery" led her into obtaining it by "easy," immoral means. "The love of ease and luxurious living," it was argued, "have so infected our domestic life that if we go on at the present rate, virtue may become a commodity to be found only among a few old-fashioned simple minded people."[21]

Another disturbing aspect of commercialization was the displacement of humanitarian concerns by market values. Even reformers who were neither socialist nor feminist found themselves appalled by the lack of "industrial conscience" among industrialists whose low wages drove women into prostitution to support themselves or their families. "We have become money worshippers," complained Clifford Roe, a well-known legal foe of prostitution. "Most of our reforms have to do with money. . . . Let us put the purity of our homes and the morals of the people back in the proper place. . . . Then we shall not wreck the lives of our girls upon the wheel of economic conditions."[22]

Prostitution itself exemplified the intrusion of market values into one of the most private areas of human existence. Although prostitution had always been a commercial transaction, the striking changes in the *scale* of its commercialization just before the turn of the century made it seem especially dehumanizing and most flagrantly immoral. It had evolved from a small-scale, informal operation to a highly organized business that reaped vast profits and maintained connections with numerous third-party agents, including liquor interests, landlords, police, and politicians. Brothels were opened "much as grocery or hardware stores were opened in legitimate trade."[23] As one reformer put it, prostitution had developed into a "man's business," with "business methods, bookkeeping, and cash registers and checks."[24] Commercialized vice had become the underworld analogue of the faceless trusts and monopolies of the legitimate business world; both robber barons and profiteers of prostitution had successfully consolidated, rationalized, and formalized their businesses. Furthermore, both were associated with crime, exploitation, and corruption; and both were politically protected and economically invisible. The connection between anxiety over prostitution and anxiety over the transition to monopolistic corporate capitalism is most clearly shown by Progressives' exaggerated portrayals of prostitution rings as invisible, conspiratorial syndicates of national, or even international, proportions.

Another facet of Progressive concern over prostitution was the fear of a "revolution in morals," which gained widespread publicity between 1895 and 1910. Prostitution was invariably viewed as either the cause or the consequence of the changing morality of the young.[25] Evidence of youthful eroticism seemed pervasive. "City youth" (a code word for *working-class youth*) was "filled with vanity and youthful indulgence. . . . Youth is extravagant to prodigality with itself," wrote one reformer. "It is drunk with its own intoxicating perfume . . . and we surround that young, passionate, bursting blossom with every temptation to break down its resistant power, lure it into sentiment, pulsating desire and eroticism by lurid literature, moving pictures, tango dances, suggestive songs, cabaret, noise, music, light, life, rhythm, everywhere, until the senses are throbbing with leashed-in physical passion."[26] The Vice Commission of Chicago explained that "the whole tendency of modern life" was to blame because it was placing "a greater strain on the nervous system of both men and women of all classes than has ever been placed at any time in the history of the civilized world."[27]

Mark Connelly argues in a recent study that the code of "civilized morality," which had infused American middle-class life for much of the nineteenth century, was beginning to be replaced by a commercial and consumer-oriented ethic. Prostitution, in defying "the prohibition of extramarital intercourse, the equation of intercourse with reproduction, and the idealization of female purity," represented a blatant challenge to this code. Reformers therefore often extended the familiar label of prostitution to encompass a wide variety of sexual behaviors affronting "civilized morality," from engaging in premarital sex to going out with men unchaperoned.[28] Even when less restricted relations between the sexes were not equated with prostitution, they were labeled "exceedingly vulgar and suggestive" and viewed as leading to prostitution. According to the Committee of Fifteen of New York, for example, the new license for sexual promiscuity made it possible for girls "to experiment with immorality without losing such social standing as they may have, thus many of them drift gradually into professional prostitution."[29]

The Victorian code was increasingly being challenged in the middle class, as shown by the enthusiastic response by American intellectuals to advocates of a freer sexual morality like Emma Goldman, Ellen Key, Havelock Ellis, H. G. Wells, and Edward Carpenter. "If society is going to hell by way of the tango, and the turkey trot and the cabaret show," wrote William Marion Reedy, "who started it in that direction? Why 'the best people.' "[30]

Nevertheless, most reformers were primarily concerned over the low morals of the working classes, particularly those of young working-class women. By 1910, a record number of single poor women had been working outside their homes as domestic servants, factory workers, waitresses, and department store salesclerks. Whereas only 9.7 percent of women had worked in the labor force in 1860, 24.8 percent of the female population had joined men in work outside the home by 1910.[31] Outside of the family home, young working women sought out amusement after work in dance halls, ice cream parlors, and saloons. Their behavior particularly offended reformers. Much to the shock of vice investigators, young women drank, danced, and kissed young men in dance halls. "By actual count," reported one investigator, "one hundred girls and boys were intoxicated. Many of the drunken girls were sitting in the corner of the hall on the laps of their equally intoxicated partners who were hugging and kissing them."[32]

In Chicago, vice investigators worried about the lake steamers on which youth gathered to dance and drink. "The bar room was filled with boys and girls," reported one investigator. "Two girls in particular who could not have been over sixteen years old were singing in drunken discord, lying in the arms of two men. Sitting at the next table was a young woman with her skirts up to her knees talking to the young men who were sitting next to her. She pounded the table with beer bottles to emphasize her remarks, and to attract the attention of other men in the bar room. In fact, the whole boat seemed filled with intoxicated boys and girls."[33]

As Connelly observes, many vice commission reports expressed the fear that large numbers of young women might be engaging in "clandestine prostitution." Any young woman who was unchaperoned and mobile could be leading a double life and behaving immorally in secret. Reformers' suspicions reflected an anxiety over changes in the position of women and a loss of traditional controls over women's behavior.[34]

Every center of urban life—dance halls, vaudeville halls, lake steamers, saloons—was depicted by reformers as a den of prostitution.[35] Some of these places did in fact live up to their lurid reputation. Saloons, the targets of special investigations by nearly every urban vice commission, promoted a great deal of prostitution. Young women who served men liquor frequently also offered sexual services in small curtained booths or upstairs "cribs."[36] Many places where the young congregated for amusement, however, probably were not promoting prostitution in the strictest sense. Antiprostitution crusaders' exaggerated concern for "city youth" reflected their fear and ignorance of the expanding working class, which, with increasing concentration in the cities, was developing more of its own social and cultural institutions.

Reformers' class bias in relation to prostitution was paralleled by their racial and ethnic prejudices. As increasing waves of foreign immigrants and southern blacks settled in major northern cities, xenophobia and racism came to dominate the discussion of prostitution.[37] Contradicting the data they had collected, Progressive reformers continually depicted the villainous ringleaders of "prostitution syndicates" as foreigners. Depending on the year and the writer, the procurer or white slaver was depicted as a "sleazy French maquereau, in black velvet trouser and silkcap," an avaricious "Russian or Hungarian Jew with a white face and long beard," or a "devious Chinese merchant who, because of his peculiar and elastic code of morals," posed a special threat to the community.[38]

Prostitutes were also typically portrayed as foreign, even though reformers' own records show the majority to have been the native-born daughters of immigrant parents. George Kneeland's 1912 investigation found that 68 percent of the prostitutes in New York City were native born and that the foreign born were in fact underrepresented in the prostitute population.[39] Although northern urban black prostitution was just beginning to proliferate, nearly all vice reports emphasized the dangerous example set by black prostitutes in front of "innocent" white children.[40] The crusade against prostitution both fueled and was fueled by antiimmigration sentiment. As early as the 1870s, one purity reformer had fumed over immigrants' attempts to achieve wealth through prostitution, and proexclusionists in California had cited prostitution as a major reason for tightening immigration restrictions.[41]

The social changes most frequently and most emotionally discussed in the context of prostitution were transformations in the middle-class family and the role of women. Contemporary concern for the well-being of the family is hardly new; many of the same complaints have appeared with predictable frequency for well over a century. At the turn of the century, concern for the family became particularly intense; profound social and economic change had in fact begun to undermine traditional patriarchal and familial values. The divorce rate was rising rapidly; between 1890 and 1910, 954,000 divorces were obtained in the United States, two-thirds of them requested by women.[42] A falling birth rate was fueling fears of "race suicide." In 1859, the American middle-class family had produced, on the average, 5.6 children; by 1890, it was producing, on the average, one less child.[43] Most important, women were entering the world outside the home in unprecedented numbers—not only single working-class women who held jobs, but also millions of middle-class women, single and married, who joined women's clubs, social reform groups, and suffragist chapters. These women, even more than their working-class sisters, truly threatened to alter the gender divisions that had helped define Victorian culture. As women outside the home, they broke down the boundary between male and female worlds. Their increasing demands for greater social, economic, and political participation were also undermining the patriarchal organization of the family and the idealized function of the home as a refuge tended by women. Reformers defended traditional "home life" as "the highest and finest product of civilization" and looked back nostalgically to the days when families were close-knit, cooperative units. "Formerly we worked, played, ate and slept at home," wrote one reformer, "but now we scarcely do any of these." Another reformer explained that "a generation or more ago, boys and girls were satisfied to get their amusements in and around the home, but the forces in the community are all centrifugal now; our homes are small, the neighborhood dance or jollification is the exception, the public dance is the rule."[44]

Suffragists were held especially responsible for the increase in divorce, the decline in births, and the loss of "home-centered" life. By encouraging other women to move outside the traditional sphere, they were placing the social order in danger. Race suicide would be a "grievous consequence" of women's concerning themselves with matters outside the home, concluded the Illinois inquiry into working women, wages, and prostitution. "Return the married woman to her home and the care of her children."[45]

In the minds of reformers, prostitution was inextricably intertwined with all such changes in family life. It was therefore cited as a cause, consequence, or sign of every change. "The surest sources of prostitution are found in broken homes," one reformer warned; others claimed that husbands' contact with prostitutes and venereal disease was one of the main reasons that so many wives were petitioning for divorce.[46] The falling birth rate, which supposedly presaged the extinction of the race, was blamed on the sterility caused by venereal infection of innocent wives and mothers. "A healthy woman," the Vice Commission of Chicago proclaimed, "living in wedlock all of her child-bearing life, under favorable circumstances for natural procreation, should have a family of ten children"; venereal disease was preventing a natural growth of population.[47] It was also contributing to race suicide by damaging the health of future generations. "Prostitution is pregnant with disease," explained reformers,

> a disease infecting not only the guilty, but contaminating the innocent wife
> and child in the home with sickening certainty—a disease to be feared with

as great a horror as a leprous plague, a disease scattering misery—and leaving in its wake sterility, insanity, paralysis, the blinded eyes of little babes, the twisted limbs of deformed children, degradation, physical and mental decay.[48]

The change in family life which reformers frequently linked with prostitution was the changing role of middle-class women. Women's entrance into the public arena, traditionally frequented only by prostitutes and other "bad" women, blurred the clear divisions between the "lady" and the prostitute. For many anti-vice crusaders—despite vehement opposition from feminists—women's activities outside the home became symbolic of whorish behavior. Women who became active in clubs and social reform, according to the "custodians of culture," risked losing their sexual purity and drifting into a life of prostitution. By absenting themselves from home, they exposed their unprotected daughters to the immorality of the street. If women would just remain at home, such tragedies need not occur.[49] Further, thought reformers, contempt for feminine domestic pursuits would inevitably lead to contempt for feminine chastity as well. As one reformer lamented, "Daughters no longer feel content to follow their mothers' lives in the home. Our system of female education which fosters a contempt for the mother that delves amongst the pots and kettles in the kitchen, while the accomplished daughter home from school, armed with her diploma, thumps away at the piano in the drawing room, must be held accountable for much of the looseness in morals and virtue."[50] The willingness of many reformers to pursue such improbable arguments reflects the deep threat posed by changing gender relations in the middle-class family.

It is within the context of changing gender relations that the panic over prostitution shown by reformers—or at least the male, middle-class social conservatives who dominated the antiprostitution movement—becomes most comprehensible. As Judith Walkowitz argues for Victorian England, focusing exaggerated attention on prostitution was for many reformers a way of avoiding more complex and compromising socioeconomic issues.[51] Prostitution was singled out because it was a visible and dramatic form of illicit sexual relation and the most stigmatized form of female existence outside of patriarchal authority and protection. While marriage, home, and family represented women's energies carefully channeled into stable reproductive relations and caretaking duties in a private sphere, prostitution represented the "lawlessness" of increasing numbers of women from all classes moving out of traditional structures and into the public sphere. This great transformation in American life, perhaps more than any other, threatened the dominant group of reformers deeply and directly.

The constellation of emotionally loaded issues associated with prostitution distorted reformers' perceptions of the prostitute herself. Typically, the prostitute was presented as one of two polarized images: the innocent victim or the sinister polluter.

The prostitute as innocent victim was viewed sympathetically: she had been coerced or tricked into vice by external forces. Contradicting their own data, reformers frequently depicted the prostitute as a young rural girl whose innocence, ignorance, and poverty had been manipulated by urban male procurers. "Many a young girl," wrote a popular sex handbook advisor, "under the promise of marriage, sometimes even under a bogus marriage, is brought into a condition of hypnotism or into a mental state that puts her in the power of the man whom she loves and respects. . . . We cannot wonder that the girl—deserted, humiliated, crushed, by the one in whom she reposed absolute confidence, cast out of society, perhaps thrust from the protection of her own father's roof—gives up the struggle and says, '*What's the use?*' "[52]

All around this helpless girl stood "men whose sole object is their subsequent exploitation for pleasure of money."[53] "Against these powerful business interests," the Vice Commission of Chicago dramatically explained,

> the liquor dealer, the house owner and his agents, the men who run the place, the furnisher of all sorts from the butcher and grocer to the dry goods houses and the supported men, against these stand the girl, usually young, feeble of will, unskilled as a worker, a lover of ease, perhaps at first deceived, and always after a time the victim of liquor, "dope," and other standards, it is obvious that the weaker factor, the girl, will be crushed in so unequal a conflict. On her falls the ignominy, the loss of health or social position and final physical and social death. While the men who profit from this vice, live on, sleek and prosperous—often so powerful in politics that even decent men dare not expose them.[54]

The Atlanta Vice Commission similarly depicted the prostitute as a "defenseless child of poverty, unprotected, unloved, and uncared for" who was brought into vice "by men who are so low that they have lost even a sense of sportsmanship and who seek as their victim a tired, lonely, and destitute girl."[55] Thus women were ruined by the "desperate, adroit and ghoulish contrivance of procurers, who cannot . . . recruit a sufficient number of victims to supply the demand of this nefarious trade."[56]

Not only male procurers, but also industrial employers were singled out as responsible for prostitution.[57] Sweatshop factories destroyed a young woman's will power, William Lloyd Garrison testified. "Between the wages of sin and the wages of the sweatshop, the simple wonder is that so many women in need can hold to lives of chastity." "Girls" were not to blame, concluded the Vice Commission of Chicago; unregulated business was the villain. "What is the natural result of such an industrial condition?" reformers asked. "Dishonesty and immorality, not from choice but from necessity . . . in order to live."[58]

The reverse image of the innocent victimized girl was that of a "vicious woman": a "willful spreader of infection."[59] This sinister polluter received no sympathy; she had gone into prostitution because of her "immoral cravings for excitement, her endless search for 'love of luxury.' " She was filled with "vanity," "desirous of idleness," and "in love with finery."[60] Lacking the "instinctive and inherent purity of mind of the normal woman," she was "degenerate, lewd, and promiscuous by nature."[61] Such immorality, as one industrial employer defensively argued, was a "state of mind."[62] The Reverend James Curry of New York agreed; immorality was natural to the prostitute. "If a girl or woman wishes to go wrong," he explained, "she will do so no matter if she is working for $3, $30, or $300 a week."[63] Low wages were not the cause of prostitutes' fate, wrote another reformer. "The mating instinct comes early to the slum girl. Overdeveloped physically, as she frequently is, while at the same time underdeveloped mentally, uninstructed, and with no knowledge of control of self, her impulses drive her to acts impossible to the girl whose parents have surrounded her with every safeguard that loving care can devise."[64] The nineteen-volume *Report on the Condition of Women and Child Wage Earners in the United States*, after demonstrating the poor working conditions that women and children suffered, concluded that women's downfall was "due to moral causes, to their inheritance and early training or to lack of training." That is, women did not become prostitutes because of industrial exploitation; on the contrary, immoral women entered those occupations from which prostitutes were drawn.[65]

The extent to which these contradictory images could coexist in reformers' minds is striking. The same vice report that blamed poverty and evil procurers for young women's downfall could also describe in vivid detail the immoral cravings that had produced the prostitute.[66] Thus reformers vacillated in their policies and attitudes toward the prostitute. For the innocent girl, they searched for environmental causes; for the prostitute, they found "natural" and individual failures: immorality, laziness, sexual overdevelopment, and feeble-mindedness. For the "wronged" girl, reformers tried to offer aid; for the degenerate prostitute, they legislated repressive laws, built reformatories to isolate her from the public, and reviled her for her impurity.[67]

Why were such polarized images of the prostitute prevalent? We can partially understand reformers' ambivalence as one instance of a larger conflict between scientific environmentalism, which viewed the poor and the socially deviant as victims of external forces, and deep-rooted moralism, which viewed them as basically responsible for their own unfortunate condition. By characterizing the prostitute as a victim, reformers were prevented from understanding that many women made rational choices to enter prostitution: that they acted upon their environment as well as being acted upon by it. Yet reformers simultaneously felt that prostitutes were in fact responsible for their own deviant behavior and had actively chosen their trade because of their lack of morality and will.

The images of the prostitute also reflect reformers' confusion over female sexuality. Many Progressives had been brought up by their Victorian forebears to believe that women were "naturally" passionless beings who would submit to sex only as a duty of marriage, at the initiative of their husbands. They could reconcile their belief in women's purity with the reality of prostitution only by depicting the prostitute either as a passive victim forced into sex or as a creature so deviant as to scarcely deserve the name of woman.

Racial, ethnic, and class prejudices also contributed to the polarized images of the prostitute. The innocent victim was typically portrayed as the embodiment of agrarian purity: white, native born, and middle-class in her manners and attitudes if not her background—potentially, if not actually, a "lady." By imagining the prostitute in this way, reformers could empathize with her as a member of their own class and as a woman who had at least tried to conform to the model of proper sexual behavior. Furthermore, by imagining her as young, rural, and innocent, they could fit her into their drama of traditional rural American society being corrupted by evil outside forces. It makes sense, then, that the reverse image of the prostitute as sinister polluter was so frequently one of a lower-class nonwhite or immigrant woman. In this version of the drama, the prostitute herself was the evil outside force, invading and infecting the body politic.

Mary Douglas has suggested in her studies in symbolic anthropology that in times of social or cultural crisis a society may feel compelled to redefine and reinforce its moral boundaries. Under such conditions, she argues, there is a "strong tendency to replicate the social situation in symbolic form by drawing richly on bodily symbols in every possible dimension."[68] Society, like a bodily organism, is viewed as endangered by all forms of external threats. "It is only by exaggerating the differences between within and without, above and below, male and female, with and against, that a semblance of order is created." Fears of pollution and contagion, she further explains, become exaggerated.[69]

Certainly Douglas's description is applicable to the response of the dominant group of reformers during the critical years of the Progressive Era. These reformers manifested a strong compulsion to create a sense of order by reinforcing older moral boundaries and defining who should remain within and without the body politic. As their world view was increasingly challenged by social, cultural, and economic change, they began to perceive themselves as a body under attack by external, contagious, and polluting forces.

The dominant voice of the antiprostitution movement was not the only voice. Socialists and many nonleftist women, while discussing prostitution in some of the same terms as other reformers, also developed their own unique symbolism of prostitution and used the topic to express radically different concerns. They tended, more than other reformers, to portray the prostitute as an innocent victim and empathetically to identify with her powerlessness.

The socialists saw prostitution primarily as the result of working women's poverty—a poverty stemming not from lack of humanitarian concern among individual employers, but from systematic exploitation under capitalism. Capitalism, they pointed out, not only forced men to sell their labor for wages; it also caused women to sell their bodies.[70] The prostitute (or white slave, as one of Joe Hill's songs sympathetically expressed) became a romanticized symbol of one of the most exploited members of the American working class.[71]

Women's approach to prostitution had its roots in the women's culture of the nineteenth century. This culture, with its broad range of autonomous organizations established for social and moral reform, emphasized the experiences uniting all women, the necessity for women to organize around the issues that affected their lives, and the potential of women to transform society. Whether or not nineteenth-century women's movements took a strong stand for "women's rights," they did tend to express, however indirectly, criticism of male dominance and sexual subjugation. Prostitution was viewed primarily as a male crime against women: it exemplified the double standard, sexual and economic exploitation, and women's political powerlessness.

A separate female tradition continued to flourish in the early decades of the twentieth century, even though some women lived outside of it and allied themselves more closely with a male point of view. Male and female reformers' attitudes toward prostitution cannot be clearly and simply distinguished; nevertheless, as chapter 4 will illustrate, numerous women's organizations across the country did develop their own analyses of prostitution and their own tactics for confronting it. To the extent that their sexual attitudes and class, racial, and ethnic prejudices allowed them, women identified with the prostitute and perceived her as victim rather than criminal. Unlike male reformers, who tended to depict the body politic as a male body being polluted by the prostitute, women tended to portray their national collectivity as a female body being raped by the men who bought, sold, and controlled the prostitute. In the end, however, women's agitation and anger against prostitution were easily ignored or redirected in the service of a larger movement that by driving prostitutes underground, made them even more vulnerable and powerless than before.

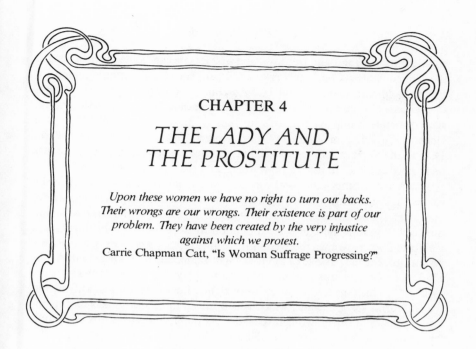

CHAPTER 4

THE LADY AND
THE PROSTITUTE

Upon these women we have no right to turn our backs.
Their wrongs are our wrongs. Their existence is part of our
problem. They have been created by the very injustice
against which we protest.
Carrie Chapman Catt, "Is Woman Suffrage Progressing?"

From the moral reform activities of the Jacksonian Era to the full-scale national campaign of the Progressive Era, organized womanhood had always figured prominently in antiprostitution movements.* Although they participated in many of the same activities as their male colleagues, they remained closely identified with their own autonomous female organizations, maintaining older forms of female reform activity, establishing new feminist responses to prostitution, and frequently manifesting motivations different from those of the civic leaders in the larger crusade.

By the turn of the century, middle-class women had established a national network of women's groups which considered prostitution to be as significant as other reforms, like temperance, suffrage, child labor laws, and protective legislation. Intellectual analyses and political writings exploring the causes of prostitution were provided by such notable women as Elizabeth Cady Stanton, brilliant theorist and president of the National American Women's Suffrage Association; Elizabeth Blackwell, first woman doctor in the United States; Frances Willard, president of the W.C.T.U.; Victoria Woodhull, radical advocate of

---

* I use the term *organized womanhood* to describe women who viewed prostitution from either a feminist or a female-identified perspective. Some women of the Progressive Era worked outside the women's rights and female reform traditions and saw prostitution through the eyes of male crusaders, whereas other women, like Jane Addams, bridged the differences at various points in their writings. Both feminists and social feminists frequently used the term *organized womanhood* to identify themselves.

equal rights, suffrage, and free love, and first female candidate for president of the United States; Charlotte Perkins Gilman, social and economic theorist; Emma Goldman, anarchist; and Jane Addams, prominent leader of the American settlement house movement.[1] By the first decade of the twentieth century, such disparate groups as women's suffrage organizations, the W.C.T.U., the General Federation of Women's Clubs, Mothers' Congresses, the Anti-Saloon League, the Sunday School Association, and dozens of female-led civic leagues had joined together to form a powerful coalition against prostitution.

Women sometimes joined with men to form a major political and social lobby for red-light abatement acts and were instrumental in seeing their passage in many states. The Chicago Women's City Club, for example, managed to obtain nineteen thousand signatures for a petition to close the red-light district.[2] In California, where women received suffrage in 1911, they were almost exclusively responsible for the passage of the Red Light Injunction and Abatement Act of 1913. The women's organizations in California playing the largest roles were the W.C.T.U., which spent $83,500 and printed three hundred thousand leaflets, and the California Civic League, which issued fifteen thousand leaflets and maintained a team of fifteen women speakers. As public acknowledgment of their "maternity" of the act, Governor Hiram Johnson honored the W.C.T.U. by giving their president, Sara Dorr, the pen with which the bill was signed. A campaign to repeal the act was soon launched by liquor and vice interests, but once again the coalition of organized California women defeated their opponents.[3]

Why did organized womanhood, with its energies taken up by so many other struggles, regard prostitution as such an important issue? Why did millions of women become involved in the campaign to end prostitution? The answers to these questions are perhaps best revealed by examining some of organized womanhood's attitudes and activities regarding prostitution which were not generally shared by male reformers.

The female reformers who attacked prostitution were inspired by some powerful personal motives that their male counterparts did not share. Many of them, like male reformers, asserted that prostitution must be abolished to protect the home; but "protecting the home" generally had a different meaning for them than it did for men. To men, it meant upholding patriarchal authority, barring women from the public sphere, and "protecting" women from knowledge of or contact with sordid realities. To women, however, it meant asserting some authority over that domain—the home—which men had supposedly granted them. At the most intimate level, prostitution threatened the security of women's homes through the infection of venereal disease. Frances Willard extended her campaign against liquor to encompass prostitution because she recognized that men's right to transmit prostitutes' venereal disease to their wives and children, like men's right to drink up their wages and abuse their wives, made a mockery of women's alleged ascendency in the home. Prostitution, then, represented not only a physical threat of infection but also a man's license, because of a sexual double standard, to inflict that threat on his wife and children and a woman's powerlessness to avert it.

Reports and investigations on venereal disease helped to cultivate a growing fear on the part of women. In 1899, for example, a conference in Brussels reported that of one hundred women who had been infected with syphilis, twenty had been infected by their husbands. In 1907, the New York Committee of Seven surveyed seven hundred physicians and discovered that nearly one-third of infected women were married and had been infected by their husbands. One doctor was led to declare that "more venereal infection exists among virtuous wives infected by their husbands than among professional prostitutes." In a confidential report to the president of the New York Suffragist Association, the Social Hygiene Association revealed that congenital syphilis—infection passed from a pregnant mother to a newborn infant—had become a "growing" problem. One of every twelve pregnant women was found to be infected. Finally, congenital blindness in newborn infants, caused by venereal infection of pregnant women, was estimated as the cause of 30 percent of all cases of blindness in New York.[4]

Whether or not these estimates are true, that women truly feared venereal infection is evident in both their public speeches and private papers.[5] "Every day," wrote one female doctor, "thousands of pure young women become infected in assuming what should be the most sacred relation on earth, that of wifehood." Eighty percent of women's "inflammation peculiar to their sex," she estimated, was caused by venereal disease.[6] When Emily Hoppin, vice president of the California Women's Clubs, declared that there was "not a home in the state that may not be affected either directly or indirectly" by the Social Evil, she was referring not only to some abstract sense of injustice but to the pervasive threat of venereal disease.[7]

Whereas male reformers typically represented the carriers of venereal infection as women, female reformers typically represented them as men. It is not surprising, therefore, that organized womanhood strenuously opposed the regulation of prostitution. Why should prostitutes be subjected to examination, they argued, "while the man who has voluntarily exposed himself to the contagion of a loathsome disease continues even after his infection by the prostitute to have business and social relations as before, with the result that innocent members of society are exposed to a dangerous and contagious disorder to which they have not exposed themselves and from which no effort is made to protect them?"[8]

Echoing Josephine Butler and other British women who had organized to oppose the Contagious Diseases Acts regulating prostitutes in England, American feminists argued that regulation discriminated against prostitutes and locked them into a life of prostitution. The members of the Chicago Women's Club passed a resolution against regulation because they felt that "the door of hope

should always be open to an unfortunate woman who wishes a better life."⁹
Women's battles to repeal or prevent the passage of legislation regulating prostitution continued into the Progressive Era, with especially strong support from
feminist organizations and the W.C.T.U.¹⁰

Whereas some men had suggested controlling venereal disease by medically
examining and regulating women, organized womanhood turned the tables by
attempting to regulate men. In California, women successfully lobbied for a
mandatory health certificate to ensure that the men women married would be
free from venereal disease.¹¹ Female reformers emphasized male, rather than
female, sexual misbehavior and attempted to regulate men's sexual conduct by
agitating for a single sexual standard and lobbying for its incorporation into law.

In women's arguments against prostitution, the issue of the sexual double
standard came up more often than any other. While it was also discussed by
some male reformers, it was far more important and more emotionally charged
for women. After all, as one feminist argued, women had for ages been "reaping
the wild oats that men have sown: from the prostitute, to the girl with an illegitimate child, to the wife with a hidden disease that she dare not even mention."¹²
One W.C.T.U. member, for example, described the double standard as "this
monstrous, barbarous, devilish doctrine."¹³ Dr. Cecile Greil, a socialist writer,
angrily criticized society's indulgence of the sexual escapades of man.

> Society smiles on his acts, calls them sport, sowing his wild oats, etc. He
> becomes a moral coward and sneak, conscious only of strong animal im-
> pulses that he need not curb and these drive him early to secret vice, to the
> brothel, to dissipation and roguery. And the crop he reaps from the wild
> oats he sows fill our streets with prostitutes, fill our foundling asylums with
> nameless babies and give him a heritage of venereal disease to wreck his
> future usefulness and hand down as a sad legacy to his posterity. He fears no
> moral code; his mothers and sisters live in a rarified atmosphere of imagi-
> nary purity that cuts him off from intimacy and the understanding which his
> mother could impart to him if she were his friend instead of a transcendental
> ideal far up on a pedestal out of his reach.¹⁴

The most blatant manifestation of the double standard was the differential
treatment of prostitutes and their male customers or the men responsible for
their "fall." One female doctor angrily asked, "If every year 40,000 men were
doomed to a miserable ignominious death as the result of a life forced upon them
in their early youth by an uncontrolled, even fostered sexuality, would not the
publication of such facts rouse a storm of wrath and indignation?"¹⁵

Women's solution to these injustices was the imposition of a single sexual
standard for men and women. As late Victorians themselves, most members of
organized womanhood interpreted equality in the sexual realm not as equal
sexual freedom for women but as equal sexual restraint for men. "Women,"
wrote one feminist,

have not been in a position to make demands of men. Until recent years men have owned even our property and our children, our legitimate children— women have always owned their illegitimate children—men have had all the education, all of the control: financial, social, and political—I believe that the first demand that we shall make of men will be the demand that men have made of us. We shall say to men as they have said to us, "If you are to come to us in that intimate relationship between man and woman, you must have lived a pure life. Your mind must not be tainted with sordid memories and the children that you give us must have every chance to be strong and healthy."[16]

Many women's organizations considered agitating for a single sexual standard as one of their top priorities. The members of one such group, the Maine Federation of Women's Clubs, even resolved at an 1894 meeting to make it their life's work.[17] The importance of a single sexual standard to female reformers is shown, not only by their work to abolish prostitution, but by their promotion of many other kinds of legislation. One of their earliest efforts was to raise the age of consent. In Ohio in 1891, for example, the age of consent was fourteen, yet a man could not be convicted of rape until he reached the age of twenty-one. Such discriminatory legislation outraged women's advocates. Frances Willard cynically noted that "it is a greater crime to steal a cow than to abduct and ruin a girl."[18] Ohio suffragists demanded that the age of consent be raised to eighteen; the legislature responded by raising it to sixteen.

When women received the vote in California, they startled the nation by recalling the first judge in San Francisco's history. After Judge Charles Weller reduced the bail of Albert Hendricks, who had been charged with the rape and assault of a young San Francisco woman, Hendricks fled the area. Outraged local women launched a recall campaign. Charging that Weller routinely charged bail of twenty-five hundred dollars for crimes against property but only two hundred dollars in rape cases, the women succeeded in recalling the judge.[19]

Women also played a significant role in campaigns to bring white slavers to justice. The Rhode Island Sarah Doyle Club petitioned and supported President Taft's proposal to obtain fifty thousand dollars to convict and punish men engaged in white slave traffic.[20] Women of the California W.C.T.U. challenged the light sentences given white slavers. For stealing a horse or saddle, they argued, a man would be sent to San Quentin; for ruining a girl's life, his case would be dismissed.[21]

Several feminists took their analysis of prostitution a step further than the critique of the double standard by pointing out similarities between the institutions of marriage and prostitution. Loveless marriages contracted for economic security were, like prostitution, a selling of women's sexual services; and marriage, like prostitution, placed women under the sexual control and exploitation of men. These arguments were not new; Victoria Woodhull, among others, had advanced them in the 1870s. "The marriage law is the most damnable Social Evil Bill—the most consummate outrage on women—that was ever conceived," she declared. "Those who are called prostitutes, whom these bills assume to regulate, are free women sexually, when compared to the poor wife. They are at liberty, at least to refuse; but she knows no such escape."[22] Charlotte Perkins Gilman went on to develop these ideas more fully in her book *Women and Economics*. By the 1890s, they were being widely debated, not only in women's rights and other radical circles, but also among such audiences as the readers of women's magazines like *Good Housekeeping* and the readers of muckraking journals like the *Arena*.[23]

A story attributed to George Bernard Shaw was widely quoted by radical feminists to express their attitudes toward marriage and prostitution as commercial transactions:

> Gentleman: Madam, would you go to bed with me for a million pounds?
> Lady: Well, for that kind of money, yes.
> Gentleman: Well, would you go to bed with me for two pounds?
> Lady: Heavens! What do you think I am?
> Gentleman: We have already established what you are, Madam; we are now merely trying to establish the price.[24]

Another male critic of marriage, Havelock Ellis, received a warm response from feminists when he argued that "the wife who married for money, compared with the prostitute, is the true scab. She is paid less, gives much more in return in labor and care, and is absolutely bound to her master. The prostitute never signs away the right over her own person, she retains her freedom and personal rights, nor is she always compelled to submit to man's embrace."[25]

Ethel Sturges Dummer, a Chicago feminist, offered an even broader definition of marriage as prostitution: "a marriage in which psychical values are ignored, even though it has legal sanction . . . based upon economics, upon the idea of possession and the inheritance of possession." She added that "any love degenerates into prostitution when one of the pair is used as a tool, not as a person."[26]

The argument that prostitution and marriage were both institutions of male exploitation and coercion was based on the awareness that prostitution was a business controlled by men. "Men are behind the whole business," asserted one woman. "With very few exceptions, almost all the women keepers of houses of ill-fame are nothing more than paid servants, there is always a man or men behind them, who are the real proprietors."[27] Adopting a Progressive view of history, some women's rights advocates argued that prostitution and traditional marriage both represented a backward stage in human evolution which subordinated the female to the domination of the male. The more advanced stage, toward which humanity was evolving, would be characterized by equality of the sexes, abolition of prostitution, and transformation of the institution of marriage. Feminists frequently described subordination in sexual terms: in both marriage and prostitution, women were sexually controlled by men. Carrie Chapman Catt, president of the International Women's Suffrage Association, returned from a trip abroad to pronounce that all over the world, "just as numberless girls were sacrificed in olden times to appease the anger of the god, so are they sacrificed today to appease the demands of men."[28]

The emphasis on women's sexual victimization led many female reformers to concentrate on cases of "white slavery," in which women were forcibly recruited into prostitution or forcibly kept from leaving it. Certain female missionaries made a name for themselves by their attempts to rescue women who were virtually being held captive in brothels. Rose Livingston, called in New York the "Angel of Chinatown," had apparently been a white slave and drug addict herself. She dedicated herself to the dangerous work of trying to rescue prostitutes from Chinatown brothels. Of small stature and slender build, Livingston took on male procurers, or cadets, and other profiteers and achieved a reputation for fearlessness owing to the numerous physical beatings and assaults she suffered in her work. Friendly with many New York suffragists, she toured suffrage chapters in small towns all over the country, speaking on the important connections between women's suffrage and women's political powerlessness to end prostitution.[29]

Even more famous was Donaldina Cameron, whose work is still marked by the presence of the Cameron House in San Francisco. Cameron came to California in 1869 at age two and lost her mother during early childhood. Inspired by stories of rescue work in San Francisco, Cameron was drawn there to assist an older woman until she took over the directorship of the Presbyterian Mission Home of San Francisco. Famous for her bold attempts to rescue young Chinese women held as white slaves, she soon became known as *Lo Mo* ("The Mother"). White slave traders called her *Fahn Quai* ("White Devil"). Throughout her long and tireless career as a missionary worker and director, Cameron challenged Chinese tongs and highbinders and established a strong relationship with the police. She investigated any suspicious situation that indicated the presence of white slavery, then demanded that the police help extricate the white slave from debt and captivity. In her mission, former prostitutes lived together with other young "Christian" women who sought to dedicate their lives to missionary work. Like the settlement workers, such missionaries created an all-female environment in which they could receive support for their work in the public sphere.[30] Hattie Rose, a prison missionary in New York, and M.G.C. Edholm, in San Francisco, also became well known for their efforts to rescue women from white slavery and publicize white slavery's existence.[31]

Many female reformers tried to guard young women from being tricked or kidnapped into prostitution. Frances Kellor launched a campaign in Chicago to identify "unsavory" employment agencies and rooming houses that attempted to recruit prostitutes. Grace Abbot, director of the Chicago Immigrants Protective League, along with the Y.W.C.A. and the National Council of Jewish Women, aided women in finding employment and lodging.[32] Other women's organizations offered aid to traveling women. Sometimes their concern became extreme. California women felt impelled to issue a national warning to all young women before the opening of the 1915 Panama International Exposition. They distributed broadsides all over the country warning young women of procurers who would be scouring the country for prostitutes to embellish the festivities of the fair. The broadside shown here was posted in a railway station in Grand Forks, North Dakota.

Women confronted not only their sexual subordination through the issue of prostitution but also their political subordination. The continuing presence of prostitution brought home to women very clearly their lack of political power. "Women with political power," wrote Jane Addams, "would not brook that men should live upon the wages of captured victims, should openly hire youth to ruin and debase young girls, should be permitted to infect unborn children—if political rights were given women, if the situation were theirs to deal with as a matter of civic responsibility, one cannot imagine that the existence of the social evil would remain unchallenged in its semi-legal protection."[33]

Suffragists argued that women could not be politically effective in causes like the fight against prostitution until they had the vote: "We women suffragists will never be content with alleviation, with half measures, with aimless and hopeless service, while we have no real power over ultimate causes; that power which only franchise can bring; only the franchise rightly used can make operative."[34] Many women seem to have assumed that once women finally obtained the vote they were sure to use it "rightly" and gain, without much further opposition, "real power over ultimate causes" of sexual inequality and sexual slavery. In so doing, they greatly underestimated the power of male-dominated institutions to divide, co-opt, and manipulate them politically.

Female reformers argued that when women obtained political power they would use it to battle corrupt male institutions and establish a morally superior social order. Sometimes female reformers' scorn for the male politicians expressed itself dramatically. When the Hartford Common Council refused to fund the publication of its vice report, suffragists raised the funds, published the report under their own names, and placed it for sale in local shopping areas. To further underscore their contempt for the male members of the council, Hartford suffragists also erected a six-foot-high signboard in front of suffrage headquarters which described each city "father's" attitude toward prostitution.[35] One woman fighting against recall of the red-light bill in California asserted that the

WARNING!

THE women of San Francisco are determined to prevent the letting of a portion of the fair grounds for the purpose of establishing houses of prostitution and are doing all in their power to stay the evil.

HOWEVER this controversy ends, one thing must be remembered. The vice that sacrifices the girlhood and boyhood of the country, and brings contamination upon innocent wives and children--that vice intends to flourish somewhere during the world's fair.

LET it be remembered that the country will be scoured for girls to supply the demand of this nefarious business, and every means that is possible for man to conceive will be used to snare and mislead these girls in order to secure them.

EVERY girl should be warned against advertisements of positions in San Francisco, for every place that is worth while will be taken, and the door that will be open for the strange girl will be the door that leads to perdition.

THE papers that do their duty to the girlhood of the nation will publish the warning, and women of every town and city who would protect the youth of the land, will sound the alarm and caution and guard the girls of their neighborhood.

A broadside distributed by the San Francisco women warning of procurers at the Panama Pacific International Exposition, 1915. Reprinted courtesy of the Bancroft Library, Berkeley, Calif.

"mothers were uprooting the weeds of injustice and immorality that the fathers of the city let grow."[36] "Is it not time," demanded one suffragist, "that mothers become law-makers?"[37] Some antisuffragists responded by arguing that if women got the vote, "bad women" would vote for the continued existence of prostitution and against the prohibition of liquor. Suffragists, however, managed to defend their position by explaining that "no class of women needs the ballot and other measures of protection more than the so-called 'bad woman,' " and that "if the ballot is an uplift for good women, it can be made an uplift for bad women."[38]

Once the newly enfranchised women of California achieved their first political victories over prostitution, they experienced a gratifying sense of power. One female lobbyist for the Red Light Injunction and Abatement Act recalled with satisfaction that after the franchise was won, "it was recognized that I represented a large party of women." The all-male legislature was beseiged by hundreds of letters written by women. The same lobbyist reported, "It was pitiable to see men get up and say: 'I am entirely out of harmony with this bill, but my constituents . . . wish me to do so and therefore I vote aye.' "[39] A female observer noted that "a political pressure to which all politicians are accustomed when corporate and financial interests are involved, made the legislators squirm unhappily when brought to bear by 50,000 organized women."[40] One suffragist declared triumphantly that women's political victories in California went to show that "what Bernard Shaw said is true, that many men are afraid of votes for women because they know if women get power they will impose on men the same sexual standards of sexual morality that men have imposed on women . . . that is just exactly what we are going to do."[41] Thus many female reformers viewed their use of the state to close red-light districts as a demonstration of their ability to make revolutionary changes in the male-dominated social order.

Organized womanhood also discussed the situation of working women in the context of prostitution, arguing that economic equality was as necessary as the vote for abolishing the Social Evil. In her book *A New Conscience and an Ancient Evil*, Jane Addams sympathetically recounted numerous stories of young women driven into prostitution out of economic hardship. She described how a factory girl, weary and discouraged from "the long hours, the lack of comforts, the low pay, the absence of recreation, the sense of 'good times' all about her which she cannot share, the conviction that she is rapidly losing health and charm," might eventually be no longer able to withstand "temptation."[42] While Addams, like many male reformers, mentioned the desire for finery as a motive for entering prostitution, she described it not as an individual fault but as a socially instilled ambition. Young women, she wrote, were raised to believe that no obstacles ought to stand in the way of financial success. Extravagant displays in department stores continually tempted poor women whose dreams of material success could never be realized. Torn by the desire for "fine" purchases and the knowledge that honest efforts could not obtain them, poor women developed a "dangerous cynicism regarding the value of virtue."[43] Similarly, Emma Goldman explained that immigrant women were especially "driven by American conditions, by the thoroughly American custom for excessive display of finery and clothes, which, of course, necessitates money—money that cannot be earned in shops or factories."[44] The perceived connection between prostitution and economic hardship led some female reformers to agitate for higher wages for working women; it led others to offer newly unemployed prostitutes charity or employment.[45]

In their discussions—whether political, social, or economic—of prostitution, female reformers, unlike their male counterparts, generally took an empathetic stance toward prostitutes which was based on instinctive feelings of identification and an expressed desire for the solidarity of all women. Organized womanhood sharply criticized the way men had divided women into "two classes . . . feeling perfectly justified with the solution of the love problem, even though it exists at the expense of a most fearful wreckage of life for the outcast class."[46] They protested the fact that "proper" ladies were "actually forbidden to have any knowledge of their fallen sisters."[47] Arguing against the Victorian belief that prostitutes served to protect decent women, one woman angrily asked her female audience, "Suppose that you knew that the sacrifice of other women protected you—it does not, but if it did—how many of you would buy your protection at the cost of the lives of other women? I do not believe that there is one."[48] A California woman addressed the question most directly when she argued for the Red Light Injunction and Abatement Act: "To that small and misguided class that desires a red-light district in order that my daughter have protection we have this to say: 'Who is to decide that the human sacrifice demanded by lechery is not to be YOUR daughter? Are you willing to give her that another man's home may be protected?' "[49]

At the most emotional and unconscious level, many women probably recognized their own social and economic vulnerability in the prostitute's plight. Aware of their own economic dependence on their husbands, women's rights advocates may well have realized that "there, but for my vicariously achieved social status and economic security in marriage, go I." Although most of these women enjoyed a fair degree of social status and economic security, they understood the fragility of a position achieved vicariously rather than through one's own efforts. What if their husbands left them or died? Then they, too, might be reduced to the extreme situation of seeking a livelihood on subsistence wages and perhaps even resorting in desperation to prostitution.

Some feminists also saw reflected in the prostitute the precariousness of their own respectability as "virtuous" women. Jane Addams, who knew how easily a woman could fall from angel to whore, argued that all women without the protection of a man could be treated as prostitutes. Women, she explained, would never achieve equality "until they recognize as one of themselves the very harlot who, all unwittingly, has become the test of their spirituality, the touchstone of their purity."[50] Prostitution lowered the status of women "because they came to be looked upon as possible harlots."[51] Just as a "Negro" might suddenly be degraded into a "nigger," beneath each woman's respectability lay a potential "whore." This deeply personal relationship of women to prostitution had no analogue among male reformers.

On occasion, women reformers could become important allies of prostitutes. In Denver, for example, the local political machine tried to force prostitutes to register publicly so that their votes could be exchanged for police protection. Angry at the political extortion, prostitutes appealed to a large political club of middle-class women to stop the police harassment. The women's club responded by campaigning against the chief of police until he was ousted in the next election.[52] During World War I, feminists offered the most sustained criticism of the abrogation of prostitutes' rights under the American Plan.[53]

Nevertheless, the barriers of class, race, and ethnic prejudice, along with political and economic naiveté, often created tensions between female reformers and prostitutes and prevented the dream of women's unity from becoming a reality. Female reformers in the 1830s had been able to empathize with prostitutes more easily because prostitutes at that time were mainly native-born white women. Early twentieth-century women, however, experienced greater distance between themselves and the racial and ethnic minorities they sought to help. Fears of unrestricted immigration, the prevalence of stereotypes about the "low morals" of other racial and ethnic groups, and the popularity of eugenics all made female reformers waver in their sympathies for prostitutes. Even Jane Addams, who generally showed concern, rather than condemnation, for prostitutes, once expressed fears about the "race deterioration which would occur as a result of immigrant prostitution." Another well-known female reformer, Anna Garlin Spencer, reminded readers that "clandestine prostitution and all manners of sin and uncleanness are matters of race culture and personal character."[54]

Another source of tension was middle-class reformers' inability to comprehend the life circumstances of poor and working-class women. Efforts to give prostitutes charity and employment tended to backfire because the assumption behind them was naive: that a prostitute would find *any* work, no matter how ill-paid and degrading, or even the mere provision of food and shelter, better than making a living from prostitution. Reformers generally persisted in seeing prostitutes as women driven by desperation into vice because they had no alternatives, rather than women making a rational choice given their limited alternatives. Because of this misperception, reformers often felt hurt or bewildered— and occasionally indignant—when prostitutes refused their aid. A Miss Kate Adams from Chicago, for example, was given "unlimited funds" to provide for every destitute prostitute she encountered. She apparently walked the streets of the red-light districts day and night; but, much to her disappointment, she found not "one application for that aid so abundantly offered."[55]

In San Francisco, women successfully closed the dance halls of the Barbary Coast, then realized that they needed to provide employment for the army of unemployed young women they had created. In response, they created an employment bureau. They were quite taken aback when they received a letter from one former dance hall girl who rebuffed their offers of domestic work.

> In regards to the employment of the dance hall girls; I wish to state as one of them that the work suggested by the majority of the club women is not any better than that offered an immigrant. Possibly you have failed to realize that the majority of these girls are young, fair-looking, well-educated, well-groomed. . . . They have had or are now maintaining a home for themselves or other relatives. . . . They are not immoral or they wouldn't be where they are, most of them are using that means of livelihood as a quicker road to a home of their own. Some of them have professions or trades, quite a few are musical; if it wasn't for the fear of ridicule or curiosity they would return to their legitimate labor. I don't believe any one of them would accept the position of kitchen mechanic. If a living wage was offered where the girls could work, meet their installments, I doubt if they wouldn't gladly accept.[56]

One San Francisco clubwoman discovered that such hostility was not an isolated case. In order to interview these young women she had to disguise herself, since they apparently "blamed the club women for the closing of the Coast."[57]

The employment bureau was a failure. Only eight dance hall girls actually applied for assistance, even though the committee made 106 visits and interviewed forty women. Only three young women were even willing to discuss other employment. The majority apparently agreed that their former work represented better employment than the "honest labor," namely, domestic work, offered by the clubwomen.[58]

While female reformers seldom expressed the loathing and horror of the prostitute that many male reformers did, their feelings of compassion were frequently mixed with condescension and self-righteousness. One member of the League of Women Voters in San Francisco, for example, expressed her ambiguous feelings when she wrote, "I feel a great step has been taken to save our young girls from seeking pleasure—I only hope and pray that our efforts were not *pearls cast before swine*."[59] Another woman reformer expressed her deeply felt identification with the sexual oppression of prostitutes, then went on to characterize them as dull, stupid, and unregenerate. Alice Davis Menken, a member of New York City's Board of Guardians and an organizer of the city's Jewish "Big Sisters," spent considerable energy trying to improve the quality of life for Jewish immigrant young women. Yet she also supported the views of eugenicists who called for the segregation of the "feeble-minded" and prevention of marriage between the "unfit"—many of whom were incarcerated prostitutes.[60] One California woman involved in the closing of San Francisco's Barbary Coast dance halls came to the conclusion that the "poor deluded creatures, their mentality is so stunted with sensuality, drink and sin, they do not realize the awful bondage they are subject to."[61]

The ambiguity of reformers' attitudes toward prostitutes may have been heightened by their sexual attitudes. Sexually repressed themselves, some female reformers may have privately envied, while publicly opposing, the sexual abandon attributed to prostitutes. One feminist, for example, felt that prostitutes represented "more living energy than any other repressed women." If only that "energy were channeled into different areas," she argued, "perhaps women would be happier."[62] Another woman declared that "the social evil was more than prostitution; it was unchastity." To her, prostitution may have represented the forbidden arena of female sexuality.[63]

Moralism showed up most clearly in interactions between prostitutes and female missionaries who devoted their lives to "rescuing and redeeming" the souls of their "fallen sisters." The rescue of white slaves performed by such missionaries as Donaldina Cameron was part of an extensive effort of such work with prostitutes throughout the country and growing out of a long-established evangelical tradition. Female missionaries ventured into brothels not only to rescue prostitutes held forcibly but to convert women who were in prostitution out of their own free will and to persuade them to leave their degrading occupation. In California, for example, Florence Roberts, converted in 1896 by a vision of her own carnality and selfishness, became known as Mother Roberts as she wandered through small Northern California towns and cities trying to rescue young prostitutes. (Interestingly, Mother Roberts's conversion occurred when her husband lost his job and she realized that she needed to become economically independent.) With extraordinary bravado, she invaded the dark dives of San Francisco's Barbary Coast. There she set up her autoharp, sang hymns, and tried, without success, to persuade prostitutes to accept Christ and receive her offers of redemption.[64]

White slavery rescue workers, like Rose Livingston and Donaldina Cameron, met with considerable success because women held forcibly in prostitution were more likely to welcome any assistance in escaping from it. But missionaries who, like Mother Roberts, tried to rescue women from more or less voluntary prostitution often found their offers of aid rebuffed. The California W.C.T.U., for example, visited brothels in Oakdale, California. Although they pleaded with the prostitutes to pray with them and come live in missionary homes, the inmates scoffed at them. Having failed to eradicate prostitution in Oakdale, the California W.C.T.U. had the police arrest the prostitutes and send them out of the county—an act that did little to improve the relationship between female reformers and prostitutes.[65]

Many female reformers noted the scorn and distrust that prostitutes directed at them. One reported that a prostitute had teasingly asked her, "Are you a reformer? Do you want to make us good girls?" One settlement worker who had visited hundreds of prostitutes honestly conceded, "We reach one in a hundred and try not to be discouraged." A. W. Elliot, a clubwoman who was president of the Southern California Rescue Mission, admitted that she had offered aid to fifteen thousand prostitutes and yet had reformed only one. "I do believe," she said, "that they love that kind of life and scoff at the reformer and kick him out if he does not get out."[66]

A few sources exist in which prostitutes themselves describe some of the reasons for their hostility; these show that prostitutes were quick to resent any trace of condescension, repugnance, or objectifying detachment in the attitudes of the women who came to "help" them. Unaware that she was talking to a "fallen sister," one female reformer explained why prostitutes must be socially ostracized; the former prostitute bitterly wrote of the conversation,

> It has been decreed that, while prostitution must go, the "vampires" must be kept outside the pale. A most peculiar logic this and one which I am utterly unable to grasp—decrying a sin and yet condemning a fellow-woman to follow it for the term of her natural life. "Surely my dear," said a noted club president to me recently, "surely you would not have us condone? If we forgive them and take them back again into decent society, *where* will the family be?"[67]

Maimie Pinzer's relationship with the prominent Mrs. Mark De Wolfe Howe represents a unique relationship between a "lady" and a "prostitute." Initially distrustful, Maimie gradually grew to love and trust the nonjudgmental Fanny Howe. Maimie wrote of Howe's letters, "I unconsciously made them a live friend, and we, the letters and I, were in league against all these ugly conditions and the letters were the only things I discussed my hatred to of things." Trusting Fanny Howe to understand her difficulty in maintaining a respectable life while impoverished, Maimie was able to expose her worst fears and deepest uncertainties. Although she met Howe only twice during twelve years of correspondence, Maimie found the friendship an essential source of support. "I did not eat lunch today to write this," Maimie wrote once to Howe, "but to write you is like a good meal, especially when I get fat letters—they make me so happy, and are so satisfying."[68]

In her letters to Fanny Howe, Maimie did express hostile feelings toward the "lady reformers" and social workers who tried to help her. She bristled at their considering her their "work" and was outraged when they read aloud her letters. "It makes me feel as if I am Exhibit A," she wrote Howe. Refusing to be an object of charity, she explained that she was unwilling to write to "persons that I feel are not interested in me as a person but in me as a question (if you know what I mean)." Basically, she distrusted reformers' capacity to understand her daily reality. Of one woman reformer, she wrote Fanny, "She has beautiful ideals and lives the life of the characters in the Sunday story books . . . if I wrote her as I do you, she would think I had gone completely daft."[69]

Maimie became particularly indignant when her benefactors wanted to name her informal shelter for young prostitutes "The Montreal Mission for Friendless Girls."—In complete disgust, Maimie, who understood these girls' lives from her own experience as a prostitute, explained, "I thank God you are not friendless, but if you were—and were 18 years old—you would no more admit it than any girl does. The kind of girl—the human jelly fish—that is willing to be classed as 'friendless' I haven't much time for . . . and I'd like to see the place I'd have walked into when I was a young girl that was known to be a haven for friendless girls." Angered by the way female rescue workers sermonized young prostitutes, Maimie asserted: "I would prefer not to write this for it sounds ridiculously egotistical but I believe I am correct and it is, that I can do more, given the time, with a girl who is on the street, toward getting her to go to work than any 10 ladies whose method of procedure is along the lines laid down by Rescue Workers."[70]

Unlike Fanny Howe, however, most women reformers never had the opportunity to know a Maimie Pinzer so intimately. Emma Goldman was an important exception. Having lived with and shared prison cells with prostitutes, her perspective on prostitution was influenced by her personal experiences with the poor as well as by her feminist and anarchist views.[71] Going beyond many other women reformers, she viewed prostitution as dependent on industrial slavery. Going also beyond socialists, she viewed prostitution as a natural outgrowth of society's devaluation of women.

Like many radicals of her time, Goldman blamed industrial capitalists for the oppression of the working class. Such economic exploitation, she argued, caused women to consider the higher wages offered by prostitution. Seasonal layoffs and job insecurity, along with subsistence wages, created conditions that made survival nearly impossible. Working women, Goldman wrote, were perceptive enough to understand that industrial slavery constituted a form of prostitution itself. "Why waste your life working for a few shillings a week in a scullery, eighteen hours a day," she asked, "when a woman could earn a decent wage by selling her body instead?"[72]

Economic conditions alone, however, did not cause prostitution, Goldman emphasized; it was inevitable in a society that treated all women simply in terms of their sex. Reformers rarely understood that "nowhere is a woman treated according to the merit of her work, but rather as a sex." The options were limited. "It is merely a situation of degree whether she sells herself to one man, in one marriage, or to many men."[73]

Goldman had only contempt for the single standard of purity which other female reformers sought. Women in America, she wrote, tragically accepted the culture's definition of their supposed asexuality and "thus became a prey to prostitution, or to any other form of relationship which degrades her to the position of an object for mere sex gratification." Denied premarital sexual activity, women were forced to wait until marriage. "To the moralists," Goldman pointed out, "prostitution does not consist so much in the fact that the woman sells her body, but rather that she sells it out of wedlock." If sexually active before marriage, a woman ruined her chances for a respectable marriage because even the "meanest, most depraved and decrepit man still considers himself too good to take as his, the woman whose grace he was quite willing to buy."[74]

Somewhat alone in her analysis, Goldman repeatedly asserted that women's lack of sexual freedom outside of marriage often made prostitution the only escape for an "already ruined" young woman. Not all women would eventually marry; did they have to remain celibate? "Human nature asserts itself regardless of all laws, nor is there any plausible reason why nature should adopt itself to a perverted conception of morality."[75]

Goldman was one of the few female reformers skeptical about the outcome of women's attempts to employ the state against prostitution. Before the raids and the final closing of the red-light districts, she pointed out, prostitutes had managed to survive within the protected confines of the brothel. Now, "the girls found themselves on the streets, absolutely at the mercy of the graft-greedy police. Desperate, needing protection and longing for affection, these girls naturally proved an easy prey for cadets." The widespread exploitation of prostitutes by pimps by the end of the Progressive Era, wrote Goldman, "was the direct outgrowth of police persecution, graft and attempted suppression of prostitution."[76]

In short, Goldman recognized that women would abolish prostitution not by enacting repressive legislation but by gaining "real power over ultimate causes"—social, political, and economic. "As to a thorough eradication of prostitution," she wrote, "nothing can accomplish that save a complete transvaluation of all accepted values—especially the moral one—coupled with the abolition of industrial slavery."[77]

For most of organized womanhood, the elimination of prostitution symbolized the dream of improving all women's lives by ending the sexual exploitation of women and challenging patriarchal values in both the private and public spheres. In attempting to legislate their own values and a single standard of sexual morality, middle-class female reformers implicitly proclaimed their right to criticize the dominant male culture and to transfer their moral superiority to the public sphere. Consciously or unconsciously, their attack on prostitution represented an attack on a male-dominated society whose legal codes and sexual politics condemned in women what it condoned in men.

While female reformers genuinely sympathized with the plight of the prostitute, they failed to perceive the implications of the laws for which they lobbied. Reform efforts such as rescue ventures proved relatively harmless, but middle-class women's attempts to employ the power of the state produced further oppression of their working-class sisters. Satisfaction with their political victories kept them from realizing that they were not abolishing prostitution but merely driving it underground, and that the power they wielded was primarily being used not against the men who bought, sold, and controlled prostitution, but against a powerless group, the prostitutes themselves. What the female reformers failed to understand was that the state—hardly the bastion of women's concerns *or* feminist values—could not and would not translate their humanistic concerns for the prostitute into social reality.

Organized womanhood in the antiprostitution campaign failed to achieve its stated goals. Although the active participation of its adherents provided a public forum for feminist grievances and created a socially acceptable way for middle-class women to enter political and public debate, their contribution did little to improve women's own status. Nor did their vital role in legislating the suppression of prostitution improve prostitutes' lives. Finally, women's ambivalent attitude toward the prostitute and their frequent insensitivity to the realities of working-class life prevented them from crossing class and cultural barriers to achieve a true sisterhood capable of challenging the class structure and gender system that supported prostitution in American society.

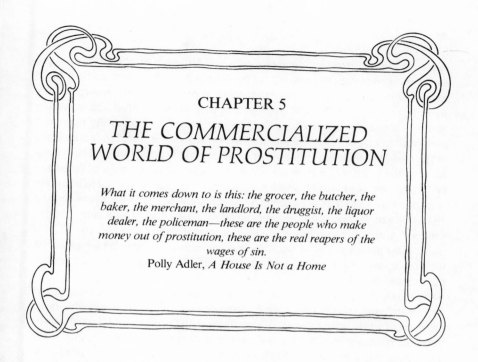

CHAPTER 5

THE COMMERCIALIZED
WORLD OF PROSTITUTION

*What it comes down to is this: the grocer, the butcher, the
baker, the merchant, the landlord, the druggist, the liquor
dealer, the policeman—these are the people who make
money out of prostitution, these are the real reapers of the
wages of sin.*
Polly Adler, *A House Is Not a Home*

Although many reformers responded to prostitution as a symbolic issue, the practice of prostitution was an unquestionable fact of daily existence for thousands of urban dwellers. Some reformers, like George Kneeland, who conducted and supervised some of the most famous vice commission investigations (in New York and Chicago), clearly articulated what others only intuited: that prostitution had grown into a highly commercialized and profitable business, which penetrated the deepest recesses of the political, cultural, and economic life of the city.[1]

In the history of prostitution, as in the history of other long-surviving institutions such as the family, it is not always easy to distinguish change and continuity. How do we know which aspects of prostitution have remained unaffected by time and which aspects have been transformed in the course of economic and social historical development?

It appears that, by the turn of the twentieth century, Americans had begun to observe very real changes in the practice of prostitution, even though they discussed many of these changes in highly symbolic ways. Although the professionalization and commercialization of prostitution had already taken place during the late nineteenth century, Progressive reformers experienced these changes as sudden and recent transformations of the "oldest profession."[2]

Despite scanty evidence for earlier periods, it is likely that early nineteenth-century prostitution differed from the more highly commercialized forms of twentieth-century prostitution in several ways. Although brothels existed in the early towns and cities, the majority of prostitutes probably practiced their trade much like the artisans who owned the tools and product of their own craft; they were the owners as well as the employees of their trade. In effect, the prostitute was an artisan of her sexual goods. She sold herself in a relatively open and unorganized marketplace. Like shoemakers who made and sold the entire fruits of their labor without an employer or middleman, the prostitute sold her goods without the interference or extensive exploitation of an employer. When the prostitute *was* employed by another individual, she usually worked in a brothel controlled by a woman, a madam. Although some of the larger towns (by the 1830s) began to designate specific neighborhoods for prostitution, "night-walkers" probably plied their trade in an informal, casual manner. In all likelihood, most prostitutes lived near or in the communities in which they practiced their trade, moving in and out of "respectable" life when economic difficulties necessitated occasional prostitution.[3]

As the sheer number of women who became prostitutes increased during the nineteenth century, several major changes took place. Increasingly, large numbers of women became part of a permanent and professional class of prostitutes. Such women searched for customers in seaports, in congested manufacturing centers, and in mining and lumber camps—wherever a large unattached male population worked. Gradually, with increased urbanization, neighborhood politics concentrated prostitution into tolerated red-light districts. There, hidden from genteel society, a large and increasingly profitable traffic and trade in women grew into a complex and commercialized business. As third-party agents began to seek a share in the profits of "vice," prostitution became deeply enmeshed in the political, economic, and cultural life of the city.

As a result of these changes, the nature and practice of prostitution, at least in the larger cities, was considerably altered. Although many women continued the patterns of entrepreneurial and casual prostitution, a new and more professionalized class of prostitutes had emerged, partly as a result of the capitalization of the trade and partly in response to society's repression of prostitution. Like the shoemakers, who lost their independence as they became industrial wage earners, the prostitute became increasingly dependent upon and exploited by third-party employers or agents who reaped the profits of her labor and paid her a "wage." As an employee in the many brothels that characterized the districts, or as an "employee" of a pimp, the prostitute found herself dominated by a new worker-employer relationship.

As prostitution, like other aspects of American society, became more commercialized, reformers noted a "strange development" across the nation. "The business enterprises for marketing girls," wrote George Kibbe Turner in his famous exposé of "The Daughters of the Poor," "have passed entirely from the hands of women into those of men." Although women also exploited prostitutes as

View of the Chicago red-light district as portrayed in a white slavery tract.
Reprinted from Clifford G. Roe, Horrors of the White Slave Trade
(London: Clifford G. Roe and B. S. Steadwell, 1911), facing p. 304.

procuresses or madams, the Vice Commission of Chicago was basically accurate in charging that *men* now owned and operated the business of prostitution. Whereas many earlier madams had owned their own businesses as lodging or boarding houses, now they increasingly worked directly or indirectly as managers for men whose financial investment gave them considerable control over the operation of prostitution as a business. The segregated district of Little Rock, Arkansas, was "typical," in that there were nineteen (white) houses, all run by women, owned by "well known and prominent male citizens."[4]

Increasingly, the relationship between the prostitute and the customer became complicated by the presence and commercial interests of middlemen, who invested in vice much as they invested in other areas of the American economy. Money still changed hands; now, however, prostitution represented widespread business and political interests that permeated nearly all aspects of urban cultural and economic life.

The gradual growth of prostitution into a large and commercialized enterprise involved enormous financial investments and generated incredible profits. In Kansas, for example, it was estimated that the red-light districts involved at least four hundred thousand dollars in capital investment; in Chicago, reformers estimated that fifteen million dollars of business revolved around the traffic in women.[5] In Storyville, the famous New Orleans red-light district, it was estimated that "over a million dollars a week, well over ten million dollars a year, probably closer to fifteen million, found its way into the stockings of the prostitutes, the cassocks of the clergymen who owned the whorehouses property, the pockets of the politicians, and the swelling accounts of the landlords."[6] As one reformer pointed out, "a girl represents as a professional prostitute a capitalized value four times greater than she would represent as a hard working industrial worker."[7]

Despite the vast sums of money involved in the business of prostitution, prostitutes rarely managed to keep even a bare fraction of the large profits. Other members of the community siphoned off the majority of their earnings. The profiteers of prostitution can be classified into two categories: those who existed "above and around" the vice districts, but whose economic participation in the trade became a vital and necessary aspect of a semilegal, tolerated vice; and those who lived within the vice districts in a semiisolated subculture of prostitution.[8]

The first group, as reformers continually noted, was heavily composed of politicians and police. Because prostitution was tolerated but not exactly legal, the trade in women required a broad range of protective services from politicians. Between 1900 and 1917, prostitution became a powerful political weapon in urban politics. Politicians tried to undermine an incumbent's "respectable" appearance by eagerly uncovering evidence of corruption at every doorstep. Incumbent politicians, for their part, sought to vindicate their political administrations from any connection with commercialized vice. The attempt to oust Tammany Hall politicians in 1901 in New York is only the most dramatic example of prostitution becoming a central issue in urban politics. To many reformers, corrupt municipal politics implicitly meant that an urban administration, through its ward system, not only catered to the needs and vices of immigrants and the poor, but also had deeply entrenched financial interests in the business of prostitution.[9]

Early in the social purity movement, the Reverend Charles Parkhurst had recognized politicians' strong *personal* and financial investment in prostitution. Precisely because the legal status of prostitution remained so vague, politicians could extort vast amounts of protection money by harassing any brothel for "infractions" of regulations. In addition, politicians frequently offered official protection to those exclusive brothels they frequented themselves. "We do not say," wrote Reverend Parkhurst with his typical cynical tone,

> that the proposition to raise any noted house of assignation touches our city
> government at a sensitive spot. We do not say that they (politicians and
> police) frequent them nor do we say it is money in their pockets to have
> them maintained. We only say (we think a great deal more, but we only say)
> that so far as relates to the blotting out of such houses, the strength of the
> municipal administration is practically leaguered with them rather than ar
> ranged against them.[10]

By the turn of the century, Reverend Parkhurst's accusations gained greater credibility as urban vice reports, "blue ribbon" committees, and muckrakers revealed the nature and extent of vice in dozens of cities. In New York, for example, reformers discovered that particular lawyers associated with the "trade" charged prostitutes exorbitant fees for settling their legal problems with local politicians.[11] In Storyville, the local newspaper found that certain parlor houses had been assessed unusually low tax rates. It seems that leading citizens and politicians had invested so heavily in these houses that they granted owners special tax breaks.[12] In dozens of cities, moreover, the connections between breweries, liquor interests, and the municipal government formed a solid wall of protection for saloons and brothels. In his investigation of Pittsburgh, Lincoln Steffens found that the white slave traffic in girls and women was controlled by ward officials; in New York, George Kibbe Turner charged Tammany leaders with the responsibility for the growth of the white slave trade. Commissioner General of Immigration Daniel J. Keefe revealed in a February 1910 report that white slave traders were frequently protected from arrest by political ties with local officials.[13]

The stiff opposition that reformers faced was both well funded and politically entrenched. In California, one reformer who led the struggle for the red-light abatement act discovered the extent of the economic and political power of the real estate interests who fought the measure. "If the public can be aroused," he wrote in a private letter, "to the fact that we have opposed to this Redlight Abatement Act exploiters of prostitution who have literally millions at stake, who have political and financial connections in all parts of the country, who have already resorted to forgery and perjury to defeat the measure, there is no question but that the bill will be overwhelmingly ratified at the polls."[14]

In Illinois, a young, idealistic district attorney discovered that his antivice prosecutions offended and threatened his political mentors. Describing the young man's encounter with these political pressures, his close friend wrote the Illinois Senate Vice Committee and described the political threats his friend had encountered. "Some years ago," he wrote, "a friend of mine was elected State's attorney in a city, which was under the political control of vicious elements." During the course of his official duties, this friend had prosecuted a procuress and her male accomplice for attempting to "ruin" a young girl. Enormous political pressure was brought upon him by politicians with "tenderloin interests." Although this young attorney had been considered a candidate for the gubernatorial nomination, he was soon informed that "without delegates from the wards in which the vice district was situated," his nomination was impossible. "In short," his friend explained,

> he discovered that unless he was willing to connive at the escape of these wretches from punishment for their despicable crime, he must bid farewell to any hope of a political career. The result showed that the vice ring was just as powerful as it claimed to be. He insisted on performing his full duty,

despite all the pressure, and the two criminals were convicted and sentenced. Not only was the nomination he sought denied to him, but he was bluntly told that the political powers saw no way in which he might succeed himself in the office of State's Attorney. Realizing that his own community was closed to him as a field of action, he felt obliged to quit the State and take up practice elsewhere.[15]

Political support of prostitution inevitably required a high degree of police compliance and corruption. Although tolerated by official authorities, red-light districts had to pay municipal "fines" to maintain official "toleration." In Kansas, for example, the vice report revealed that seventy-eight houses in one red-light district paid monthly fines of $1,374, whereas another district paid combined fines of $1,334.50. The average annual revenues to a major city in Kansas from such forced fines often amounted to as much as forty thousand dollars. In some cases, the police did not even bother to cite houses for disorderly conduct or other minor infractions. The madams simply paid local authorities a weekly visit with their "fine" money.[16]

In Minneapolis, such police corruption became particularly blatant when the city closed its brothels and the police department could no longer count on extortion and bribery for its "toleration of vice." In their vice commission report, which considered reopening the segregated district, many officials testified to the widespread police corruption that the tolerated district had formerly generated. Such a district, they explained, "corrupts and demoralizes the police and offers endless opportunities for blackmail and extortion." They further substantiated their opposition to segregated districts with stories of respectable girls who had been denounced to the police as prostitutes out of revenge or jealousy. Such girls, unprotected by brothel bribes, were sometimes then arrested as prostitutes.[17]

Local police officers in the growing black neighborhoods of northern cities extorted such exorbitant bribes from black brothels that they became known as the "Czars of the Tenderloin." In New York, an ordinary parlor house "contributed" about five hundred dollars to a new precinct captain and thereafter gave fifty dollars every month as another "contribution" to local police officers. One owner of a parlor house paid thirteen plain-clothes men ten dollars each per month, and two patrolmen five dollars each per month as well; this was in addition to local police and ward officials.[18]

Good relations with the police smoothed the daily workings of the traffic in women. As one saloon keeper in Portland, Maine, explained, "If you are a good fellow, set up drinks and cigars, and throw in a little [sexual] business on the side there will be no trouble with the policeman on the beat; there will be no trouble to a place right down in town."[19] In some cases, owners of brothels became so cozy with local police officials that they knew when their local patrolman was going to be transferred before he ever received official notification from his superiors.[20]

And, on occasion, police were not above using their official authority to take advantage of a "little business." One investigator filed the following report:

> Wabash Avenue. October 31 at 2:30 A.M., place crowded at this hour, and several persons were intoxicated. Two strangers, who had the appearance of being farmers, were with two prostitutes. They complained to the waiter that he had overcharged them and . . . were ejected from the saloon. Later they returned with two officers who called the waiter and spoke a few words to him.
>
> The officer then turned to the farmers and told them to "beat it or they would be arrested." The men appeared surprised, and finally left as one of the officers was about to hit one of them with his club. The two officers then entered the cafe, and holding their hands over their stars, went to the rear closet, took their uniform coats off, and put on ordinary coats, which were much too small for them. They then took off their helmets and sat down with the same prostitutes. They did not pay for their drinks. Investigators recognized them as being the two who were patrolling the district.[21]

Rank-and-file police had little economic or professional investment in enforcing rules against prostitution. In fact, most chiefs of police consistently favored the regulation of vice. Since most police departments were decentralized,[22] however, they responded to local political interests.[23] Police "lists" of brothels and streetwalkers, for example, grossly underestimated the number of both in a given district. Protection of prostitution meant higher incomes. Looking the other way, moreover, helped maintain order and stability in the vice district.[24]

The second group of profiteers, those living within the subculture of prostitution, had a large and varied membership. In every district, for example, certain beauty and manicure parlors agreed to cater exclusively to a "disreputable" clientele and their specific cosmetic needs. In exchange, they charged prostitutes outrageous prices for exclusive service. In the same way, druggists who sold prostitutes morphine and cocaine reaped handsome profits. Hotel owners who permitted streetwalkers to bring customers to their rooms profited greatly from the nightly rental fees. When prostitutes brought customers to a furnished room, they also had to provide the landlady with a small "commission" in exchange for the continued use of the room. In some towns, local authorities required periodic physical examinations of prostitutes. In return for a rather superficial and superfluous inspection, doctors issued certificates of health in exchange for high fees.[25]

Many other individuals exacted small commissions for simply "steering" customers to one particular woman or brothel. "Nightliners," bartenders, waiters, chauffeurs, and cabdrivers were all part of an informational network that profited from the existence of prostitution. Cadets, if they succeeded in seducing or persuading a woman to enter a brothel, received a commission from either the owner or madam of the house.[26]

In addition to such steerers, many young boys learned the profession by earning money as a "messenger boy." One investigator for the Vice Commission of Philadelphia reported the following conversation with such a sixteen year old.

> "You know you're in the red light district now. Would you like to go to see some of the women?"
> "How do you know where the women are?"
> "Know? Why that's my business to know . . ."
> "How does that come about?"
> "All the women in the houses telephone to the office when they want something. We run errands for them, buy chop suey, take messages, buy things for them, and do anything they want us to. If it were not for this business, the office could close up."[27]

Pimps formed another class of men who lived off the earnings of prostitutes. Sometimes they were distinguished from cadets, who "sold" women to brothels but did not then continue to make money off them; at other times the terms *pimp* and *cadet* were used interchangeably. The New York Committee of Fifteen defined a typical cadet or pimp as "a young man, averaging from eighteen to twenty-five years of age, who after having served a short apprenticeship as a 'light house,' secures a staff of girls and lives upon their earnings. His occupation is professional seduction."[28] Although pimps became much more central to the practice of prostitution *after* the closing of the brothels, they nevertheless comprised the most significant group of individuals living as parasites on the prostitute. Although madams never permitted pimps to live in the brothels, it was not uncommon for madams to split the prostitutes' earnings between themselves and the pimps. In other cases, pimps took most of a streetwalker's income and returned a pittance of her earnings to her.

In most brothels, prostitutes' wages were further diminished by the custom of "splitting" half of all earnings with the madam. In a one-dollar house (considered medium-priced), supporting eighteen inmates, each prostitute earned about twenty-one dollars a day. Since the madam received half of each woman's earnings, she could earn over fifty thousand dollars in a year. In addition, many inmates cynically learned that madams required them to buy their clothing and furniture from peddlers and dealers, who charged exorbitant prices and then gave kickbacks to the madam. The Vice Commission of Chicago pointedly described how "An inmate of ——— avenue said she had to buy a kimona for $15.00 from a man who came to the house which could be bought over the counter for $3.00. The Madame received $9.00; the salesman, $6.00."[29]

Although the madam realized sizable earnings throughout the year, she, in turn, had to pay a substantial part of *her* income to the men who owned the actual real estate in which the business was conducted. Given the legally ambiguous status of prostitution, landlords rented their property "for immoral purposes" at two to three times the normal rental rate. In some cases, several businessmen formed "combines," which collectively owned and operated a group of "houses."[30]

During hearings in Washington, D.C., over the possibility of passing an abatement law, a Mr. W. S. Duffield, representing the Colored Citizens' Association of South West Washington, testified how men had combined their money to build a row of twelve three-story "houses" in his neighborhood. His information, he claimed, came straight from the precinct captain. Angry at the establishment of brothels in his neighborhood, close to his girls' school, Mr. Duffield pointed out how such financial investments would "call for a large number of female help, most naturally young women, and as their life has not been a very easy one at best, when brought in such close contact with an apparent life of ease and luxury and fine clothes, there is no question but that it would appeal to them. We will be the dumping ground."[31]

The rental of property for prostitution proved to be a very profitable financial investment. In one house, for example, which had fifteen inmates, a landlord realized $6,454 each month from his real estate investment. Since most property owners tended to cultivate close ties with local politicians, they were generally left alone—despite the passing of the red-light abatement laws and "tin plate" ordinances.[32]

Another large group of profiteers involved in prostitution were saloon keepers, brewery owners, and anyone else involved in the sale and distribution of liquor. Breweries, for example, sometimes forced indebted saloon keepers to establish a string of available prostitutes on their premises in order to stimulate more drinking and attract a wider clientele. Prostitutes were instructed to require each customer to buy a drink so as to avoid appearing a "cheapskate." Saloon keepers, for their part, gave each prostitute a small commission for the number of drinks their customers consumed each evening. In some cases, saloon owners similarly received kickbacks from the hotel that their "girls" used in their trade. Most saloon keepers readily conceded that they made their greatest profits from the drinks bought by customers who accompanied prostitutes to the rear booths or upstairs rooms used for sexual activities.[33]

With so many powerful interest groups reaping financial rewards from the practice of prostitution—politicians, police, real estate agents, landlords, and owners of saloons and breweries—reformers faced serious economic resistance in their attempts to close down the red-light districts. Not all businessmen, of course, supported prostitution. On the contrary, many small businessmen feared the potential depreciation of their small stores' property if a neighborhood became filled with prostitutes. Or they feared that customers would hesitate to patronize a store that was located in the center of a district. As the Hartford Vice Commission pointed out, however, nearly every aspect of prostitution had become profitable to someone, somewhere: "There was profit in selling girls to houses, profit in selling their services, profit in selling clothes to them and liquor to their customers."[34] In sum, a very large part of the urban community had become involved, either directly or indirectly, in the commercialized business of prostitution.

The location for much of this business between 1890 and 1918 was the red-light district—a segregated area in which various forms of vice were "tolerated." In theory, of course, vice was limited to the district, "thereby protecting other neighborhoods from its manifestations." In fact, prostitution was mainly practiced in poor neighborhoods, which frequently overlapped with or included the designated red-light district. In some cities, police tried to keep track of the districts by keeping lists of brothels and requiring a license or certificate. In Lancaster, Pennsylvania, for example, local authorities kept careful track of the twenty-seven houses they discovered in their midst.[35] In large cities, however, it was often impossible to keep accurate records. In one edition of a New Orleans blue book, a guide to brothels in the famous Storyville district, 247 more names appeared than were registered on the police rolls. Records on prostitutes themselves, such as the lists of names, photographs, and certificates of health kept in some cities, were even less complete. In the South in particular, most Mexican and black prostitutes were never registered or even officially noted by the police. One investigator estimated that, at best, one-sixth of all prostitutes were officially regulated by the practice of segregated prostitution.[36] In small towns or cities, as one prostitute recalled, "segregation was a name only, not a fact. . . . Vice flourished in all parts of the city [Kansas City]; wine rooms were wide open for anyone having the price of a drink; private houses and assignation houses abounded—and the roadhouses ran full blast for twenty-four hours a day."[37]

The commercialization and visibility of prostitution varied widely across the country and reflected the historical development of the cities in which prostitution grew. In the larger cities, commercialized vice had reached a highly organized and visible presence. In its prime, for example, Storyville supposedly had 230 sporting houses, 20 assignation houses, and two thousand prostitutes. In some cities, such as New York or Chicago, investigators estimated that from four thousand to fifteen thousand prostitutes actively practiced their trade. Streetwalking and the presence of pimps also began to characterize the largest and most infamous districts.[38] In smaller towns and cities, however, prostitution remained less visible and had not yet developed into the extensive business described in the larger urban areas. For example, in Superior, Wisconsin, a typical small district, twenty brothels paid fifty dollars a month in fines, practically licensing fees. Part of the fines went to the court and part to a drug clerk who sold three hundred and fifty dollars' worth of drugs monthly to the district. In such towns and cities, probably fewer than a hundred women became involved in prostitution.[39]

It was the red-light district, however, with all its gaudy advertisements for drink, gambling, and sex, that created the most visible evidence of American urban prostitution. Some of the more infamous districts in the country, though hardly typical in the smaller cities and towns, had already achieved national reputations as dens of legalized vice: New Orleans's Storyville, San Francisco's Barbary Coast, Denver's Market Street Line, Baltimore's Block, Chicago's Levee, and New York's Bowery, Five Points, and Tenderloin. These sporting resorts, with their streets lined with brothels, saloons, and hotels, the air filled with the odor of tobacco and liquor and the sounds of blaring music, windows framed by images of women making obscene gestures, gave Americans their most distasteful and frightening picture of the segregated vice district.

In many cities, regulations controlling music, lights, and stoop-calling became a common part of attempts to minimize the visibility of public prostitution. In Chicago, for example, where several officially segregated red-light districts existed simultaneously, police regularly published "Rules Governing the Regulation of Vice," in which injunctions were included against: persons between three and eighteen years of age in a brothel; under-age brothel inmates; forcible detention of girls in brothels; women entering certain houses without male escorts; prostitutes wearing short skirts, transparent gowns, or improper attire in the public rooms; males who lived off the income of a prostitute entering a brothel; prostitutes soliciting from houses; signs, lights, or obscene pictures on the outside of a house; and swinging doors on parlor houses.[40]

Because "respectable society" wished to avoid visible evidence of prostitution, vice was generally concentrated, rather purposefully, in the poorest neighborhoods, where residents, mostly renters, had the least political clout. One former chief of police in Chicago, for example, issued a semiofficial statement to the effect that persons "involved in prostitution who confined their business to the west of Wabash Avenue and to the east of Wentworth Avenue would remain immune from police harassment." Predictably, this neighborhood was largely composed of black residents.[41] Although some reformers worried about the effects that prostitution would have on black youth, they did little to alter the economic and social barriers that barred black residents from other neighborhoods.

In New York, segregation of vice similarly pushed prostitution into the neighborhood pockets of recent black immigrants from the South. "The wide open city" of Harlem in the twenties originated in the Progressive Era. In the 1890s, the Reverend Charles Parkhurst had attempted to "clean up" the "Black Tenderloin" but had met fierce and implacable resistance. By the turn of the century, most of New York's prostitution had become increasingly concentrated in black and poor ethnic neighborhoods.[42] In his autobiography, the Reverend Dr. Adam Clayton Powell, Sr., of the Abyssinian Baptist Church, remembered living surrounded by the sights and sounds of prostitution. Finding rooms in a cold-water

flat, he recalled hearing "prostitutes over me and all around me." His congregation, moreover, often included "large numbers of pimps, prostitutes, keepers of
dives and gambling dens." Outside the church, "harlots would stand across the
street on Sunday evening in unbuttoned Mother Hubbards soliciting men as
they left our service."[43]

For many young black girls, prostitution was never an alien occupation. All
around them, they had watched black women survive by selling themselves.
Other jobs paid less, moreover, and often involved poorer working conditions.
The number of black prostitutes in the Bedford Reformatory in New York demonstrated that black women were probably arrested more frequently than white
women and that black women were overrepresented in the prostitute population. Like black women, Japanese, Chinese, and Mexican women also were
overrepresented in the prostitute population because they found fewer avenues
of economic survival available than did working-class women of other
backgrounds.[44]

Red-light districts provided employment other than prostitution for many
black women and men. In Chicago, for example, nearly all the domestics of
brothels were black women, and the majority of musical entertainers in saloons
and parlor houses were black men. In her autobiography, *Lady Sings the Blues*,
Billie Holiday described how she first made a living as a domestic in a "cat
house."[45] In New Orleans, some of the finest jazz musicians in the country, such
as Jelly Roll Morton, revolutionized American music while working in brothels.
The "professors," as black musicians were known, were frequently required to
compose "dirty lyrics" to excite male customers. Given the environment in which
jazz developed, it is hardly surprising that whites early identified jazz with prostitution and other forms of "low life."[46]

The extent of racial segregation of prostitution varied widely from one city to
the next. Hattie Rose, a New York white slavery fighter, found that "black and
tan" clubs existed on the side streets of New York's red-light districts. In such
clubs, both black and white women practiced prostitution in the same houses. In
Kansas, however, the vice report revealed that houses were segregated by color.[47]
The city of Little Rock was so segregated that separate reports on prostitution
were issued for white and black prostitution. In New Orleans, segregated black
and white houses stood side by side in the same district. Black men, however,
were not permitted to patronize either "color" house. After 1917, when the government officially closed down Storyville, separate black and white areas of prostitution emerged in different parts of the city. In San Francisco, some "cribs"—
large buildings in which prostitutes were virtually caged in small cubicles four by
six feet—dealt with the issues of race and ethnicity in a unique way. The top
floors of the building was allocated to French, English, and American women,
whereas the lower floors were relegated to Chinese, Japanese, and Mexican
women. Prices varied according to the race and nationality of the prostitute. Not

surprisingly, the top floors cost customers more than the lower floors, which housed women of stigmatized races.[48]

Procurers in all states made serious attempts to import women of different races and nationalities into brothels of all kinds. Healthy and attractive young black women were often desired in the northern brothels. Jane Addams noted that procurers often advanced the boat fare to black girls from the South, promising them domestic work. When the girl arrived, however, she was put into a "questionable" house and forced to pay back her debt.[49]

In general, however, red-light districts reflected the particular racial and ethnic composition of the region in which they were situated. Although the population of prostitutes was quite mobile, it still tended to reflect the community in which the women lived.[50] Thus, visitors and "chair warmers" usually observed women drawn from the poorest racial or ethnic social groups in the area: the extreme concentration of "colored" prostitutes in the Cotton Belt, "half breeds" along the southern border, Japanese and Chinese along the western coast. In eastern cities, investigators noted the high visibility of women from eastern and southern European immigrant groups, along with heavy concentrations of black women recently arrived from the South. In the Midwest, most of the smaller cities reported predominantly rural, white native-born prostitutes.

The red-light district at the turn of the century differed from modern "tenderloin" areas in several important ways. First, the district was characterized by the open presence of brothels. Although some prostitutes worked in cabarets, in saloons, and on the streets, the brothel system of prostitution was *the* distinguishing feature of the red-light district. Second, because the district received official toleration, brothels were free to advertise their wares with considerable abandon.[51]

In the largest cities, blue books—published guides to prostitution—directed the visitor who "hopped" around the district to particular services. The first blue book guide to New Orleans apparently appeared in 1895 and was distributed until 1915. The Storyville blue books carried the following motto: "Order of the Garter: Honi Soit Qui Mal Y Pense (Evil to Him Who Evil Thinks)."[52] In Chicago, a guide also appeared, bearing the title, *The Sporting and Club House Directory, Chicago: Containing a Full and Complete List of all Strictly First Class Clubs and Sporting Houses.*[53]

Inside the blue books, the visitor found descriptions of each house in the district, its price and the particular service and "stock" it offered. The following description of Madame Lulu White's House, at the corner of Basin and Bienville Streets, was a typical blue book advertisement.

> Nowhere in this country will you find a more popular personage then Madame White, who is noted as being the handsomest octoroon in America.
> . . . Aside from being a handsome woman, her mansion possesses some of

the most costly oil paintings in the Southern country. Her mirror parlor is also a dream. There's always something new at Lulu White's that will interest you. "Good time" is her motto. There are always ten entertainers who get paid to do nothing but sing and dance.[54]

Another advertisement described the delights the well-bred visitor could find at May Evans's establishment, another famous Storyville parlor house: "Miss Evans is one woman among the fair sex who is regarded as a jolly good fellow, and one who is always laughing and making all those around her likewise. While nothing is too good for May she is clever to all who are in contact with her. Miss Evans also has the honor of keeping one of the quietest establishments in the city, where beautiful women, good wine and sweet music reign supreme."[55] Some blue books went so far as to imply the kinds of sexual entertainment the houses offered. One establishment, for example, hinted that female homosexual entertainment was available.[56] Another house let it be known that they offered an "international" fare, a variety of sexual practices that one could obtain for a special price:

> Mrs. Emma Johnson, better known as "parisian Queen of America," needs little introduction. Emma's "House of all Nations," as it is commonly called, is one place of amusement you can't very well afford to miss while in the Tenderloin District. Everything goes here. Fun is the Watchword.
>
> Business has been on such an increase at the above place of late that Mme. Johnson had to occupy an 'Annex.' Emma never has less than twenty pretty women of all nations, who are clever entertainers. Remember the Name, EMMA JOHNSON.[57]

In Chicago, pamphlets raved about the fabulous resorts on Dearborn Street. The "comforts to be found within the walls of that sumptuous house," they assured the visitor, would relieve men of "other worries." No one, they boasted, need "feel the chill of winter nor the heat of summer in this place."[58]

In addition to such blue books, prostitutes and madams—especially in less-populated districts—found other ways of advertising their wares. Young boys were paid to stand on street corners and distribute cards advertising a particular house. Behind the windows of low-priced brothels, prostitutes indicated what kinds of services were offered by visibly sucking their thumbs. Outside the brothels, a "lighthouse," usually a young boy, supplied potential customers with information on available sex practices while watching for sudden and unexpected police raids. In return for a commission, bartenders and saloon keepers offered to direct potential customers to houses where visitors could obtain and afford their desired services.[59] The most important advertisement, however, as the Chicago vice report emphasized, was "the district itself. The lighted street, the sound of music, the shrill cries, and suggestive songs of the inmates and entertainers, all of these features tend to bring the business to the attention of the public and to spread the news to other towns and cities."[60]

Working the streets was considered by many prostitutes to be the most dangerous and brutal form of prostitution. "Don't ever be fool enough to go into the streets," one young girl was warned by an experienced prostitute.[61] The dangers of customer and police harassment made street prostitution a particularly formidable and degrading occupation. It was in the largest cities, like New York or Chicago, that streetwalking and street prostitution had already become widespread.[62] In his semiautobiographical novel, *Jews without Money*, Michael Gold described the scenes that he witnessed as a child. "The East Side of New York," he wrote,

> was then the city's red light district, . . . There were hundreds of prostitutes on my street. They occupied vacant stores, they crowded in flats and apartments in all the tenements. The pious Jews hated the traffic. But they were pauper strangers here; they could do nothing. . . . They tried to shut their eyes. We children did not shut our eyes. We saw and knew. On sunshiny days the whores sat on chairs along the sidewalks. They sprawled indolently, their legs taking up half the pavements. People stumbled over a gauntlet of whores' meaty legs. . . .
>
> The girls winked and jeered, made lascivious gestures at passing males. They pulled at coat-tails and cajoled men with fake honeyed words. They called their wares like pushcart peddlers. At five years I knew what it was they sold.
>
> The girls were naked under flowery kimonos. Chunks of breast and belly occasionally flashed. Slippers hung from their feet; they were already ready for "business."[63]

Other prostitutes worked on excursion boats or met men at dance halls and took them to nearby hotels. In some cases, "occasional," or clandestine, prostitutes took their customers to rooms in assignation houses, rooming houses, or hotels that were known to be available for "immoral purposes." As police increasingly closed down the red-light districts, however, women tended to rely upon massage parlors, call-girl flats and other safer and more private forms of prostitution.[64] Some towns prohibited actual districts. As one prostitute from a small town recalled, "The attitude of the town was too puritanical to permit wide-open, publicly recognized houses of ill fame. There were boarding houses, dress making shops, hand laundries and the homes of working men whose wives added to the family finances by occasional prostitution."[65]

In the larger towns and cities, the theater became associated with prostitution during the nineteenth century. Lower-class prostitutes were permitted to use the third tier for making connections with customers. Meanwhile, on the first tier, expensively dressed prostitutes mingled with the fashionable clientele for the same purpose.[66]

From the literature of the period, it appears that a significant amount of prostitution centered around the saloon. This impression may be due to the prohibitionist bias of many of the writers of vice reports. Nevertheless, it does seem that many prostitutes who were not attached to a brothel became in some formal way linked to a particular saloon. In 455 saloons investigated by the Vice Commission of Chicago, an investigator was solicited by prostitutes 236 times and counted 928 prostitutes soliciting other men. "Waitresses" who worked the saloons were given a meager salary, compensated by commissions on their customers' drinks. The profit on liquor, moreover, was exceedingly high. A twenty-five-cent pint bottle of beer usually brought a 178 percent profit. When sold in the private upstairs rooms used for prostitution, the same bottle made a 250 percent profit for the owner.[67] Each waitress earned about three dollars a day from liquor commissions, which, when combined with her small salary, equaled three times the earnings of a domestic worker.

Because saloons offered more than simply liquor, they frequently advertised their services as well. Printed cards distributed by lighthouses extolled the "joys to be found within." In case an unfriendly patrolman approached the saloon, the lighthouse pressed a concealed electric button.[68]

In some saloons, prostitutes offered quick sexual services to customers in private booths surrounded by tables and other booths. Waiters asked unescorted men if they wished a "lady companion for the evening." One investigator from Hartford, Connecticut, described his surprise when he learned that

> sexual immorality was habitually practiced by them there. Seeking advice
> from the waiter, one of our detectives was told to "Go Ahead; nobody will
> come near this booth while the curtains are drawn;" The girls said "I told
> you so; it is done in these booths every day." Three of the other booths were
> occupied at that time and the conversation in one corroborated the reputa-
> tion of the place. Those entering the second floor invariably ask the waiter if
> there are vacancies on the floor above. The upper rooms are preferred on
> account of their greater privacy.[69]

From the same report, it is clear that waiters and saloon keepers smoothed the process for the prostitutes who brought in a constant stream of customers: "As soon as a couple enters a booth, a waiter can be called by a bell and indicator. He does not come until called. On approaching the booth, he regularly shuffles his feet and then pauses before opening the curtain."[70]

In addition to the booths and upstairs rooms, saloons frequently provided "vaudeville" shows in rear rooms. Such shows regularly included sexual acts designed to create more interest in immediate sexual gratification. Half-naked, stripping dancers encouraged male customers, already plied with drink from waitresses, to accept prostitutes' offers.[71]

In addition to offering the sexual services of female prostitutes, it appears that saloons attracted male homosexuals or actual male prostitution. The Vice Commission of Chicago referred to vaudeville performances in "which men impersonate women and solicit men for 'perverted practices.' "[72] Allusions to male homosexuality or transvestism are vague and veiled behind euphemisms. One report referred to a form of "mental aberration too disgusting to discuss," which involved four men of wealth and social standing. The Hartford report stated that such practices were "practiced extensively."[73] One messenger boy, less concerned with euphemisms, offered the following observations: that after Philadelphia had closed its brothels, an increased number of male homosexuals had appeared in the saloons, or, in his words, "there are a lot of 'fairies' (sexual perverts) hanging around the tenderloin. They usually go after the messenger boys first."[74] Until further research is completed, however, it will not be clear to what extent female or male same-sex liaisons took place either in or near the segregated brothel district; nor is it clear how much male prostitution was practiced in these same neighborhoods.

In retrospect, it seems evident that the segregated district, with its sale of sex and titillating promises of satisfaction, constituted the most blatant and commercialized form of prostitution during the first decade of the twentieth century. Like many other elements of the American economy, however, the business of prostitution during this period was in a state of transition. Whereas the legacy of small-scale entrepreneurs in the trade lingered in small towns, prostitution in large cities had become increasingly rationalized, professionalized, commercialized, and consolidated into larger business enterprises. Equally important, as cities began closing the districts, new forms of prostitution began replacing the public forms of prostitution so typical of the segregated district.

Just as many American reformers sought to control, or at least stabilize, the growing power and wealth of corporate structures in the "legitimate" business world, they also sought to eliminate the worst aspects of commercialized prostitution. For those who profited from prostitution, however, these reforms represented serious economic interference; for commercialized vice already supported and created an entire urban subculture based on the sale of sex. Some, as those just described, lived off prostitution from a distance, even though their livelihoods depended on or were elevated by their parasitical relationship to prostitution. Others lived within the subculture itself, where the view from within was shaped by the daily realities of the practice of prostitution.

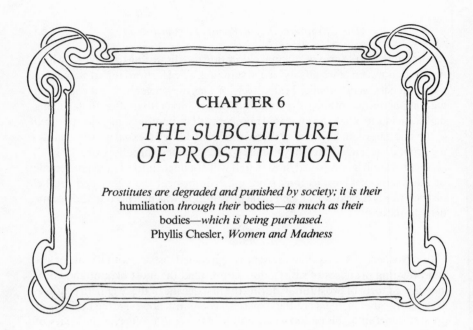

CHAPTER 6

THE SUBCULTURE
OF PROSTITUTION

Prostitutes are degraded and punished by society; it is their humiliation through their bodies—as much as their bodies—which is being purchased.
Phyllis Chesler, *Women and Madness*

From the outside, commercialized vice represented "big business" for those who reaped its profits and for the reformers who sought its demise. For the individuals who lived or worked within the district, however, the view was somewhat different. What was the subculture of prostitution like for those people who worked on the "underside" of American urban life?

The brothel was the center for much of the subculture of prostitution. The report of the Vice Commission of Minneapolis emphasized that the "business of Public Prostitution has become commercialized and the brothel is the recognized center of this abhorrent commerce."[1] In Philadelphia, reformers found that approximately half of 3,311 interviewed prostitutes either resided in or worked in brothels.[2] Most important, the brothel came to represent the most flagrant example of tolerated prostitution. Since much of the data collected about prostitution from this era focused on this particular institution, we can at least gain some view into the daily life of certain prostitutes. Data on brothels also provide us with a richer sense of the class stratification that characterized prostitution (typical in nearly all periods of history) and allow us to recreate the kind of public prostitution whose historical demise meant the growth of new and more familiar forms of the trade.[3]

Not all brothels were alike. Reflecting the class distinctions of the rest of society, brothels catered to the economic interests and budgets of different clientele. Every city, for example, boasted several expensive five- and ten-dollar parlor houses that attracted wealthy men, who used the facilities much as a gentlemen's social club.[4] There, they made political connections, met their associates, and relaxed in an atmosphere of exquisite food, wine, and women. One-dollar houses catered to the interests and budgets of middle-class men, and fifty-cent houses and cribs heavily relied on the working-class "stiff" for their clientele. As the Kansas vice report explained, "A few [brothels] were equipped with expensive furniture and furnishings including the finest of upholstered chairs, well chosen paintings and costly rugs, while a large number of others were hovels of repulsive squalor."[5]

The success or failure of a high-priced parlor house ultimately rested on the central figure of the establishment, the madam. Viewed from an occupational point of view, the position of a madam required extreme competence in business and political matters as well as managerial, personnel, and communication skills.

Her first priority was to maintain a profitable business. This meant balancing income with expenditures for municipal fines, commissions to procurers, doctors' bills, and, most significantly, high rents. Given the ambiguous legal status of prostitution, the madam also had to possess a high degree of political tact and diplomacy.[6] She had to learn, for example, the fine art of adapting to local political practices in order to insure the political protection of her house. Since some of the high-priced sporting houses doubled as clubs where the local political and economic elite met to exchange necessary information and negotiate informal deals, an intelligent madam invariably became privy to the inner workings of her community. A reputation for absolute silence was essential; for example, she had to protect the identities of her customers. In the event of a customer's sudden illness or accident while in her house, a madam would have the person removed to a more respectable location before notifying police or family. A successful madam, moreover, never greeted her clientele in public; she traded her silence for the continued political protection of her business. In some cases, some madams became silent partners in the local power structure; they knew too much for any local politician to shut their establishments down.[7]

Running a house with four to twelve inmates required skillful management.[8] In a sense, the madam managed a small business; she checked on the servants who prepared meals for the inmates and herself, made sure that sheets in all rooms were changed several times during an evening, maintained an adequate supply of fine wines and liquors, and oversaw repairs. In addition, the madam interviewed, hired, and fired servants, maids, musicians, and prostitutes who worked in her house. Since local patrons always demanded "new faces," a good businesswoman periodically sought new prostitutes. Such interviews could be grueling. One prostitute found that her credentials from Kansas City were no match for the "proper" behavior and dress required in the "Ice Palace" in Chicago. There, the haughty madam reluctantly took her in because she possessed youth, good looks, and manners that "might" be transformed into an appropriately elegant employee of a sporting resort. Older or less attractive women, or women whose racial or cultural background offended the gentlemen of a particular region, frequently found employment in "first class" houses impossible to obtain.[9]

Since most madams formerly had worked as prostitutes, they were usually familiar with the problems young prostitutes faced in their work, and the petty quarrels and jealousies that periodically erupted between inmates of the houses.[10] It was the madam's responsibility to prevent such problems from interfering with the business of the house. Quite naturally, she became a confidante and counselor to her "girls." Frequently called "mother" by her employees, she learned to placate their worries and help them solve their problems.[11]

The madam's relationship with the inmates, however, was necessarily ambiguous and complex. As one investigator pointed out, "Madams become the advisor and friend of the girls, while at the same time she drives them to the utmost to earn larger profits for the houses." She was, in fact, both friend *and* exploiter of her "girls."[12]

Among other aspects of their work, madams also had to maintain a good reputation through constant advertisements. To maintain their clientele, madams often kept lists of customers and sent out periodic announcements of changes in address or changes in their "stock." One madam in New York sent out a neatly folded announcement that read, "Kindly call at our old place of business as we have a Beautiful Spring Stock on view."[13]

To maintain a fresh supply of prostitutes, madams offered good commissions to procurers who replenished their house. Patterned after some of the famous European and British brothels of the nineteenth century, some American parlor houses specialized in the defloration of young virgins, flogging, and assorted sexual activities never enumerated because investigators found them too "lewd" to discuss. In the society column of the New Orleans *Mascot* appeared the following comment: "It is safe to say that Mrs. Thewer can brag of more innocent girls having been ruined in her house than there were in any six houses in the city."[14]

Madams took special pride in creating an extravagant (frequently ostentatious) display of gilded glamor for their wealthy clients. One investigator in Portland, Maine, described the luxurious interior of a high-priced house, meant to make wealthy men feel comfortable:

> I learned that there are fourteen rooms in the house, located on the second and third floors. On the second floor is a private parlor which the madame has handsomely furnished. On the same floor is another room fitted up with Dutch furnishings which she calls her Dutch room. It contained a handsome rug, large library table, an assortment of steins; and around the entire room is a plate rail on which she had numerous Dutch steins of various designs. A large sum of money has been spent fitting up this room, and the madame told me it was used for a very exclusive class of men who spend much money for wine and such as that. On the other side of the hall is a long

room furnished in solid mahogany, containing a handsome pianola and a Victrola and adorned with gorgeous draperies and several pictures. The madame said it cost her several thousand dollars to furnish that one room. On the third floor are located the private apartments of the madame and the rooms of the three sporting girls that she has whose names are Katherine, Ethel and Edith. She told me she was looking for another girl because the three she had were not sufficient to meet the demand of her house.[15]

In some establishments, men were also offered the opportunity of viewing special "circuses" or "shows" designed to stimulate more business. Since contemporaries found these exhibitions too "vulgar" or too "lewd" to describe, one can only speculate as to their content. It is known, however, that men frequently spent as much as fifty to seventy-five dollars for such exhibitions.[16]

Although the few such exclusive clubs and houses tended to glamorize the profession, they did offer reasonably well-paying work for young and attractive women. For madams, the work provided an opportunity to attain a position of responsibility, to gain a fairly high standard of living, and occasionally to achieve a certain degree of desired celebrity.

Some of the madams who either managed or owned the establishments they ran *did* in fact become local, or even regional, celebrities. In Storyville, the name Lulu White became synonymous with high-priced parlor houses. Born on a farm in Selma, Alabama, this black woman passed herself off as a "West Indian" in Storyville society. Her famous "Mahogany Hall" became one of the most notorious and expensive sporting houses in New Orleans. Unfortunately, Lulu White permitted herself to become involved with a "fancy man" who disappeared to Hollywood with her savings of $150,000.[17]

Another well-known madam who achieved a certain degree of upward mobility through her profession was Josie Arlington (born Mary Deubler). She became famous for the luxurious mansion she established, a sporting house that boasted "lewd" live sexual acts, special services, and exhibitions of all kinds. Having first worked as a local prostitute, Josie Arlington supported her family on her earnings. After managing a low-priced house characterized by constant brawling, she parlayed her talents into the establishment of "The Arlington" on Basin Street, with the intention of creating the grandest bordello in the district. During the last years of her life, Josie Arlington built herself a red marble tomb with a cross on the back and a statue of a kneeling woman whose arms are filled with flowers. In front of the doors of the tomb stands a "beautifully executed statue of a young girl . . . in an attitude of knocking at the door." Legend has it that the statuary was to symbolize that Josie Arlington had never permitted a virgin to be ruined in her house.[18]

One of the most famous parlor houses in the United States was founded by the Everleigh sisters in Chicago. Born in Kentucky, they both married, left their husbands, and subsequently enjoyed brief stage careers. During the 1898 Trans-

Mississippi Exposition, they opened their first brothel and then moved their business to Chicago. The Everleigh Club became one of the most exclusive sporting houses in the nation. The club boasted a fifty-dollar entrance fee and required a formal calling card or letter of introduction. Serving the best champagne and liquors, the Everleigh Club became famous for glamorous bedrooms furnished with marble inlaid beds, surrounded by ceiling and wall mirrors, as well as such special attendants as barbers and masseurs.[19]

Despite—or perhaps due to—the illicit nature of their work, most madams seem to have viewed their achievement with pride and satisfaction. From an occupational point of view, the role of a madam offered responsibilities and business opportunities normally denied women because of their gender identity. Unlike other women, madams engaged in political wheeling and dealing, faced the daily responsibilities of personnel and "hotel" management, and gleefully shattered the boundaries of "proper" feminine sexual behavior. As the infamous San Francisco madam Sally Stanford was later to remark about her profession, "It doesn't take much to produce a good merchant of cash-and-carry love; just courage, an infinite capacity for perpetual suspicion, stamina on a 24-hour-a-day basis, the deathless conviction that the customer is always wrong, a fair knowledge of first and second aid, do-it-yourself gynecology, judo—and a tremendous sense of humor."[20]

Despite the flamboyant behavior and comments made by many madams, most expressed conventional concerns for their economic security and took their responsibilities as seriously as a businessman who runs a hotel. In describing a madam who catered to a prairie clientele in Canada, one male customer commented that

> Pearl Miller was easily the most successful whore Calgary ever had. I think her secret of success was that she ran a clean and happy joint. . . . She really acted more like a hostess than a whore. You know, she'd visit with you, have a drink with you though I never saw her drunk. She kept her eye on her girls and tried to run a real nice place where you liked to return. If you didn't think where you were, you could easily imagine you were in a boarding parlor with ordinary lodgers, with Pearl being the landlady looking after things.[21]

Repudiating the moralistic perspective of reformers, madams looked upon their business ventures as a means of earning a decent livelihood. The goals of material success and economic security were socially legitimate; only the means of reaching them were "illegitimate." One madam in Chicago, for example, viewed the three flats she managed with her sister as a business venture and a secure way of earning a livelihood. Catering to an upper-class clientele, she charged five dollars for a typical visit and seven or ten dollars for extra services. When interviewed by an investigator, however, "Edna" wanted to sell her business. For years she had been supporting her ailing parents with her annual earnings of six thousand to seven thousand dollars. She now wanted to retire, maybe buy an orange grove in California, and lead a respectable, quiet life. In her published memoirs of her life as a successful madam, Pauline Tabor similarly viewed her work as a business venture, a means toward a socially acceptable and respectable end. She, too, wished to retire with sufficient cash to insure a secure old age.[22]

In most memoirs published by former madams, there appears an irreverent attitude toward society's hypocritical "morality," combined with a rather conventional and pragmatic perspective on one's business as a means toward upward mobility; in fact, the desire for future respectability mingles with a genuine disgust for society's sexual purists. As the irrepressible Sally Stanford noted in her autobiography, "Madaming is the sort of thing that happens to you, like getting a battlefield commission or becoming the Dean of Women at Stanford University. But I have never been the least bit touchy or sensitive about it . . . never. Many are called, I always say, but few are chosen; and for me it has been a steppingstone to bigger and more profitable things."[23]

Pauline Tabor, who became a prostitute when she was left penniless with two children to support, eventually opened a notorious brothel during the depression. She, too, shared other madams' attitudes—attitudes that cross the decades to emphasize some of the continuity in the history of prostitution. Explaining her occupation as a madam in Bowling Green, Kentucky, Tabor wrote; "To compound such felonies against society's code of ladylike behavior, I was a mercenary. I was a sex merchant for the same basic reason that motivated other people to peddle pills, groceries, clothing, toys, cars and all manner of their wares—to make money and acquire the better things of life."[24]

In theory, the exclusive brothels run by these businesswomen created and sustained a sexual fantasy for their customers. The madam and the extravagant surroundings were supposed to create the feeling of entering a specially sexual world in which the customer became a part of an erotic and sensual atmosphere. Prostitutes received training in the art of flattering their customers and convincing them of their desirability: "The girl must be kept gay and attractive. . . . She must smile and laugh and sing and dance or she becomes a 'has been.' "[25] One Storyville prostitute recalled greeting each customer with some exclamation of affection: " 'My you so han'some, why you no come before,' I say 'you jus' my type.' T'ings like dat day don' mean nawthing, be de man like dees, hah?"[26]

A prostitute in such an exclusive sporting house was supposed to be an accomplished actress, demonstrating at every instant the customer's irresistibility through dramatic declarations of passion and excitement. Even the language of the trade, "turning a trick," reflected the hoax that the prostitute was perpetrating on the customer.

According to survivors of the Storyville district, however, such fantasies were rarely sustained. Sex was a commodity, and the prostitute understood and exploited that fact. One prostitute characterized sexual relations in a high-class house in the following manner: "I lay on de bed, and he do what he want. Ees nawthing, you know—maybe wan, two minutes. Si! I can make heem do eet queeker, but mo' all de time eet ees not necessary. He ees queeck by himself."[27] Apparently not all customers found such mechanical sex, without an aura of fantasy and illusion, very satisfactory. One wealthy gentleman who frequented Storyville's high-priced houses for over twelve years, and also had visited brothels all over the world, concluded that American prostitutes lacked all pretense at creating sexual fantasies. "I consider the quality of sex in Storyville," he sniffed, "to constitute an indictment against the American man's taste and degree of civilization." In comparison with American prostitutes, he continued,

> foreign whores somehow managed to feign an attitude that leads you to believe, at least for the moment of intercourse, that you have their attention and that they are interested in seeing that you have a pleasant time. While they never do it for free, they always seem just a little surprised when you give them the money . . . as though they'd forgotten about this crass detail. They have, how shall I describe it, pride in their workmanship. Some at times show a certain art consciousness, as though in recognition of the possibilities of the development of substantial aesthetic qualities in sexual congress.[28]

If high-priced parlor houses sometimes failed to conform to popular expectations of "native craftsmanship," middle-priced houses and fifty-cent cribs never promised anything but the most expedient and efficient opportunity for immediate sexual relief. Just as the high-priced parlor houses created a pretense of luxury—fine wines, extravagant surroundings, stunningly attired young women—and provided a variety of circuses and exhibitions to appeal to cosmopolitan and even kinky tastes, the average one- or two-dollar brothels, which catered to a middle-class clientele, offered surroundings and sexual practices suitable to the tastes and budgets of their clientele.

Descriptions of middle-class establishments are rare; investigators apparently found the extremes of high-priced parlor houses and low-priced tenements or cribs more interesting to investigate. One prostitute described the informal ambience of such middle-class "joints" that catered to the average working man. "The prostitutes," she wrote,

> sat around in their underwear or wrappers, drank beer, joshed a lot in country talk, felt at home with the simple horny guests that came to them with dusty shoes and derbys. There was a morality about these places that mirrored the words of the whores and their guests. They were Mama and Papa fuckers, doing it mostly the straight and traditional American way, as they had been raised. Frenching was talked and joked about, but rarely asked for

*Missionary (foreground) and prostitutes standing outside a Chicago brothel.
Reprinted from Clifford G. Roe,* Horrors of the White Slave Trade
(London: Clifford G. Roe and B. S. Steadwell, 1911), facing p. 336.

or offered. The Italian Way, entry through the rear, was kind of a joke
carried over from farm boys experimenting on themselves and each other,
considered a sign of depraved city sinning. Memories of Bible lessons and
sermons on Babylon and hellfire from their country churches was still there
in the middle class whorehouse.[29]

Particularly in small towns and in the Midwest, the young women who "worked"
these houses represented a local, native population. Unlike the variety of racial
mixtures found and requested in the largest coastal cities, the madams and most
of the prostitutes in the small towns "were of native stock, corn-fed Kansas girls
and hustlers who had come from broken down farms and small ranches. Some
had been deserted by a railroad brakeman or boss carpenter, who moved on,
leaving them with no rent money or food."[30] If a prostitute had real ambition, she
left such towns for the large cities to apply for work in the high-priced brothels.

Unlike the fanciest sporting houses, which were frequented by a wealthy and
politically powerful clientele, the middle-class whorehouses catered to the needs
of "all those who figured the cost of their spending. . . . The clerk, the wagon
husky, the logger, the husband who wasn't getting it properly at home . . . he
could come to have his ashes hauled, his wick dipped—both expressions popular
in these middle-class joints." Although many of the customers may have asked
for sexual practices refused to them at home, "the idea of flogging for fun, or

being stomped on by high heels, or a daisy chain in a middle class whorehouse was like spitting on the flag or drawing a mustache on Martha Washington's picture."[31]

It was in tenement houses and cribs that investigators found the horrendous conditions that characterized low-priced prostitution. In New York, one cheap joint was described as follows:

> A large wooden bench was placed against the wall of the receiving parlor. Business was very brisk at the time the investigator entered. The bench was full of customers crowded close together, while others, who could not be accommodated with seats, stood about the room. At the foot of the stairs which led to the bedroom above, a man was stationed. Every time a visitor came groping his way down the stairs, the businesslike and aggressive announcer would cry out, "Next!" At the word, the man sitting on the end of the bench nearest the stairs arose and passed up. As he did so, the men on the bench moved along and one of the men who was standing took the vacant seat.[32]

Unlike the pretentious wealth exhibited in the best parlor houses or the sturdy, comfortable atmosphere of a medium-priced house, most low-priced tenements and cribs contained a few old leather couches in a small receiving room. The rooms were "dirty, the loose creaking floors [were] covered with matting which [was] gradually rotting away, the ceilings [were] low, the windows small, the air heavy and filled with foul odors . . . the atmosphere heavy with odors of tobacco and perfumes, mingled with fumes of medicine and cheap disinfectants."[33]

In the cribs that dotted the southwest and western coast, the working conditions were even worse than in the eastern tenements. A "cowyard whorehouse" was a three- or four-story tenement with long halls lined with cubicles or closets. Sometimes as many as 250 women crowded into these separate small cubicles. "Crib whores," mostly Chinese and black women, also worked in small shacks where they were virtual prisoners of the man who stationed himself in the front reception room. In the back, the prostitute worked in a small room surrounded by a basin, a washstand, and a small bed with a strip of oil cloth at the end of it. For "two bits" the customer was briefly washed and permitted to take off only his shoes.[34]

Although little research or investigation has been done on the customers who frequented brothels, one still wonders about the expectations and experiences of the men who visited the "houses of ill fame." Former madams emphasize that what they sold was not sex per se but a variety of other intangible products— such as companionship for lonely men, the illusion of being admired for one's sexual prowess, the escape from an unhappy wife to a flattering prostitute. As Sally Stanford noted in her autobiography,

> I learned that men came to a place such as mine not for sex but for a whole batch of other reasons; to talk about their troubles, their wives' infidelities;

to sleep off a drunk; to find out if there were any new wrinkles; to get laughs from jokes that were clinkers elsewhere; to find sweethearts and even wives; to escape from the cops; to get advice on the cure of social diseases; and some to get a good cup of coffee and a plate of ham and eggs when everything else was closed.[35]

In some cases, a young boy's first experience occurred in a brothel. Brought by his father to Lulu White's "Mahogany Hall," one "gentleman of means" recalled his first sexual encounter. His experience, like the few others existent, reveals a sense of disappointment, deception, and disillusionment.

The instant we stepped inside that door, it became apparent that, though ornate, the taste reflected in the furnishings and decore was just miserable. . . . Lulu White, herself, greeted us after we'd been announced by a Negro doorman . . . she was a monstrosity . . . laden with diamonds worn not selectively but just put on any place there seemed to be an inch to accommodate them. She wore a red wig that hardly pretended to be natural in color. . . . Lulu was obviously Negro. Her efforts to appear cultured were quite ludicrous. Her quick smile was as fake as the color of her wig.[36]

After being invited into the parlor, the father and his son were introduced to the dozen prostitutes lounging on sofas and chairs. Lulu picked one of the girls dressed in the most "revealing" clothes and said, "Rita, this is M'sier Rene. You take him and see that he has a real good time." The son sipped some champagne, tipped the "professor," and proceeded upstairs with his "lady companion." His expectations, influenced by his prior knowledge of such exclusive establishments, were high: "I was nervous—not because of the fact that I was about to have a sex experience, but because I expected something quite sensationally evil and was conscious of being a guest in a world-renowned den of iniquity."[37] His actual experience, however, revealed the disillusioning fact that he had bought the sexual services of a woman who, justifiably, cared nothing about him:

The young lady, apart from a certain studied theatricality, was just as ill-informed and gauche as she could be. She led me upstairs to a bed-room of medium size, dominated by a fourposter bed, quite dusty looking—the drapes, I mean. She got out of her clothes and invited me to do the same. She approached and seized my genital organ in one hand, wringing it in such a way as to determine whether or not I had the gonorrhea. She did this particular operation with more knowledge and skill than she did anything else before or after. I was not taken aback, because I had already heard about this part of the procedure from many people, including my father. She washed me with some foul-smelling disinfectant and lay down on the bed, inviting me to mount her. This I proceeded to do, and the mechanical procedure that followed endured for perhaps a minute. She then washed me and herself again, politely asked me if there would be anything else, and when I thanked her and said no, she asked for ten dollars. I apologized, telling her I didn't know whether the money was paid to the girl or to some cashier at the close of the evening. Back in the parlor, I found my father still conversing with Lulu.[38]

If exclusive clubs frequently failed to sustain the sexual fantasy they promised, the more modest establishments, lacking gilded surroundings, emphasized efficiency instead of illusion. In an interview with Al Rose, one "typical" working-class man recalled his own experiences in a medium-priced brothel. "Naturally," he explained, "as a wage laborer I couldn't afford those luxury places on Basin Street. . . . The real truth is, though, that an evening in any house, no matter what the going rate was reported to be, it always cost you as much as you had in your pocket." As in the higher-priced sporting houses, a few dances mixed with a couple of drinks preceded the evening's sexual activities. "The player piano," he recalled, "only had *fast* tunes. . . . It seemed like everything they did was fast, especially take all your money and get you out of there so they could take on more customers."[39]

After dancing with several women, each of whom whispered the special treatment he would receive, he was led upstairs to the "boudoir." Like his wealthy counterpart quoted earlier, he, too, felt cheated by the experience.

> You wouldn't believe how fast those girls could get their clothes off. Usually they'd leave on their stockings and earrings, things like that. A man usually took off his trousers and shoes. New girls didn't give you a second to catch your breath before they'd be all over you trying to get you to heat up and go off as soon as possible. . . . When it came to the actual act, though, the routine was standard. . . . I think the girls could diagnose clap better than the doctors at that time. She'd have a way of squeezing it that, if there was anything in there, she'd find it. Then she'd wash it off with a clean wash cloth. She'd lay on her back and get you on top of her so fast, you wouldn't even know you'd come up there on your own power. She'd grind so that you almost felt like you had nothing to do with it. Well, after that, she had you. She could make it get off as quickly as she wanted to . . . and she didn't waste any time, I'll tell you. . . . I'd say that the whole thing, from the time you got in the room until the time you came didn't take three minutes.
>
> Then she'd wash you off again, and herself. Then she'd get dressed, without even looking at you . . . you could see she was already thinking about nothing but getting downstairs. But she'd be smiling, though, as if everything was just fine and she'd had a good time. . . . In fact, from the time you'd come in the front door of the house until you'd be back out on the banquette hardly even took more than fifteen minutes.[40]

Like the wealthy, but disenchanted, patron of the Basin Street mansions, this man experienced continued alienation during encounters with prostitutes. "I was never satisfied," he explained,

> I don't mean that I thought the girls had cheated me, but I always had the feeling afterwards that life had cheated me. I always had the feeling that

there must be something—more fun, you know. . . . Of course, they'd drain me off. I'd be depleted and enervated—but I never had the feeling of satisfaction that I was always looking for. The truth is that a man wants something more from a woman than that—and it's not easy to find even outside a district. Most all the married women you run across are just a different kind of whore. But a man keeps looking for somebody he can just feel—well, like he isn't always *alone*.[41]

Given the alienation and dissatisfaction that some men apparently experienced in all brothels, regardless of the price, one wonders why they kept returning to the district. Some men apparently found in prostitution a temporary, if unsatisfactory, escape from their loneliness. Young clerks in New York replied that they sought companionship with prostitutes to offset the "dullness of their lives." In Lancaster, Pennsylvania, the vice commission found that college boys, eager for new sexual experiences, sought prostitutes when they could not find women in their own social milieu. Predictably, married men commented that they sought sexual practices that they felt or knew would offend their wives.[42]

Since reformers focused most of their attention on prostitutes, a profile of the customers is impossible to re-create. If more recent twentieth century data reflect this earlier period, it is likely that a majority of the men were married, young, or middle-aged; they sought in prostitutes sexual practices forbidden at home, the illusion of companionship, a congenial club environment, or an escape from marital, family, or work difficulties.[43] Examples cited since the thirties, which rely heavily on psychological explanations, tend to emphasize clients' needs for anonymous sexual relations—including the need to feel superior to someone, anyone.[44]

It is interesting to note that the American Social Health Association, which has studied male customers since the 1930s, has determined that whereas only 10 percent of men in the thirties asked for any sexual activity other than "straight" relations, nearly nine out of ten male customers in the 1960s requested oral sex or "half and half," a combination of oral and "straight" sex. They also noted that both prostitutes and clients in the sixties expressed greater comfort and fewer "vulgar epithets" in discussing oral sexual activity.[45]

Although prostitution may seem a deviant marketplace, it is important to remember that there are always reasons behind the demand and supply in any market relation. Judging from the more recent research cited above, it seems likely that men in 1910 asked for relatively common forms of sexual relations. With more women willing to engage in such sexual activity today, the sexual requests may have changed in relation to what many women outside the world of prostitution still find unpleasant or about which they still feel inhibited.

Although prostitution offered some women a means of survival or better-paying work than they could otherwise obtain, it also exposed them to physical risk and emotional strain. These problems were most severe for streetwalkers and women working in low-class "dives" and cribs. These women faced frequent brutality and police harassment from which prostitutes in high-priced establishments were politically protected. Their inadequate and precarious means of support exposed them, more than other prostitutes, to the medical problems most common to the poor: tuberculosis, tonsillar infection, and malnutrition. Crib prostitutes also saw more than the four or five customers that high-priced prostitutes entertained in one evening. The squalor of the surroundings, combined with the quantity of the customers she served (from thirteen to thirty), made the low-class prostitute's work an intolerable, inhumane, and debilitating experience.[46]

Even in less extreme situations, however, prostitutes had to deal with risks to their health and job security and assaults on their self-respect. For example, whereas some customers searched for genuine companionship and felt disappointed, many prostitutes looked upon men's desire for genuine warmth and human contact as an outrageous expectation. Prostitutes knew they were supposed to be "superior wives," offering temporary nurturance and refuge while flattering men's egos. In reality, however, they deeply resented men's desire to "buy their soul as well as their body." One young prostitute found such pretense particularly difficult. She hated the fact that customers "expect the same willing, responsive service from the woman whose body they have bought as they do from the waitress who serves their dinner."[47]

A prostitute therefore found it necessary to defend against this intrusion on her personal self while engaged in the most personal and intimate sexual acts. For prostitutes, having sexual relations with customers for whom they felt physical disgust was a daily fact of life. From fragmentary evidence, it appears that some prostitutes used morphine to immunize themselves against these interactions and to soften the hard-edged reality of their daily work. Morphine could be obtained through certain druggists or doctors who acted as suppliers to prostitutes. Although drug addiction among prostitutes did not receive a great deal of attention, it was probably more prevalent than realized; when arrested, many imprisoned prostitutes suddenly became seized with violent withdrawal symptoms. One female worker with prostitutes noted that prostitutes in workhouses smuggled in morphine or cocaine in pies, oranges, and chewing gum.[48]

The percentage of prostitutes addicted to drugs is difficult to estimate. At Bedford Reformatory, 5.7 percent of 647 prostitutes were found to be using drugs. The superintendent of police of Philadelphia, however, estimated that closer to 50 percent of prostitutes working in the districts used drugs. The use of cocaine—since its discovery twenty years before as a surgical anesthetic—had spread to many criminal subcultures. One rescue worker stated that 7 out of 229 prostitutes she had encountered were "confirmed opium users." When brothels were closed, some municipal reformers noted that pimps began selling opium and cocaine to recoup their losses.[49] In her description of her life as a prostitute, Maimie Pinzer recalled that she, too, had been addicted to "m___."[50] In sum, though drug addiction was not as closely tied to prostitution as it is today, evidence suggests that it was a growing problem that investigators and reformers were just beginning to observe and acknowledge.

Another major occupational hazard was venereal disease. Estimates of infected prostitutes varied widely. One female reformer guessed that forty thousand prostitutes died every year as the result of venereal infection.[51] In one New York study, 20.56 percent had clinical manifestations of venereal disease. After testing, however, only 10 percent were actually found to be infected.[52] One writer estimated that 60 to 70 percent of all active prostitutes eventually became infected while plying their trade. Another study at Bedford Hills of 200 prostitutes revealed that only 13.5 percent of prostitutes were free from venereal disease. Yet another study concluded that 74 percent of active prostitutes in San Francisco tested by the new Wasserman laboratory procedure were found infected. Venereal infection was not limited to women who practiced the trade constantly. Maimie Pinzer, plagued with illnesses throughout her impoverished young womanhood, lost an eye to syphilitic infection.[53]

Pregnancy was a particular problem that prostitutes encountered in their work. Although contemporary sexual handbooks still described women's fertile period as during and after menstruation,[54] prostitutes were apparently aware of the accurate female fertility cycle and used such well-known contraceptive methods as "packing with sponges" and douching. Nevertheless some prostitutes still became pregnant. If they carried their children to term, they frequently found a "baby farm" where an older woman, sometimes a former prostitute, took care of prostitutes' children. Prostitutes also had access to quack doctors, who parasitically lived off the women's medical problems. Pharmacists and doctors provided a "black pill which, if taken for three days and with hot baths, usually brought a girl around."[55] Although statistics are unavailable, it is likely that the many deaths associated with prostitution might have resulted from some of the medicines and procedures used for abortion. Another gynecological problem that prostitutes may have experienced was chronic pelvic congestion, caused by excessive sexual intercourse without orgasm, an uncomfortable condition for which prostitutes now frequently seek medical help.[56]

Suicide was also associated with prostitution. Sensationalized newspaper accounts frequently described the despair that led prostitutes to take their own lives. The prevalence of suicide among prostitutes is difficult to determine. One study of prostitutes working in brothels found that 11 percent of the women had attempted suicide at least one time.[57] Nearly all memoirs of madams and prostitutes have emphasized the periodic despondency and despair that prostitutes experience when hopes of marrying fail, when dreams of achieving some form of upward mobility disintegrate, or when women feel trapped in a hopeless situation.[58] Maimie Pinzer, while struggling to avoid returning to prostitution, experienced periods of deep depression as she tried to live on subsistence wages in a variety of jobs. She eloquently described the plight of such estranged, alienated, and impoverished young women when she wrote, "When the seasons change as they are doing now—I feel the smallness of my life and I get terribly discouraged for need of many things makes me wonder if after all it is worthwhile to struggle as I do."[59]

Another major occupational hazard for prostitutes was their own aging. A young, white, attractive woman could easily find employment in a number of reasonably well kept houses. But as a woman grew older, as the scars and bruises of a difficult occupation gradually destroyed her health and looks, she faced the grim certainty of downward mobility in her occupation. Like the athlete who depends on his or her youthful strength or looks for early career advancement, the prostitute could look ahead only to a bleak future. If she had a pimp, he might drop her. A madam might similarly let her go. Without any training or skills, she might at best marry; at worst, she might be forced into the fifty-cent houses or into streetwalking, where older and less attractive women finally plied their trade.[60]

Finally, prostitutes faced continual social and community ostracism in a society that viewed them as a social evil, a pariah. How did prostitutes cope with such moral ostracism from the dominant culture? Did they care? Did they feel victimized by society? Were they contemptuous of middle-class "sexual hypocrisy"? Did they internalize society's view of themselves and believe in their worthlessness? Or did they find means of achieving self-esteem despite their socially degraded status?

Available evidence points in several directions. Maimie Pinzer, for example, expressed a strong will to achieve respectability and continually worried about etiquette and other rules of behavior. Very early in life, and throughout her experiences as a prostitute, she aimed at elevating her self-esteem and achieving respectability.

> I can recall distinctly that I was ever on the alert as a girl to learn the things that distinguished "nice" people from the other kind. I don't know just why I thought this desirable inasmuch as I didn't show any desire to live as "nice" people did—but I can recall hundreds of times when I would meet a man—son of "nice" people—& he, thinking to come down to the level of a girl of my sort would either express himself coarsely or in language that would not be considered good English by "nice" people—and I would take great pleasure in correcting him, thinking to show him that it wasn't necessary to come down—I would come up. In this way, I learned much—often it wasn't their speech, sometimes their mannerisms at or away from the table—but I knew all this because I wanted to know and nothing escaped me.[61]

Despite her aspirations for a respectable and refined life, however, Maimie, like many other prostitutes during this period, maintained a rather cynical attitude toward conventional definitions of respectability. "Respectability," she realistically noted, "too often means a cheap room with cheap surroundings." Faced with constant unemployment, imminent impoverishment, Maimie further confided, in a letter to Fanny Howe, "I just cannot be moral enough to see where drudgery is better than a life of lazy vice." Struggling to maintain a "straight" life, she further explained, "I am absolutely honest with you . . . I can't stand this any longer. It is a struggle each day. . . . My trouble," she described, "is that I am a working girl who has lived like a 'lady' and it's hard to curb my desires and live as the working girl should."[62]

Prostitutes and madams *did* have to defend themselves in some way against the dominant culture's judgment of their occupation. In her memoirs, Pauline Tabor most articulately described the process of acculturation which led her from a respectable background to owning a successful brothel.

> Fortunately, the human spirit is not easily destroyed. It instinctively builds defenses against attack. In my case, I soon developed protective armor of cynicism about my fellow man. The once naive Pauline Tabor, like an old soldier, just faded away. She was replaced by a hard-nosed, cash-on-the-line madam who operated on the philosophy that all God's children have feet of clay. That philosophy, I might add, was firmly founded on the knowledge that many of the gentlemen who snubbed me in public were patrons of my house; that many of the public officials who cried out the loudest against vice were the first in line to accept supposedly "soiled money" in return for closing their eyes to the vice against which they crusaded; that many of the respectable ladies who scorned me and my profession were failures as wives, frigid females whose sex-starved husbands turned up at my door to buy an illusion of love and human warmth they couldn't find in their own homes. So in time I learned to ignore the barbs of a disapproving society, and I was able to laugh all the way to the bank.[63]

Some prostitutes, of course, grew up in the tenderloin districts, barely exposed to conventional ideas of "virtue." Life at home blurred with the practice of prostitution. One young girl in Storyville, for example, was the daughter of a prostitute and one of her former "tricks." Growing up in a cheap brothel, she learned before five how to prepare opium and how to wash off her mother's clients. At seven, she began performing sexual acts for clients. Soon after, her virginity was auctioned off for $7.75. Later, she became a waitress, continued to "turn a few tricks," and eventually married. When asked how she viewed her early life, however, she breezily replied, "I ain't ashamed of what I did, because I didn't have much to do with it." She then went on to explain what seemed to be a typical attitude of many prostitutes: "I know it'd be good if I could say how awful it was and like crime don't pay, but to me it seems just like anything else—like a kid whose father owns a grocery store. He helps him in the store. Well my mother didn't sell groceries."[64]

Another survivor of a Storyville crib explained how her background never prepared her to view prostitution as anything but another means of survival. The daughter of former black slaves who had become poor menial workers, she had never been exposed to any theoretical difference between prostitution and "decent" sexual relations. When asked when she had first started having sexual relations with men, she replied, "Shit! I don't know when I started. I been fucking from befo' I kin remembuh. Shit yes! Wit my ol' man, wit my brother, wit d' kids in da street."[65]

One vital means of support which helped prostitutes face any stigma or brutality they encountered in their trade was the subculture of prostitution itself. Although most aspects of the culture remain to be uncovered by further research, fragmentary evidence suggests that red-light districts, although in a state of transition, still offered women a certain amount of protection, support, and human validation. Logically, a woman new to the subculture might have felt sensitive about her stigmatized status, particularly if she had not grown up in the district or if she hailed from a family or community from which she had already received significant social ostracism. The process of adapting to the district, or "the life" as it is called, involved a series of introductions to the new argot (*cribs, lighthouses, johns, tricks*, etc.), the humor, and the folklore of the subculture.[66]

Judging from past and present evidence, it is likely that the subculture of prostitution offered valuable ways of helping women to defend against social devaluation. Typically, prostitutes maintained an attitude of defensive superiority toward "respectable" members of the rest of society: they joked about the "charity girls" who freely gave away sexual favors, and they derided the "respectable" wives of their customers. In particular, they expressed contempt for the "respectable" domestic and factory workers who worked for subsistence pay, endured poorer working conditions, and often had to submit to sexual harassment by their bosses. Most frequently, they reserved their worst epithets for the "nosy" reformers who wanted to "save" prostitutes by destroying their means of support and running them out of town.[67]

Within the subculture, the new prostitute learned to assume both a new identity and a defensive social attitude. The literature abounds with an interesting initiation rite in which all new prostitutes changed their name as they entered a brothel.[68] Perhaps the change of name helped to insure further privacy from family. Or, perhaps women simply chose to adopt more flamboyant names appropriate to their trade, such as "Violet" or "Sugarplum." Yet the strong emphasis on the entire initiation suggests something more important: for the novice, as well as for the initiated, the change of name was a means of bonding to a subculture considered deviant and degraded by the dominant culture. When one prostitute entered a brothel, for example, she repeatedly found all the "girls bustling with suggestions for her new name."[69] It was as if a new name (as in a nunnery) made a new claim on the individual's loyalties to her past through the purposeful elimination of an older identity. Interestingly, the new name never included a

Superstitions particular to brothel life offered additional strength to a sub-culture that remained distant from the dominant culture. As one prostitute re-called, many of the day's activities were guided by superstitious beliefs. "At Ma-dame C's," she wrote, "it was considered bad luck for a man to come in and then leave without spending money. To remove the curse from the house it was the custom for the girl who let him out of the door to spit on his back."[74] In addition, such superstitions may have allowed prostitutes to act out hostile feelings toward their male customers. Other superstitions included injunctions against using one's own name and bringing a cat inside a brothel. Placing wine on the sidewalk or readjusting a wall mirror supposedly brought more customers. If a woman was rejected by the first evening's customer, her luck was certain to be bad for the near future. If a woman performed fellatio, bad teeth or a rotten stomach would result if she swallowed any sperm.[75]

Prostitutes also explained to novitiates the legends that accounted for much of the argot. *Red-light*, for example, derived from the early railroad days in Kansas City, when a brakeman, who carried a red lantern signal lamp, would hang it outside the whorehouse while engaged inside. The dispatcher then knew where to find the brakeman, as well as any other member of the train's crew, when the train was ready to pull out. The origin of *hooker* was attributed to the many women who became camp followers in General Hooker's army during the Civil War.[76]

Prostitutes also shared the daily worries and problems they faced as room-mates living in the same house. Recalling the days of running an illegal brothel during the thirties, Pauline Tabor emphasized that "a madam and her girls are cut off from the normal society in which they once moved. . . . As a result, they tend to 'adopt' each other as a family. Although they indulge in gossip, petty jealousies, and quarrels, they develop a sense of loyalty and concern for one another's problems—a tolerant acceptance of human faults which sometimes even extends to the customers they serve."[77] The myth of the "whore with a golden heart" probably originated *not* from what prostitutes did for men, but from what they did for one another. When a woman could not pay for her child's care at a baby farm, the other women chipped in to help her out. When one prostitute became pregnant and lost her baby, the women surrounded her with all the nurturance "of her own sisters and mother."[78] In effect, women living together could, under certain conditions, create a surrogate family life in which both deep caring and fights sustained and bonded the entire group together.

It is also true, however, that prostitutes did develop a rather widespread repu-tation for generously tipping other workers such as maids or bartenders, taking in stray dogs, with whom they developed extremely close and loving ties, and acting like the mythical "whore with a golden heart." While some scholars might argue that the prostitute was acting out of guilt for her sins,[79] there may be other explanations closer to the daily realities of these women's lives. Maimie Pinzer's

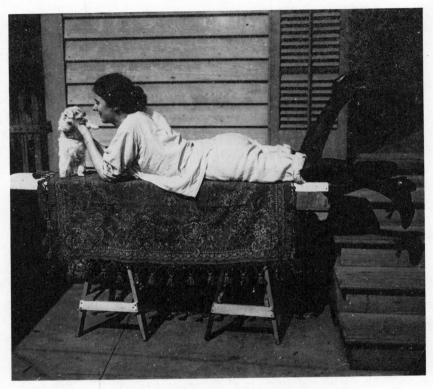

*A Storyville prostitute playing with her pet dog, c. 1900. Photograph by E. J.
Bellocq. Reprinted by permission of Lee Friedlander.*

letters, for example, were filled with lengthy and affectionate references to her
much beloved dog, Poke—alongside pages of despair and expressions of despondency and alienation. A majority of the well-known photographs taken by
E. J. Bellocq of Storyville prostitutes depict the women posed with a favorite
canine pet.[80] Given the alienated nature of prostitutes' work, their frequent estrangement from their families, it should not be surprising that the women would
express their tenderness and generosity with whom they felt most comfortable—
animals, other menial workers who would not judge them, and especially one
another.

Prostitutes who "worked" the most expensive houses also shared with each
other the joys of buying clothing they had never been able to afford. Poring over
gowns that peddlers brought, driving around the city in their most stunning
attire, these women enjoyed and experienced a sense of shared wealth and status.
Although some high-priced prostitutes tried to dress like other wealthy women,
it has long been a tradition for prostitutes to identify their trade by wearing

special attire. (Interestingly, many of the aspects of "whorish" appearance have inevitably become part of "respectable" women's appearance: make-up, wigs, drawers, shaving of bodily hair, boots, short skirts, etc.)[81] For prostitutes, the distinguishing marks of their trade reinforced the sense of belonging to a particular subculture.

What bonded most prostitutes together, ultimately, was their collective view toward the rest of society. The "snide, smug, respectable" people "out there" were viewed as hypocrites: not the judge and jury of people's morals, but rather a collective "enemy" who used "bribery, dishonesty, lies, corruption in high places, and swindled taxpayers." As one madam explained, "The grocer had fixed scales; the priest was exiled for buggery with his choir boys, the businessman who led a reform party owned half the worst houses in town, and people never felt they got a 'just price' for any merchandise."[82] In a sense, then, prostitutes, like reformers, criticized the commercialization and corruption of American society.

Despite their alienation from the dominant culture, prostitutes shared certain values with it. Dreams of upward mobility—of earning sufficient money to buy a small cottage and enjoy a happily married life, or of becoming a wealthy madam—pervaded the subculture of prostitution. Furthermore, the numerous forms of prostitution reflected class distinctions in the larger society which prostitutes often guarded jealously. As one young prostitute explained these class differences, "The social gulf between the first-class courtesan and those who have become the dregs of prostitution is as great as the gulf between the sheltered woman in her home and the streetwalker."[83] At the bottom of the social scale was the streetwalker or the prostitute who worked in one of the low-class cribs; at the top was the courtesan, the kept woman whose livelihood was insured by a gentleman of means. Other women, under economic duress, would find such gentlemen and make "dates" with them, as did Maimie Pinzer. As she pointedly explained to Fanny Howe, no one would ever have known she was a prostitute; she dressed and behaved as a lady while on her dates, and she took care to avoid prostitutes on a lower social level than herself:

> You need never fear that I would get into some public place; I don't have to do that; I wouldn't ever have to do that. As long as I have my mind and can use my tongue, such extreme measures are unnecessary. I never did that before, never did anything even 1/10 as low and consider that the last gasp. I never associated with low women—I don't think I ever met to talk to the second time a woman who was publicly known to live other than she should, I shun such people. Even girls who did no worse than I couldn't claim acquaintance with me.[84]

Many prostitutes expressed extremely conventional social preferences and values when they actually found a potential mate. As Sally Stanford noted, the running of a brothel never challenged her basic morals or sense of propriety. Honesty was essential in all dealings, particularly when the work of a prostitute was a series of sexual lies. As she claimed, "the path to my bedroom is paved with all the legalities and the marriage license comes first with me."[85]

The relationships that some prostitutes in the larger cities formed with pimps mirrored in an exaggerated form some of that heterosexual conventionality. Such relationships posed a great problem, however—pimp domination over streetwalkers or prostitutes attached to saloons was a particular horror of prostitution. Albeit small by today's numbers, the growing group of pimps had already begun to develop their own particular culture: they gathered in gambling resorts during the evening while their women "worked the streets or saloon," and maintained tyrannical and brutal control over the women. "It is an unwritten law among these men," explained the Rockefeller Commission, "that the authority of the individual over the woman or women controlled by him is unquestioned by his associates to whatever extreme it may be carried." Social reformers were bewildered by the pimp/prostitute relationship.[86] Prostitutes, moreover, rarely offered any reasonable explanations. "Arrei," a former prostitute, explained, "Well shit, you know how 'tis wide dese heah who's. Evvy one of dem got a man she give all her money. I ain't no diffen' I give *mah* man mah money. One time I buy a gos back suit, an' you know what he do? He punch me in d' head an' tell me he don' need no suit he need money. Aft' dat I jes give him mah money. Ah doan know why. Ah jest give him mah money."[87] Fortunately for Arrei, her man saved her earnings and bought a barroom over which they continued to live "like ma'ied folks."

Was it simply a custom to have a pimp if unattached to a brothel? Was the relationship maintained by force alone? What function did these early pimps play in prostitutes' lives?

In some sense, the pimps offered many of the same services to prostitutes which madams had proffered in brothels. Like madams, they maintained an ambiguous relationship with the prostitute: they exploited her while offering her some of the genuine physical and emotional protection a woman needed outside of the brothel system.

Pimps "took care of their women," by demonstrating how they could earn a better living. As one pimp several decades later argued, "I take her to a dress shop, beauty parlor, and dentist, and remove her moles. I show a girl that she's been wasting her life working for peanuts and giving it away."[88] At the same time that a pimp "helped" his woman, of course, he also reaped the profits of her income.

Despite the exploitative and brutal nature of the relationship, the pimp seemed to provide a primary emotional relationship for some prostitutes. Given that prostitutes had experienced an unusually high incidence of "broken" or "troubled" homes in their childhood, some women perhaps found emotional relief in feeling needed and wanted, if only for their earnings, by one central figure in their lives. As George Kneeland remarked after analyzing the pimp/prostitute relationship in New York, "A spark of affection lives at the heart of this ghastly relation."[89] Such affection, however, was usually one-sided.

Cadets and pimps generally came from the same economic backgrounds, even neighborhoods, as prostitutes. "Everywhere," wrote George Kibbe Turner, "the boy of the slums has learned that a girl is an asset which, once acquired by him, will give him more money than he can ever earn and a life of absolute ease." Turner's observations were confirmed by Clifford Roe, assistant state's attorney in Chicago, who indicted 150 boys for procuring girls for prostitution.[90] As Emma Goldman noted, "It is not the cadet that makes the prostitute. It is our sham and hypocrisy that creates both the prostitute and the cadet. . . . Why is the cadet more criminal or a greater menace to society than the owners of department stores and factories, who grow fat on the sweat of their victims, only to drive them into the streets?"[91] Like the prostitute, the cadet or pimp found in the trade an illegitimate means of achieving the socially acceptable goal of material wealth. Next to the slum landlord who rented real estate for prostitution, the pimp was a mere pauper. Nevertheless, his personal relationship with the prostitute mirrored the individual subjugation of women to men.

The story of a former cadet named Marc, who was born in the 1880s, is somewhat typical. Like many prostitutes, Marc was born and raised in an atmosphere in which prostitution was a daily fact of his existence: "My ol' lady—it wan't no secret—was a whore in Dauphine Street, and tha' where I was born—in a little house on Dauphine Street in the French Quarter. It's still there. . . . I don't know who my ol' man was. Just another trick, *you* know. Anyway, the ol' lady died in 1903 from the clap."[92] Like many poor children, Marc became dissatisfied with the meager earnings he made from selling newspapers and dreamed of making a fortune through some other means. "When I was fifteen years old," he recalled, "I started thinkin' I better think about doin' somethin' else, because I couldn't be sellin' papers all my life."

In exchange for a commission, he began "steering" customers to a particular prostitute. By the time he was seventeen, he had "eight broads turning tricks" for him. "I was making about three hundred a week clear." His major job: "I'd have to lay each one of 'em once or twice a month."

Like many pimps, Marc spent a great deal of time at certain saloons where cadets drank, gambled, and boasted of the jewels they could buy with earnings from their "broads." Unlike many pimps, however, Marc refused to gamble and invested his money in solid real estate, which permitted him to enjoy economic security in his old age. By illegitimate means, Marc found economic security and respectability. He expressed no regrets: "I got this bar. I got a fine house with a big yard . . . I don't care that I made mine pimpin'. . . . How was I gonna make it, selling papers? I was in business like anybody else, and I run it good.

Better than the rest of 'em. I wan't no lush. I didn't take dope an' I didn't gamble. What's wrong with that?"[93]

To the pimps, prostitutes, and madams who based their livelihood on prostitution, *nothing* was "wrong with that." Barred from "legitimate" means of achieving the American Dream, they found alternative ways of securing the conventional goals that other Americans also craved: upward mobility and material success.

One cannot, and *should not*, however, equate the life of a prostitute with that of a pimp. There were—and are—essential differences that transcended the similarity of their class origins and emphasized their gender differences. Due to a double standard of sexual morality, the prostitute suffered great ostracism and brutality, while the pimp parasitically lived off her earnings. Whereas a man gained a certain degree of self-esteem and status by "making it" as a pimp in the slums, few poor families praised a young woman for achieving economic security through prostitution. Many members of the poorest classes might envy, or even admire, the cadet for his ability to circumvent the blocked mobility that faced the unskilled male worker, but few people offered sympathy to the young slum girl who sold herself rather than achieving respectability and security through marriage.

In sum, a prostitute became the victim of a pimp's brutality and exploitation, and not his partner in economic business. Only a few prostitutes ever achieved the kind of material wealth and independence of which pimps could boast. Wherever the prostitute worked, a legion of parasites lived off her earnings. The prostitute, like women outside the subculture, suffered the stigma and degradation imposed by male sexual exploitation and patriarchal sexual values.

To "polite" society, cadets, prostitutes, and madams comprised an alien and deviant subculture that threatened to undermine the purity of American society. But was this subculture—and the political and municipal crime and corruption it generated—*so* different from the dominant "respectable" culture?

Looking back at her own experience in the business of prostitution, Pauline Tabor did not think so.

> Many of these experts seem to view prostitutes and madams as a special kind of human animal—as a breed apart from the rest of society. This is not so. We are not different than the rest of God's children. We are subject to the same emotions, the same ambitions, the same despairs, the same pain, the same weaknesses, the same hunger. The only basic difference is that the society from which we come puts us in a different, untouchable category—an ostracized class of "fallen women" who, if we are lucky and make our fortune, magically are socially cleansed and become respectable once again.[94]

In fact, there *were* many similarities between this "deviant" subculture and the dominant culture. Prostitution mirrored the rest of society in several significant ways.[95] By the early twentieth century, the United States had become an increasingly rationalized and commercialized society.[96] Prostitution, too, had become a well-organized and commercialized business in the largest cities. Much of American business and industry had become concentrated into fewer and fewer trusts and monopolies. Much of prostitution, as well, had become owned and operated by a handful of powerful politicians and businessmen. In all areas of American business, men "hustled" one another to achieve power and wealth. In the subculture of prostitution, prostitutes and cadets "hustled" customers for their last penny. Despite the concentration of wealth into corporate structures and the gradual loss of entrepreneurial mobility, many average American workers still hoped to achieve individual "possession and private ownership of the valuable things." For most of the underworld, "making it" was also a lifelong obsession.

By the early twentieth century, many important human relationships in American society (labor, professional services, marriage), had become governed by a "cash nexus." Prostitutes' relationships to customers, madams and cadets were also largely governed by commercial concerns. Alienation and loneliness in American society were met by corporate efforts to sell happiness through the advertisement of material goods and the creation of new needs and services. Prostitution, too, falsely promised to eliminate individual alienation and loneliness for the right price.

Although prostitution seemed seedier and more sordid than other aspects of American society, it also embodied many values taken for granted in other arenas of American life: efficient, but impersonal, service; the commercialization of human relationships; the subjugation and devaluation of women by men; and the exploitation of the many for the benefit of a few.

As Americans investigated the subculture of prostitution, they discovered a microcosm of their own daily prostitution for the almighty dollar. Only some reformers or observers consciously recognized the similarities because prostitution sold *sex*, as opposed to less sacred products of the new industrial order. Viewed from the outside, from the reformers' perspective, the subculture of prostitution seemed to be one of the greatest social evils in American society. For the poor, and particularly for women, however, survival or upward mobility was frequently blocked by their class and gender status. Viewed from below, then, prostitution offered an illegitimate, frequently brutal and degrading means of achieving *socially acceptable* goals in a society that valued material acquisition, expected upward mobility, and judged an individual's worth on his or her ability to achieve both.

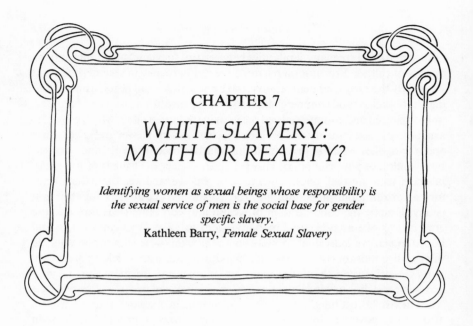

CHAPTER 7

WHITE SLAVERY: MYTH OR REALITY?

Identifying women as sexual beings whose responsibility is the sexual service of men is the social base for gender specific slavery.
Kathleen Barry, *Female Sexual Slavery*

Why did women enter prostitution? During the early years of the twentieth century, when social scientific studies fired the country's imagination, many reformers tried to answer this question by gathering evidence on economic and social factors: the low wages paid to women in the labor force; the generational conflict between children and parents of immigrant families; the crowded, unsanitary, and emotionally explosive conditions under which the poor lived; and the diseases, alcoholism, and chronic unemployment that wrecked such homes.[1] Others attempted to link prostitution to inherited strains of physical or mental degeneracy.[2]

Alongside these theories, however, another explanation—that hundreds of thousands of women were being captured and sold into prostitution as "white slaves"—was gaining increasing public attention and causing a nationwide panic that reached its height during the years 1911–15.[3] In the quiet of their homes, middle-class families devoured journalistic accounts of the ruin of young women at the hands of sinister procurers armed with poisoned needles and drugged drinks. Young girls, the headlines screamed, were being sold into virtual sexual slavery.[4]

Did white slavery actually exist, and, if so, how did it differ from ordinary prostitution? The question itself is extremely controversial and bound to be debated for years to come. In her recent book, *Female Sexual Slavery* (a well-documented study of the continued existence of white slavery in contemporary America and elsewhere), Kathleen Barry has noted that most Americans today are extremely reluctant to acknowledge this "invisible crime."[5] Denial of white slavery's existence today is accompanied by a denial of its existence in the past. Most historians have assumed that the white slavery described by reformers of the Progressive Era was merely a myth that expressed certain tensions, fears, and conflicts in American society.[6]

To Progressives, *white slavery* in its most specific sense meant the selling of women's bodies (the "traffic in women") for the purposes of prostitution. For many reformers, it further implied the use of force or coercion to bring a woman into prostitution and also to keep her from leaving it. Definitions often became blurred, however, and one cannot always be sure whether reformers or journalists were describing sexual *slavery*, in which a woman was bought, coerced into prostitution, and held against her will, or forms of prostitution in which a woman did in fact exercise some degree of choice. Mark Connelly notes that whereas some reformers attempted to distinguish the problem of white slavery and the larger problem of prostitution in general, others went so far as to declare the two synonymous and to claim, as authors of white slave narratives did, that between 40 and 100 percent of the prostitutes in the United States were white slaves.[7] Similarly, the term *white slaver*, defined during the period as "any man or woman who traffics in the sexual life of any woman or girl for financial reward or gain," was sometimes also used to describe pimps who seduced women and then kept them in prostitution by force.[8]

The problem with rigidly separating white slavery and "voluntary" prostitution is that even a prostitute who had not been forcibly captured and sold might be brought into, or kept in, prostitution through some form of coercion by individuals who in some way made a profit from her.[9] Perhaps a more useful way of distinguishing white slavery from other forms of prostitution during this historical period is to imagine a continuum along which varying degrees of force were used to bring a woman into prostitution and keep her there. At one end was white slavery, in which a maximum amount of coercion was used to sell a woman's body for profit and in which a woman possessed nearly no avenue of escape. In essence, she was a sexual slave. At the other end of the spectrum were the more routine and casual forms of prostitution in which a woman might participate, not because she chose it out of a plethora of attractive alternatives (hardly the case), but because prostitution, under certain circumstances and conditions, might have appeared a better means of survival than other available choices. In between these two extremes existed forms of prostitution in which varying amounts of choice and coercion produced neither a totally passive victim nor an actor who could freely choose her own destiny. In using historical materials from this period, I have carefully tried to separate cases involving maximum coercion from cases that, though labeled as "white slavery," involved more casual forms of prostitution located at other points along the spectrum.

Documenting, describing, and analyzing the subject of white slavery is a difficult task for the historian. First, there is the contemporary disbelief in the existence of white slavery, which the reader must be willing to suspend. The very absence of the subject of white slavery from our standard historical texts further undermines the credibility of its historical or contemporary reality. (It is important to remember, however, that historians have long neglected many other significant aspects of the female historical experience.)

Furthermore, the idea of white slavery seems to provoke in many readers' minds the response that prostitutes *wanted* to enter prostitution. The idea that men would or could sell women's bodies so counters normative ideals of gentlemanly conduct that people are reluctant to believe women's own testimony today. A tendency to deny the historical and current reality of male violence against women and to hold women responsible for their own victimization— shown in the frequent accusations that rape victims or battered women have provoked violence against themselves—is also at work in the reluctance to acknowledge the reality of forced prostitution.

The historical sources available for examination further complicate the discussion. In their attempt to eliminate prostitution, reformers tended to exaggerate the extent of white slavery to prove the evils of uncontrolled and openly tolerated red-light districts. One suffragist, for example, advised her female audience not to worry about exaggerating stories that dealt with white slavery. "Remember, ladies," she warned, "it is more important to be aroused than to be accurate. Apathy is more of a crime than exaggeration in dealing with this subject."[10] The effect of such exaggerations is that the more sensationalized accounts of sexual slavery during the period tend to undermine the credibility of an entire historical phenomenon.

In addition to reformers who exaggerated for political purposes, some entrepreneurs so sensationalized the subject for profit that one is tempted to believe white slavery existed only in the minds of greedy film makers. Such films as *Traffic in Souls* dramatized cadets trapping girls from stores, railway terminals, and steamship piers with sufficient titillation to reap profits from the sexual slavery of women. Other films, which highlighted the more lascivious aspects of white slavery, similarly excited the public's imagination. Legends grew around such episodes as a policeman finding a note, "Help me—I am held captive as a white slave,"—supposedly written by a raped and drugged young white slave held in a brothel. Several books that sensationalized the more erotic details of seduction and entrapment by white slavers gained significant public attention. Reginald Kauffman, one of these authors, became well known for his book *The House of Bondage*. One of his typical stories describes a girl who arrives in a large city and is drugged by a "thickly accented German Jew." After her virginity is "robbed" from her, she is sold to a madam who is beholden to some mysterious organization. The major themes of the child victim, the immigrant villain, and the conspiratorial white slave rings (embellished with pornographic details) were typical of Kauffman's tales. Other authors, too, contributed to the public hyste-

A typical melodramatic portrayal of a man procuring a white slave.
Reprinted from Clifford G. Roe, Horrors of the White
Slave Trade *(London: Clifford G. Roe and B. S. Steadwell, 1911), facing p. 48.*

ria and oversensationalism of white slavery. Finally, posters appeared in conspicuous places in major urban areas with the warning: "Danger! Mothers beware! Sixty thousand innocent girls wanted to take the place of sixty thousand white slaves who will die this year in the United States."[11]

Alongside this sensationalized material stand other accounts from the period which strongly attempted to discredit the idea that white slavery ever existed at all. Politicians, police, liquor interests, and property owners tried to convince the public that white slavery was simply a fantasy born of reformers' overactive imaginations.[12]

Despite this mixed record, a careful review of the evidence documents a real traffic in women: a historical fact and experience that must be integrated into the record. Testimony given by escaped prostitutes, convictions of white slavers after the passage of the Mann Act in 1910 (prohibiting the interstate traffic of women for the purpose of prostitution), and data and conclusions drawn from federal studies on white slavery, along with results of investigations undertaken by the Federation of Women's Clubs, the W.C.T.U., rescue workers, and the National Vigilance Committee, all lead to the conclusion that the sale of some women into sexual slavery is an inescapable fact of the American past.

White slavery was not a phenomenon peculiar to American society during the Progressive Era. History records numerous examples of extensive trade in women's bodies for financial profit in both European and Asian civilizations.[13] Nor did the term *white slave* originate in the United States. Rather, factory workers first used this term during the early industrial era in England, and later in America, to describe their "slavery" to wages and industrial discipline.

The idea of white slavery as it was defined during the Progressive Era first gained wide currency in England during the latter half of the nineteenth century. While fighting the Contagious Diseases Acts in the 1880s, Josephine Butler also discovered a traffic in women from London to Brussels. Meanwhile, other countries in Europe gradually discovered that an international trade in women existed within their own national boundaries as well. In 1877, the first international recognition of the traffic in women occurred at an international abolitionist conference in Geneva, Switzerland. There, reformers publicly revealed how carloads of young women had been transported across Europe for the purpose of prostitution.[14]

In 1885, white slavery received widespread publicity when British reformer William Stead scandalized England with an article he penned in the *Pall Mall Gazette* titled "The Maiden Tribute of Modern Babylon." Having infiltrated fashionable brothels, Stead became enraged by the traffic in young girls. In order to prove that a child could easily be purchased for white slavery in Great Britain, Stead arranged to buy a thirteen-year-old girl for "service in a nice home." Her parents, he later assured his readers, had understood the immoral purpose behind his offer and had been paid a pound for their daughter. The result was that Stead was arrested and imprisoned for three months for his involvement in the exposé.[15]

American social purity reformers and members of the W.C.T.U. were shocked by the stories that Stead and other British reformers brought to the United States during the 1870s and 1880s. Inspired by the muckraking activities of their British counterparts, American reformers soon took up the banner of both the "new abolitionism" and the fight against white slavery. *Union Signal*, the official organ of the W.C.T.U., published a shocking account of the white slave trade that had invaded the lumber camps of Wisconsin and Michigan.[16]

By 1902, recognition of the traffic in women had become so widespread that France invited other nations to an international congress for the suppression of the white slave trade. A treaty was formulated that bound member nations to suppress the traffic in women. In May 1904, a majority of the nations signed the treaty; the agreement was ratified by the United States in 1905 and officially proclaimed by President Roosevelt in 1908. Until the revised immigration law of 1907, the Mann Act of 1911, and the various states' white slave acts, however, American authorities did not seriously interfere with the flow of white slavery.[17]

From 1885 to 1915, increasing numbers of prominent individuals expressed a belief in the existence of white slavery and a commitment to stopping it. Former abolitionists, who had rejoiced at the end of black slavery, now joined forces with "social purity" reformers to battle the new slavery. O. Edward Janney, chairman of the National Vigilance Committee for the Suppression of White Slavery, and E. W. Sims, U.S. district attorney, agreed that white slavery constituted "real slavery." Stanley Finch, chief of the Bureau of Investigation of the Department of Justice, even asked Congress to accept the slavery amendment in the Constitution as the basis for legislation against white slave trade.[18] Clifford Roe, the fiery U.S. district attorney of Chicago who was hailed as the William Lloyd Garrison of the antiprostitution movement, never wavered in his belief that the white slave trade posed a serious threat to women. "Chicago," he dramatically declared,

> at last has waked up to a realization of the fact that actual slavery that deals in human flesh and blood as a marketable commodity exists in terrible magnitude in the city today. It is slavery, real slavery, that we are fighting. The term "white slave" isn't a misnomer or a sensational term conjured up by sensational newspapers. The words describe what they stand for. The white slave of Chicago is a slave as much as the Negro was before the Civil War, as the African is in the districts of the Congo, as much as any people are slaves who are owned, flesh and bone, body and soul, by another person, and who can be sold at any time and place and for any price at that person's will. That is what slavery is, and that is the condition of hundreds, yes, of thousands of girls in Chicago at present.[19]

Mabel Gillespie, head of the Boston Women's Trade Union League, also believed in the threat of forcible procurement into prostitution. Writing to Stella Frandlen at the national headquarters, she explained that one of the league's important duties was to guard the meeting halls of working women from potential white slavers.[20]

In some cities, vice commissions worried about the white slave trade infiltrating their own communities. In Minneapolis, a city from which white slaves were allegedly sold to Chicago and New York, the Minneapolis Vice Commission concluded that "nearly every city is infested with its agents and everywhere these connect themselves with corrupt ward politicians and more secretly with men 'higher up' who give them police protection or immunity in exchange for votes." In 1909 Daniel Keefe, commissioner general of immigration, stated that "enormous business is constantly being transacted in the importation and distribution of foreign women for purposes of prostitution. . . . In some cities the traffic is more or less connected with local political conditions, and the police and other municipal authorities are either implicated or else helpless to assist in even the partial eradication of the evil." In short, the belief in white slavery was widespread among public officials.[21]

Whether increasing public concern about white slavery coincided with an actual increase in white slave traffic is difficult to determine. As a clandestine operation, the white slave trade obviously did not keep tidy historical records of its activities. Moreover, the statistical records kept by the Bureau of Immigration and other federal agencies, which described deportations and arrests for white slave trade activity, were not begun until after white slavery had received wide publicity. All other data that might indicate the extent of the trade—such as court records, police records, or journalistic accounts—are only proof of increased public awareness of the problem rather than evidence of increased growth of the trade itself.[22]

Nevertheless, the actual existence of white slavery, as opposed to merely a widespread belief in it, is supported by abundant records of criminal convictions. For example, from June 1910 to January 1915, 1,057 persons were convicted of white slavery in the United States.[23] Harriet Laidlaw's "scrapbooks" contain numerous newspaper and magazine clippings that describe hundreds of convictions for white slavery as well as affidavits filed both by victims of white slavers and by detectives who infiltrated groups of white slavers.[24]

At first, American investigators concentrated on the international white slave trade. Along with their European counterparts, they argued that the international trade was a response to the demand for a constant flow of women into legalized brothels in countries that regulated prostitution. They further argued that the international trade fulfilled an even more bizarre function; it catered to the sexual fantasies and cravings of men for women of different racial and national origins. Thus, white slave fighters argued that American women received a warm welcome and a high price in cities of the Orient; East European girls found themselves installed in parts of South America; and French women ended their journey as high-priced prostitutes in the fancy parlor houses of American vice districts.

The importation of foreign girls and women into the United States received an enormous amount of public attention. As a result, American officials conducted investigations that attempted to identify the number of imported white slaves and the cities through which they entered and to determine whether an organized traffic in women actually existed. As one would expect, estimates of the number of imported white slaves into the United States varied widely. Theodore Bingham, author and former police commissioner of New York, guessed that two thousand foreign girls annually entered the American vice market. Edward Sims, basing his estimate on data received from police raids on houses of prostitution, put the number as high as fifteen thousand. Finally, the Immigration Commission's report to the United States Senate on the white slave trade summarized its findings by stating that "in the opinion of practically everyone who has an opportunity for careful judgment, the number of girls imported runs well into the thousands each year."[25]

Far easier was the task of identifying the ports through which white slaves entered. Detectives of the federal government estimated that half of the white slaves in the United States originated or entered the business in New York City. Other cities whose deportation rates indicated a high incidence of white slavery included San Francisco, San Antonio, Cleveland, Boston, and Chicago. Montreal and Seattle were also cited as common ports of entry.[26]

The procurers, importers, and madams who organized and controlled the activities of the white slave trade accumulated enormous profits as a result of their efforts. Who they were was a question of great concern to many American reformers. A majority of international procurers, it was surmised, were of French, German, and Polish origin. In their examples of the domestic slave trade, reformers often pointed to Jews and Italians as the primary "foreign" villains who recruited young girls into prostitution. In fact, however, of men convicted under the Mann Act, 72.5 percent were native-born Americans, 11.5 percent were Italians, and 3.5 percent were Russians.[27]

Investigations by various state and federal commissions and reform groups revealed that white slavers used several methods to lure foreign women into the United States. Agents within the country generally had representatives abroad who procured women through promises of marriage, better employment, or payment to their families. Letters seized from such foreign associates reveal the objectification and commercialization of the female body which characterized the traffic in women: "I can assure you," one correspondent wrote, "that I have found a woman the likes of whom you can never find; young, beautiful . . . and who fully decided to leave. You can well understand I gave them a song and dance. . . . I will send you her photograph. Her beautiful teeth alone are worth a million."[28]

To secure entrance into the country, foreign women were often declared the wives or relatives of the procurer who accompanied them. Sometimes they were "booked" to a "friend" who turned out to be a notorious madam. Procurers took great pains to teach women how to answer the questions that customs officials would ask them. At other times, procurers met boats of arriving immigrants and carefully searched for young women who entered the country without family. Offers of employment and shelter would be made. However a young woman was procured, she would find herself sold to the owner of a house of prostitution. She would then be "broken in" and virtually imprisoned in a "house."[29]

The testimony of a young French girl given at a trial in Seattle gives a detailed and representative account of such foreign procurement. When asked by the court to recount her life history from the time she left her parents to work in Paris, until her arrest as a prostitute in America, the young woman gave the following testimony. The story bears retelling:

> When I was employed in a delicatessen store two men called to buy something and left. I met them again on the street some time later, and they asked to be allowed to accompany me home, which I refused. Next time they met me they took me to a cafe and treated me. They told me they knew a man who was looking for girls to do some kind of work which paid better money than I was getting at the store, but they would not tell me what kind of work it was. They also told me that the man was very rich and asked me how I would like to marry a rich man. . . . Later they sent me a message to come to a certain place on the street, saying they had something for me. After my work was done I went to the designated place and met three men—the two I had met before and a third one, who was Emil Chaillet. . . . He induced me to go with him and stay with him, promising to make me very happy. I asked him how he would make me so happy, and he told me he would marry me, so I went to the hotel and stayed with him ever since. I was not even allowed to go back for my clothes or let anyone know where I was.
>
> At first he treated me very kindly for about a month while I lived with him; then he told me he would put me in a place where I could make plenty of money, but did not say how. He told me that we were going to America, but I did not know where.
>
> We left Paris. . . . I travelled with him as his wife. . . .
>
> The first time he told me about the kind of business I was to do was on the boat from Liverpool, but I was so young—I was only seventeen—I did not understand what it meant. He explained about it; how they lived in houses of prostitution; but I had no idea about what it really meant, even after his explanation. I was helpless. I could not tell my misfortune to anybody. I was afraid he might do me some harm.
>
> When we arrived at Montreal we stayed there one day and then he placed me in a house of prostitution. . . . I stayed there seven months. . . . he compelled me to give him every cent of my earnings . . . which I had to do, as I was very much afraid of him. He once blackened my eyes in Montreal because I went to the theater with another girl and did not practice prostitution. . . .
>
> He told me he was taking me to Seattle to practice prostitution, as the exposition was on there and that I could make as much money there as in Fairbanks by prostitution . . . and we were arrested at Tacoma.

I am very anxious to return to my father and mother and my sister. This man, Emil Chaillet, . . . or whatever his name is, actually kidnapped me. I had no idea what awaited me. The men who first met me actually sold me to Chaillet, as he later told me himself that he gave them some money for bringing me to him. . . . Since Chaillet put me in a house of prostitution at Montreal I have earned more than $2,000, but he kept all that money; he forced me to give the money to him.[30]

The story related by the arrested French girl was by no means unusual. The use of lies and force to procure foreign women into prostitution was common practice.[31] As the immigration commission pointed out in their report on white slavery, such imported white slaves felt particularly vulnerable and helpless as prostitutes. "The alien woman," they emphasized, "is ignorant of the language of the country, knows nothing beyond a few blocks of the city where she lives, has usually no money, and no knowledge of the rescue homes and institutions which might help her."[32]

Of all the foreign girls and women imported into the United States, Chinese and Japanese women probably suffered the cruelest treatment and enslavement. In part, this resulted from the strong antagonism against Asians prevalent on the West Coast. It is also true that Asian women made extremely inexpensive and easy targets within their own country. The first traffic in Chinese women apparently began during the middle of the nineteenth century.[33] Around 1854, six hundred women were imported from China by the Hip-Yee Tong. Finding Chinese women for importation was not a difficult task. The extreme impoverishment and destitution among most families made daughters a serious liability in prerevolutionary China. Just as some parents actually broke their children's limbs to seek charity, certain families welcomed promises of marriage and payment for their daughters, even when they suspected that the girls might be sold as concubines within China.

The number of Chinese prostitutes on the West Coast apparently so offended Californians that the importation of Chinese women for "immoral purposes" was outlawed in California in 1870. After the Chinese Exclusion Act of 1882, white slavers had to devise new means of importing Chinese women into the United States for prostitution. Bribing or blackmailing immigration officials were some of the "business methods" commonly used. Due to the difficulty of securing passage for such women, the prices of Chinese white slaves skyrocketed.[34]

In most recorded cases, Chinese girls continued to be purchased from their families. One Chinese man, for example, paid a family $140 for their daughter by promising to send her to school in America. Given the feudal and patriarchal attitudes toward women at the time, the daughter had little choice but to obey her parents. Passing the customs officers as father and daughter, or using a forged certificate of citizenship, the procurer then forced the young girl into prostitution in Boston. Soon after, he made a handsome profit by selling her to a Chinese woman for three thousand dollars.[35]

In another documented case, a Chinese mother made arrangements for her daughter to be married in a distant city. Instead, the procurer transported the bride-to-be to the United States. "One thousand five hundred and thirty dollars were paid for me," the girl later recalled, "I saw the money paid and I . . . was placed in her den. They forced me to do their bidding, but I cried and resisted. I did not want to live this life. They starved me for days, tying me where food was almost in reach of me . . . then they beat me time after time and threatened to kill me if I did not behave right."[36]

Stories such as these were told to missionaries who received runaway slaves at rescue homes in San Francisco and Berkeley. In addition, such rescue workers and missionaries learned that false promises of marriage and outright kidnapping were indeed the most common methods of importing Chinese women into "yellow" slavery. In many cases, the procurers had made contracts with parents which had no legal status in the United States; nevertheless, Chinese tongs, or organized Chinese political societies in the United States, attempted to enforce these contracts between procurers and Chinese families.[37]

A white slave market soon grew around Dupont Street in San Francisco. There, Chinese white slaves were directly brought from ships to endure a humiliating physical examination by potential buyers. In an apartment called the "Queen's Room," young girls were subjected to the kind of dehumanizing objectification that Africans had experienced upon landing in the hands of southern auctioneers.[38] Many of these girls, often as young as eleven and twelve, ended up as slaves of the infamous crib system—viewed by one reformer as the worst form of American sexual slavery. He described the cribs as "small rooms opening into inner passages by means of a barred window and door, which is kept locked by the manager, the key being given to men as they apply to him. Within these little cells, scantily furnished, are kept young girls, most of them Chinese and Japanese, but some of them European and American. They have little light or air, are rarely allowed to leave their rooms, and the manager receives the money."[39]

Occasionally, when these girls managed to escape, members of tongs, or of the white slave trade, spread throughout northern California, searching for runaway slaves and returning them to their "owners." Thus, in many respects, Chinese white slaves became virtual chattel. Sometimes they did not even understand that they were "owned" by someone else until they found a rescue home or missionary that helped them escape their pursuers.[40] Such women, as the Immigration Commission recognized in their report, had "become real slaves . . . and unless some man . . . is ready to marry them, their position is practically that of permanent slavery." In other words, unless a woman, like a black slave in the nineteenth century, could buy her freedom—and legend has it that some did—she remained the property of her procurers.[41]

Although the importation of foreign girls and women probably accounted for only a small percentage of white slavery in the United States, the international traffic in women received an inordinate amount of publicity. Perhaps this resulted from the contemporary xenophobic attitudes that characterized the period. Many Americans felt more comfortable in attributing the traffic in women to foreign influences than in facing the social implications of domestic white slavery that existed within the United States. Such traffic could be dismissed as a problem of uncontrolled immigration. If only immigration laws would exclude more foreigners, many Americans reasoned, the international white slave trade would cease to be an *American* problem. The domestic white slave trade, however, which recruited young American women for prostitution, posed a far more threatening moral problem.

As increasing numbers of young women left their homes to work in distant towns and cities, they frequently carried with them a provincial perspective of the world "outside," which sometimes made them easy targets for the panderers and procurers whose livelihood depended on selling white slaves to certain brothels. Many young women actually disappeared and were never heard from again. Frantic parents placed advertisements in newspapers begging authorities for information concerning the welfare of their daughters.[42] When unidentified young women's bodies were brought to city morgues, police received hundreds of letters from inquiring and despairing parents of runaway girls.[43] Hattie Rose, a fiery white slave fighter in New York, described the many letters she received from parents concerned that their daughters had become the victims of white slavers.[44] In New York City alone, 1,439 girls disappeared in one year.[45] Police estimated that 20 percent of the girls (ages fourteen to seventeen) reported missing were never seen again.[46] The very fact that Americans began noting the disappearance of young female runaways attests to the probable generational conflict between daughters and families or to the new independence that some women sought away from their families. Such disappearances simply fueled the fears of family disintegration and uncontrolled female sexuality. Where did young women go? Did they simply run away from troubled homes and find other living arrangements in distant cities? Most likely; but such runaways, separated from their families, became easy targets for white slavers in urban vice districts (like today's runaway teenagers who are "turned out" by pimps in America's large cities).

Both reformers and prostitutes asserted that brothel owners and procurers resorted to coercion when insufficient numbers of voluntary prostitutes were available.[47] Former prostitutes told federal agents that an innocent young girl was viewed as particularly desirable because the "house" did not have to share her earnings with a pimp. Proprietors of brothels would pay a procurer up to one thousand dollars for such an attractive and potentially profitable "item."[48]

Of great concern to Americans obsessed with monopolies was whether a nationally organized traffic in women existed. Their attempts to find out whether or not corporate interests had consolidated the traffic in women met with mixed

results. The Massachusetts report, for example, found that there was no organized white slavery and that all dealings in white slavery were private business
ventures.[49]

A more complicated conclusion was reached in the city of New York. On
January 3, 1910, Judge Thomas C. O. O'Sullivan of the Court of General Ses-
sions of New York charged a grand jury with the duty of determining whether
such a syndicate existed in the United States. Chaired by John D. Rockefeller,
the jury returned an interesting verdict. On the one hand, they found no evidence
of a *formal* organization of white slavers. They did discover, however, that the
people involved in the market tended to associate with one another through an
informal network of social relationships. "It appears," the "presentment" read,
"that from indictments found by us and from testimony of witnesses that a traf-
ficking in the bodies of women does exist and is carried on by individuals acting
for their own individual benefit, and that these persons are known to each other,
and more or less associated."[50]

In addition, the jury revealed the existence of a "mutual benefit" association
whose members included gamblers, procurers, and "keepers of disorderly
houses." Many of these members were found to have agents and representatives
in various cities of the country. The purpose of the organization, the jury decided,
was the mutual "protection" of its members from police detection.[51] "Mutual
benefit societies" with less sinister purposes, however, were a common institution
among new immigrants to American cities.

As a result of their investigations, the Grand Jury also found that agents
stationed in other states contacted New York white slavers to receive and give
current prices of "stock" and trade methods of procurement. They additionally
discovered that white slavery existed through the mutually beneficial and profitable connections between the traders and the police. In fact, as a result of the
Grand Jury investigation, New York "traffic" came under such scrutiny that one
white slaver admitted that "two years ago he could have sold them all the girls
they wanted at $5 or $10 apiece" (whereas now he would not risk selling one in
New York for one thousand dollars). Nevertheless, the Grand Jury's investigators managed to secure fifty-four indictments and revealed the specific details of
several transactions, including that of four young women sold to agents, two of
whom were from a "black and tan" dealer and two of whom were under eighteen
years of age.[52]

Unfortunately, the public never received the actual details or conclusions of
the Rockefeller Grand Jury. A delayed statement released to the press implied
that the jury had found no evidence of organized traffic in women. The next day,
June 29, 1910, newspapers across the United States carried misleading stories
indicating that no evidence of *white slavery* had been discovered. As a result,
both the American public and future historians were seriously misled. Those
attempting to discredit the idea of white slavery would henceforth cite the news-

paper report of the jury's conclusions and dismiss other accounts as sensationalism and hysteria.[53]

The Rockefeller Grand Jury presentment had in fact documented the existence of an extensive, informal white slave trade across the country. Additional investigations by other municipal agencies and reformers confirmed their findings.[54] A federal investigation by the Committee on Interstate and Foreign Commerce even submitted evidence indicating the presence of an organized syndicate that had headquarters and clearing houses in eight states.[55]

Once the Mann Act was passed and cases on white slavery began to come before the courts, the Department of Justice, as well as the American public, began to fear the spread of white slavery throughout the United States. Between 1910 and 1913, 337 convictions were obtained in cases involving white slavery, and 35 cases ended in acquittals.[56] Granted that some of these cases may have involved blackmail against a man and that other cases may have simply reflected a young woman's willingness to cross state lines with a man, there is nevertheless strong evidence of a white slave trade and its operations. In fact, many federal authorities were genuinely shocked by the cases that appeared before them. Stanley Finch expressed his horror at finding that girls transported "solely for the purposes of prostitution were treated as mere articles of merchandise for the profit of those who handled them and who were willing for the profit involved to sacrifice the bodies and souls of their victims."[57] Although some women's groups argued that judges gave too lenient sentences to white slavers, the existence of the white slave trade was not in question in court.

These and other investigations into white slavery revealed the business methods that accompanied the selling of women. A procurer would be paid for his efforts, according to the woman's age and attractiveness, with one fixed sum or a percentage of her earnings. The seductive methods employed by procurers filled the vice commission reports and reformers' publications and were reinforced by prostitutes' and white slavers' testimonies. False promises of marriage, mock marriages that had no legal status, and deliberate attempts to entangle a woman in financial debt or emotional dependency were some of the most commonly known methods of procurement. Other devious and ingenious strategies for recruiting potential prostitutes were not so different from those used today on contemporary teenage runaways. In Boston, procurers searched court records for the names of young women on probation who might want to leave the jurisdiction and the vigilant eyes of a probation officer. Women procurers also searched the charity wards of local hospitals for indigent girls recovering from accidents or illnesses. An offer of employment would be made and the girl would be taken to a house of prostitution.[58]

Employment agencies often served as a means of procuring young women for prostitution. Women who responded to advertised positions as domestics might be sent to a local sporting house. One young woman, for example, was sent by an employment agency to work as a nurse at a sanitarium for elderly people. The "sanitarium" turned out to be a parlor house to which other innocent women had been sent. Another woman, who responded to an advertisement offering employment as a lady's companion for a European vacation, found herself lured into a wealthy madam's "vice resort." A young woman from Connecticut responded to an advertisement for work and received a letter that provided her with an address to which she might apply. When she entered the building, however, her clothes were seized and she was thoroughly drugged.[59]

Although municipal officials sometimes tried to curb these practices, lucrative payoffs attracted all kinds of accomplices to the act of procurement. Cabdrivers, for example, received commissions from proprietors of vice resorts for delivering unsuspecting female passengers to their building. This practice apparently so scandalized citizens in Chicago that the city council felt compelled to pass an ordinance prohibiting the transportation of any unwilling person in public vehicles to a "house of ill fame."[60]

Unsuspecting girls and women were sometimes procured at railway and bus stations, a situation that motivated travelers' aid associations and immigrant protective groups to provide assistance to young women who traveled alone. Women panderers, posing as concerned social workers, would offer newly arrived girls shelter and employment. Instead, the girl would find herself sold as a white slave in a local vice district. One male panderer went so far as to drag a married lady from a train into his carriage. Counting on the public's devaluation of a woman's emotionality, and over the woman's hysterical protests, he explained to onlookers that she was only his deranged wife.[61] Most often, panderers simply stalked the locations where young women congregated at work or for pleasure. In his report on prostitution in New York, George Kneeland described how procurers waited for young women at movie theaters or at dance halls.[62]

In the literature of the period, girls were continually warned of the dangers of meeting strange men, accepting a drink containing "knock out drops," and waking up to discover that they had been "ruined."[63] In their attempts to recruit new prostitutes, however, procurers more frequently played upon the specific psychological, social, and economic needs of young women. Italian women, for example, were promised marriage; Jewish women were promised good employment. "If the girl is one of the 'love sick kind,' " one procurer testified, "they pretend they are in love with her, and in most cases, they promise to marry her. If the girl is looking for a job, they're always 'Johnny on the Spot' with an offer of a good position. The fellows offer girls employment to their liking, which of course is a trick, which they never intend to carry out. The whole idea is to get the girl's confidence and the fellow will say anything to do this."[64] If appeals to ambition, affection, or vanity failed, however, procurers were not above relying on the famous knock out drops and brute force. As a former procurer admitted, "We use any method to get them. Our business is to land them and we don't care how we do it. If they look easy we tell them of the fine clothes, the diamonds and all the money they can have. If they are hard to get, we use knock out drops."[65] As the Rockefeller Grand Jury concluded, procurers used every method to exploit young women's economic, psychological, and social needs. "With promises of marriage," they wrote, "of fine clothing, of greater personal independence, these men often induce girls to live with them, and after a brief period, with threats of exposure or physical violence force them to go upon the street as common prostitutes."[66]

Other cases of procurers tricking or forcing women into white slavery can be found in court records, newspapers, and other journalistic sources of the period.[67] For example, a Bertha S. was taken to a parlor house by an Emmanual Grove and placed there for four weeks. During that time she earned four hundred dollars for him, seeing thirty men a day for fifty cents apiece. Later the case came to court when Grove slashed her with a knife because she had appropriated five dollars for badly needed new shoes.[68] The Rockefeller Grand Jury also described "an indictment and conviction where the defendant by such promises induced a girl of fifteen to leave her home and within two weeks put her on the streets as a common prostitute."[69] Many examples of white slavery which described the seduction of country girls, of immigrant girls who did not understand the language, of working girls who sought some form of amusement, or of women simply walking on the street, offered further evidence of a traffic in women.[70]

Some of the stories that appeared in *The New York Times*, for example, described the most stereotyped cases of white slavery. On December 26, 1913, Alois Marein, treasurer of the Rosenstock Chemical Company, reported to the police that his sister Margaret had escaped an attempt to drug her while she was shopping. After she returned home, she found a needle in her coat. The needle had not entered her arm, and her brother identified the needle as belonging to a hypodermic syringe.[71] In Canada, the *Regina Register* reported in 1909 that a brothel owner had recruited two Polish immigrant girls for housework and then forced them into prostitution. He was sentenced to four years in the penitentiary at hard labor.[72]

In her study of prostitution, Jane Addams found other examples of white slavery. Marie, the daughter of a Breton stonemason, believed she was going to join a theatrical troupe, but was instead forced into prostitution. In another case, two men induced a Polish girl who was searching for her mother to leave a New York train at South Chicago. Young immigrant women were susceptible to procurement especially if they had no immediate family ties or did not know the language. Jane Addams worried most about their particular plight. "It is obvious," she wrote, "that a foreign girl who speaks no English, who has not the remotest idea in what part of the city her fellow countrymen live, who does not know the police station or any agency to which she may apply, is almost as valuable to a white slave traffiker as a girl imported directly for the trade."[73]

In one publicized case, a man forced his legal wife to earn their livelihood by prostituting herself to other men. Reformers were particularly shocked by this story, which seemed to symbolize the worst aspects of "marital prostitution":

> One man who married a woman and forced her into prostitution used to take her about the Mexican labor camps. He would strip her and put her into a box car to which he charged admission for Mexican and Negro laborers. In one case, the girl several times broke away from her exploiter, but was each time brought back. On each occasion she received a severe beating and finally when the pimp threatened to kill her she again ran away and escaped, but was caught and severely slashed about the arms and face with a razor. This necessitated her transfer to a hospital. One hundred eight stitches were required to close her wounds. Upon recovering, she again came under the man's influence and resumed soliciting on the street.[74]

Women who made it their "calling" to rescue white slaves from red-light districts provide perhaps the richest documentation of the experiences of white slaves. In San Francisco, Donaldina Cameron became famous for her rescue work with white slaves.[75] In New York, Hattie Rose, who remained in correspondence with several well known suffragists in the state, spent her days documenting, analyzing, and trying to rescue the victims of the traffic in women, especially in Chinatown. Having been a white slave herself, she dedicated her life to rescuing women who experienced similar degradation and humiliation.

In February 1910, Rose described a case that revealed that one of the more sensationalized methods of procurement did, in fact, occur:

> Louise Elbert, 17 years of age, an orphan, was in a home when some girl in Chinatown wrote to her telling her that a maid was wanted; and the matron of the home, without investigation, sent Louise on. With the address given her she landed in Chinatown. One morning at 10 o'clock, this girl who had induced Louise Elbert to come with her, was bargaining with 4 Chinamen as to which one would buy her. This took place at 16 Doyer Street. Just passed in time to hear some one sobbing, went in, and demanded the girl. I took her to Miss Miner's Home at 165 West 10th Street.* She is at present at her own home.[76]

In May, Rose documented what many reformers had already suspected: the forced prostitution of wives.

> Lillian King, 18 years of age living at 152 O Street, Southern Boston. She is married. This man to whom she is married, put her on the streets to lead an immoral life and to give him the money obtained by doing so. I found her on the Bowery and took her home to Boston. She is now at home with her mother.[77]

In the same month, Rose described a case where a young woman had been led into white slavery by a girl friend, apparently not an uncommon occurrence:

---

* I assume "Miss Miner" refers to the well-known Maude Miner, who, as probation officer and director of the Bedford Home, attempted to help prostitutes through prevention and rescue efforts.

Marcella Feavue, 17 years of age, living at 14 Delaware Street, Easton, Penn. Found her in Chinatown. She told me that she had been led there by a girl friend who wrote to her, saying that she could find plenty of work in New York. This girl told Marcella that she was married when, in fact, she was but living an immoral life in Chinatown. I found Marcella locked up in a room. I watched the house for two days and nights when a woman, who was cleaning the house at 11 Pell Street, told me that Gypsy Gordon was buying Marcella Feavue for $50. I reported this to the Woman's Society. They had the place raided. They took Gypsy, Marcella, and two other young girls. A trial was held. She was found guilty and sent to the Penitentiary for three months. Marcella is now home and working.[78]

While some young women most certainly fell victim to the deceptions practiced by white slavers, one must still ask *why* they seemed so susceptible to these methods in the first place. It seems inconceivable that all these women could have been as naive as they were portrayed. What psychological, social, or economic needs caused them to place themselves in danger of being victimized?

In part, their susceptibility stemmed from the same factors that caused some poor women to consider prostitution a better alternative than other problems and options they already faced, such as troubled families, economic destitution, desire for adventure. (These will be explored in depth in the next chapter.) The desire to engage in casual flirtation, to receive affection, to feel protected, to experience the much heralded "love at first sight," and to experiment with sex on a limited basis probably contributed to young women's susceptibility to procurers' claims of love and promises of marriage. Some young women, as William Stead noted, "are just a little silly, just a little flirtatious, and just a little romantic. They have heard of love at first sight and they think they are a trifle smarter than the other girls when they pick up a chance acquaintance with a strange visitor in town."[79]

Marriage, moreover, represented both the affectional and economic protection many young women sought in a society that blocked their own independent upward mobility. Thus, from a context of feeling unloved or economically unprotected, some women may have consciously or unconsciously chosen to tempt and tease fate by placing themselves in what turned out to be dangerous situations.

Once a woman had been procured and sold, the "breaking in" process would begin. If the procurer had not already sexually seduced the young woman, the madam would usually arrange to have her drugged and raped by an accommodating customer. Included in "breaking in" were instructions on what to say and do and how to avoid arrest. Sometimes, as procurers recalled, the other prostitutes and the madam attempted to convince the white slave of the advantages of her position:

There is such an air of comraderie about the madame that the young girl is usually relieved of her embarrassment and the landlady usually admits that

> she is the owner of a house where nice men come and pay liberally for their entertainment. That it is possible for the girl to always wear beautiful gowns and have plenty of money, to say nothing of the dandy times she will have. Then the other girls are brought into the picture and they bring all their persuasive power to bear.[80]

Not surprisingly, some young women bitterly and violently refused to submit to male "guests" even when beatings and other forms of coercion were employed. To prevent a white slave from escaping, the madam or pimp took away her street clothes and money. In exchange, the young woman received flimsy transparent gowns in which she could not enter the street. In essence, she was given a glamorous prison uniform. Locked inside her room, the young woman would be carefully watched. She now represented a financial investment that her owner was not about to forfeit. Only after a madam felt certain that a young entrapped woman felt too disgraced, too intimidated, or too demoralized to escape, would she be granted the freedom to leave the house by herself.[81]

Theoretically, a white slave could accumulate enough money to escape or to purchase her freedom. This was exceedingly rare, however, due to the elaborate credit system—much like the sharecropping credit system of the postwar South—employed in most houses. Half of her earnings as a prostitute went to the "house." In addition, she had to pay back the fee or commission that her procurer had received for her. She was also required to pay exorbitant prices for the jewelry and flimsy gowns she was given as part of her costume—often at four times the regular price she would have paid elsewhere. Room and board, charged at twice the rate of a boarding house also kept the white slave wholly indebted and without cash of her own.[82] Asked why she had not escaped from the house in which she was kept a white slave, a young Irish woman explained:

> Get out! I can't. They make us buy the cheapest rags, and they are charged against us at fabulous prices; they make us change outfits at intervals of two or three weeks, until we are so deeply in debt that there is no hope of ever getting out from under. Then, to make matters worse, we seldom get an accounting oftener than once in six months, and sometimes then months or a year will pass between settlements, and when we do get an accounting it is always to find ourselves deeper in debt than before. We've simply got to stick, and that's all there is to it.[83]

Another young woman explained in night court why she had been unable to leave the house where she had been imprisoned: "With kimonos and silk stockings and clothes and the rest, they got me way in debt. I wanted to get out of that place, but they wouldn't leave me go. They claimed it was all because I owed so much money and said, 'You can't get out when you're in debt to us.' "[84]

Despite these very objective obstacles, one still feels justified in asking why white slaves perceived escape as such an impossible alternative. After all, the physical bondage that characterized white slavery never constituted a totally closed system of imprisonment. And, white slavery *was* different from black slavery in important ways. White slavery never achieved the institutional or cultural organization of the southern plantation. From the outside, reformers were justified in wondering why white slaves did not escape more often.

To consider this question, it is helpful to view white slavery as the prostitute herself might have experienced it. First of all, the white slave had been procured against her will and had usually been the victim of some form of violence or seduction; thus she felt some degree of helplessness at the hands of her captors. Threats of physical violence were also used to intimidate a newly initiated prostitute. Procurers and madams showed her examples of beaten and razor-slashed prostitutes to maintain her docile acceptance of her new role. Pimps, too, frequently used such physical violence to keep prostitutes from leaving the trade.[85] One prostitute explained to a female reformer why she could no longer leave prostitution. "He threatened to put a bullet through me or to cut my face if I told and I didn't dare to tell." Such examples, by no means uncommon, could not escape new prostitutes' attention.[86]

The sustained intimidation and brutality that kept such women immobilized is clear from Rose's description of the following case of white slavery. Mary Crane, a Bowery girl, had been "put on the street by a man named Michel O'Connor," who "demanded from her $15 every night." When she refused to "work" one evening, he beat her and gave her a black eye. Rose had Michel O'Connor arrested. He was found guilty and was sentenced to one year imprisonment and a fine of $500.[87] As is evident from this man's sentence, the punishment for white slavery, as many feminists of the period argued, was not overly severe.

The Vice Commission of Philadelphia, although it uncovered little evidence of women who had been forced into prostitution, found that a number of prostitutes were indeed coercively kept in their trade. Pimps and madams, it pointed out, had "pull" with the police and made it impossible for prostitutes to count on police protection. It further emphasized the terrifying threat of physical retribution that prostitutes invariably suffered from their pimps: "All this" it concluded, "constitutes for hundreds of girls a kind of white slavery that breaks down their will and courage and effectually prevents the success of any desire to quit the business."[88] Another investigation of five white slave cases further documented the fact that the pimp/white slave relationship resulted in serious physical and psychological terror for women. The pimp, investigators noted, had become an increasingly integral part of the white slave trade:

> Now this system of subjection to a man has become common. The procurer
> or pimp may put his woman into a disorderly house, sharing profits with the
> "madam." He may sell her outright, he may act as an agent for another man;
> he may keep her, making arrangements for her hunting men. She must walk
> the streets and secure her patrons, to be exploited, not for her own sake, but
> for that of her owner. Often he does not tell her even his real name. If she

tries to leave her man, she is threatened with arrest. If she resists, she finds all
the men about her leagued against her; she may be beaten; in some cases
when she has betrayed her betrayer she has been murdered.[89]

Without friends or nearby family, and without knowledge of rescue homes,
missionaries, or other avenues of escape, some women simply did not know
where to go. Many were estranged from their families and friends and knew that
any return to them would be accompanied by whispered rumors or met with
explicit contempt. When white slaves did manage to escape, procurers who had
been alerted throughout the underground grapevine frequently found and returned them to their "owners." Prostitutes also feared going to the police. Madams would have the police arrest the escaped white slave. Identified as a thief,
she would then be returned to pay the considerable debts she still owed. Prostitutes also feared the retribution that resulted from involving the police. After
testifying against her procurer, one former prostitute was killed by a bomb ex-
plosion in her apartment.[90]

In addition to the external obstacles that prevented escape, some prostitutes
may have become gradually immobilized by their own internalized self-hatred
and guilt. Like the battered wife or rape victim who has been conditioned to
blame herself for her victimized condition, the white slave may have internalized
negative societal attitudes toward "fallen" women and felt personally responsible
for her situation. The initial feelings of shame and disgrace that some young
prostitutes experienced indicate the extent to which they blamed themselves for
their own condition. As Maude Miner explained, "The severe condemnation of
society only degrades her further. She finds herself cut off by her friends and
family; through being constantly decieved she loses faith in human nature; she
loses respect even for herself. . . . This demoralization of character constitutes
the real slavery of prostitution."[91]

As Kathleen Barry has pointed out in her study of contemporary sexual slavery, it is not part of women's training to design well-laid plans of battle such as
those men learn in sports or in the military. Women who were forced into prostitution survived as best they could, as Barry points out, in a haphazard manner,
and without the confidence of escaping forces that appeared larger and more
powerful than themselves. "Surviving," writes Barry, "is not written into the code
of socialized female behavior."[92]

As the white slave gradually became acculturated to the subculture of prostitution, escape probably seemed less and less possible. The prostitute might have
adopted the defensive and hostile antisocial attitudes generally associated with
individuals who are labeled deviant and marginal outsiders. Breaking out of
such a subculture—the slang, habits, customs, attitudes, rules, and expectations—
could have proved increasingly difficult. The subculture, moreover, now offered
the most immediate solutions to a woman's need for economic and social protection. Each day, the options offered by the society "outside" seemed less accessible, less attractive, and more remote.[93]

Was white slavery a real system of slavery? The answer depends on the definition of the term. If we mean by slavery the psychological and physical dehumanization of an individual through another's ownership of his or her physical freedom, then white slavery should be considered a form of slavery. As the Wisconsin vice report pointed out, white slaves were imprisoned by economic, physical, and psychological dependency. "The prostitutes," it summarized,

> are made to feel absolutely dependent on the "madam" and "pimps" for everything they need, and are sometimes threatened with more or less severe violence in cases of any mutiny. In this way they soon lose all ambition in life and following the path of least resistance, they resort to drink and drugs to palliate their unfortunate position, subordinating themselves to any men or women who will relieve them of responsibility and care of themselves until they are finally cast off. This is the now generally accepted definition of the term "white slavery" and is as real a moral slavery and results in as real a form of physical subservience, as if the prostitute were, indeed, controlled by the bolts and bars and brute force of her owner.[94]

How much did white slavery contribute to women's entering prostitution? When 6,309 prostitutes during the Progressive Era were asked why and how they entered prostitution, only 7.5 percent listed white slavery or extreme coercion as the cause (see Table 1). Since most of the prostitutes interviewed were working in brothels, on the streets, or in prisons, and since any actual white slaves were unlikely to be available for interviews, the true percentage of women forced into white slavery might perhaps be somewhat higher. It may be safely assumed, however, that white slavery, though it did exist, was probably experienced by less than 10 percent of the prostitute population.

Why, then, did white slavery figure so largely in explanations and descriptions of prostitution during the Progressive Era? One obvious reason for its popularity was its lurid and melodramatic appeal. Stories of underground intrigue, crime, seduction, and sex provided virtually pornographic entertainment to a late Victorian reading audience. The idea of white slavery also served, however, to deflect attention away from the very real social and economic factors that led women into prostitution. The class guilt of middle-class Americans for conditions that gave rise to prostitution was projected onto a few villainous white slavers, typically represented as foreigners. Furthermore, the white slavery explanation, more than any other, emphasized women's passivity. With their own class presumption of women's supposed sexual purity, many middle-class Americans could not imagine a woman voluntarily entering prostitution. As one writer explained, "We know that no innocent young girl ever would or ever could go there of her own free will—those who are there are enticed—those who employ these artifices are men—devils in the guise of men."[95]

Finally, white slavery, as the most extreme and coercive form of prostitution, elicited the most extreme expression of the emotional reactions and symbolic associations triggered by prostitution in general. As American society began to assume its modern industrial character, women increasingly left their urban or rural homes to become proletarianized in the cities. Once there, they became a profitable item not only for white slavers but for other corporate interests, such as factory employers and media managers. Citizens who felt threatened and were appalled by the trends of commercialization, dehumanization, and moral corruption in American society could see in the traffic in women a symbol of everything that they deplored. Those who felt increasingly dominated by corrupt political machines and faceless industrial trusts may have identified with the white

Table 1
Studies and Surveys Concerning White Slavery

Author: Study	# of prostitutes interviewed	# who listed white slavery as cause of entry into prostitution	% of entire study who listed white slavery as cause of entry into prostitution
Street cases	1,106	6	0.5
Other institutions	610	21	3.4
Katherine Davis: Bedford study (reformatory prostitutes)	647	2	0.3
Vice Commission of Chicago: women inmates	30	9	30.0
Maude Miner: prostitutes	1,000	256	25.6
Vice Commission of Chicago: dance hall prostitutes	40	3	7.5
Vice Commission of Chicago: juvenile delinquents	2,241	107	4.8
Kansas Vice Commission	525	59	9.3
Bridgeport Vice Commission	110	10	9.0
Totals	6,309	473	7.5

Sources: Bridgeport, Conn., Bridgeport Vice Commission, *Report and Recommendations of the Bridgeport Vice Commission* (Bridgeport, 1916), pp. 76–77; Chicago, Ill., Vice Commission of Chicago, *The Social Evil in Chicago: A Study of Existing Conditions, with Recommendations* (Chicago: Gunthrop Warren, 1911), pp. 170, 171, 174; Katharine Bement Davis, "A Study of Prostitutes Committed from New York City to the State Reformatory for Women at Bedford Hills," in George Kneeland, *Commercialized Prostitution in New York* (1913, reprint; Montclair, N.J.: Patterson-Smith, 1969), p. 225; Fred Johnson, *The Social Evil in Kansas* (Kansas City., Mo., 1911), p. 16; Maude Miner, *The Slavery of Prostitution* (New York: Macmillan, 1916), p. 27.

Note: There are several problems that should be noted in regard to the figures offered about white slavery. In most surveys, different categories were used in questioning. Thus, in one questionnaire, "forcible seduction" is a category used to indicate white slavery, whereas in another survey, the actual term *white slavery* appears. In choosing which figures to use here, I have been particularly conservative and have used only those categories that indicated actual involuntary introduction into prostitution. Second, it is important to note that most vice reports offered conclusions that significantly differed from the statistics they had collected. Reformers assumed that there was more white slavery than actually appeared in the figures or, at least, that more women would blame other people for their "downfall."

slave as a passive victim of uncontrollable and sinister forces. For organized womanhood in particular, the sale of women into forced prostitution constituted the most extreme form of the commercial and sexual exploitation of women and provided the most vivid representation of female subjugation and degradation in society.

There is much that remains unclear about white slavery and requires additional research. Yet it *is* clear, despite the sensationalism and the necessary qualifications, that a trade in women, however small, existed, and, according to Barry, continues to exist wherever women have been sufficiently devalued and discriminated against to become easy targets for physical and economic coercion.

A prostitute in Storyville, c. 1900. Photograph by E. J. Bellocq.
Reprinted by permission of Lee Friedlander.

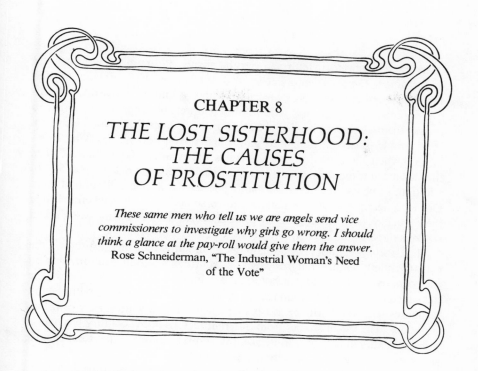

CHAPTER 8

THE LOST SISTERHOOD: THE CAUSES OF PROSTITUTION

These same men who tell us we are angels send vice commissioners to investigate why girls go wrong. I should think a glance at the pay-roll would give them the answer.
Rose Schneiderman, "The Industrial Woman's Need of the Vote"

Despite the national hysteria over white slavery, the vast majority of women who practiced prostitution were not dragged, drugged, or clubbed into involuntary servitude. How do we know this? Because prostitutes of the Progressive Era, in response to reformers' questioning, described the actual economic, social, sexual, and familial difficulties influencing their decision to practice prostitution.

For far too long, historians have accepted and perpetuated sex-stereotyped images of women as passive, helpless people incapable of taking responsibility for themselves. To describe women as active participants in their own lives is not to ignore the very real social and economic oppression they suffered. Poor women had little power to create or alter the bleak options they faced. Nevertheless, they were capable of choosing, amidst an array of intolerable options, their means of survival. Most women *chose* to enter prostitution—not because they were mentally deficient, not because they suffered unresolved Oedipal complexes, not because they were the helpless victims of sinister procurers or greedy industrialists, not because they were the passive objects of abstract "push/pull forces"—but because they perceived prostitution as a means of fulfilling particular economic, social, or psychological needs.

The data available to create a profile of prostitutes are somewhat problematic.[1] The survey procedures used by urban vice investigators created many difficulties. Former pimps and prostitutes penetrated the red-light districts to interview prostitutes in brothels, dance halls, and saloons. Social workers also interviewed prostitutes in reformatories and prisons. Posing as fellow prostitutes or customers, the investigators believed they had won the confidence of their subjects. Whether this is true, we will never know. A number of seasoned investigators noted that prostitutes gave reformers unreliable information, either to protect themselves or to have a joke at reformers' expense.[2] Benjamin Reitman, for example, observed that both pimps and prostitutes enjoyed lying to reformers when filling out their questionnaires. "They laugh," he explained, "when they tell me how they answered 47 questions incorrectly out of a possible 50." In addition, some social workers probably interfered with the collection of data. One investigator pointed out that prostitutes sometimes hesitated before listing their previous occupation (often because they had none). In some cases, social workers directed the women to write down *Houseworker*.[3]

These surveys cannot provide definitive quantitative data on prostitutes of the early twentieth century, but they are a rich source of descriptive information on the economic, social, and psychological conditions that prostitutes faced. The data are useful despite their limitations in that certain demographic patterns and responses reappear with consistent frequency across a wide variety of urban situations. The use of studies from different regions of the country provides a more general, but probably more accurate, portrait of prostitutes than could a single study of one city's prostitute population.[4]

In reformers' accounts, the prostitute is most frequently portrayed as poor, rural, very young, single, childless, and sometimes foreign born. The reality, however, is more complex, adding to and sometimes contradicting these descriptions.

The surveys do suggest that a large majority of prostitutes came from the working class. Most of the prostitutes in New York's Bedford Reformatory study came from working-class families, as indicated by the blue-collar occupations of their fathers (see Table 2).[5] The same study also showed that many of the prostitutes' mothers (22.4%) worked outside the home while their daughters were young children (see Table 3). Since in 1900 only 6 percent of women in America were working for wages outside the home and prejudices against married women working were especially strong, it is almost certain that these mothers worked out of economic necessity.[6] The additional income they earned constituted an essential portion of the family economy.

Reformers' frequent references to prostitutes' record of early juvenile delinquency, families with a slightly higher than average number of children, paternal desertion or death at an early age, mothers cohabiting with a series of different men, and family histories of incest, severe alcoholism, tuberculosis, and chronic unemployment also suggest that most prostitutes came from blue-collar neighborhoods and/or working-class families; such experiences, while not restricted to the poor, probably occurred most commonly among the poor.[7]

The class *origins* of prostitutes tell only part of the story, since women, unlike men, obtained their class status vicariously throughout their lives. Both a son and a daughter carried their father's class affiliation. After marriage, however, a daughter assumed her husband's class status, and if she were widowed or deserted, her class status again changed. Without life insurance, a rather modern invention designed to protect against such sudden tragedies, women were generally incapable of maintaining the economic support their husbands had provided.

An unusually high percentage of prostitutes came from situations in which the family economy of either their original family (family of origin) or their newly created family (family of procreation) had been severely disturbed. Many of the prostitutes, therefore, came from families that were not originally destitute; rather, certain conditions had disrupted the entire family's means of survival.

Two popular stereotypes about prostitutes' backgrounds depicted the young foreign-born girl who, having just stepped off the boat, supported herself and her family through prostitution, and the innocent rural girl whose arrival into the urban industrial world caused her fall from grace.[8] Theodore Dreiser's *Sister Carrie* helped to popularize and perpetuate the "fall of the country girl" myth.

These images, despite their popularity, did not correspond to the facts. In 1900, the background of prostitutes varied widely throughout the United States. On the West Coast, a high proportion of prostitutes came from recent Chinese and Japanese immigrant populations, but in many other areas the proportion of prostitutes who were immigrants was much lower: in Kansas, for example, 95 percent of the prostitutes were native-born Americans, and in the South, particularly New Orleans, most prostitutes were reported to be native-born black or Creole.[9]

In 1858, William Sanger's study of prostitutes in New York had asserted that half of the prostitutes were recent immigrants to the United States. In 1911, however, a combined study of 2,364 prostitutes in New York showed foreign-born women to be *underrepresented* in the prostitute population; they contributed 28 percent of the prostitutes but represented 40 percent of the New York City population. Native-born women (a category including daughters of foreign-born parents, or first-generation Americans) were overrepresented; they constituted 60 percent of the New York City population but composed 72 percent of the prostitute population.[10]

One institution, Bedford, gave statistics on native-born daughters of foreign-born parents as a separate category. These show that first-generation Americans constituted roughly one-third of the incarcerated prostitutes, approximately their proportional representation in the New York City population. Foreign-born women, however, contributed only one-quarter of the prostitutes at Bedford (as compared to their 40 percent representation in the New York population). Thus it appears that *native-born women of foreign parentage were more likely to become prostitutes than were foreign-born women.*[11]

Table 2
A Study of Prostitutes at Bedford:
Occupations of Inmates' Fathers

Professions		*Mechanical Trades (continued)*	
Architect	2	Carpenter	13
Civil engineer	1	Carriagemaker	1
Black preacher	1	Cooper	1
Lawyer	1	Electrician	2
Minister	1	Engineer (railroad)	4
Music teacher	1	Engineer (stationary)	15
Musician	2	Gas fitter	1
Physician	2	Glazier	1
Surveyor	2	Hardwood polisher	1
Trained nurse	1	Ironworker	8
Veterinary surgeon	1	Machinist	7
Total	15	Mechanic	3
		Painter	14
Self-employed		Plasterer	1
Brewer	1	Plumber	3
Contractor	5	Printer	6
Fruit dealer	2	Slate roofer	1
Horse dealer	4	Stonecutter	2
Hotel keeper	2	Stonemason	9
Livery stable keeper	1	Terra cotta worker	1
Peddler	8	Tinsmith	2
Saloon keeper	11	Walking delegate	1
Shopkeeper	29	*Total*	114
Total	63		
		Clothing Trades	
Business Positions		Cap maker	4
Insurance agent	2	Cloak maker	2
Milkman	1	Designer	2
Real estate agent	4	Finisher of corsets	1
Salesman	21	Presser	6
Total	28	Tailor	22
		Total	37
Mechanical Trades			
Blacksmith	6	*Other Trades*	
Bricklayer	3	Baker	2
Brickmaker	1	Barber	8
Builder	5	Bartender	2
Cabinetmaker	2	Basket maker	1

Reformers often assumed that the "new immigrants" (Eastern and Southern Europeans and Italians) were primarily responsible for prostitution. The data they collected, however, revealed that foreign-born women of such backgrounds were in fact underrepresented in the prostitute population. Using the 1911 case study of 2,364 prostitutes, we find interesting comparisons among foreign-born Jewish, Italian, Irish, French, Canadian, and English prostitutes. Those ethnic groups that tended to emphasize family solidarity and female chastity—Jews,

Table 2 (*continued*)

Other Trades (*continued*)		Domestic Positions	
Butcher	10	Coachman	7
Carpet layer	1	Cook	9
Cigar maker	10	Elevator man	1
Draughtsman	1	Gardener	3
Mat maker	1	Janitor	5
Photographer	1	Porter	3
Reed and rattan maker	1	Waiter	7
Shoemaker	10	*Total*	35
Watchmaker	1	Foreman	7
Weaver	2	Asst. Supt. Life Ins. Co.	1
Total	51	Conductor	2
		Sea captain	5
Clerical Positions		*Total*	15
Bookkeeper	3		
Clerk of court	1	*In Public Service*	
Excise officer	1	Fireman	5
Total	5	Lighthouse keeper	1
		Mail carrier	1
Laborers		Policeman	5
Derrick rigger	1	Soldier	5
Electric light trimmer	1	*Total*	17
Employed on boats	11		
Employed on railroad	12	*Miscellaneous*	
Farmer or farm hand	34	Collector	1
Hod carrier	3	Gambler	1
Laborer	40	Sandwich man	1
Miner	3	Telegraph operator	1
Stableman	3	Ticket speculator	1
Street sweeper	2	Undertaker	3
Teamster	18	*Total*	8
Watchman	4		
Total	132	"Does not work on account of kidney trouble and fainting fits"	1
		Unknown	7
Mill and Factory Positions		No statistics	99
Factory	13	*Total*	107
Mill hand	7		
Total	20	*Grand Total*	647

Source: Adapted from George Kneeland, *Commercialized Prostitution in New York* (1913; reprint, Montclair, N.J.: Patterson-Smith, 1969), pp. 215–16.

Irish, and Italians—were underrepresented in the foreign-born prostitute population.[12]

What the underrepresentation of immigrants in the prostitute population probably reflects is the attempt of "new immigrants" to re-create the strict family and community controls that they had known in their former villages or communities. Their American children, however, particularly those of mixed parentage, encountered a different set of values and expectations in the "new country."

Table 3
Commercialized Prostitution in New York, Bedford Cases

Occupation of Mother	Number of Prostitutes
Actress	1
Canvasser	2
Charge of hotel linen room	1
Cook (6 colored)	10
Day's work	46
Domestic-general housework (6 nonwhite)	9
Dressmaker	4
Factory operative	11
Housekeeper	4
Janitress	13
Laundress	17
Midwife	6
Milliner	1
Market woman	1
Nurse	9
Peddler	2
Small shopkeeper	7
Tailoress	1
Total	145

Total number of cases: 647
Percentage of occupied mothers: 22.4

Dreams of upward mobility, generational conflict between children and parents over new customs, and the gradual disintegration of family and community ties may have contributed to more deviant activities on the part of daughters of foreign-born parents. In the case of mixed parentage, family and community ties might further have been weakened.[13]

Reformers' surveys also contradict their own assumptions that most prostitutes were rural born. Of the women in New York's Bedford study, 82.48 percent had been born in an American city. Those not originally from New York were more likely to have come from another city (22.9 percent) than from the country (17.4 percent). When asked why they had moved to New York, 78 percent said they had come to "live with family" (usually relatives), and 26 percent said they had been looking for "work" or "easier work." It appears from this and other studies that an increasing number of young women were moving from city to city, often "just for pleasure."[14]

Investigators did not often inquire into prostitutes' religious backgrounds. The little information available shows primarily that religious background varied widely from region to region, with Protestantism predominant among prostitutes in the Midwest and Catholic or Jewish affiliation more common in cities like New York, where a larger Catholic or Jewish population resided.[15]

Most prostitutes had received little education. Studies generally found that very few prostitutes had entered high school; many had not finished even the primary grades; and many were "barely literate."[16] Unfortunately, the reasons why prostitutes left school so early were not investigated in most cases. From other evidence, however, it seems likely that, as Maimie Pinzer discussed earlier, they left school to support a fragile family economy torn apart by the death or desertion of one parent or by chronic unemployment.

One theme that appears with unusual frequency in prostitutes' life histories is that of families "broken" by divorce, desertion, or the death of one or both parents. In 1858, William Sanger found that over half of the two thousand prostitutes he studied were orphans. Fourteen percent of the prostitutes in the Bedford study had already been orphaned by the time they were admitted to the institution. Twenty-six percent of the women had lost their fathers and 30 percent had lost their mothers—18 percent before the age of fourteen. In all, two-thirds of the 647 prostitutes had grown up without one parent for a part of their childhood, and 14 percent had no parents at all.[17] Between 1907 and 1915, another study in New York found that, of 378 prostitutes, 25 percent had no parents and 60 percent came from "broken homes."[18]

In contrast, the *Summary Report on the Condition of Women and Child Wage Earners in the United States* found a much lower percentage of broken homes among working women who were *not* prostitutes. In the ready-made clothing industry, for example, only 18.1 percent of working women had experienced the death, desertion, or divorce of one or both parents. For the glass, cotton, and silk industries, the figures averaged about 17 percent. Since prostitutes had been employed in a much wider variety of occupations (including no former occupations), these figures are not comparable with the studies of prostitutes' lives. Nevertheless, this national sampling of working women *does* provide one point of reference by which to judge the high incidence of broken homes in prostitutes' pasts. A comparison of the collective profile of prostitutes with that of the women studied in the report of working women shows that both groups of women in fact share many of the same life experiences and backgrounds. The single exception, however, is that prostitutes did seem to experience more frequent breakdowns in their family's economy or social relations.[19]

Although prostitutes were usually portrayed as single women, many had in fact married and raised children. Thirty percent of the Bedford prostitutes were married, separated, or divorced, and an even higher percentage of married women was reported in some other states. In Massachusetts, 300 prostitutes claimed 109 children among them, a ratio found in surveys of other areas as well.[20]

Contrary to popular notions, most prostitutes had *not* lived alone in boarding homes before entering prostitution. Although an increasing number of young women were leaving their families and living on subsistence wages in boarding houses, this had not yet become a common pattern. In fact, most studies reveal that the vast majority of prostitutes had lived at home with their families or husbands before practicing prostitution.[21]

Although investigators often failed to inquire about prostitutes' religious or educational backgrounds, they rarely missed an opportunity to collect data describing the sexual history of each woman. For most prostitutes, their first sexual contact ("offense") was not associated with prostitution. Of sixty-six prostitutes studied in Hartford, twenty-five listed their first partner as a boyfriend or acquaintance; twenty-two said that their first sexual contact had been with a total stranger; and the remainder listed family members, friends of their family, or, for two of the women, an employer—an experience possibly indicating the sexual harassment so common to women who worked in factories or department stores or as domestics. The average age of the women's first sexual contact was between fifteen and eighteen years.[22]

One or two years after their first sexual contact, these women began practicing prostitution, usually between seventeen and twenty-one years. In some cases, a change in consciousness occurred during this short interval. Their new "sporting" life brought them into contact with occasional or full-time prostitutes. Gradually they became aware of the potential money-making possibilities in the sexual favors they were "giving away." As the famous madam Pauline Tabor later recalled, she began questioning her "charity" and "decided to start merchandising sex instead of giving it away." In other instances, young women felt they had been ruined by their first sexual contact or were "locked out" of the family home for their sexual transgressions (Table 4).[23]

The age at which prostitutes were interviewed by investigators (whether in institutions, on the street, or in brothels) usually fell between twenty and twenty-three years. Most women admitted to institutions seemed to average about twenty-two years of age. Nearly every study emphasized that the average number of years which most prostitutes practiced their trade rarely exceeded five or six years.[24]

What happened to these women during their late twenties and thirties? Unfortunately, there is very little evidence which documents their life cycle after prostitution. Certainly, some prostitutes must have died of venereal disease, suicide, and other occupational hazards of their trade. But of the others? We can only speculate that some women found economic security in marriage and hid their former life behind a veil of respectability. Former madams such as Pauline Tabor and Sally Stanford later described prostitutes who found husbands, "went straight to suburban homes and did damn well at it," "went to college," "became marriage counselors," "became further involved in dope or crime," or "saved sufficient money to attend college."[25] In his study of Storyville, Al Rose described at least one prostitute who married a salesman who had peddled clothes to the brothel. Other evidence, drawn from a registration of prostitutes between 1871 and 1896 in Copenhagan, suggests possible futures which American prostitutes faced. Twenty canceled their registration due to marriage, 135 returned to relatives, and 10 became the wards of private persons or institutions.

A very small minority of former prostitutes may have secured their "fortune" as a wealthy madam (a very popular brothel myth). Most women, like Maimie Pinzer, probably faced the continuing options of marriage, prostitution, or unskilled menial work at subsistence wages. Given prostitutes' attitudes toward "respectable" work, it is likely that most of these women found economic security in marriage or continued practicing their trade. As their attractiveness waned with age, however, they could no longer "work" the expensive brothels and were forced downward into cheap fifty-cent houses or into the streets.[26]

In addition to securing demographic data from prostitutes, investigators also asked the women why they had turned to prostitution. Unfortunately, it appears that prostitutes had to select their answers from categories created by the surveyors. It seems unlikely, for example, that prostitutes would have described their reasons in the language drafted by reformers: "tired of drudgery," "love of luxury," or "born bad." As "opinions," moreover, these data are not reliable in any statistical sense. It is also important to remember that most women probably chose "the last straw" which influenced their decision, a fact which obscures the many overlapping social, economic and psychological factors involved in most women's choices.

Nevertheless, prostitutes' answers *do* provide interesting insights into their own perceived reasons for entering their trade. When the most frequently chosen answers are tabulated (Table 4) from several major studies, we gain a closer look at the way prostitutes regarded their own decisions. Although reformers provided the "reasons," prostitutes were free to choose whichever answer best suited their personal experience.

All of the women could have blamed their "fall" on procurers or economic destitution, knowing that reformers widely believed in these twin evils. Yet of 3,117 prostitutes, only 2.8 percent specifically cited white slavers and 11.3 percent accused men (lovers, seducers, etc.) of having actively forced, seduced, or betrayed them into prostitution.* The issue of white slavery and forced prostitution has been discussed in the preceding chapter. The other two most frequently listed reasons for entering prostitution were bad home conditions (17.2 percent), probably reflecting the breakdown of family relations or family economy, and low wages or economic necessity (15.5 percent). Several other reasons reflected financial pressures or ambitions: death or desertion by a husband (10.2 percent);

---

* Reformers asked fewer women about the full range of causes that led them to prostitution. That is why the responses and the number of women differ from the study of 6,309 women cited in the previous chapter, who were specifically asked about white slavery. Nevertheless, in both cases, the percentage of women citing white slavery is usually less than 10 percent.

Table 4

Studies and Surveys Concerning Major Causes
of Prostitution

	Bedford Study	New York institutions (1)	New York street cases	Kansas	Chicago 30 inmates	Chicago dance hall prostitutes	Chicago prostitutes, streetwalkers, or in saloons	Bridgeport, Conn.	TOTAL	Percentage of total number of answers given
No. of prostitutes questioned	647	610	1106	525	30	40	49	110	3117	
No. of answers given	671	1011	1436	525	33	28	30	179	3913	
Own choice, "easy money," tired of work	241	86	149	90	3	1	3	—	373	9.5
Economic need	32	246	175	70	6	14	3	51	607	15.5
Desire for more money	38	27	135	—	2	2	4	50	258	6.6
Bad home conditions	297	141	182	—	2	2	4	48	676	17.2
Desire for pleasure	58	65	103	—	—	—	—	—	227	5.8
Death of or desertion by husband	55	115	152	87	4	3	—	—	416	10.6
Support of husband	—	—	—	10	—	—	—	—	10	0.25
Lonely, bored	5	—	19	—	—	—	—	—	24	0.6
"Naturally bad"	—	2	116	—	2	1	—	—	121	3.0
"Bad" friends	75	108	16	42	—	—	—	—	287	7.3
Betrayed, deceived, seduced	13	113	245	72	—	—	—	-	443	11.3
White slave	2	21	6	59	9	3	2	10	112	2.8
Ignorance	10	6	—	—	—	—	—	20	36	0.9
"Ruined anyway"	11	38	45	—	1	—	4	—	99	2.5
Drink and drugs	29	43	38	91	3	—	—	—	204	5.2
Not educated for other work	—	—	—	—	1	—	—	—	2	0.05

Sources: Bedford Study, New York institutions, and New York street cases data obtained from Kneeland, Commercialized Prostitution in New York (1913, reprint; Montclair, N.J.: Patterson-Smith, 1969), pp. 235, 251, 259; Kansas data from Fred Johnson, The Social Evil in Kansas (Kansas City, Mo., 1911), p. 16; Chicago data from the Vice Commission of Chicago, The Social Evil in Chicago: A Study of Existing Conditions, with Recommendations (Chicago: Gunthrop Warren, 1911), pp. 167, 171, 173; Bridgeport data from Bridgeport, Conn., Bridgeport Vice Commission, Report and Recommendations of the Bridgeport Vice Commission (Bridgeport, 1916), pp. 76–77.

Note: Table 4 suggests that fewer prostitutes were victims of white slavery than does Table 1, which includes studies and surveys that asked, in some cases, only about white slavery; that is why Table 1 includes a higher number of prostitutes who were interviewed. Not as many women were asked about all the causes contributing to their entering prostitution. In any case, the percentage of women who described themselves as victims of white slavery was usually below 10 percent in most surveys. More specific figures being "tired of drudgery" and wanting "easy money" (9.5 percent); and wanting "more money" even though it was not a necessity (6.5 percent).

From these sources, the major causes of prostitution begin to emerge with greater clarity: economic factors (actual poverty, fragile family economies, need for supplemental income, lack of or contempt for other occupational options, and rising economic expectations) and social and personal problems experienced in family life (emotional deprivation, generational conflict, and a double standard of sexual conduct for women).

The *Summary Report* concluded that "poverty, whether it be the result of a low family income or of insufficient wages for a girl living by herself, touches the question of immorality in many ways. It decides the girl's companionships, her amusements, her ability to gratify without danger her natural and reasonable tastes, her very capacity for resistance to temptation."[27] By defining poverty in its widest cultural and social sense, the report recognized an important fact: that prostitution was not simply "caused" by poverty but represented an integral part of culture determined by poverty. Poverty directly affected women's choice to enter prostitution in several important ways. The low wages paid to women workers, the sudden changes in family income status, and the desire for upward mobility were some of the most important economic factors influencing women's decision to practice prostitution.

Put quite bluntly, women generally profited economically from prostitution, even when they also suffered the social cost of family or community ostracism. At least for a young and reasonably attractive woman, prostitution represented economic survival and sometimes, as we shall see, upward mobility. In their former occupations, prostitutes had earned from four to six dollars a week.[28] These wages differed little from those of other working women of the period. The *Summary Report* found the average weekly wage for 1,600 department store and factory women to be $6.67. In the four industries in which most female industrial workers were employed—men's ready-wear clothing, glass, cotton, and silk—the same study reported that from two-fifths to two-thirds of those women sixteen years of age and over earned less than six dollars in a representative week.[29]

By every contemporary standard, such low wages represented a subsistence standard of living. The *Summary Report* conservatively estimated that a young working woman needed $3.80 for shelter, $ .38 for clothing, $1.49 for carfare, leaving $ .37 for amusements. Since most authorities agreed that a working woman needed a weekly wage of nine dollars—especially if she lived alone—most working-class women were clearly underpaid.[30] Industrialists justified their subsistence wages by arguing that women worked simply for "pin money" and were already supported by their families or husbands. Manufacturers further exploited women as a cheap source of labor by hiring them for seasonal work, which left them unemployed and unsalaried for months at a time. "It is a commercial proposition with us," shrugged one manufacturer.[31] Despite the testimony of prostitutes who complained of their former subsistence wages, industrial employers continued to argue that there was no connection between low wages and vice. Since most unions refused to train women for skilled jobs—fearing their competitive labor and the lower wages they had been forced to accept over the years—women workers found little support for their demands for higher wages.

As a prostitute, however, a woman's weekly earnings soared. The average brothel inmate or streetwalker received from one to five dollars a "trick," earning in one evening what other working women made in a week.[32] When comparing "women's wages" with the weekly income of prostitutes, it is not surprising that some women chose prostitution for its economic benefits. "Is it any wonder," mused members of the Vice Commission of Chicago, "that a tempted girl who receives only six dollars per week working with her hands sells her body for twenty-five dollars per week when she learns there is a demand for it and men are willing to pay the price?" Prostitution was profitable. As the ubiquitous crusader William Stead noted, "the peculiar temptation of a woman is that her virtue is a realizable asset. It costs a man money to indulge in vice but for a woman it is money in the pocket."[33]

Prostitutes recognized this simple truth. One young woman explained, "I was broke and had no work. I had nobody here and I didn't know what to do. He offered a room and I took it."[34] Another prostitute who gave her family her entire wages but received none in return for her own amusements, replied, "Do you suppose I am going back to earn five or six dollars a week in a factory, and at that, never have a cent of it to spend for myself, when I can earn that amount any night, and often much more?"[35]

Earning more money than other working women, however, was not a sufficient reason for prostitutes to risk the social isolation and ostracism that frequently accompanied a life "in the trade." The personal and social costs of joining a deviant subculture had to be offset by some other compelling motivation.

The disturbance of a fragile family economy by death, desertion, or divorce was a situation that frequently created such need. In many working class families, each member—including the mother as well as any grown children—contributed to a family economy that barely supported their survival. From the *Summary Report* it appears that American daughters continued to view their earnings as part of a family economy. When they married, they similarly contributed their salary to their "family of procreation." Over 90 percent of female workers during the early part of the twentieth century gave all of their earnings to their families. Such wages, significantly, often represented a vital portion—from one-fourth to two-fifths—of the family's combined income.[36] The vast majority of women did *not* work for "pin money." "It is evident," the *Summary Report* noted, "that the amount these workers retain for their own individual use is too small to account for their going to work. In the main, their earnings go into the family fund, from which they are fed and clothed, but no part of which is looked upon as particularly theirs."[37]

What happened to an already fragile family economy in the case of death, desertion, or divorce? This was the situation in many prostitutes' families. Since prostitutes experienced an unusually high incidence of troubled or "broken" homes, their families had probably suffered the loss of a significant part of the family economy. The death or desertion of a working father or husband, for example, created severe economic crises in working-class homes. Like Maimie Pinzer, some daughters were pulled out of school to help support the family. Although they contributed to the family economy, they usually received little or no money of their own for clothing or social amusements. The net effect was a daughter who worked six days a week and was bitterly resentful at the loss of the few amusements she had previously enjoyed.[38]

The life histories of prostitutes reveal the extent to which such family economic crises contributed to women's choices. A twenty-five-year-old Swedish prostitute recalled that when her mother died she had to leave home at the age of sixteen to find work. Finding employment as a servant, she became an involuntary sexual partner of the husband of her mistress. When caught and later discharged, she found a position as a nurse to an invalid woman whose husband demanded occasional sexual favors as part of her work. After her father left the city in which she was employed, she felt she could become a full-time prostitute without disgracing the only living member of her family. When asked why she became a prostitute, she replied, "For the money that was in it." Without any family, she also experienced a sense of loneliness and worthlessness. The lack of family, however, gave her freedom to "get paid" for what her employers had already required: sexual favors. "Nobody really cares what becomes of me," she said, "so why should I starve to be decent? Only one week this year have I made less than $30 and so far I haven't spent a cent on doctors either."[39]

Another prostitute revealed the difficulties in her family's economic and social life. Her father did not work and her mother had fallen ill. In addition to the four dollars that the young daughter earned from flower-making, she supplemented her income by "hustling" on the side.[40] A crisis in the family economy also resulted when a wife became widowed or was deserted by her husband. A twenty-two-year-old admitted that her life was easier as a "widow with means" kept by a wealthy married businessman than as an unskilled menial laborer working six days a week for subsistence wages. By entertaining her benefactor one or two evenings a week, she was free to entertain other young men for additional income as well.[41]

Writing to the Illinois Senate investigation on the relationship between low wages and prostitution, another widow described the impossibility of supporting herself and her child on a typical female worker's salary of six dollars a week. "I am a widow with a little girl to support," the letter began,

> and I am employed in one of the largest department stores on State Street and give my time from 8:15 to 6:00 p.m. and at present I am doing two persons' work for the small salary of six dollars a week and I know I am doing my duty to my employer. Now, I must clothe my little daughter and myself, pay rent and buy food. My expenses for the day: ten cents car fare, five cents lunch, ten cents child's lunch, 50 cents a day for rent, 30 cents for supper: I make $1.15. Now I am obliged to do a little sewing in the evening after I have worked hard all day to try and make my expenses, and my health is not very good, and I am not able to do very much in the evening. Now where is the money to buy clothes and books for the child's education? And if a clerk does not look just so, she is sent home. How can you expect a woman to take care of a child and herself on $6 a week? No one can blame a girl or anyone for doing wrong when they are obliged to work for such wages. . . . I kindly ask you to withhold my name.[42]

The loss of a husband's employment frequently created a crisis in the family economy. It was not easy for an unskilled wife to support the entire family on "women's" wages. One woman explained to the Hartford investigators: "My husband lost his position; we were starving. I went out first with the grocer in my own home; then a baker; finally I drifted into it [prostitution]. At first it hurt my husband, but after a short time he stopped looking for work and depended on me. That settled it. I left him and went to Springfield for a while. After I heard that he had left town, I came back. I wouldn't trust any man now."[43] A street-walker who solicited a Chicago investigator similarly explained that she had only recently begun working the street because of money needed after her husband's serious illness.[44]

The seasonal employment that plagued working-class men also caused women to search for means of supporting their families. Maimie Pinzer, for example, became exasperated at her first husband's alternating periods of seasonal layoffs and subsistence wages. To help support them, she secretly "dated" men of "means."[45]

Such "occasional" prostitution has always been part of the history of the trade. As the Wisconsin vice report revealed, many women during the early years of the twentieth century quietly slipped into and out of prostitution as economic need required. Daughters who wanted or needed more spending money, widows who had to support their families on subsistence wages, wives who attempted to compensate for a husband's sudden unemployment, and working women who were laid off during the slack season of the trade could acquire "easy money" through the practice of occasional prostitution. Katharine Davis found that only 59.50 percent of the prostitutes she studied at Bedford practiced the trade on a permanent basis. Of streetwalkers interviewed in New York, however, 95 percent practiced prostitution fairly steadily.[46]

That many poor women viewed prostitution as an important means of supplementing their income is evident from literature of the period. One female reformer noted that German and Swedish domestic workers commonly supplemented their salary through occasional prostitution. A dance hall prostitute explained to an underground investigator in Chicago that the $6 weekly wage she earned in the basement of a department store did not cover her basic expenses. To supplement her income, she therefore "hustled" three nights a week at a dance hall. Another saleswoman, Jennie, came from Pittsburgh to find work in Akron, Ohio. After five months of starving on $6 a week (she was totally self-supporting), she agreed to be kept by a man in an apartment in the East End, but still kept her position in the store. During the annual winter layoff at a packing plant, another young female worker said she was unable to find another job. To survive, she began going to cheap hotels for money with a man she had met at a local picnic.[47]

It was not unusual for women who occasionally practiced prostitution to continue supporting their families. One woman explained that ever since her father had died, she had been supporting an invalid mother and two smaller children on her subsistence wages. In addition, she "kept company" with a young man several times a week to increase her weekly income. In her study of industrial female workers, Elizabeth Butler found that many young women who had continued to help support their families while working outside the home also supported them as occasional prostitutes. Rose, one young prostitute whom Butler interviewed, was employed at a ribbon counter in a department store. With a mother and two sisters dependent upon her wages, she began supplementing her income by occasional prostitution. When the management discovered her activities, she was fired. She later joined a brothel in Ohio, from where she continued to send money to her family.[48] Most women attempted to hide their activities from the families they supported. At least one young woman who earned four dollars a week at a retail store told her family that she was earning a weekly wage of nine dollars to camouflage the fact that she received $5 a week from a married man for her occasional favors.[49]

In addition to the inadequate pay that women received for "women's work," many prostitutes favorably compared prostitution to the other occupations available to working-class women. Many of these occupations (dance hall hostess, waitress, department store clerk, factory worker, domestic worker) made the difference between "pleasing" male customers or male employers and occasional prostitution seem rather arbitrary. A former waitress turned prostitute explained to the Illinois Senate Committee on Vice:

> You wait on a man and he smiles at you. You see the chance to get a tip and you smile back. Next day he returns and you try harder than ever to please him. Then right away he wants to make a date, and offer you money and presents if you'll be a good fellow and go out with him. And if you refuse

and he stops coming in, the boss jumps on your neck and wants to know why you are losing his customers. Then the next thing there's a new girl in your job and you're out on the street. For my work in the restaurant I get $3.00 a week and my meals and a few dimes each day in tips just enough to pay my room rent and for my laundry. If I didn't pick up a little money on the side, I'd have to go naked. If it wasn't for my folks, I'd quit bluffing and get into the game right.[50]

The poor working conditions found in these occupations, along with subsistence wages, greatly contributed to young women's dissatisfaction with "respectable" work. Saleswomen who earned six dollars a week, for example, were required to dress as fashionably as their wealthy customers—an impossible task on their wages. Many prostitutes, on the other hand, could afford expensive clothes on the higher wages they earned.[51]

Sexual harassment added further insult to women's subsistence wages. In order to obtain, or even retain, a low paying job, many young women found that they were expected to extend sexual favors to their male employers.[52] In several of her jobs, Maimie Pinzer encountered such sexual harassment. Greatly in debt, Maimie began working for a tailor, doing his books every night. In one letter, she wrote:

When I had worked for ten nights, knowing it would be $5.00, and it would pay the debt to the real estate man in Phil., I asked for it. And then a few things happened. This man had always been apparently interested only in my work there, and I hadn't the least idea that he might become "fresh"— and then I wasn't sure, because what he said might have been only meant in kindness. . . . Then, the night I wanted the $5—I worked a bit longer . . . and he came in from the front of his store and said I had better quit, as no doubt I was hungry. I remarked that I was, and that I'd like him to pay me. He came over then to the desk, and he point-blank—without a word of introduction—made a proposal to me that I go up to the city with him and he would give me "a couple of five spots."

I was so surprised I couldn't think quick enough to say something, and I think now that he took my silence for a sort of consent. And before I could say Jack Robinson, he had me tight in his arms. Of course, I struggled and screamed—and in a few seconds was out on the street, leaving behind several things. Seemingly no one heard me, because next door several men were standing listlessly. When I told the folks, [the people Maimie happened to be living with at this point in her working life], Mr. Arons advised that I should say nothing to anyone else about it, because he [her employer] is a very coarse man, and to justify himself, might say bad things about me that would make me leave town—as this is a very small village.

The next evening, Mr. Arons stopped into his store to get my sun umbrella and little handbag, and also the $5.00—and he refused *point-blank* to give them to him, and said he would give them to me if I called. And somehow, to date, I have not had the courage to go for them . . . I really think he would make life here impossible for me if I troubled him. He has been in business here for eighteen years, and I feel his word would have some weight. As usual—after all this happened, I learned that some years ago this same man received a horse whipping from the husband of a respected lady here whom he insulted and *assaulted*, perhaps as he did me. Really, what with this experience, I feel as though I had been thru a fire. I am almost stripped of everything, and I can't see how I could have helped it.[53]

Later, when Maimie was working in a New York firm writing letters, she again encountered sexual harassment on the job. As she explained to Fanny Howe in one letter, she had just finished the day's work when the last mail arrived and she conscientiously decided that two of the pieces needed immediate answers. She finished the last two letters, and started to leave, feeling satisfied that she had done more than her share. "Everyone but the manager had gone when I got up to go," she explained,

He asked me if I had answered the necessary letters, and I said yes. He said, "Wait until I look them over." As he did, I saw him making two piles, I knew he was going to say I had to answer one of them. I felt myself getting hot and then cold—because it was not just. I was very tired and hungry and it was 6:30. And I felt I was going to cry, so I walked to the door. And he sprang up, and said, "You! finish this work or you needn't come back." Surely I could not afford to lose my position—but you can't understand how terrible it is to feel you must have to take such treatment. He grabbed me by the arm and jerked me back. And I just couldn't control myself—and I picked up a heavy letter file and went after him. . . . When I began to think calmly, I saw what I had done was going to cost me my position. And the terror of being in the position I was in last spring [the episode described above] frightened me so. I began to explain to him how tired I was, and how the extra work was wearing on my nerves. . . . And then he started in to say how I had tried to impress the New York office and finally "worked my way into the manager's attention"—and then he said he supposed I'd kept a few 'dates' with him, and that I only made an ass of myself, etc. etc. He heaped abuse on me; and when I could stand it no longer, I told him that he had no right to accuse me of being friendly with the N.Y. manager, as I gave him no reason to believe I was the sort. And he laughed insinuatingly and said he could have made a "hit" with me too, had he cared to, but he didn't go in for "one-eyed women"*—and I didn't wait to hear any more but came home.[54]

Maimie's outrage at being unfairly accused, in addition to the actual sexual harassment that she encountered on the job, was not uncommon. Jean, a college-educated woman with whom Maimie eventually formed a small multigraphing firm, had experienced sexual harassment while attempting to forge a career as a reporter. In describing Jean's background to Mrs. Howe, Maimie explained that

---

* Maimie wore a patch over the eye she had lost to syphilitic infection.

she found that being a girl—and a rather nice-looking one—was making her position there unbearable. The man she was directly under made advances to her; and whether he meant well or not, it was entirely repulsive to Jean, for he is a man of perhaps fifty or sixty, and a big, redfaced, fat, coarse type. (I've seen him.) Jean had to resign, she couldn't stand him. It was about that time I met her.[55]

As a result of the sexual harassment women frequently encountered at work, some women workers may have come to the conclusion that sexual purity was a privilege unavailable to the poor. The idea of prostituting oneself for low wages may have appeared absurd when compared with the higher wages offered by outright prostitution.

In the industrial trades, women faced particularly arduous working conditions. Seasonal layoffs in the millinery, dressmaking, embroidery, and fur and food processing trades constantly threatened women's economic security. In addition, the hours which women worked were generally long and tedious. The customary working day for women in Pittsburgh industries, for example, was approximately ten hours a day. Unlike men, moreover, many women returned home to face the unpaid work of child rearing and housework.[56]

Factory work left little energy for domestic or leisure activities. Poor ventilation, crowded working conditions, and uncontrolled noise and humidity levels combined to enervate factory operatives' strength. One young female worker described the tedium of her working life as follows: "We only went from bed to work and from work to bed again . . . and sometimes if we sat up a little while at home we were so tired we could not speak to the rest and we hardly knew what we were talking about. And still, though there was nothing for us but bed and machines, we could not earn enough to take care of ourselves through the slack season."[57] The monotony of factory work endangered women's health as well. A young working woman named Sadie Frowne described her experience in a factory. "The Machines," she said, "go like mad all day, cause the faster you work the more money you get. Sometimes in my haste I get my finger caught and the needle goes right through it. It goes through quick, though, so that it does not hurt much. I bind up the finger with a piece of cotton and go on working." As Jane Addams noted, the effect of long working hours and tedious work combined to create strong human needs for escape through, for example, entertainment, amusement, and alcohol. Sadie Frowne explained that "the Machines are run by foot power and at the end of the day one feels so weak that there is a great temptation to lie right down and go to sleep. But you must go out and get air, and have some pleasure. . . . Sometimes we go to Coney Island, where there are good dancing places and sometimes we go to Ulmer Park to picnics. I am very fond of dancing, and, in fact, all sorts of pleasure."[58] In contrast, prostitution, in some women's eyes, appeared to offer the sporting life itself as work.

Prostitutes who had formerly worked as domestic servants also complained of the working conditions of that occupation. In addition to sexual harassment from husbands, domestic workers complained of their hours: they worked from sunrise to nine in the evening, leaving precious little time to socialize with their peers. Because they received room and board, their wages were considerably lower than other female workers. On the average, most domestic servants earned three dollars a week. With no place to entertain male visitors, except in the kitchen, domestic servants often felt isolated from the social world of other young working people. They rarely frequented the dance halls, ice cream parlors, and bars, which attracted young factory workers.[59]

I have emphasized the particular difficulties which domestic servants and factory operatives faced because these two occupations accounted for the highest percentage of prostitutes' former occupations.[60] Since 40.4 percent of female workers in the United States in 1900 were employed as domestic servants, it should not be surprising that a high percentage of prostitutes had formerly worked as domestics.[61] Many women were increasingly entering the manufacturing industries, so it is also reasonable to assume that the second largest group of prostitutes had been employed in that capacity. The Bureau of Labor *Summary Report* similarly pointed out that women in the industrial trades were only slightly overrepresented in the prostitute population.[62]

Some female occupations appear to be overrepresented or underrepresented in the prostitute population. In a study comparing prostitutes' former occupations with the percentage of women employed in that particular vocation, it was found that certain factors, such as whether or not work was seasonal, affected whether women in a particular occupation turned to prostitution. Laundresses, for example, one of the poorest classes of female employees, were found to be underrepresented in the New York City prostitute population, probably because they had year-round work.[63]

Even more interesting is that women employed in the higher-paying occupations appeared in nearly all studies of prostitutes. (Whether or not they were overrepresented or underrepresented is impossible to tell.) The Committee of Fourteen *Department Store Investigation Report* of New York revealed that the *highest*, and not the lowest, paid saleswomen most often turned to prostitution.[64] Theatrical workers, office workers, telephone operators, typists, and stenographers—all of whom received higher wages than domestic or factory operatives—appeared with a surprisingly high degree of frequency among the lists of prostitutes' former occupations.[65]

Some prostitutes had never been gainfully employed at all. The Hartford study of sixty-six prostitutes revealed that twenty had been married and never before employed. A Chicago study of thirty prostitutes similarly found that three women had never before worked for payment.[66]

Although it appears that prostitutes' former occupations differed little from other working women, they may have felt particularly contemptuous of their employment as unskilled and menial workers. When the Vice Commission of Chicago pointed out that some prostitutes viewed their work as "the easiest way," it may have expressed an opinion with which many prostitutes would have agreed. In George Bernard Shaw's play, *Mrs. Warren's Profession*, the heroine presents a prostitute's perspective on exploitation: "Do you think we were such fools as to let other people trade in our good looks by employing us as shop girls, or barmaids, or waitresses, when we could trade them in ourselves and get all the profits instead of starvation wages? Not likely."[67] Did prostitutes during the Progressive Era agree with this perspective? Did they consciously view prostitution as less exploitative than other kinds of work?

Certainly, we can never actually know how most prostitutes felt about their work. Interviews with the women, however, provide some indication of their attitudes. A twenty-three-year-old prostitute interviewed by the Illinois Senate Committee, for example, liked to pose as a "respectable wealthy woman" during her annual lavish trips to Atlantic City. Delighting in mingling with "society" on money earned as a prostitute, she pointed out that she had never been able to earn enough money for a vacation by "honest work."[68]

Another young prostitute, who lived in a furnished room where she received her customers, expressed similar disdain for respectable women's work. She had left her job as a waitress in another city so that her parents would not discover her new occupation. Asked why she would not consider working as a domestic servant, she answered, "I'll live fast and die early rather than become somebody's kitchen slave. Restaurant work is bad enough, but I won't be a dog in anybody's kitchen." Having never married, this twenty-six-year-old, whose fierce pride kept her from becoming a servant, stated that she had never met a man whom she wished to live with—either as a wife or as a mistress. Another prostitute explained why she detested the life of a domestic servant. "The ladies," she explained, "when they got money to hire servants imagine they have some form of dog to kick around, and I don't want to be kicked around."[69]

One formerly married young prostitute, whose husband had stopped supporting her, found employment as a house servant. After visiting a "low life" café one evening, she began to consider the "money making possibilities" in prostitution. Earning more in one night than she had earned in two weeks as a domestic, she swore that she would never "work" for a living again. May, a sixteen-year-old prostitute, left home and employment at a department store. When asked why she had turned to prostitution, she replied that "hustling was easier." Tantine, a nineteen-year-old who solicited a Chicago investigator stated that she had just started to "hustle because it was easier than waiting on tables for one dollar a day."[70]

A consistent theme that prostitutes voiced during interviews was that prostitution offered "easier" work than other available occupations. Flora, age twenty-two when committed to a home for wayward girls, learned at a Brooklyn department store "how easily she could get money by not working hard." Another young prostitute, addicted to heroin, told Hartford investigators that she had wearied of being a waitress in a cheap restaurant. "I grew tired of the continual drudge in a restaurant; and too many chances were given me," she explained. Eight months later, she married and supported her husband with her earnings as a prostitute. Paulette, a prostitute who had worked in a department store, felt that her employer expected women to be partially supported by men anyway: "After I had been working two months," she testified, "I left the position. If a girl in a store wears soiled clothing, they will tell her about it. You have to work in a department store for years and years before you get anything. While in the store, I heard of a case of a good girl getting six dollars a week. She asked for more money. She said she couldn't live on that. The man said, 'Can't you get some-body to keep you?' "[71]

What was "easier" about life as a prostitute? Some women noted the shorter hours worked by prostitutes. As a rule, prostitutes worked from nine in the evening until two in the morning. During the morning they slept and during the afternoon their time was their own. In some brothels, meals were cooked and served by servants. In addition, laundry facilities and maids were often provided in the best brothels. One eighteen year old who had quit her five-dollar-a-week job began earning thirty-five dollars a week at a brothel. After splitting the cus-tomary "half" with the madam, buying the required lavish clothing, and purchas-ing the necessary cosmetics and medical services, she was just as broke as she had been in her former occupation. She now enjoyed a higher standard of living, however, which included well-made clothes and regular meals. Another prosti-tute, who quit working in a laundry and her occasional hustling on the side for full-time work in a sporting house, similarly boasted of the improvement in her standard of living:

> I felt that if I was right in a house, I would be able to take care of myself, take care of my health and everything better than where a girl worked every day and had to see people on the outside at night. . . . As far as having respect of people goes, I wasn't anymore respected in that line than in any other line. I was sporting just the same anyway. . . . If I am in a house I can get my rest, and I am not out late at night. I can rest and I don't have to get up early in the morning. I am provided with good board and with a good room and I am able to look after my health.[72]

Although many other prostitutes faced extreme brutality and serious health hazards in their trade, it is nevertheless important to note that prostitution was viewed by *some* women as an "easier" and upgraded lifestyle. During the 1909 shirtwaist strike in New York, for example, the well-known Industrial Workers of the World (I.W.W.) organizer Elizabeth Gurley Flynn recalled that when the young female strikers were jailed, the "prostitutes in jail jeered at their low wages and told them they could do much better at *their* trade."[73] For other women, it may have been clear from the start that prostitution was "easier" than any other available employment.[74]

Higher wages and the possibility of better working conditions made prostitution "attractive" to poor women precisely because it offered the promise of social and economic mobility. For young men at the turn of the century, the American dream of upward mobility and material success still seemed an accessible goal. The legend of Horatio Alger's meteoric climb to wealth and power through hard work and frugal living had become an integral part of American folklore. Although educated along with boys and exposed to the same myths, most girls were never expected to achieve fame and fortune by their own efforts. Instead, a female's best chance was to "catch" an upwardly mobile young Horatio Alger and vicariously enjoy his status and wealth as *Mrs.* Horatio Alger. How to accomplish this feat was a secret passed on from one generation of women to the next—a young woman had to cultivate her physical appearance and learn the gentle art of bartering sexual favors for the promise of future social and economic security in marriage.[75]

Because of their class *and* their gender, working-class women found themselves barred from social and economic competition. The effect of such blocked mobility frequently results in innovative strategies of circumventing obstacles or in self-destructive behavior.[76] In order to achieve the socially prescribed goals of social status and material wealth, women frequently resorted to deceptive means, not the least of which was to "catch" a husband through coy and manipulative behavior.

Many young women came to view prostitution as a step toward such upward mobility. Through practicing occasional or full-time prostitution, they hoped to earn sufficient money to buy the proper clothes to attract a promising husband. Daughters of immigrants, in particular, rebelled against the idea that one should dress according to one's "class." The urge to dress like a "lady" was exceedingly strong. The Committee of Fourteen *Department Store Investigation Report* in New York found that clothes were nearly an obsession of the better-paid workers.[77]

The Vice Commission of Chicago interviewed several prostitutes who explained that their desire for more money came *not* from abject poverty but from a desire for a new hat, new shoes, or a general wish to improve their appearance. A nineteen-year-old Polish factory worker told the Illinois Senate Committee that she had sex relations with men at work for money or articles of clothing. Boasting of the twenty pairs of silk stockings she had accumulated, she nevertheless viewed a respectable marriage as the ultimate goal of economic and social security: "I got to get out of this place and meet some guy, and marry him before my folks get wise," she explained. "If my father knew he'd kill me." A Polish laundry worker who earned a weekly wage of seven dollars was deserted by her husband. She justified her occasional prostitution with the statement that "men don't hunt in laundries for wives."[78]

Reformers who worked with prostitutes soon discovered that prostitution did in fact symbolize potential upward mobility to many young women. Maude Miner quoted a young prostitute as explaining, "I thought I'd get style like the other girls do. . . . I saw them dress swell and make nice money." A sixteen-year-old prostitute who lived at home and had no job claimed that "it was the easiest way to get money and fine clothes." One reformer pointed out that dance halls became so attractive to working-class women because they offered the opportunity of meeting college men sowing their "wild oats."[79]

In their memoirs, both Pauline Tabor and Sally Stanford pointed to the number of young women who had viewed *and* used prostitution as a means of upward mobility. "Rosie," a prostitute who worked for Tabor, "was just one of a number of my girls—and I guess that several hundred worked for me at one time or another over the years—who used prostitution as a stepping-stone to a better, more prosperous life in a society from which they had once retreated." Rosie left Tabor's house with a hefty bank account and returned to college. Later, she worked as a teacher, married, and raised a family of four children.[80] Sally Stanford, having left behind her life as a prostitute for a career as a famous madam in San Francisco, retired as a prosperous restaurant owner in Sausalito, California.[81]

With her typical insight and candor, Maimie Pinzer, too, perceived the limited options a young woman faced in her desire for a decent and upwardly mobile life. While attempting to go "straight," under the tutelage of a social worker named Mr. Welsh and her faithful correspondent Fanny Howe, Maimie looked for work but found that few jobs were available to a one-eyed unskilled woman. Although she was aware she could find menial work, she frankly confessed, "Of course there is scrubbing of floors and dishwashing to be considered—and since I wouldn't do that, it is plain to be seen, I do not *sincerely* want to go to work."[82] Nevertheless, Maimie did try her hand at an array of jobs, from addressing envelopes to soliciting ads. In each case, subsistence wages, exhausting hours, and sexual harassment from employers resulted in greater despondency and deprivation. Describing her reasons for quitting the letter addressing business, she admitted, "I refused to work for $3.40 from sun-up to sun down." To ease her hunger during these periods of impoverishment, she drank hot water, counted every penny, and complained to Fanny Howe of the poverty that kept her from acquiring any new clothes or enjoying any social amusements.

Wavering between her new "respectable life" and her memories of being a "lady" by dating men for cash, Maimie honestly revealed her dilemma: "I spent 3 days in despair thinking of ditching it all and taking up again the life of least resistance." Without the financial assistance of her new friends—Mrs. Howe and social workers who continually kept her afloat—Maimie knew she would refuse to live indefinitely as a pauper. "My trouble," she wrote Fanny Howe, "is that I am a working girl who has lived like a 'lady' and it's hard to curb my desires and live as the working girl should." Considering the plight of women like herself, Maimie rhetorically asked in one letter,

> Then what do girls do, who not only haven't a good appearance, thru a like affliction [her eye], and who aren't able to see as well as others, yet who haven't been gifted with intelligence enough to pick up an education suffi-ciently good to get positions such as . . . [I] have had? I don't know ex-actly what they do, unless they resort to living as I did formerly; or perhaps marry; or if they do work, are laundresses, potato peelers, scrubwomen. And perhaps, instead of feeling any pride because I have been able to pick up a little knowledge, I should regard it as a "dangerous thing," since it takes me out of the class that I've every reason to believe I should be in.[83]

With her strong desire for self-improvement and education, Maimie could not bear to live an impoverished and deprived life. Even when she established an actual business in Montreal, the Business Aid Bureau, Maimie found that "all the forces of the Business world in Montreal are arranged against a woman develop-ing a real business . . . in spite of that I am going to work up a real Business that will be a Big Money maker."[84]

For the many young women who found their ambitions blocked by their gender and class, marriage of course represented the most respectable path to economic security. In describing her first marriage, however, Maimie bitterly complained of her disappointment with the seasonal layoffs that her husband experienced. "When I married him," she confessed to Fanny Howe, "It was as a sort of anchor. I was living more or less uncleanly; I had lost my eye and weighed 96 pounds—and I reasoned it all out as one would a business proposition." Later, when his continual unemployment failed to support them, Maimie con-fided her disillusionment: "When I saw how useless trying to use him to earn any more than a bare meagre livelihood was, I gave up in disgust as I began to see that I was still attractive to men, I began to use what charms I might possess to make it possible to have a few of the luxuries which had become necessities."[85]

When life became too difficult, Maimie temporarily moved into her childhood sweetheart's hotel apartment, where she wrote ecstatically about her aesthetic surroundings and comfortable living quarters. Later, after founding a home for girls like herself in Montreal, she in fact married her childhood sweetheart. De-spite her genuine affection for him, she had carefully scrutinized his earning capacity before the marriage: "The thought came to me—why shouldn't I keep up the friendship with him . . . and though Ira is but a boy, he might some day be in good financial circumstances—for he is a very earnest and hard worker and earns from $50 to $75.00 a week. . . . And, too, I like Ira much better than Albert [her first husband]."[86]

Maimie's desire for a cultured and comfortable life became insistent: "I feel a gnawing discontent all the time," she wrote, "because I see so much that I desire, I envy the women I see on the street and I haven't even the courage to work in the office with the clerks there who are all so well dressed." Acknowledging the liabilities she faced as a woman, Maimie voiced her envy of men's position in society: "I wish I was born a man. I know what I'd do this morning. I'd button up my coat and jump on the tail end of a train and steal a ride to wherever it was going and when I'd get there I'd stop to consider, 'What next?'"[87]

Like other working-class women of the period, Maimie accurately perceived her options for survival: marriage, unskilled labor at subsistence wages, or prostitution. She had tried all three and ended up marrying a second time when she last wrote to Fanny Howe. Her experience underscores the differences that men and women faced when they considered their economic security. The Illinois Senate Committee, for example, described the different "success stories" of a brother and sister from the same small town. The brother became a successful businessman. The sister first found work as a clerk, where she was seduced and later abandoned by her employer. Each new position she found required that she have "immoral relations with the employer." After finally gaining employment as a saleslady, she found that she could not support herself on six dollars a week. She eventually "yielded" to a fellow worker and began "sporting" for extra money. With another ambitious female friend, she set up a small flat where they received male patrons and enjoyed a thriving business. Like her brother, the sister had become a successful businesswoman. He, however, could enjoy the social status denied her.[88]

Although economic factors directly or indirectly caused much prostitution, many prostitutes had in fact listed "personal reasons" such as "bad family conditions" as the major reason why they turned to prostitution. Family life, of course, cannot be separated from economic factors; many troubled or "broken" families resulted from the unrelenting pressures caused by a fragile family economy. For the daughters and wives who experienced such economic deprivations, certain social and personal problems, originating in the family, affected their choice to turn to prostitution.

In some prostitutes' backgrounds, for example, there was a history of incestuous sexual activity. Maimie Pinzer, it will be remembered, had first been sexually assaulted by her uncle. The Vice Commission of Chicago cited 47 girls out of 2,241 institutionalized females who had first been seduced by a member of their family (19 by their father). Thirty-two out of seventy-two girls brought before the Juvenile Court of Chicago similarly revealed a history of incestuous sexual behavior. Jennie, a nineteen-year-old prostitute who was interviewed by the Vice Commission of Chicago, said that her own brother had first raped her. She soon after got in "trouble" (not specified) and left home. After arriving in Chicago and living with an old man and his wife, she found herself pregnant with a baby that died at birth. When interviewed, Jennie worked in a laundry room and solicited at night at cheap hotels for one and a half dollars.[89]

Since incest was, and continues to be, a widespread sexual taboo, one must ask whether young girls who had been raped, seduced, or sexually initiated by a member of their own family experienced deep internalized feelings of guilt, shame, and humiliation. If so, they may have continued to view themselves as unworthy individuals who were already "ruined." As a result, prostitution could have appeared as an appropriate occupation for one who was already "tainted." Interestingly, Gail Sheehy's contemporary study of prostitutes in New York in the early 1970s similarly revealed a high percentage of prostitutes who came from broken homes and had experienced incest at a relatively early age.[90]

Many of the young women who later became prostitutes also had a history of alcoholism in their families, which may indicate a degree of parental neglect in early childhood. By adolescence, many of the girls already had a history of juvenile delinquency as well.[91] A young prostitute explained to Hartford authorities how early identification with delinquent and "deviant" groups influenced her perspective on life: "I slipped when I was a kid, and believe me my mother put me in a home. I did not know a thing when I went in, but I was wise when I came out. Girls there told me how to make money and lots of stuff. I came out educated. I stayed home for a bluff for a while, but I hate my mother and _____ made up her mind and we beat it together. I am of age now and they can't stop me now."[92]

Prostitutes frequently voiced their contempt for their parents and home life. In many cases they may have been rebelling against overly strict parents who permitted them too little social freedom. In addition, the stories of incest and alcoholism point to deprivation of parental love and affection. When prostitutes stressed their "loneliness" or "need for company" as a reason for entering prostitution, they may have been describing a history of emotional deprivation and parental neglect.

In her study of juvenile females brought before night court for prostitution, Maude Miner found that many of the girls had been on the street since they were children, taking care of themselves as best they could, while avoiding the violent tantrums and abuse of drunken parents. The Portland, Maine, vice report similarly noted how young female children were left adrift in rooming houses and in apartments by neglectful parents who could no longer take care of their children. Although somewhat melodramatic, Stephen Crane's portrait of *Maggie* accurately pictured the plight of a daughter reared by a broken and alcoholic mother who gave her daughter little love or support. When Maggie sought emotional comfort with a man she met through her older brother, her mother disowned her.[93] It is not surprising that, with their families torn by unemployment, early death, divorce, desertion, alcoholism, and disease, some young women felt strong human needs for love and affection and sought that companionship with young men. Unfortunately, such attachments all too often ended in abandonment by a man not interested in marriage. Frequently, families disowned and "locked out" their daughters.[94]

The sexual double standard that condemned young women for the same sexual activity permitted men resulted in many tragedies. One unmarried young mother bitterly complained of her sole responsibility for the child that had resulted from a love affair: "He doesn't have any of the trouble or disgrace; why should I have to support the baby and bear all the disgrace?" Another prostitute, who had worked for a pimp, similarly attacked the double standard: "If they want to stop this 'white slave' business, why don't they get the fellers? He got six months and I got three years; it ain't straight."[95]

Without the financial support of a family, a single woman faced the bleak prospect of attempting to support herself on subsistence wages or turning to prostitution. As one madam of a brothel testified after twenty-two years in the business, prostitutes were the result of "low wages" and having been "thrown out on the world without a home. They haven't any companionship and they naturally fall into prostitution for the sake of company and companionship."[96]

Some prostitutes admitted that early love affairs led them to later prostitution. Much bitterness was evident in these stories. One prostitute, for example, explained that she had kept company with a man who later abandoned her. "I was in love with a fellow," she said, "and kept company with him because he could not marry until his mother died." After the mother's death, however, the woman discovered that her lover had already married another woman. Soon afterward, she started drinking. "Never again," she said when asked about marrying. "I don't care what becomes of me."[97]

Given the emotional deprivation that some prostitutes experienced in their family life, what did prostitution offer to ease their "loneliness" or "need for company"? From the few pieces of evidence available, one can only speculate about what kinds of psychological need prostitution might have fulfilled.

Although brothel inmates tended to be somewhat transient, there are stories of close and supportive friendships between young women who lived together in houses. A prostitute from Hartford explained how important her friendship with another prostitute had become: "My mother died when I was born. My father has always been a rummy and I had to get along the best I know how. I longed for company. Then I met a girl older than me. She taught me how to get money. She is true blue. We live together." Another prostitute was described by investigators as "always alone" until she went "public with her favors." When interviewed, she emphasized her two good friends, also prostitutes, all of whom went "around together."[98] Despite its potential brutality and exploitation, prostitution offered the immediate promise of other women, or a procurer or pimp who *promised* marriage and endless devotion.

Case studies from the period richly illustrate the various family problems that led women to consider prostitution as a better alternative to living at home. In a study of 229 "wayward" girls, the death of one or both parents had resulted in sudden impoverishment and consequent deprivation for the daughters in the families. Jennie, one of these interviewed young women, had lost her mother when she was two years old. Her father had tuberculosis and was an alcoholic. Her stepmother evidently took little care of her. At fifteen, Jennie was committed to a home after having "improper relations with boys." A Mrs. Brown, who was widowed and had five children, earned $2 a day sewing. After eight years of living as a pauper, the mother was stricken with tuberculosis and became unable to work. She now depended on the earnings of her eldest daughter, aged eleven. The daughter became "wild" and began running around with a sexually promis-cuous crowd. Arlena, another committed "inmate," began working when her father deserted the family when she was seven years old. Her mother remarried but the stepfather died when Arlena was ten. The mother worked outside the home. At fifteen, Arlena was committed to a home with a child of her own.[99]

An important theme reappearing throughout the letters to Fanny Howe was Maimie Pinzer's total estrangement from her family. The loss of her father at thirteen had changed Maimie's life. Forced out of school to support the family, Maimie battled with her mother over her right to have money of her own. She also hated her mother's ignorant and insinuating condemnations of her cravings for a becoming appearance and an active social life. Such generational conflict, especially between immigrant parents and their daughters, was a commonly noted problem during the period.

After Maimie began working at a department store, she experienced tre-mendous relief at having access to her own money. After she was imprisoned in a "home" for her "incorrigible" behavior with men, her family shunned her—even when she went "straight" and demonstrated her willingness to lead an impover-ished, though respectable, life. "They all hate me," she confided to Mrs. Howe, "I must be somehow at fault or why doesn't one of them like me?" Her immigrant family was headed by a mother who, like the other children, could not forgive Maimie her past. Maimie tearfully confided, "I've got 3 brothers, a mother and many uncles and aunts and I can't turn to one of them and my brother said he'd consider I'd done the family a kindness if I would get off the Earth."[100] Unwilling to return to her native Philadelphia for fear of ostracism, Maimie attempted to transcend their rejections through hard work and a respectable marriage. Al-though she willingly rushed to her family's side during emergencies, she sadly discovered that they shunned her requests for aid when she found herself in dire straits.

Only later, as an adult who had gained a degree of self-esteem through the aid of Mrs. Howe and others, was Maimie able to reconstruct her life. Founding a home for girls like herself, she easily recognized the problems that affected the young women with whom she generously shared her own apartment. Maimie understood, like Jane Addams and other enlightened reformers, how many of these young women had been rejected by their families for their "sexual transgressions." A peer counselor way before her time, she was sensitive to the emotional deprivation that many of her "girls" had suffered in impoverished, diseased, and embattled homes, and she provided a warm and nurturing environment for many young women. Unlike the "nosy" reformers she detested, Maimie worked day and night to find employment for the young women who slept in her bed, ate her food, and became part of her new surrogate family until she remarried.

Examining the causes that had led these girls to her doorstep, Maimie concluded that the presence of some loving family member or adult was an important deterrent to prostitution. Many girls, she noted, led impoverished lives. Yet only some became prostitutes. Based on her own experiences and on those of the girls she aided, Maimie decided that the lack of *felt* or *demonstrated* love was an essential factor in these girls' lives. "I am sure I lacked love," she wrote to Howe in one of her letters. "Many girls before they give themselves over to the sinful life, have the love of their parents, but people of the sort they spring from—as were my people—are singularly undemonstrative and often it isn't for lack of love, that the girls go astray, as much as for some evidence of it, which in the sinful life, they get in abundance—of a sort of course."[101]

In examining the background of poor women who became prostitutes, the overlapping economic, social, and psychological factors that influenced their choices become clearer. But what of the women who hailed from more comfortable homes? Were they subject to similar or different sources of stress? Although reformers tended to sensationalize and overestimate the number of young middle-class girls and women who were turning to prostitution, available evidence indicates that some proportion of prostitutes came from well-to-do families. Whether this was a growing phenomenon is difficult to determine. The Bedford study revealed that nearly one-quarter of their institutionalized prostitutes had come from homes that could be described as low and high white-collar (see Table 2). The Bridgeport report indicated that a "number" (never specified) of the prostitutes they interviewed came from comfortable, "nice" homes. The Vice Commission of Chicago described a prostitute from a wealthy family who had been an inmate in a brothel for three years. Her parents thought she had a respectable job in another city and each week the daughter sent them ten dollars to save for her future. Unfortunately, no reason was given for her entry into prostitution.[102]

In a talk before the General Federation of Women's Clubs, George Kneeland, the director of vice investigations of several cities and author of *Commercialized Prostitution in New York*, warned his audience of the small, but ever growing, number of women from comfortable homes who were joining the ranks of prostitutes.[103] Kneeland's interpretation of this phenomenon was that young women who became prostitutes were rebelling against their parents' rigid morality. An expanded explanation is that such women may have tended to act out their hostility and aggressiveness *not* through violent means, but through the pursuit of forbidden areas of sexual activity. Prostitution, in other words, may have represented one way in which a woman could aggressively flaunt her sexuality and rebel against family or society.

In 1858, when William Sanger asked two thousand prostitutes why they had become prostitutes, one-quarter chose the category labeled "inclination."[104] Perhaps these answers simply reflected the women's internalization of society's judgment of them as "naturally depraved." It is possible, however, that some women actually thought they would enjoy "a sporting life." Fifty years later, a small number of prostitutes still replied that they had turned to prostitution because "they liked the sporting life," "for the fun of it," or "for pleasure" (see Table 4). In memoirs written by madams during the twentieth century, there are sporadic references to prostitutes who stood out from other women because they actually enjoyed the work. A common sexual fantasy of American females is working as a prostitute. What is fantasized, however, is the opportunity to take an *active* and controlling initiative in giving and receiving sexual pleasure, not the lack of choice in customers, the physical dangers, the potential brutality, and the probable social ostracism.[105]

The fact that a few women desired to taste "the sporting life" is not evidence of the glamorous or exciting life offered by prostitution. On the contrary, prostitution was often accompanied by familial and community ostracism, the danger of disease, and the prospect of declining earning capacity. Given societal prohibitions against the free expression of female sexuality, however, prostitution falsely promised the distinct opportunity of gaining sexual or affectional pleasure and definitely provided an avenue for shattering the proper boundaries of female sexual conduct.

Judging from evidence drawn from later periods, the presence of middle-class women in prostitution may also be explained by the family ostracism they suffered as the result of their sexual transgressions. Pauline Tabor described the sequence of events that brought a young middle-class woman to her famous brothel in the 1930s. After high school, the young woman had an affair with her boss and became pregnant. Thrown out by her parents, abandoned by her employer, the young woman found employment with another family. Meanwhile, her baby died, and she decided to leave her home town in eastern Kentucky. She soon settled in Louisville, worked in an office during the day, and supplemented her meager income at night as a prostitute.[106]

In other words, those young women who challenged the sexual double standard, like their working-class counterparts, may have found themselves without financial or emotional support from their families. If, in addition, they internalized their families' opinion of themselves, they, too, may have experienced themselves as moral lepers who properly belonged among the prostitute population. Incest, alcoholism, and child abuse in middle-class families may also have contributed to young women's search for love and companionship outside the home, resulting in rejection by their families.

No one cause, but a variety of interconnecting economic, social, and psychological factors, influenced women's choice to practice prostitution. Low wages created a need for supplemental income, while poor working conditions in other occupations motivated women to find "easier work." But some women turned to prostitution while others, equally impoverished, did not. Within the working class, *both* prostitutes and nonprostitutes faced the same limited and bleak occupational prospects. *Both* prostitutes and nonprostitutes found their economic and social mobility blocked by their class status and gender identity.

Since prostitutes differed little from other women in the working class, except for a higher incidence of family instability, the lack of family or good family relations may have been an important factor in many women's decision making. Most women, whatever their class, who lacked the support of a family economy found survival difficult on the wages paid for "women's work." The breakdown of a family economy often created a sudden acute need for income. Furthermore, to practice prostitution, women had to risk familial rejection. Thus it is probably not coincidental that women from broken homes or the daughters of immigrant families more frequently turned to prostitution than did the foreign-born women or daughters of closely knit families. Without close family ties, such women may have lacked the familial restraints and controls that kept other women from entering prostitution. If no one seemingly cared, or if family bonds were sufficiently torn by constant generational conflict, a daughter may have felt free to choose an illegitimate means of achieving upward mobility. Finally, some women may have turned to prostitution after having already been ostracized by their families and labeled as moral deviants for engaging in sexually promiscuous behavior, whether out of a desire to experiment sexually or out of feelings of deprivation resulting from the pressures of a fragile family economy or disrupted family relations.

By looking at accounts of prostitutes' lives, we can see how poor women attempted to work out strategies of survival from the bleak options available to them: marriage contracted for an economic protection that often proved to be temporary or illusory; alienating, exhausting, or dangerous work accompanied by the pressures of sexual harassment and performed for subsistence wages; and full-time or casual prostitution. While reformers set prostitution apart from other conditions in poor women's lives and dramatized it as a fate worse than death, they failed to see what prostitutes themselves recognized—that the sporting life, in the promises it offered and the reality it delivered, was not much different from its alternatives. Reformers' emphasis on prostitution as *the* "Social Evil" obscured the many other "social evils" of sexual and economic exploitation that poor women faced. Such a limited perspective polarized prostitute and reformer and made the crusade against prostitution ultimately self-defeating.

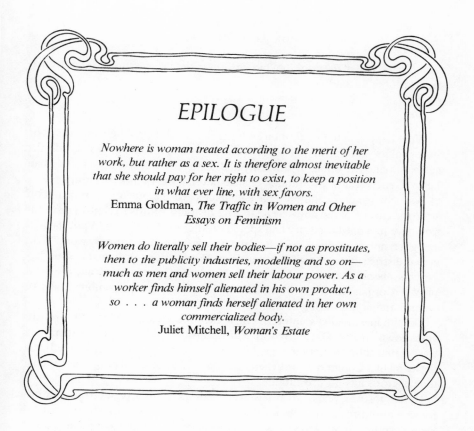

EPILOGUE

Nowhere is woman treated according to the merit of her work, but rather as a sex. It is therefore almost inevitable that she should pay for her right to exist, to keep a position in what ever line, with sex favors.
Emma Goldman, *The Traffic in Women and Other Essays on Feminism*

Women do literally sell their bodies—if not as prostitutes, then to the publicity industries, modelling and so on— much as men and women sell their labour power. As a worker finds himself alienated in his own product, so . . . a woman finds herself alienated in her own commercialized body.
Juliet Mitchell, *Woman's Estate*

Despite Progressive reformers' relentless moral efforts to eliminate prostitution from American life, the closing of the red-light districts scarcely banished commercialized sex from the urban landscape. On the contrary, prostitution has remained an ineradicable and seemingly permanent fixture of the commercialized sex marketplace.

It is one of the ironies of history that much of Progressive legislation—aimed at creating a more rational, efficient, and orderly society—backfired in ways never imagined by Progressive reformers. The effort to create a properly sober and "Americanized" society, for example, resulted in the criminal chaos and social disorder associated with Prohibition. Similarly, the attempt to eliminate prostitution from American society drove the Social Evil underground, where it became more closely yoked to liquor, drugs, theft, and increased violence.

Part of the Progressive legacy is that the state began to assume the role of parent to the dependent, the needy, and the deviant. As a result, the state responded paternalistically to the needs of people and neglected their rights as individuals.[1] Such was the case with prostitution. Stigmatized as criminals, prostitutes never personally profited from the Progressive effort to eliminate prostitution. That is one of the ironic but bitter truths of the Progressive Era's confrontation with the Social Evil.

What happened to prostitution after the closing of the red-light districts? The history of prostitution in the twentieth century is complex and quite naturally the subject of another book. With scanty and scattered evidence, however, we can begin to suggest how prostitution changed during the twentieth century.[2]

Both change and continuity have characterized the practice of prostitution since the closing of the now-legendary vice districts. Efforts to control prostitution have remained arbitrary and sporadic. After the First World War, the federal government gradually withdrew its appropriations for "sanitary work." Tolerated districts did not reappear, however. Prostitution—scattered and underground—became associated with new "tenderloin" areas or speakeasies and provided organized crime with enormous profits from the combined sale of women and liquor during Prohibition.

Despite increased law enforcement, some brothels survived the Progressive crackdown on vice. During World War II, however, the army again attempted to systematically protect the armed forces from prostitution. In 1941, the Interdepartmental Committee for Venereal Disease Control set up programs to coordinate efforts against prostitution.

In the postwar years, when fewer brothels seem to have survived, law enforcement of prostitution assumed a rather capricious pattern. As in the nineteenth century, most Americans and politicians reluctantly acknowledged the presence of a "necessary evil," which periodically shifted to different "tenderloin" areas—usually the neighborhoods of the transient poor. Politicians tolerated (or ordered crackdowns on) prostitution in response to public outrage (or the political exigencies of an election).

Such arbitrary law enforcement—exacerbated by a dizzying array of conflicting local statutes—created a permanent "scatter syndrome," first witnessed by Progressive reformers after the closing of the first large red-light districts. Depending on the political climate and changing local statutes, prostitutes and pimps participated in a constant hide-and-seek game with law authorities as they fled one city, where police were cracking down, for another, where the atmosphere was more lenient and congenial.

Prostitution has retained many of its familiar characteristics despite the traumatic transformations of life in the twentieth century. Attitudes toward prostitution, for example, reflect the Progressive legacy in significant and familiar ways. The practice of the trade is still viewed differently depending on the class position of the observer. Although prostitution has lost the powerful symbolic meaning it possessed during the Progressive Era, it is still viewed by many Americans as a rather alien, immoral, and, now, criminal activity. To many feminists, prostitution still represents the quintessential form of sexual exploitation of women in a masculinist society. The call to end prostitution recalls an earlier generation of women similarly concerned with both the symbolic and the real female oppression represented by prostitution. To other feminists, the continued presence of prostitution represents an important index of the gender and class discrimination that women continue to face sixty years later.

The trade itself also has enduring characteristics. Women who sell their bodies continue to suffer from a double standard of social and criminal justice. Prostitution remains an enormously profitable business, with most of the profits siphoned off by men—pimps, taxi drivers, members of organized crime, liquor dealers, physicians, and real estate speculators. As during the early twentieth century, prostitution still reflects social class stratification and caters to every man's budget. Private clubs, massage parlors, call girls, and streetwalkers make sexual services affordable to nearly all potential customers.[3]

Fierce class distinctions continue to divide the prostitute population. The call girl who earns $100 for a "champagne trick" views the streetwalker with contempt. And while the protected brothel in which prostitutes formed a "lost sisterhood" is gone, prostitutes continue to help one another in significant ways and to maintain a number of lesbian relationships.[4]

The recruitment of prostitutes has not changed appreciably. Pimps "turn out" young women, promising them the same emotional and financial security that cadets offered in 1910. Forced prostitution, moreover, has not disappeared. As Kathleen Barry has ably documented in *Female Sexual Slavery*, a widespread domestic and international trade in women's bodies forces thousands of women into prostitution. White slavery still exists.[5]

Similarly, the perspective of the prostitute on her trade has not altered significantly. The view that prostitution represents yet another and perhaps easier form of work is widely shared by many prostitutes. The illusion that prostitution may provide a certain degree of upward mobility continues to play an important role in the recruitment of young women into the trade.[6]

Many of the changes in prostitution have been merely superficial. For example, the "key" club brownstones in New York, which double as exclusive brothels, are merely the twentieth-century counterparts of the famous red-light parlor houses of an earlier era. "Private" membership status offers these upper-class men the kind of police protection provided to gentlemen of an earlier era.[7]

Technology has changed some superficial aspects of the practice of prostitution. The car has complemented the steady growth in streetwalking; the telephone has made call girl networks possible while offering protection from police harassment. Credit cards have replaced the famous brass checks once used in parlor houses. Revolving mirrors, waterbeds, vibrators, and other electrical "toys" have replaced the feathers and other accoutrements of an earlier period.

Prostitution, however, has also changed on a more fundamental level. From most indications, the sexual activity requested is of a kinkier nature than during the earlier twentieth century, with a new emphasis on sadomasochism.[8] The protective red-light district in which the subculture of prostitution once flourished has disappeared. Streetwalking, as noted earlier, has become the predominant means of solicitation. Today's pimp therefore occupies a central role in the recruitment, practice, and profits of prostitution. In fact, as organized crime has increasingly moved into drugs and pornography, the pimp has assumed an even tighter grip over his individual "stable." Indeed, it is nearly impossible for a woman to ply her trade independently on the street for fear of trespassing on some pimp's territory.[9]

Significantly, the degree of violence associated with prostitution has increased since the closing of the red-light districts. In addition to police brutality, prostitutes have endured brutal beatings and razor slashings meted out by organized crime and pimps. As streetwalkers accompany strange men to unsupervised hotels, they occasionally encounter unpredictable assaults by deranged customers.[10]

The kinds of violence and exploitation associated with contemporary prostitution are varied and horrifying. On occasion, authorities have exploited prostitutes' legal vulnerability for official ends. In July 1979, for example, the C.I.A. conceded that it had used prostitutes in San Francisco "safe houses" to extract information from potential informants. The C.I.A. also used both pimps and prostitutes in drug-related mind control experiments, knowing they had little recourse to legal authorities.[11]

Fear of violence frequently makes escape impossible or unimaginable for many contemporary prostitutes. A case in point surfaced during a House Republican investigation into illegal welfare payments. After finally escaping her husband (a member of one of the nation's largest motorcycle gangs), a Houston woman testified about gang life and prostitution. "Mary," age twenty-eight, explained that this cycle gang was involved in a white slavery market as well as in a multimillion dollar drug racket. Members of the gang lured hitchhiking girls— often as young as fourteen—into their gang by offering them rides. "This is her first mistake," the woman testified. "When she does that she becomes involved in a white slavery market. Often the first ride with a biker will take the girl to a club meeting where she will be sexually abused by each club member. That night for her, the drugs and booze are free. After that she is expected to earn her keep for the club." Most of the cycle women were forced to work as topless dancers, waitresses, prostitutes, or drug sellers. Within the gang, women found themselves trapped in an endless cycle of degradation and danger. They were forced to carry all the drugs and guns "so if anyone gets caught and goes to jail, it's her." When "Mary" could no longer bear her husband's daily beatings (punishment for her refusal to participate in a wife-swapping arrangement), she attempted to escape. "I was bound with tape around my wrist, elbows, knees and ankles and then my wrists and ankles were bound for five days. Each day I was beaten when my husband woke up. I was kicked until my entire body was swollen."[12]

In addition to the greater victimization of prostitutes by violence, there has been a dramatic change in the kinds of women drawn into the commercialized market. Most prostitutes during the early twentieth century came from poor families and, as we noted, from families particularly torn apart by divorce, death, desertion, sexual abuse, and concurrent changes in the family economy.

Today, a majority of prostitutes still enter prostitution from similar backgrounds. Yet, there have been changes. Prostitution, as this book has continually emphasized, tends to *mirror changes in the family, women's lives, and sex roles.* With a growing divorce rate, an increased number of women of all classes engaged in wage labor, and the precarious nature of family relations, more American women have become vulnerable to sudden and unpredictable proletarianization and impoverishment. As a result, new strata of women have entered the commercialized marketplace. Exposés of suburban wives walking New York pavements to supplement family income represents only the most sensationalized and "newsworthy" part of this story.

Young female college graduates, unable to find employment after graduation, increasingly work in massage parlors while searching for other jobs or employable skills. Students also support their education through prostitution. On the campus of one famous major university, work-study grants were drastically cut during the early 1970s. Several students detailed the elaborate call girl network into which upper-division, graduate, and law students had been recruited. Their customers—bank executives, campus administrators, and faculty—paid one hundred dollars per evening for the pleasure of a coed's cultural and sexual companionship. Faced with the prospect of losing educational opportunities, these women judiciously chose to "work" four or five evenings a month, just enough to offset the work-study grants they had lost. Naturally, many of these privileged women viewed prostitution as a temporary step to professional status. Nevertheless, the choice was not free of danger. To avoid the harsh reality of their encounters, some of the women turned to heroin. Some also feared, with good reason, that if they refused a "date," the "coordinator" might resort to blackmail to keep them employed as local hookers.[13]

The entry of young teenagers, particularly runaways, into the sex market represents the greatest change in the practice of prostitution. It is estimated that in the late 1970s, five hundred thousand teenagers ran away annually. Approximately fifty thousand girls annually arrive in the city of New York alone.[14]

The dangers that runaway teenage girls face are staggering. Alone in a new city, they constitute easy targets for pimps. Their lack of confidence and deep self-hatred—frequently fueled by rape or incestuous assault at home—soon becomes reinforced by degrading experiences with customers, beatings from pimps, and drug addiction. Escape is nearly impossible. Under age, and engaged in criminal activity, these young girls refuse the help of agencies that will send them home. One girl explained why so few will leave the pimp who "turned them out": "They have a way of making you like them . . . and you don't care anymore." Turning approximately thirteen tricks a day, these girls soon find that the promises of a glamorous lifestyle are illusory and serve only to enhance the pimp's profits. Nevertheless, the world of the pimp, who turns out these "pro babies" for pornography or prostitution, provides a marginal and temporary alternative to starvation or an unacceptable home life.[15]

A New York priest who helped runaway girls at a New York crisis center described the backgrounds and experiences of these young women. Seventy percent of the runaways had been sexually abused by their families—an experience bitterly remembered and noted by Maimie Pinzer and other prostitutes who worked during the Progressive Era. Burdened with low self-esteem, these girls frequently believe that they deserve what they get. Working 14 hours a day, moving in and out of cars and sleazy hotels, they face constant danger. Two hundred prostitutes were murdered in New York City in 1978.[16]

The streets of all major American cities are now heavily populated by young prostitutes who constitute a new class of proletarianized women. In the San Francisco Bay Area, where sociologist Marilyn Neckes interviewed "street kids," a minimum of five hundred young prostitutes can be seen walking San Francisco streets on any afternoon and at all hours of the night. Many of these young women arrive from all over the country by hitchhiking or by bus. Recruitment, as Neckes points out, is easy. "A man will see a young girl at the bus station or on the street who looks lost. He'll start talking to her, ask to take her to dinner—which is probably a hamburger—then offer her a place to stay. After a few days, the girl becomes attached and the man may say, 'I'm broke, what are we going to do? I know you can make money on the streets.' . . . And the girl becomes a prostitute." The options are limited. "Who can they turn to?" asks Neckes. "They don't want to go home, they're afraid of being picked up by the police and this guy is threatening them. So they go out on the streets." Neckes's suspicion that runaways turn permanently to prostitution was confirmed by her research, which revealed that 65 percent of adult prostitutes had been runaways.[17]

The persistence of prostitution puzzles some Americans. During the twentieth century, women have attained greater sexual freedom as well as more occupational opportunities. More women today participate in and are available for premarital and extramarital sexual activity without paying the penalties once exacted by the double standard; more than half the women in the United States are currently in the labor force, many of them working in occupations that were unavailable to turn-of-the-century women. Where, then, does the supply of prostitutes come from?

Despite the sexual and occupational changes in twentieth-century women's lives, it should be understood that the basic class structure and gender system that supported the existence of prostitution during the Progressive Era have not changed substantively. Despite the much touted achievements of a few token women in university or business careers, the majority of women today are still channeled into a sex-segregated labor force: nearly two-thirds of working women are occupying clerical, sales, or service jobs, generally characterized by monotonous work and low pay. In 1980, women were making fifty-nine cents for every dollar earned by men. "Pink-collar" work may offer the "perks" of vicarious association with white collar professionals in clean office environments, but the female factory worker in overalls brings home a larger paycheck and need not spend it simulating a "white collar" appearance. The earnings of the pink collar worker, moreover, are unconscionably inadequate to support the growing number of female-headed households, which have resulted from a growing divorce rate and the decrease in extended family relations. Even more important, there is still a large pool of unskilled women for whom prostitution continues to represent more lucrative, "easier" work than domestic or other unskilled labor.[18]

The sexual freedoms that twentieth-century women have attained—such as increased control over fertility and increased societal tolerance for female sexual activity outside of marriage—are important but have not eliminated the sexual exploitation of women. Women's sexuality is now reified, degraded, exploited as a commodity, and both portrayed and acted upon as a target for violence. As a result, women's sexual choices and sexual expression continue to be restricted and distorted.

Ironically, the expansion of the female labor market and the "sexual revolution" have served corporate interests far better than the real needs of women. Pink collar workers, for example, have provided a cheap labor force to maintain a bureaucratized corporate economy—while still performing unpaid labor expected of women in the home. The sexual objectification of women's bodies has become one of the most common practices of advertising as well as the basis for an immensely profitable pornography industry. Given these conditions, it is hardly surprising that some women reject blocked avenues of economic mobility and turn to their bodies—already objectified by their own culture—as a means of supporting their children, supplementing inadequate wages, or trying to acquire the socially legitimated goals of upward mobility and material comfort.

Contemporary policies toward prostitution are in many ways a political legacy of the Progressive Era. Laws against prostitution in contemporary America are based on the Progressive belief in prohibition—that society can and should prohibit the practice of prostitution. Such law enforcement has particular consequences. American cities spend astronomical portions of revenue in constant combat against the prostitute. All across the nation, large numbers of women are daily jailed at great public expense and dumped out again, only to be arrested and jailed again as prostitutes.[19]

Prostitution laws, as Marilyn Neckes has emphasized, are selectively enforced against women and not men.[20] Among prostitutes, laws are selectively enforced against the most powerless individuals, the streetwalkers, drawn disproportionately from the ranks of racial minorities, the poor, the very young, and the drug-addicted. It is no accident, for example, that black women are arrested for prostitution ten times more frequently than white women.[21] Fancy private clubs, massage clubs, and call girls may escape police detection or have sufficient funds to acquire adequate police protection, but the streetwalker is least equipped to evade the police and ends up paying the heaviest penalty for society's prohibition of prostitution.

The law is not neutral: it reflects social values and enforces social norms. Furthermore, the legislation of morality becomes tricky when conflicting interests must be appeased. As sociologist Jennifer James points out, "Authorities have found themselves making moral laws to satisfy one group, then not enforcing these laws to satisfy another group, and, finally, selectively enforcing the laws to satisfy a third group."[22]

Certainly this has been the case with prostitution. Progressive reformers successfully passed laws against prostitution for the benefit of the middle class, which viewed prostitution as a symbol of a threatening new urban social order. These laws have been arbitrarily enforced depending on whose neighborhood prostitutes invaded, which businessmen did or did not profit from prostitution, or which politicians faced elections and required evidence of renewed efforts to eliminate visible corruption. Arbitrary law enforcement has in turn encouraged questionable practices among the police, such as entrapment.[23]

Prostitution is not an entirely victimless crime: both society and the prostitute suffer from its continued existence. Certain segments of society are more immediately affected: the children in ghettos and barrios who are too early exposed to the flashy clothes of the pimp and the glamorous attire of the prostitute; the taxpayer; the customer who is "rolled" or brutalized by pimps or prostitutes; the respectable poor who find their neighborhoods plagued with the crime and drug addiction which accompany prostitution.

One example particularly highlights how prostitution affects the poor. In June 1979, indignant residents of West Oakland, California, a largely black neighborhood, marched to eliminate prostitutes from their neighborhood. "We are victims of prostitution," their picket signs read, and they sang "We Shall Overcome." Residents explained that they worried about their children being exposed to prostitutes. "They even proposition the priest!" exclaimed one bitter resident. Another neighbor explained why police tolerated prostitution in *their* neighborhood. "The prostitutes are here," she bitterly noted, "because it's a low income neighborhood and many people think that anything goes here." Having been kicked out of numerous other areas, however, the prostitutes defended their right to work. One prostitute said of the residents: "They got a m——f—— job an' I got my own job." Another prostitute defiantly responded, "They're not going to get rid of us."[24]

Even if the residents were successful in eliminating the prostitutes from their *particular* neighborhood, what then? As one protester explained, "I marched for two years trying to get the hookers off [Berkeley's] University Avenue. I'll join the [residents'] march but I hope it doesn't send the hookers back to Berkeley." But then where to? Here again we see the scatter syndrome, begun during the Progressive Era, which has now become a permanently futile, unproductive, and costly pattern in American urban life.

Interestingly, the question of whether or not society is victimized by prostitution due to venereal disease has become a relatively unimportant issue. Whereas turn-of-the-century reformers genuinely feared the relationship between the spread of venereal disease and prostitution, most authorities today agree that the use of the birth control pill, the decreased reliance on the condom, and the extensive sexual activity among the young largely accounts for the contemporary epidemic spread of venereal disease. Prostitutes, some of whom frequently live on a steady diet of penicillin, are not so likely to be viewed as polluters of society's health.[25]

How is the prostitute victimized by society? First, she suffers from class and gender discrimination, which limits her options early in life. Second, she is brutalized by pimps, harassed by police, and ostracized by society. Finally, she suffers from a double standard of social and criminal justice which renders her a criminal while her customer generally escapes social condemnation. As a member of a realtively powerless group in society, she has neither the political nor the social power to control her fate—if she escapes her pimp, it is a rarity; if she maintains long-term upward mobility, it is an exception to the rule.

Solutions to the problem of prostitution depend on whether prostitution is viewed as an ineradicable part of the human condition. Those who have suggested that prostitution be legalized are in basic agreement with their Victorian forebears that prostitution is, in the end, a necessary evil. The attempt to create segregated sexual ghettos in which women service customers (with the state assuming the role of the pimp) is the modern analogue of regulated prostitution in the nineteenth century. The Eros Center in Hamburg and the legalized brothels in Nevada are examples of the loss of civil rights (restricted mobility) that legalized prostitution has brought prostitutes.

During the 1970s, the first unions of prostitutes, along with many feminists, called for the decriminalization of prostitution.[26] Without laws against prostitution, they argued, pimps would lose a certain degree of their control over the trade and the drugs and violence associated with an underground criminal activity would quite naturally decrease. Decriminalization has gained strong support from those who believe that the double standard that punishes women for prostitution should be abolished. Unlike legalized prostitution, decriminalization would not create a class of permanently and publicly stigmatized women; unlike prohibition, it would not maintain a class of criminal outcasts.

Several researchers have suggested that a variety of reforms should ideally accompany the withdrawal of legal statutes. Marilyn Neckes, for example, has argued that mass arrests for obstruction of sidewalks and loitering should be discontinued because they are not enforced against male clients; safe houses for runaways should be established in high crime and high prostitution areas; counseling and medical services especially tailored to the needs of prostitutes should be established; a twenty-four-hour hotline for prostitutes and runaways in urgent need should be created; educational and job training programs and work education furlough programs should be available to prostitutes; "streetworkers" should be employed to reach out to prostitutes; and the only statutes involving prostitution that should remain on the books are laws involving pimping or child protection.

Despite these proposals, many proponents of decriminalization acknowledge that it is only a temporary solution that remedies the worst aspects of prostitution and leaves untouched the fundamental sexual and economic exploitation of women. An alternative solution to such reforms is the forced rehabilitation of prostitutes, such as that practiced in postrevolutionary China, Russia, and Cuba. In these countries, former prostitutes were placed in special institutions in which they were trained in new skills and taught to regard themselves not as moral pariahs but as victims of sexual and economic exploitation. After their rehabilitation, they reentered society as skilled, or at least semi-skilled, workers. Many Americans, however, view such measures as coercive and authoritarian. Rehabilitation programs are based on the socialist assumption that prostitution is not an individual moral failing and that society owes the prostitute complete rehabilitation. Such ideas counter the strong strain of individualism in American social thought which basically regards each individual as responsible for his or her destiny.

Ultimately, America must find its own, indigenous solution. Were the Victorians right when they termed prostitution a necessary evil? Or do we accept the "normalcy" of prostitution—along with rape, pornography, and wife battering—merely because it exists within a familiar culture that presumes female inferiority and inequality?

As we continue to investigate the seemingly infinite means of organizing human economic and sexual activity, we may yet gain a glimpse of a future in which sexual and economic egalitarianism seem as normal as does the contemporary devaluation of women in our society. Only when this egalitarianism is attained will prostitution truly be relegated to the American past.

NOTES

CHAPTER 1

1. Arthur Calhoun, *Social History of the American Family*, 1:135; C. F. Adams, "Some Phases of Sexual Morality," *Proceedings of the Massachusetts Historical Society*, 2d ser. 6 (1891):509–10; *Diary of Cotton Mather* (1911; reprint ed., New York: F. Ungar, 1957), p. 126. For a more detailed discussion of illicit sexual relations in the colonial era, see Emil Oberholzer, Jr., *Delinquent Saints* (New York: Columbia University Press, 1956), pp. 254–55.

2. Calhoun, *Social History*, 1:211, 333; Mary Ryan, *Womanhood in America from Colonial Times to the Present*, p. 74; Joan Scott and Louise Tilly, "Women's Work and the Family in Nineteenth-Century Europe."

3. The term *sexual slavery* was used by Adolph F. Niemoeller, *Sexual Slavery in America*, to refer to involuntary, coercive sexual relations; see especially pp. 49–60. Ulrich B. Phillips, *Life and Labor in the Old South*, p. 58; Fernando Henriques, *Prostitution and Society*, vol. 2, *Prostitution in Europe and the New World*, p. 245.

4. *Diary of Cotton Mather*, p. 126.

5. Oberholzer, *Delinquent Saints*, p. 142.

6. Carl Bridenbaugh, *Cities in the Wilderness* (New York: Knopf, 1960), pp. 71–73, 226, 229, 388; Carl Bridenbaugh, *Cities in Revolt, 1743–1776* (New York: Knopf, 1955), p. 160; Howard Woolston, *Prostitution in the United States prior to the Entrance of the United States into the World War*, p. 24.

7. Dixon Wector and Larzer Ziff, eds., *Benjamin Franklin: Autobiography and Selected Writings* (New York: Rinehart, 1969), p. 64, quoted in Ryan, *Womanhood*, p. 95.

8. Walter Blumenthal, *Women Camp Followers of the American Revolution* (Philadelphia: MacManus, 1952).

9. The effects of early capitalist commercialization and later industrialization are most succinctly described in Ryan, *Womanhood*. The literature of early moral reform movements illustrates the effects of working women's wage and sexual exploitation outside the home; see *Advocate of Moral Reform*, published from 1835 to 1860.

10. This pattern becomes evident particularly in community studies; see Mary Ryan, *Cradle of the Middle Class: The Family in Oneida County, New York, 1790–1865* (Cambridge: At the University Press, 1981).

11. Richard Evans, "Prostitution, State, and Society in Imperial Germany."

12. The effects of a large floating male population on the frontier in creating a demand for prostitution appear in many sources and studies; see, for example, Marcia Rittenhouse Wynn, *Desert Bonanza*; Charles Clegg and Lucy Clegg, *The Legends of the Comstock Lode*; Shirley Clappe, *The Shirley Letters from the California Mines*; the following manuscript collections: ABP, ABeP, CBP, THP, JNP, SRP, SSP.

An interesting Canadian community study describes the conflicts between families and prostitutes as the prairie towns became "civilized," which has many American parallels; see James Gray, *Red Lights on the Prairies*. For a history of western prostitutes themselves, see Jacqueline Barnhart, "Working Women."

13. Richard Hofstadter, *Violence in America* (New York: Vintage, 1971), p. 447; Bridenbaugh, *Cities in the Wilderness*, pp. 72, 388; Bridenbaugh, *Cities in Revolt*, pp. 121, 316, 317, 318; Pauline Maier, *From Resistance to Revolution* (New York: Knopf, 1973), p. 5.

14. Woolston, *Prostitution*, pp. 25, 204; George Kneeland, *Commercialized Prostitution in New York*, p. 152; Willoughby Cyrus Waterman, *Prostitution and Its Repression in New York City, 1900–1931*, p. 14.

15. Editorial, *Mascot*, p. 37.

16. Bridgeport, Bridgeport Vice Commission, *The Report and Recommendations of the Bridgeport Vice Commission*, p. 15.

17. William Acton, *The Functions and Disorders of the Reproductive Organs in Youth, in Adult Age, and in Advanced Life: Considered in Their Social and Psychological Relations* (Philadelphia, 1865), p. 133, quoted in Barbara Berg, *The Remembered Gate*, p. 84.

18. The ideological and proscriptive definition of male and female sexuality in the nineteenth century is best described and interpreted in G. J. Barker-Benfield, *The Horrors of the Half-Known Life: Male Attitudes toward Women and Sexuality in Nineteenth-Century America*, and "The Spermatic Economy"; Ann Douglas Wood, "The Fashionable Diseases"; Carroll Smith-Rosenberg, "Puberty to Menopause"; Carl Degler, "What Ought to Be and What Was"; Carroll Smith-Rosenberg and Charles Rosenberg, "The Female Animal."

19. William Edward Hartpole Lecky, *History of European Morals*, 2:282–83.

20. James Finley, Chaplain of Ohio Penitentiary, 1848, quoted in Cynthia O. Philip, *Imprisoned in America: Prison Communications, 1776 to Attica* (New York: Harper & Row, 1973), pp. 53–54. For a discussion of the early nineteenth-century view of the "fallen woman," see Barbara Hobson, "Seduced and Abandoned."

21. Nathaniel W. Chittenden, *Influence of Woman upon the Destinies of a People: Being an Oration of Salutatory Addresses Delivered at the Annual Commencement of Columbia College* (New York, 1837), p. 17, quoted in Berg, *Remembered Gate*, p. 80.

22. See Barker-Benfield, *Horrors*, chaps. 11, 23, and Charles Rosenberg, "Sexuality, Class, and Role in Nineteenth-Century America."

23. Anne Firor Scott, *The Southern Lady*, pp. 45–80; Al Rose, *Storyville, New Orleans*, p. 170; Lucy Hirata, "Free, Enslaved, and Indentured Workers in Nineteenth-Century Chinese Prostitution," p. 9; Henriques, *Prostitution*, 2:263; A. B. Hart, *The Southern South*, p. 152; Frederick Bancroft, *Slave Trading in the Old South*.

24. This argument is presented in detail by Mary Elizabeth Perry in her study of prostitution in sixteenth-century Seville, " 'Lost Women' in Early Modern Seville."

25. John McDowall, *Magdalen Report*, reprinted in *McDowall's Journal* 2 (1834).

26. *Advocate of Moral Reform* (1835), pp. 1–2, quoted in Berg, *Remembered Gate*, p. 186.

27. Charles Christian, *A Brief Treatise on the Police of the City of New York* (New York, 1812), p. 16, quoted in Berg, *Remembered Gate*, p. 181.

28. *McDowall's Journal* 1 (1834):36, quoted in Berg, *Remembered Gate*, p. 181; and McDowall, *Magdalen Report*, p. 39, quoted in Berg, *Remembered Gate*, p. 178.

29. *New York Female Benevolent Society, First Annual Report* (1834), pp. 20–24, quoted in Berg, *Remembered Gate*, p. 181; *Second Annual Report, Advocate of Moral Reform* (September 1835):72, New York, quoted in Nancy Cott, *The Bonds of Womanhood* (New Haven: Yale University Press, 1977), p. 152.

30. Two excellent articles that have explored the motivation and practices of early female moral reform societies are Carroll Smith-Rosenberg, "Beauty, the Beast, and the Militant Woman," Mary Ryan, "The Power of Women's Networks." See also Berg, *Remembered Gate*, and Cott, *Bonds of Womanhood*.

31. *New York Female Benevolent Society, First Annual Report*, pp. 20–24, quoted in Berg, *Remembered Gate*, p. 181; Lydia Maria Child, *Letters* (Boston, 1882), p. 207.

32. For a wealth of examples of such challenges, see Berg, *Remembered Gate*, chaps. 8–10.

33. The best account of both the reglementarian and social purity movements' perspectives, practices, and institutional history can be found in David Pivar, *Purity Crusade*. See also Roland

Wagner, "Virtue against Vice," p. 9; Linda Gordon, *Woman's Body, Woman's Right*, chap. 6.

34. John Warren, *Thirty Years' Battle with Crime*, p. 39.

35. William Sanger, *History of Prostitution*, pp. 575–627.

36. Warren, *Thirty Years' Battle*, p. xi.

37. Sanger, *History*, pp. 415–575.

38. Illinois, Senate Vice Committee, *Report of the Senate Vice Committee*, p. 887.

39. See Pivar, *Purity Crusade*, p. 52; Woolston, *Prostitution*, p. 27.

40. John Burnham, "Medical Inspection of Prostitutes in America in the Nineteenth Century."

41. For a discussion of individualism in the American reform tradition, see Richard Hofstadter, *The Paranoid Style in American Politics and Other Essays*.

42. Maude Glasgow, "On the Regulation of Prostitution, with Special Reference to Paragraph 79 of the Page Bill," p. 2.

43. Edwin Seligman, *The Social Evil, with Special Reference to Conditions Existing in the City of New York: A Report under the Direction of the Committee of Fifteen*, 2d ed. (New York: Putnam, 1912), p. 115.

44. See Judith K. Walkowitz, *Prostitution and Victorian Society*.

45. For a detailed discussion of women's role in the social purity movement, see Gordon, *Woman's Body, Woman's Right*, chap. 6.

46. Lexington, Ky., Vice Commission of Lexington, *Report of the Vice Commission*, p. 30. Also see Illinois, *Report*, p. 13.

47. Clara Cleghorne Hoffman, speech in *Report*, International Council of Women, assembled by the National Women Suffrage Association (Washington, D.C.: NWSA, 1888), pp. 283–84, quoted in Gordon, *Woman's Body, Woman's Right*, p. 118.

48. Belle Mix, *Marital Purity*, pamphlet no. 2, National Purity Association, n.d., p. 4, quoted in Gordon, *Woman's Body, Woman's Right*, p. 120.

49. Vernon Mosher Cady, "The Sex Hygiene Exhibit," p. 19.

50. Illinois, *Report*, p. 42.

51. Hartford, Hartford Vice Commission, *Report of the Hartford Vice Commission*, p. 30.

CHAPTER 2

1. Aaron Powell, *The National Purity Congress*. This collection contains the most representative ideas and attitudes of the social purity movement.

2. For a partial list of titles and dates of publication, see Howard Woolston, *Prostitution in the United States prior to the Entrance of the United States into the World War*, p. 150. The first city to have a standing vice commission was Pittsburgh. Its Morals Efficiency Commission, which grew out of a post–Civil War study of prostitutes titled *The Pittsburgh Survey*, was replaced in 1913 by the Public Bureau of Morals.

3. George Kibbe Turner, "The Daughters of the Poor"; "The Rockefeller Grand Jury Report"; U.S., Congress, Senate, *Reports of the Immigration Commission, Importation and Harboring of Women for Immoral Purposes*. See also discussion of religious and muckraking efforts of Lincoln Steffens, Charles Parkhurst, and William Stead in Roland Wagner, "Virtue against Vice," pp. 54 ff.

4. A study of *Reader's Guide* articles indicates that only fifteen articles on prostitution appeared during the years between 1905 and 1909. Between 1910 and 1914, however, one hundred and forty-five articles appeared. By 1918, the number of articles diminished to twenty-five; Wagner, "Virtue against Vice," p. 153. For a representative sample of groups involved in a major American city, see Chicago, Vice Commission of Chicago, *The Social Evil in Chicago*.

5. Mark Thomas Connelly, *The Response to Prostitution in the Progressive Era*, pp. 84–86.

6. Minneapolis, Vice Commission of Minneapolis, *Report of the Vice Commission to His Honor James C. Haynes, Mayor*, p. 24.

7. Julius Rosenstirn, *Our Nation's Health Endangered by Poisonous Infection through the Social Malady: The Protective Work of the Municipal Clinic of San Francisco and Its Fight for Existence* (San Francisco: Town Talk Press, 1913), pp. 16–18; and Julius Rosenstirn, *The Municipal Clinic of San Francisco.* See also Neil Larry Shumsky, "San Francisco's Municipal Clinic," for a detailed study of the interest groups involved in this debate.

8. Shumsky finds that the business community exerted enormous power in the initial support, and then demise, of the clinic. Business in general was quite concerned with the *costs* of prostitution; see Ray H. Everett, "The Cost of Venereal Disease to Industry."

9. Maude Glasgow, "On the Regulation of Prostitution, with Special Reference to Paragraph 79 of the Page Bill," p. 1323.

10. Philadelphia, Vice Commission of Philadelphia, *A Report of Existing Conditions, with Recommendations to the Honorable Rudolph Blankenburg, Mayor*, p. 19.

11. Brand Whitlock, quoted in "The Futility of the White Slave Trade Agitation as Brand Whitlock Sees It," p. 286.

12. Decriminalization has become the goal of several well organized, contemporary unions of prostitutes; see Guy Roche, "The Emergence of Militant Prostitution in America."

13. Editorial, *Vigilance*, p. 28; Portland, Portland Vice Commission, *Report of the Portland Vice Commission to the Mayor and City Council of the City of Portland*, p. 31; Woolston, *Prostitution*, p. 31.

14. For a detailed description of legislation and other reforms undertaken or proposed by the many groups and prominent individuals working against prostitution, see Connelly, *Response to Prostitution.*

15. A summary of the most commonly suggested recommendations made by vice commissions can be found in Woolston, *Prostitution*, p. 268, and in Joseph Mayer, "Social Legislation and Vice Control," *Social Hygiene* (July 1919): 337.

16. Woolston, *Prostitution*, p. 245.

17. Substantial evidence for this argument may be found in an important article by Steven Schlossman and Stephanie Wallach, "The Crime of Precocious Sexuality," pp. 82–85.

18. Sarah Cory Ripley, "The Case of Angeline," p. 255. See also changes and continuity in attitudes toward female delinquents in Eric Schneider, " 'A Fountain of Corruption.' "

19. Schlossman and Wallach, "Precocious Sexuality," p. 70.

20. Maude Miner, "Two Weeks in the Night Court," p. 229.

21. Ibid., p. 230.

22. Maude Miner, "The Community's Responsibility for Safeguarding Girls," p. 11.

23. *Survey* (November 15, 1913), p. 325; letter in ESDP, folder 385.

24. "Probation for Girls Who Err," pp. 349–50; Miner, "Two Weeks," p. 231; Maude Miner, *The Slavery of Prostitution*, p. 178.

25. Jessie Hodder, quoted in Eleanor Glueck and Sheldon Glueck, *Five Hundred Delinquent Women*, p. 9.

26. Woolston, *Prostitution*, p. 254.

27. Massachusetts, *Report of the Commission for the Investigation of the White Slave Traffic, So Called.* In her scrapbook, the well-known New York suffragist Harriet Laidlaw kept a clipping in which a judge, circa 1911, declared that most prostitutes were mentally deficient; Harriet Laidlaw, "Scrapbook."

28. Katherine Davis, quoted in letter to Hartford, Hartford Vice Commission, *Report of the Hartford Vice Commission*, p. 71.

29. Paul Allen Mertz, "Mental Deficiency of Prostitutes."

30. Miner, *Slavery of Prostitution*, pp. 43, 47. Also see Katharine Davis, "A Study of Prostitutes Committed from New York City to the State Reformatory for Women at Bedford Hills," p. 183.

31. Maude Royden, *Downward Paths*, p. 125.

32. Massachusetts, *Report*, p. 42.

33. Ibid., p. 29.

34. C. C. Carstens, "The Rural Community and Prostitution," p. 267.

35. Maimie Pinzer's complete letters to Fanny Howe are in MWHP. A full chronology of her life and experiences appears in the introduction to an abridged and edited version of her letters; Ruth Rosen, historical editor; Sue Davidson, textual editor, *The Maimie Papers*.

36. The story of Maimie's imprisonment appears in letter no. 75, November 27, 1913, Rosen and Davidson, eds., *The Maimie Papers*, pp. 191–98.

37. Ibid.

38. Ibid.

39. Ibid.

40. Ibid.

41. Miner, "Two Weeks," p. 229.

42. Miner, *Slavery of Prostitution*, p. 227. Judith Walkowitz also points out how repressive legislation enacted in the Contagious Diseases Acts in England helped create a more professional class of criminal outcasts; see Judith K. Walkowitz, "The Making of an Outcast Group."

43. Clarice Feinman, "Separate Penal Institutions for Women."

44. Anna Garlin Spencer, "The Age of Consent and Its Significance," p. 406; Miner, *Slavery of Prostitution*, p. 128.

45. Illinois, Senate Vice Committee, *Report of the Illinois Senate Vice Committee*, p. 52.

46. Jane Addams, *A New Conscience and an Ancient Evil*.

47. Chicago, *Social Evil*, p. 76.

48. James Rolph Papers, box 8, folder 6, California Historical Society, San Francisco.

49. For a more detailed discussion of the abatement acts, see Willoughby Cyrus Waterman, *Prostitution and Its Repression in New York City, 1900–1931*, pp. 22, 29.

50. Franklin Hitchborn, "Arguments," Hitchborn Papers, Bancroft Library, University of California, Berkeley. Hitchborn was a member of the Northern California Campaign Committee for the Red-Light Abatement Bill.

51. J. L. Davis to Franklin Hitchborn, April 1914, Hitchborn Papers, in which Davis, as a member of "Committee of One Hundred for the Suppression of Commercialized Vice, St. Louis," describes abatement acts of St. Louis and other cities.

52. Charles Lathrop to J. E. White, 1913, in Chester Rowell Correspondence, Bancroft Library, University of California, Berkeley.

53. Woolston, *Prostitution*, pp. 32, 239; Waterman, *Prostitution*, p. 34. For typical measures enacted by thirty-eight cities, see Mayer, "Social Legislation," p. 337.

54. Woolston, *Prostitution*, pp. 124, 249, 258.

55. Bridgeport, Bridgeport Vice Commission, *The Report and Recommendations of the Bridgeport Vice Commission*, p. 19.

56. Hartford, *Report*, p. 67.

57. The following is a partial list of cities in which vice commissions resulted in the closing of red-light districts; from Joseph Mayer, *The Regulation of Commercialized Vice*, p. 11: Atlanta, 1912; Baltimore, 1915; Bay City, 1913; Bridgeport, 1915; Chicago, 1912; Cleveland, 1915; Denver, 1913; Elmira, 1913; Grand Rapids, 1912; Hartford, 1912; Honolulu, 1917; Kansas City, 1913; Lancaster, Pa., 1914; Lexington, 1915; Little Rock, 1913; Louisville, 1917; Minneapolis, 1913; Newark, 1917; New York City, 1916; Philadelphia, 1913; Pittsburgh, 1914; Portland, Me., 1915; Portland, Ore., 1913; Richmond, 1914; St. Louis, 1914; Shreveport, 1917; Springfield, 1915; Syracuse, 1913; Toronto, 1913.

58. Harriet Laidlaw, "Testimony and Addresses on Segregation and Commercialized Vice," p. 17.

59. Letter, *New York Evening Journal.*

60. Whitlock, quoting anecdote in "Futility of White Slave Agitation," p. 287.

61. Letter.

62. Louisville, *Report of the Vice Commission*, p. 17; Baltimore, Baltimore Vice Commission, "The Abolition of the Red-Light District," pp. 181–83.

63. Given the hostile relationship between prostitutes and investigators, as well as the dangers of admitting to practicing prostitution during police crackdowns, one must question the validity of these answers. Some of the women who "lived with men," "worked," or "married" may still have been plying their trade; Baltimore, "Abolition," pp. 181–83. In a later study, Walter Reckless, *Vice in Chicago*, points out that no substantial evidence exists to document the immediate aftermath of the closings of the red-light districts on prostitutes.

64. Waterman, *Prostitution*, p. 150; Reckless, *Vice In Chicago*, pp. 105, 137, 159; Hartford, *Report*, pp. 15, 24; Louisville, *Report*, p. 29; Illinois, *Report*, p. 48.

65. As a result of the closings, police used all kinds of new and old laws to arrest prostitutes. Woolston summarizes arrest records from Oakland, Calif., New York City, and Boston, showing the heightened arrests, as well as the fact that enforcement varied from city to city. In Boston, for example, one-third of arrested women were imprisoned. In New York, of 1,952 convicted prostitutes, 63.5 percent went to the workhouse, 14.1 percent went to a reformatory, 3.3 percent received suspended sentences, 13.2 percent received probation, and 5.5 percent went to prison; Woolston, *Prostitution*, pp. 125, 249, 258.

66. Evidence of this transformation appears in contemporary studies of twentieth-century prostitution; see Charles Winick and Paul M. Kinsie, *The Lively Commerce*. Another study demonstrates how pimps became involved in prostitution only when police were forced to crack down on tolerated prostitution; James Gray, *Red Lights on the Prairie.*

67. Reckless, *Vice in Chicago*, pp. 69, 74, 89.

68. Lavinia Dock, *Hygiene and Morality* (New York: Putnam and American Social Hygiene Association, 1910).

69. Katherine Bement Davis, *Social Hygiene and the War*; Fred Baldwin, "The Invisible Armor," *American Quarterly* 16 (Fall 1964): 432–44.

70. David Pivar, "Morality and Liberty: The Development of a National Policy towards Prostitution, 1868–1921," paper, California State University, Fullerton, p. 18. In his detailed, institutional study of World War I and prostitution, Pivar demonstrates how the social hygiene movement eclipsed the older abolitionist movement. He also analyzes the "American Plan" in an important study titled, "Cleansing the Nation."

71. A good source of sexual attitudes and moral proscriptions is the sexual handbook, Winfield Scott Hall, *Sexual Knowledge.*

72. Mary Macy Dietzler, *Detention Houses and Reformatories as Protective Social Agencies in the Campaign of the United States Government against Venereal Diseases* (Washington, D.C.: Government Printing Office, 1922), pp. 3, 4, 47, 56. See also Pivar, "Cleansing the Nation."

73. Pivar, "Morality and Liberty," p. 22.

74. Ibid., p. 17.

75. Ibid., p. 24. Pivar discusses the different course the British social hygienists took, advocating free, voluntary clinics and the rejection of campaigns aimed at prostitutes.

76. Kay Ann Holmes, "Reflections by Gaslight"; Woolston, *Prostitution*, p. 25. In their study of prostitution after the Progressive Era, Winick and Kinsie point out that the United States remains the single nation that attempts to prohibit prostitution by punishing the prostitute—despite rhetorical claims to the contrary; Winick and Kinsie, *The Lively Commerce*, p. 288.

77. The term *sex/gender system* is used particularly by anthropologists to describe the allocation of power or access to power between the sexes. It was coined by Gayle Rubin, "The Traffic in

Women: Notes on the 'Political Economy' of Sex," in *Toward an Anthropology of Women*, ed. Rayna R. Reiter (New York: Monthly Review Press, 1975).

78. A comparable experience in the history of the birth control movement is brilliantly documented by Linda Gordon, *Women's Body, Woman's Right*.

CHAPTER 3

1. George Kneeland, *Commercialized Prostitution in New York*, p. 25. For similar descriptions, see Howard Kelly, *The Double Shame of Baltimore*, p. 3; Howard Woolston, *Prostitution in the United States prior to the Entrance of the United States into the World War*, p. 273; Chicago, Vice Commission of Chicago, *The Social Evil in Chicago*, p. 25.

2. John P. Peters of St. Michael's Church, New York City, *New York Sun*, October 1901.

3. Stanley Finch, "The White Slave Traffic." Finch was the Special Commissioner for the Suppression of the White Slave Traffic. Baltimore city officials similarly declared, "We are on this battleground to fight for our boys and our girls, for the family and for the state"; see Roland Wagner, "Virtue against Vice," p. 182.

4. Emma Goldman, "The Traffic in Women," p. 19.

5. See, for example, the sense of alarm registered by Maude Glasgow, "On the Regulation of Prostitution, with Special Reference to Paragraph 79 of the Page Bill," p. 1323.

6. In his study of prostitution in contemporary Beirut, Samir Khalaf points out how the beginnings of urbanization and industrialization produce cultural and social normlessness, which in turn shapes the modern forms of urban prostitution. The society that he describes bears striking similarities to that of the United States during the Progressive Era; Samir Khalaf, *Prostitution in a Changing Society*.

7. U.S., Bureau of the Census, *Thirteenth Census*, 1910, p. 186.

8. Richard Evans, "Prostitution, State, and Society in Imperial Germany," p. 106.

9. Donald Meyer, *The Positive Thinkers: A Study of the American Quest for Health, Wealth, and Personal Power* (New York: Doubleday, 1965), p. 30. This argument is based on particular work in the sociology of deviance: Howard Saul Becker, *Outsiders*; Joseph Gusfield, "Moral Passage"; Joseph Gusfield, *Symbolic Crusade*.

10. Becker, *Outsiders*, p. 12.

11. Historical works that explore these changes in Americans' lives include Jean Quandt, *From the Small Town to the Great Community*; R. Jackson Wilson, *In Quest of Community*; Samuel Haber, *Efficiency and Uplift*; Robert Wiebe, *The Search for Order, 1877–1920*; William O'Neill, *The Progressive Years*.

12. Mark Thomas Connelly, *The Response to Prostitution in the Progressive Era*, p. 99.

13. J. D. Holmes, "Vice and Wages," p. 701.

14. U.S., Bureau of the Census, *Report on Crime, Pauperism and Benevolence*; Chicago, *Social Evil*, p. 297.

15. Edwin Seligman, *The Social Evil, with Special Reference to Conditions Existing in the City of New York: A Report under the Direction of the Committee of Fifteen*, 2d ed. (New York: Putnam, 1912), p. 8; O. Edward Janney, "A General Point of View," p. 12.

16. Katherine Bement Davis, "A Study of Prostitutes Committed from New York City to the State Reformatory for Women at Bedford Hills," p. 333.

17. Louise de Koven Bowen, "Dance Halls," p. 282.

18. Louisville, Louisville Vice Commission, *Report of the Vice Commission*, p. 20.

19. Woolston, *Prostitution*, p. 307.

20. John Warren, *Thirty Years' Battle with Crime*, p. 118.

21. Ibid.

22. Clifford Roe, *The Great War on White Slavery*, p. 220. In a sense, these reformers were

reacting, however ambivalently, against the "Gospel of Success" literature so popular during these years; see Moses Rischin, *The American Gospel of Success* (New York: New Viewpoints, 1974).

23. Mrs. T. P. Curtis, *The Traffic in Women*, p. 6. See also Otto Wilson, *Fifty Years' Work with Girls, 1883–1933*, p. 18; Davis, "A Study," p. 204; Kneeland, *Commercialized Prostitution*, p. 51; George Kibbe Turner, "The City of Chicago"; Ellen Henrotin, "The Ravages of Prostitution," EHP, for reformers' reactions to the new large-scale commercialization of prostitution.

24. George Kibbe Turner, "The Strange Woman."

25. See Daniel Scott Smith, "The Dating of the American Sexual Revolution," p. 332, O'Neill, *Progressive Years*, p. 114.

26. Cecile L. Greil, quoted in "Sex O'Clock in America," p. 114.

27. Chicago, *Social Evil*, p. 199.

28. Connelly, *Response to Prostitution*, pp. 8–9, 17–19.

29. Seligman, *The Social Evil*, p. 11.

30. William Marion Reedy, quoted in "Sex O'Clock in America," p. 113.

31. W. Elliot Brownlee and Mary Brownlee, *Women in the American Economy* (New Haven: Yale University Press, 1976), p. 3.

32. Kneeland, *Commercialized Prostitution*, p. 70.

33. Seligman, *The Social Evil*, p. 11.

34. Connelly, *Response to Prostitution*, pp. 40–41.

35. Ibid., p. 17.

36. Jane Addams, *A New Conscience and an Ancient Evil*, p. 205; Chicago, *Social Evil*, p. 4; Wisconsin, Wisconsin Legislative Committee, *Report and Recommendations for the Wisconsin Legislative Committee to Investigate the White Slave Traffic and Kindred Subjects*, p. 100.

37. For an early discussion of nativist reaction, see Roy Lubove, "The Progressive and the Prostitute." See also Susan Reverby, "Sex O'Clock in America."

38. "White Slave Revelations," p. 596; George Kibbe Turner, "The Daughters of the Poor," p. 45; "Chinese Slavery in America," p. 290.

39. Connelly, *Response to Prostitution*, p. 63, quoting Kneeland, *Commercialized Prostitution*, p. 101. See also chapter 8, "The Lost Sisterhood: The Causes of Prostitution."

40. See, for example, Kneeland, *Commercialized Prostitution*, p. 45.

41. Warren, *Thirty Years' Battle*, p. 4.

42. Chicago, *Social Evil*, pp. 41, 225, 261.

43. O'Neill, *Progressive Years*, p. 106.

44. Robert H. Bremner, John Barnard, Tamara K. Hareven, and Robert M. Mennel, eds., *Children and Youth in America: A Documentary History, 1866–1932*, 3 vols. (Cambridge, Mass.: Harvard University Press, 1971), 2:365; C. C. Carstens, "The Rural Community and Prostitution," pp. 271, 221. At a White House Conference on Care of Dependent Children, the fear of the family falling apart was pervasive; see Bremner et al., *Children and Youth*, p. 365.

45. Illinois, Senate Vice Committee, *Report of the Senate Vice Committee*, p. 23.

46. Carstens, "Rural Community," p. 271.

47. Chicago, *Social Evil*, p. 299.

48. Ibid., p. 25. For additional discussion of the fear of venereal disease reflected in the antiprostitution campaign, see Connelly, *Response to Prostitution*, chap. 4, "Prostitution, Venereal Disease, and American Medicine."

49. Mary Virginia Hawes Terhune [Marion Harland], "The Passing of the Home Daughter," pp. 225, 261.

50. Warren, *Thirty Years' Battle*, p. 37.

51. Judith K. Walkowitz, *Prostitution and Victorian Society*.

52. Winfield Scott Hall, *Sexual Knowledge*, p. 128.

53. Kneeland, *Commercialized Prostitution*, p. 56.

54. Chicago, *Social Evil*, p. 36.

55. "Atlanta Vice Commission Reports," p. 29.

56. Harriet Laidlaw, "Testimony and Addresses on Segregation and Commercialized Vice," HLP.

57. Nearly all published vice reports pointed to the starvation wages paid young working women as *one* of the basic causes of prostitution; see Felix Adler, "Testimony," 2:18; Henry Rogers, "Relations of Low Wages to Vice," Illinois, *Report*, p. 913; "Wages and Sin"; Chicago, *Social Evil*, pp. 44, 281.

58. William Lloyd Garrison, "Relations of Poverty," pp. 398–405.

59. L. Abott, "Care of Vicious Women," *Outlook* 104 (May 1913): 101; Frederick Bierhoff, "The Problem of Prostitution and Venereal Diseases in New York City."

60. Chicago, *Social Evil*, p. 45; Wisconsin, *Report*, p. 109; Fred Johnson, *The Social Evil in Kansas*, p. 4; Seligman, *The Social Evil*, p. 149; Kneeland, *Commercialized Prostitution*, p. 52; Illinois, *Report*, pp. 140, 332.

61. Hall, *Sexual Knowledge*, p. 128.

62. "Wages and Sin," p. 622.

63. James Curry, quoted in "Are Low Wages Responsible for Women's Immorality?" p. 402. The U.S. Commissioner of Labor denied any relationship between "wages and sin" in U.S., Commissioner of Labor, *Working Women in Large Cities*, pp. 13–76.

64. Sarah Cory Ripley, "The Case of Angeline," p. 252.

65. U.S., Congress, Senate, *Report on the Condition of Women and Child Wage Earners in the United States*, vol. 15, *Relation between Occupation and Criminality in Women*, pp. 93, 114.

66. Chicago, *Social Evil*, pp. 44, 45. Note also that the Vice Commission of Minneapolis report, while listing wages and other problems of working women, also found it necessary to list the "looseness of discipline," "entertainment," "diversion," and "foreign elements" contributing to the general "lowering" of "moral standards"; Minneapolis, Vice Commission of Minneapolis, *Report of the Vice Commission of Minneapolis to his Honor James C. Haynes, Mayor*, p. 77.

67. Turner, "Strange Woman," p. 28.

68. Mary Douglas, *Natural Symbols*, p. vvi.

69. Mary Douglas, *Purity and Danger*, p. 4. See also Carroll Smith-Rosenberg, "Beauty, the Beast, and the Militant Woman"; Walkowitz, *Prostitution and Victorian Society*.

70. Leftist analysis of prostitution has a long tradition; see, for example, Karl Marx and Frederick Engels, *The Communist Manifesto*, ed. A.J.P. Taylor (Harmondsworth: Penguin, 1967), pp. 100–101; August Bebel, *Die Frau und der Sozialismus* (East Berlin, 1964), pp. 207–42. See also Leonora O'Reilly, LOP, folder 168. William O'Neill points out that, to many leftist intellectuals, the prostitute became romanticized as the antithesis of bourgeois morality; see William O'Neill, *Echoes of Revolt*, p. 186; "Wages and Sin," p. 263.

71. Joe Hill, "The White Slaves," quoted in Wagner, "Virtue against Vice." In separate studies of nineteenth-century female reform associations, Smith-Rosenberg, in "Beauty," and Walkowitz, in *Prostitution and Victorian Society*, have demonstrated how female reformers symbolized male domination of women by male invasion of the female body. For the Jacksonian Era moral reformers of Smith-Rosenberg's study, the invasion was that of seduction and rape. For the British female opponents of the Contagious Diseases Acts studied by Walkowitz, the invasion most strikingly depicted was that of the speculum used in compulsory medical examinations of prostitutes. In the Progressive Era, women used even more images of violation: "white slavery," and the invasion of venereal disease into their bodies and their homes.

CHAPTER 4

1. See especially Elizabeth Blackwell, *Rescue Work in Relation to Prostitution and Disease*; Victoria Woodhull, "Tried as by Fire," in *The Victoria Woodhull Reader*, ed. Madeleine Stern

(Weston, Mass.: M & S Press, 1974); Charlotte Perkins Gilman, *Women and Economics* (New York: Harper & Row, 1966), pp. 28, 171; Emma Goldman, "The Traffic in Women"; Jane Addams, *A New Conscience and an Ancient Evil*, p. 197. See also articles by such well-known female activists as Julia Ward Howe, Antoinette Brown Blackwell, and Dora Webb in Aaron M. Powell, ed., *The National Purity Congress.*

2. "Antivice Program of a Woman's Club."

3. For further information on this exhaustive campaign, see "The Abatement and Injunction Law," *Woman's Bulletin* 2, no. 2 (August 1913): 29–31; Frank Woodly, "Story of Red-Light Abatement Law," *Woman's Bulletin* 12, no. 11 (June 1914): 28–29; Mrs. Dorcas James Spencer, *A History of the Woman's Christian Temperance Union of Northern and Central California*, p. 95; *Survey* 30 (May 3, 1913):163.

4. Professor Fournier, "Rapports préliminaires," p. 13, quoted in Edwin Seligman, *The Social Evil, with Special Reference to Conditions Existing in the City of New York: A Report under the Direction of the Committee of Fifteen*, 2d ed. (New York: Putnam, 1912), p. 58. Maude Glasgow, "On the Regulation of Prostitution, with Special Reference to Paragraph 79 of the Page Bill"; Prince Morrow, "A Plea for the Organization of a 'Society of Sanitary and Moral Prophylaxis,' " p. 1075; American Social Hygiene Association, "A Confidential Statement Prepared for Mrs. James Lee Laidlaw by the American Social Hygiene Association"; Stanley Finch, "The White Slave Traffic."

5. See letter from Katherine Haughton Hepburn to *Survey* 24 (1910): 637–38.

6. Mary Ritter, "The Social Evil and Its Prevention," p. 17.

7. Mary Gibson, *A Record of Twenty-five Years of the California Federation of Women's Clubs, 1900–1925* (San Francisco, 1927), pp. 131–32.

8. Glasgow, "Regulation," p. 2.

9. Henrietta Frank and Amalie Jerome, *Annals of the Chicago Women's Club for the Forty Years of Its Organization, 1876–1916*, p. 242. The idea that regulation would end women's chance at a second life after being a prostitute was echoed by Harriet Laidlaw, "Testimony and Addresses on Segregation and Commercialized Vice." See also Ethel Sturges Dummer to Bertha Lowell, ESDP, for feminist reasons for opposing segregation. Dummer, a well-known Chicago reformer in probation and World War I "protective activity" for prostitutes and a prolific writer of articles on women's status and probation, wrote that Maude Royden's *Woman and the Sovereign State*, a study of the regulation of vice in Europe, had convinced her of the discrimination against women such regulation would bring.

10. See "A Vicious Experiment Fails," *White Ribbon Ensign* 7, no. 8 (June 1913): 4.

11. "Recall League of San Francisco," *California Woman's Bulletin* 1 (1913): 13.

12. For some male reformers' arguments for a single standard of sexual morality, see Joseph Mayer, *The Regulation of Commercialized Vice*, p. 50; Winfield Scott Hall, *Sexual Knowledge*, pp. 128, 147; Wisconsin, Wisconsin Legislative Committee, *Report and Recommendations for the Wisconsin Legislative Committee to Investigate the White Slave Traffic and Kindred Subjects*, p. 117.

13. Lucy Blanchard, quoted in Southern California W.C.T.U., *Minutes of the Thirty-third Annual Convention, Southern California W.C.T.U.* (Los Angeles, 1915), p. 36.

14. Cecile Greil, quoted in "Sex O'Clock in America," pp. 113–14.

15. Glasgow, "Regulation," p. 95. For more women's criticism of the double standard, see Spencer, *History*, p. 160; Addams, *New Conscience*, p. 197.

16. Katherine Houghton Hepburn, *Woman Suffrage and the Social Evil*, p. 16. See also W. A. Muhlenberg, *The Woman and Her Accusers*, Rose Baruch, "Sex Hygiene," *Woman's Bulletin* 2, no. 2 (August 1913): 26.

17. Karen Blair, *The Clubwoman as Feminist*, Ph.D. dissertation, California Institute of Technology, Pasadena, California, p. 201.

18. Frances Willard, quoted in Norton Mezvinsky, "The White Ribbon Reform, 1874–1920," Ph.D. dissertation, University of Wisconsin, 1959.

19. "Recall League," p. 13.

20. Jane Croly, *History of the Women's Club Movement in America* (New York, 1898), quoted in Blair, *Clubwoman as Feminist.*

21. "Recall League," p. 13.

22. Woodhull, "Tried as by Fire."

23. Jessie Williams, "The New Marriage," p. 184; "Prostitution within the Marriage Bond," p. 68.

24. Charles Winick and Paul M. Kinsie, *The Lively Commerce*, p. 46.

25. Havelock Ellis, quoted in Emma Goldman, "Traffic in Women."

26. Ethel Sturges Dummer, "The Responsibility of the Home"; Ethel Sturges Dummer, "Some Thoughts on Love and Marriage," p. 20.

27. Mrs. T. P. Curtis, *The Traffic in Women.* See also "Man's Commerce in Women," *White Ribbon Ensign* 7, no. 12 (October 1913): 1.

28. Carrie Chapman Catt, quoted in Hall, *Sexual Knowledge*, p. 309.

29. Rose Livingston's reports and documents (ca. 1915) concerning her activities appear in HLP, folders 151, 152.

30. Carol Green Wilson, *Chinatown Quest.* See also Donaldina Cameron, *Strange True Stories of Chinese Slave Girls.*

31. For documents on Hattie Rose, see HLP, A–63, box 9. See also M.G.C. Edholm's personal account of her work, *Traffic in Girls.*

32. See Estelle Friedman, *Their Sisters' Keepers.*

33. Addams, *New Conscience*, p. 192.

34. Harriet Laidlaw, "The Woman Voter," HLP, folder 152.

35. *Survey* 27 (1912): 1665, and *Survey* 31 (1913): 73.

36. "Recall League," p. 13.

37. Dora Merrill, "A Protection for Girls in Ohio."

38. Mrs. Seward Simons, *California Woman's Bulletin* 1 (1913): 27, and Hester Grifith, "President's Letter," *Southern California White Ribbon* 23 (1911): 5. For more details on this debate, see Mrs. H. W. Ferlong, "Do California Women Want Suffrage?" *Federation Courier* 2, no. 6 (April 1911): 13, and "The Bad Woman's Vote," *Woman's Bulletin* 1, no. 10 (April 1913): 27.

39. Katherine Farwell Edson, "Woman's Influence on State Legislation."

40. Mary Coolidge, "California Women and the Abatement Act," p. 739.

41. Edson, "Woman's Influence," p. 7.

42. Addams, *New Conscience*, p. 77; see also chap. 3, "Amelioration of Economic Conditions." In her well-known novel, *The Long Day*, Dorothy Richardson popularized the belief that girls were the victims of economic exploitation and therefore prey to prostitution when she had her heroine say, "The factories, the workshops, and to some extent the stores of the kind I have worked in at least, are recruiting-grounds for the tenderloin and 'red-light' districts. They send annually a large consignment of delinquents to their various and logical destinations. It is rare indeed that one finds a female delinquent who has not been in the beginning a working girl"; Dorothy Richardson, *The Long Day*, p. 276.

43. Addams, *New Conscience*, p. 205.

44. Goldman, "Traffic in Women," p. 28.

45. For descriptions of female reformers' attempts to offer charity and employment to prostitutes, see Friedman, *Their Sisters' Keepers*; *Report*, 1914, League of Women Voters Collection, California Historical Society, San Francisco; U.S., Congress, Senate, Committee on the District of Columbia, *Abatement on Houses of Ill Fame*, p. 50 (hereafter referred to as Kenyon Hearings); Letter, *New York Evening Journal*, January 27, 1914; "Dayton."

46. Ellen Henrotin, "Some Thoughts on Life and Love," EHP. Mrs. Henrotin, the wife of a Chicago banker, was an activist in urban reform and the second president of the General Federation of Women's Clubs.

47. Rheta Childe Dorr, *What Eight Million Women Want*, p. 193.

48. Helen Henrotin, "Position of the Prostitute in Society," p. 8.

49. "Red-Light Injunction and Abatement Act," *Woman's Bulletin* 3, no. 1 (September 1914): 6.

50. Jane Addams, quoted in Southern California W.C.T.U., *Minutes*, p. 36.

51. "The Church and the Magdalen," *White Ribbon Ensign* 7 (1912): 1.

52. Addams, *New Conscience*, p. 195.

53. See Katharine Bement Davis, *Social Hygiene and the War*. I thank David Pivar for making me aware of this publication. See also Pivar, "Cleansing the Nation."

54. Addams, *New Conscience*, p. 25; Anna Garlin Spencer, "The Danger of Estimates," p. 19. See also Laura Garrett, "Over-emphasis on the Social Evil," p. 17. Garrett argued that prostitution should be dealt with by eugenicists rather than by social hygienists.

55. Kenyon Hearings, p. 50.

56. Letter, 1914, League of Women Voters Collection, box 2, folder 2, California Historical Society, San Francisco, cited in Gayle Escobar, "The Protection of Virtue."

57. Sue Cobble, "The Redeeming of the Prostitute," p. 17.

58. Report, League of Women Voters Collection.

59. League of Women Voters Papers, box 4, folder 3, California Historical Society, San Francisco, California.

60. Friedman, *Their Sisters' Keepers*.

61. Report, League of Women Voters Collection.

62. Chicago, Vice Commission of Chicago, *The Social Evil in Chicago*, p. 36.

63. Ritter, "The Social Evil," pp. 16–18.

64. Florence Roberts, *Fifteen Years with the Outcast*. See also Spencer, *History*, p. 134, on Mary Daswell, who did similar work in the small mountain towns in the foothills of the Sierras. Some valuable sources on women's rescue work include information on the Florence Crittendon homes, travelers' aid homes, halfway houses, "midnight missions," etc.; see Otto Wilson, *Fifty Years' Work with Girls, 1883–1933*; Muhlenberg, *The Woman and Her Accusers*; California Federation of Women's Clubs, "President's Report."

65. Southern California W.C.T.U., *Minutes*, p. 84.

66. Tessa L. Kelso, *Clause 79*; H. J. O'Higgins, "Case of Fanny"; A. W. Elliot, "Is White Slavery Nothing More than a Myth?" *Current Opinion* 55 (November 13, 1913): 348.

67. *Madeleine*, p. 320.

68. Ruth Rosen and Sue Davidson, *The Maimie Papers*, letter 72, p. 188.

69. MP, letter 91; Rosen and Davidson, *The Maimie Papers*, letter 104, p. 285; letter 9, p. 22.

70. Rosen and Davidson, *The Maimie Papers*, letter 118B, p. 340; letter 93, p. 253.

71. Emma Goldman, *Living My Life*, p. 141.

72. Goldman, "Traffic in Women," pp. 19, 20.

73. Ibid., p. 20.

74. Ibid., pp. 24, 25, 26.

75. Ibid., p. 25.

76. Ibid., pp. 30–31.

77. Ibid., p. 32.

CHAPTER 5

1. The nature and effects of commercialized vice are best summarized in George Kneeland, *Commercialized Prostitution in New York*.

2. See for example, Louisville, Louisville Vice Commission, *Report of the Vice Commission*, or U.S., Congress, Senate, Committee on the District of Columbia, *Abatement on Houses of Ill Fame*; (hereafter referred to as Kenyon Hearings).

3. In her study of mid-nineteenth century prostitution in England, Judith Walkowitz provides

some of the only exhaustive data and models of such casual neighborhood prostitution; see Judith K. Walkowitz, *Prostitution and Victorian Society*. Barbara Hobson, "Seduced and Abandoned," helps confirm my speculative impressions in the American context.

4. George Kibbe Turner, "The Daughters of the Poor," p. 61; Chicago, Vice Commission of Chicago, *The Social Evil in Chicago*, pp. 27, 71, 113; Little Rock, Little Rock Vice Commission, *Report of the Little Rock Vice Commission and the Order of Mayor Chas. E. Taylor to Close All Resorts in Little Rock by August 25, 1913*.

5. Fred Johnson, *The Social Evil in Kansas*, p. 2.

6. The Vice Commission of Chicago obtained these figures by multiplying the number of prostitutes on police lists by the average number of men each woman saw, times the average price of each visit. In addition, they included the following figures: "rentals of property and profits of keepers and inmates, $8,476,689; sale of liquor in houses, flats, and profits of inmates on commissions, $2,915,760; sale of liquor, disorderly saloons only, $4,307,000; total profits (annual) from business of prostitution in Chicago, $15,699,449"; Chicago, *Social Evil*, p. 113, quoted in Al Rose, *Storyville, New Orleans*, p. 30.

7. "Organized Vice as a Vested Interest."

8. Ibid., p. 293.

9. For detailed study of such political intrigue, see Roland Wagner, "Virtue against Vice."

10. Charles Parkhurst, *Our Fight with Tammany*, p. 6.

11. Tessa L. Kelso, *Clause 79*; Kneeland, *Commercialized Prostitution*, p. 62.

12. *Mascot* (New Orleans), October 22, 1892, p. 57.

13. Howard Woolston, *Prostitution in the United States prior to the Entrance of the United States into the World War*, p. 237; Adolph Niemoeller, *Sexual Slavery in America*, p. 140; "White Slave Revelations," p. 597; O. Edward Janney, *The White Slave Traffic in America*, p. 31.

14. Franklin Hitchborn to Chester Rowell, April 17, 1914, Rowell Correspondence, 1887–1946, Bancroft Library, University of California, Berkeley. Hitchborn was corresponding secretary for the Northern California Campaign Committee for the Red Light Abatement Bill.

15. Illinois, Senate Vice Committee, *Report of the Senate Vice Committee*, p. 837.

16. Johnson, *Social Evil in Kansas*, pp. 1, 2; Woolston, *Prostitution*, p. 234.

17. Minneapolis, Vice Commission of Minneapolis, *Report of the Vice Commission to His Honor, James C. Haynes, Mayor*, p. 53.

18. "Reminiscences of John T. Hetbrick," pp. 46–47, 73; Otto Wilson, *Fifty Years' Work with Girls, 1883–1933*, p. 19; Kneeland, *Commercialized Prostitution*, p. 146.

19. Portland, Citizen's Committee of Portland to Investigate the Social Evil, *First Report of the Citizen's Committee to Investigate the Social Evil*, p. 38.

20. Kneeland, *Commercialized Prostitution*, p. 147.

21. Chicago, *Social Evil*, p. 156.

22. Kenyon Hearings, pp. 28–35; Woolston, *Prostitution*, p. 129.

23. A good study of police response to urban crime may be found in Mark Haller, "Historical Roots of Police Behavior."

24. Kneeland, *Commercialized Prostitution*, p. 160; Chicago, *Social Evil*, pp. 147, 151, 152, 153, 160.

25. Kneeland, *Commercialized Prostitution*, pp. 40, 44, 49.

26. Ibid., pp. 13, 14; Massachusetts, *Report of the Commission for the Investigation of the White Slave Traffic, So Called*, p. 25; Kenyon Hearings, p. 55; Philadelphia, Vice Commission of Philadelphia, *A Report of Existing Conditions, with Recommendations to the Honorable Rudolph Blankenburg, Mayor*, p. 12; Maude Miner, *The Slavery of Prostitution*, p. 9.

27. Philadelphia, *Report*, p. 79.

28. Edwin Seligman, *The Social Evil, with Special Reference to Conditions Existing in the City of New York: A Report under the Direction of the Committee of Fifteen*, 2d ed. (New York: Putnam, 1912), pp. 183, 184. See also the section on pimps in chap. 6.

29. Chicago, *Social Evil*, pp. 77, 87.

30. Ibid., pp. 77, 87; Kneeland, *Commercialized Prostitution*, pp. 117, 119.

31. Kenyon Hearings, p. 56.

32. Kneeland, *Commercialized Prostitution*, p. 127.

33. Ibid., pp. 37, 38; Chicago, *Social Evil*, p. 131.

34. Hartford, Hartford Vice Commission, *Report of the Hartford Vice Commission*, p. 73.

35. Lancaster, Lancaster Vice Commission, *A Report on Vice Conditions in the City of Lancaster*, p. 17.

36. Woolston, *Prostitution*, pp. 103, 106.

37. *Madeleine*, p. 63. It has been necessary for me to distinguish among many so-called memoirs of prostitutes, which, like slave narratives, were frequently rewritten by abolitionists, but nevertheless contained important information on slavery. I have discounted most prostitutes' memoirs I have read. I am using *Madeleine* as evidence because I believe the story has an authentic and plausible narrative, and the well-known Judge Ben Lindsey probably extracted this information from a young woman or created a composite profile. In any case, the facts of her story are congruent with other statistical and survey material of the period, and I therefore have used careful judgment in selecting this document as representative of many young women's lives as prostitutes.

38. Chicago, *Social Evil*, p. 34.

39. *Survey* 31 (1914):512.

40. Wagner, *Virtue against Vice*, p. 167; Hartford, *Report*, p. 102; Woolston, *Prostitution*, pp. 105, 108.

41. Chicago, *Social Evil*, p. 38.

42. Gilbert Osofsky, ed., *The Making of Harlem: Negro New York, 1877–1920* (New York: Harper & Row, 1971), p. 146; New York City, Committee of Fourteen, *A Summary of Vice Conditions in Harlem*.

43. Adam Clayton Powell, Sr., *Against the Tide*, pp. 49–57, quoted in Osofsky, *Harlem*, p. 14.

44. See chapter 8, "The Lost Sisterhood: The Causes of Prostitution."

45. Chicago, *Social Evil*, p. 38; Billie Holiday, *Lady Sings the Blues* (New York: Lancer, 1972).

46. Rose, *Storyville*, pp. 103–23.

47. Hattie Rose, quoted in HLP, folder 150; Johnson, *Social Evil in Kansas*, p. 3.

48. Little Rock, *Report*, p. 24; Rose, *Storyville*, p. 67; Herbert Ashbury, *The Barbary Coast*.

49. Jane Addams, *A New Conscience and an Ancient Evil*, p. 169; Francis Kellor, "Assisted Emigration from the South: The Women," *Charities* 15 (1905):12–13.

50. *Survey* 30 (1913):257–59; Woolston, *Prostitution*, p. 45.

51. For more expanded descriptions of the districts, see Rose, *Storyville*; Philadelphia, *Report*; Kneeland, *Commercialized Prostitution*; Stanley Finch, "The Federal Campaign against the White Slave Traffic," p. 13; Emma Goldman, *Living My Life*, 1:356; and Bridgeport, Bridgeport Vice Commission, *The Report and Recommendations of the Bridgeport Vice Commission*, p. 58. More contemporary descriptions of modern tenderloin areas may be found in Charles Winick and Paul M. Kinsie, *The Lively Commerce*.

52. Winick and Kinsie, *The Lively Commerce*, p. 132.

53. *The Sporting and Club House Directory, Chicago: Containing a Full and Complete List of all Strictly First Class Clubs and Sporting Houses* (Chicago: Ross and St. Clair, 1889).

54. Rose, *Storyville*, p. 145.

55. *The Blue Book* (New Orleans, 1910).

56. Rose, *Storyville*, p. 140.

57. Ibid., p. 145.

58. Chicago, *Social Evil*, pp. 78–79.

59. Kneeland, *Commercialized Prostitution*, pp. 12, 73; "A Guided Tour of Storyville, 1914," in Rose, *Storyville*.

60. Chicago, *Social Evil*, pp. 124–25.

61. *Madeleine*, p. 55.

62. Some writers estimated that for every known or visible prostitute, there existed yet another

hundred prostitutes; M. L. Hedengfeld, "The Control of Prostitution and the Spread of Venereal Disease," *Journal of the American Medical Association* 42 (1905):308.

63. Michael Gold, *Jews without Money* (1930; reprint ed., New York: Avon, 1965), p. 15.

64. The Massachusetts Vice Commission estimated that at least 22 percent of prostitution took place in established brothels, and another 28 percent took place in hotels and lodging houses that functioned as brothels; 20 percent were unknown; 4 percent listed as "out of doors"; Massachusetts, *Report*; see also Chicago, *Social Evil*, pp. 73, 74, 215; Kneeland, *Commercialized Prostitution*; Howard Kelly, *The Double Shame of Baltimore*, p. 8; Baltimore, Baltimore Vice Commission, *Baltimore Vice Report*, pp. 7, 19; Finch, "Traffic," p. 12; Hartford, *Report*, p. 31.

65. *Madeleine*, p. 11.

66. Claudia D. Johnson, "That Guilty Third Tier."

67. Chicago, *Social Evil*, p. 73.

68. Ibid., p. 122.

69. Hartford, *Report*, p. 28.

70. Ibid., p. 29.

71. Chicago, *Social Evil*, p. 129.

72. Ibid., p. 126.

73. Hartford, *Report*, p. 37.

74. Philadelphia, *Report*, p. 5.

CHAPTER 6

1. Minneapolis, Vice Commission of Minneapolis, *Report of the Vice Commission to His Honor James C. Haynes, Mayor*, p. 6.

2. Philadelphia, Vice Commission of Philadelphia, *A Report of Existing Conditions, with Recommendations to the Honorable Rudolph Blankenburg, Mayor*, p. 6.

3. Lancaster, Lancaster Vice Commission, *A Report on Vice Conditions in the City of Lancaster*, p. 17; George Ryley Scott, *Ladies of Vice*, p. 98.

4. Philadelphia, *Report*, p. 5.

5. Fred Johnson, *The Social Evil in Kansas*, p. 98.

6. For a more detailed explanation of the legal ambiguities surrounding prostitution during this period, see Kay Ann Holmes, "Reflections by Gaslight."

7. Pauline Tabor, *Memoirs of the Madam on Clay Street*, is a memoir of Tabor's successful high-priced brothel in Kentucky during the 1930s. Much of the discussion of the occupation of a madam derives from Tabor's detailed description of her management of such a house in Bowling Green long after the red-light districts were closed. Her alliances with local politicians, however, enabled her to run a first-class house like those in the red-light districts during the Progressive years. Another source for the management of a high-priced parlor house is Charles Washburn, *Come into My Parlor*, which documents the rise and management of the most famous "sporting houses" in the United States at the turn of the century. Also see *Madeleine*; Sally Stanford, *The Lady of the House*.

8. The number of inmates in brothels varied widely. It appears that the average number of inmates was about five or six; Louisville, Louisville Vice Commission, *Report of the Vice Commission*, p. 55.

9. *Madeleine*, p. 127.

10. Tabor, *Memoirs*, pp. 99–125; *Madeleine*, pp. 65, 80–81, 113–14.

11. George Kneeland, *Commercialized Prostitution in New York*, p. 92.

12. Ibid., p. 92. How madams managed to combine these two roles in the past is not evident from historical sources. A recent study of modern brothel life suggests that madams are masters of verbal manipulation and, as a result, can extract loyalty from prostitutes whom they daily exploit; see Robbie Davis Johnson, "Folklore and Women."

13. Kneeland, *Commercialized Prostitution*, p. 11.

14. Quoted in Charles Winick and Paul M. Kinsie, *The Lively Commerce*, p. 132.

15. Portland, Citizen's Committee of Portland to Investigate the Social Evil, *First Report of the Citizens' Committee to Investigate the Social Evil*, p. 45.

16. Kneeland, *Commercialized Prostitution*, p. 15.

17. Al Rose, *Storyville, New Orleans*, p. 40.

18. Ibid., p. 48.

19. See Washburn, *Come into My Parlor*, passim.

20. Stanford, *Lady of the House*, p. 10.

21. James Gray, *Red Lights on the Prairies*, p. 20.

22. Chicago, Vice Commission of Chicago, *The Social Evil in Chicago*, p. 82; Tabor, *Memoirs*, pp. 285–295.

23. Stanford, *Lady of the House*, p. 9. Also see *Madeleine*, who later became a madam.

24. Tabor, *Memoirs*, p. 100.

25. Kneeland, *Commercialized Prostitution*, p. 15.

26. Oral interview in Rose, *Storyville*, p. 164.

27. Ibid.

28. Oral interview in ibid., p. 155.

29. Nell Kimball, *Her Life as an American Madam*, p. 109. The plagiarism that marks this book has justifiably prompted scholars to question the authenticity of all its material. Its graphic descriptions of brothels—taken from earlier authors and observers—should not be totally dismissed, however, since this description of the middle-class brothel corresponds to other imagery found in Tabor, Stanford, *Madeleine*, and other first-hand accounts. It thus may be considered an important historical source, but one from which every piece of evidence should be evaluated by the scholar in light of other sources of the period.

30. Kimball, *Her Life*, p. 109.

31. Ibid.

32. Kneeland, *Commercialized Prostitution*, p. 16.

33. Ibid., p. 5.

34. Hartford, Hartford Vice Commission, *Report of the Hartford Vice Commission*, pp. 23–24.

35. Stanford, *Lady of the House*, p. 72.

36. Oral interview in Rose, *Storyville*, p. 154.

37. Ibid., p. 155.

38. Ibid.

39. Oral interview in Rose, *Storyville*, pp. 161–62.

40. Ibid.

41. Ibid., p. 162.

42. Kneeland, *Commercialized Prostitution*, p. 110; Lancaster, *Report*, p. 19.

43. Johnson, *Social Evil in Kansas*, p. 3; Chicago, *Social Evil*, p. 81. In an article on prostitution, Albert Ellis has suggested that a married man seeks a prostitute whose appearance in no way reminds him of his wife. In this way, the man can freely indulge his sexual desires without tainting the "purity" of his wife; Albert Ellis, "Why Married Men Visit Prostitutes." Unfortunately, very little is actually known about the male patrons of prostitution. Then, as now, male patrons did not receive much public attention.

44. Charles Winick, "Prostitutes' Clients' Perception of the Prostitutes and of Themselves," and Winick and Kinsie, *The Lively Commerce*, p. 204; Tabor, *Memoirs*, p. 143.

45. Quoted in Winick and Kinsie, *The Lively Commerce*, p. 206.

46. Hartford, *Report*, pp. 23–24; Chicago, *Social Evil*, p. 98.

47. *Madeleine*, p. 72.

48. Chicago, *Social Evil*, pp. 184–85; Tessa L. Kelso, *Clause 79*, p. 14.

49. For Bedford, see Kneeland, *Commercialized Prostitution*, p. 186; for Philadelphia, see Phil-

adelphia, *Report*, p. 143; for cocaine, see *The Wayward Girl and the Church's Responsibility*, and Philadelphia, *Report*, p. 143.

50. It is not clear if Maimie became addicted to morphine as the result of her "sporting life" or as the result of the numerous surgical operations she had undergone; see Ruth Rosen and Sue Davidson, *The Maimie Papers*, pp. 31, 53.

51. Maude Glasgow, "On the Regulation of Prostitution, with Special Reference to Paragraph 79 of the Page Bill."

52. Kneeland, *Commercialized Prostitution*, p. 195.

53. Howard Woolston, *Prostitution in the United States prior to the Entrance of the United States into the World War*, p. 54; Albert Guilard, "Physical States of Criminal Women," *Journal of the American Institute of Criminal Law and Criminology*, May 1, 1917; Woolston, *Prostitution*, p. 54; Rosen and Davidson, *Maimie Papers*, p. xxii.

54. Winfield Scott Hall, *Sexual Knowledge*, p. 215.

55. Kimball, *Her Life*, p. 87.

56. Oral interviews with contemporary prostitutes conducted by the author in 1978; names withheld on request.

57. S. D. Ball and G. H. Thomas, "A Sociological, Neurological, Serological, and Psychiatric Study of a Group of Prostitutes," *American Journal of Insanity* 74 (1918):647–66.

58. See Tabor, *Memoirs*, pp. 113–28; Stanford, *Lady of the House*, p. 159; *Madeleine*; Rosen and Davidson, *Maimie Papers*, passim.

59. Rosen and Davidson, *Maimie Papers*, letter 67, p. 179.

60. The fact of a prostitute's downward mobility was mentioned and described in nearly all the literature of the period. It was of special concern to reformers who felt horrified at the sight of aging, diseased women plying their trade in cribs or on the street.

61. *Maimie Papers*, letter 98, p. 277.

62. Ibid., letters 21–22, p. 56; letter 52, pp. 141–42.

63. Tabor, *Memoirs*, p. 25.

64. Oral interview with "Trick Baby" in Rose, *Storyville*, pp. 148–49.

65. Oral interview with "Carrie," in ibid., p. 159.

66. Erving Goffman, *Stigma*, directed my attention to some of these questions of a "labeled," or stigmatized, individual. Goffman's work on the integration into a subculture provides a solid framework for discussing the values of those who lived within the subculture of prostitution.

67. See Norman R. Jackman and Richard O'Toole, "The Self-Image of the Prostitute"; Winick and Kinsie, *The Lively Commerce*, p. 39. See also chapter 4, "The Lady and the Prostitute."

68. See, for example, *Madeleine*, p. 62. In addition, nearly all the vice commissions commented on this phenomenon. See also Jeanne Cordelier, *"The Life"*, p. 103.

69. *Madeleine*, p. 62.

70. Michelle Zimbalist Rosaldo, "Women, Culture, and Society."

71. See, for example, Kimball, *Her Life*, p. 107; Alexandre Jean Baptiste Parent-Duchatelet, *De la prostitution dans la ville de Paris, considérée sous le rapport de l'hygiene publique, de la morale, et de l'administration;* Tabor, *Memoirs*, p. 18; Gail Sheehy, *Hustling: Prostitution in Our Wide Open Society* (New York: Delacorte, 1973), p. 61; Winick and Kinsie, *The Lively Commerce*, p. 70.

72. Winick and Kinsie, *The Lively Commerce*, p. 187.

73. Ibid., p. 43.

74. *Madeleine*, p. 144.

75. Winick and Kinsie, *The Lively Commerce*, p. 44. See also D. J. Winslow, "The Occupational Superstitions of Negro Prostitutes in an Upper New York State Brothel," *Folklore Quarterly* 24 (1908):294–301.

76. Kimball, *Her Life*, pp. 90, 202.

77. Tabor, *Memoirs*, p. 100. Also see Cordelier, *"The Life"*, p. 115.

78. *Madeleine*, p. 63.

79. See Winick and Kinsie, *The Lively Commerce*.
80. Rosen and Davidson, *Maimie Papers*, pp. 115–48, 241–42, 283–84; E. J. Bellocq, *Storyville Portraits: Photographs from the New Orleans Red-Light District, circa 1912* (New York: Museum of Modern Art, 1970).
81. See Fernando Henriques, *Prostitution and Society*, a lengthy history of prostitution all over the world, in which he describes authorities' or prostitutes' attempts to identify themselves through special armbands, signs, or attire.
82. *Madeleine*, p. 213; Gail Sheehy, among other writers on prostitution, has consistently emphasized the "class snobbery" and distinctions between the independent courtesan or today's call girl, an occupation which has been highly glamorized, and the larger number of prostitutes who worked or work for someone else under extremely inhumane conditions; see Sheehy, *Hustling*.
83. Rosen and Davidson, *Maimie Papers*, letter 27, p. 77.
84. Kimball, *Her Life*, p. 76.
85. Stanford, *Lady of the House*, p. 207.
86. "The Rockefeller Grand Jury Report," p. 472; Chicago, *Social Evil*, p. 184.
87. Rose, *Storyville*, p. 160.
88. An important older study of pimps is by Benjamin Reitman, *The Second Oldest Profession*, p. 230; a more recent study is Christina Milner and Richard Milner, *Black Players*. Both studies, however, deal with the pimp-prostitute relationship after the closing of the red-light districts.
89. See chapter 8 for a profile of prostitutes' backgrounds; Kneeland, *Commercialized Prostitution*, p. 88.
90. George Kibbe Turner, "The Daughters of the Poor," p. 59; "White Slave Revelations," p. 596.
91. Emma Goldman, *Living My Life* 1:30–31.
92. Oral interview with "Marc" in Rose, *Storyville*, pp. 150–51.
93. Ibid., pp. 151–52.
94. Tabor, *Memoirs*, p. 215.
95. David Matza uses the term *cultural overlap* to describe the similarities between the deviant subculture and the dominant culture in his work, *Becoming Deviant*, p. 81.
96. See Robert Wiebe, *The Search for Order, 1877–1920*, for an analysis and description of the increasing rationalization, commercialization, and bureaucratization in American society during the late nineteenth and early twentieth centuries.

CHAPTER 7

1. Most of the vice commission reports, as well as the popular literature, emphasized such environmental factors, even though they still concluded that morals was *a*, or *the*, basic determining factor.
2. Massachusetts, *Report of the Commission for the Investigation of the White Slave Traffic, So Called*, p. 68.
3. See Mark Connelly's excellent cultural study of white slavery in chap. 6 of *The Response to Prostitution in the Progressive Era*.
4. See, for example, Harriet Laidlaw, "Traffic in Women," who repeatedly quotes from *San Francisco Bulletin* accounts of use of poisoned needles to reduce girls to unconsciousness on ferry boats, near movies, and in other places. Laidlaw's "Scrapbook" contains clippings from the *Evening Sun* and the *New York Tribune* which document stories of girls snatched off streets and drugged with poisoned needles.
5. See Kathleen Barry, *Female Sexual Slavery*, for a theoretical and documented case study of white slavery in contemporary society.
6. See Connelly, *Response to Prostitution*, chap. 6, for an example of this approach to white

slavery. While I find his analysis of white slave narratives insightful, I disagree with his assumption that the white slave scare was simply mass hysteria with no basis in fact.

7. Ibid., p. 130.

8. Massachusetts, *Report*, p. 1.

9. U.S., Congress, Senate, *Reports of the Immigration Commission, Importation and Harboring of Women for Immoral Purposes.* Minneapolis, Vice Commission of Minneapolis, *Report of the Vice Commission to His Honor James C. Haynes, Mayor*, p. 75; "The Rockefeller Grand Jury Report," p. 472.

10. Harriet Laidlaw, "The A.B.C. of the Question," p. 1.

11. "The White Slave Films"; "Is White Slavery Nothing More than a Myth?"; "Popular Gullibility as Exhibited in the New White Slavery Hysteria"; Reginald Kauffman, *The House of Bondage*; Reginald Kauffman, *The Girl That Goes Wrong*; the poster is described in *Survey* 30 (May 3, 1913): 5.

12. See discussion of the presentment of the Rockefeller Grand Jury later in this chapter.

13. Vern Bullough, *The History of Prostitution*, p. 174; Fernando Henriques, *Modern Sexuality* (London: Macgibbon and Kee, 1968), p. 174.

14. Edwin Seligman, *The Social Evil, with Special Reference to Conditions Existing in the City of New York: A Report Prepared in 1902 under the Direction of the Committee of Fifteen*, 2d ed. (New York: Putnam, 1912), p. 196.

15. Roland Wagner, "Virtue against Vice," p. 27; Bullough, *History of Prostitution*, p. 181.

16. *Union Signal*, February 17, 1889, pp. 8–9.

17. Adolph F. Niemoeller, *Sexual Slavery in America*, p. 195; as concern over white slavery increased, states began passing their own laws. *McClure's* 35 (July 1910):348, reported that nine states had already passed their own white slavery laws. Unfortunately, the Mann Act became a means for women to blackmail men when the Supreme Court ruled in the Diggs-Camminetti case in 1917 (*U.S. Reports* 242 [1917], cases adjudicated in Supreme Court) that the Mann Act could be used to prosecute men for taking women across state lines for "immoral purposes," not simply for prostitution. This weakened the strict interpretation of the Mann Act; see legal arguments in *The New York Times*, November 14, 1915, p. 14.

18. Edwin Sims, "The White Slave Trade Today," p. 47; O. Edward Janney, *The White Slave Traffic in America*, p. 13. Stanley Finch, "The White Slave Traffic," HLP.

19. Clifford Roe, former United States District Attorney in Chicago, quoted in E. Norine Law, *The Shame of a Great Nation*, p. 143.

20. Mabel Gillespie to Stella Frandel, Women's Trade Union League Papers.

21. See Minneapolis, *Report*, p. 94, and "Five 'White Slave' Trade Investigations," p. 347. Stanley Finch estimated that twenty-five thousand women and girls were annually procured in the United States and that fifty thousand men and women were actively involved in contributing to the traffic in women; Finch, "White Slave Traffic."

22. For an interesting discussion of "waves of panic," such as those stemming from white slavery publicity, see Daniel Bell, "The Myth of Crime Waves."

23. Maude Miner, *The Slavery of Prostitution*, p. 118.

24. See, for example, the article from the *New York Tribune*, July 27, 1916, in HLP; The Vice Commission of Chicago also gave strong evidence for the widespread organization of white slavers; Chicago, Vice Commission of Chicago, *The Social Evil in Chicago*, pp. 170, 176.

25. Theodore Bingham, *The Girl That Disappears*, p. 15; Sims, "White Slave Trade Today," p. 49. The reason that deportations for the white slave trade were so low during the Progressive Era is that the Supreme Court in the Kellor case ruled that only the importation, and not the harboring, of young girls was a constitutional basis for immigration exclusion; U.S., Senate, *Reports of the Immigration Commission*, p. 60. The conclusions of the Immigration Commission were based on extensive and well-researched investigations. Their agents interviewed madams, physicians, prostitutes, panderers, police, and court officials. Furthermore, their research covered San Francisco; Seattle; Portland, Ore.; Salt Lake City; Ogden, Utah; Butte; Denver; Buffalo; and New Orleans.

26. Niemoeller, *Sexual Slavery in America*, pp. 139–41; U.S., Senate, *Reports of the Immigration Commission*, p. 60; Bingham, *The Girl That Disappears*, pp. 30–31. George Kibbe Turner, perhaps reflecting the xenophobia of the white slave scare, identified the major origins of the international white slave trade as Austria, Russia, Poland, Paris, and New York. He charged that New York was particularly involved in directing women to South America; George Kibbe Turner, "The Daughters of the Poor," p. 45.

27. U.S., Bureau of Immigration, *Report No. 540 12/201*; U.S., Senate, *Reports of the Immigration Commission*, p. 62; Ernest A. Bell, *Fighting the Traffic in Young Girls*, p. 188; Clifford Roe, *The Great War on White Slavery*, p. 101; Harvey Woolston, *Prostitution in the United States prior to the Entrance of the United States into the World War*, p. 45.

28. U.S., Senate, *Reports of the Immigration Commission*, pp. 88, 101.

29. Ibid., pp. 69, 73.

30. Ibid., p. 102.

31. Other significant examples of tricking foreign women into prostitution can be found in Miner, *Slavery of Prostitution*, p. 108; Clifford Roe, *Panders and Their White Slaves*, p. 210.

32. U.S., Senate, *Reports of the Immigration Commission*, p. 76.

33. The research on early importation of Chinese white slaves is based on the very fine work of Lucy Cheng Hirata, "Free, Enslaved, and Indentured Workers in Nineteenth-Century Chinese Prostitution." For further information on testimonies and contracts on white slaves, see Committee of the Senate of the State of California, *The Social, Moral, and Political Effect of Chinese Immigration* (Sacramento: State Printing Office, 1876).

34. Hirata, "Free Workers," p. 17.

35. U.S., Bureau of Immigration, *Report 541 34/220*.

36. M.G.C. Edholm, "A Stain on the Flag," p. 165.

37. Ibid., p. 159; U.S., Congress, Joint Special Committee to Investigate Chinese Immigration, *Report* (Washington, D.C.: Government Printing Office, 1877), p. 286. See also C. Shepherd, "Chinese Girl Slavery in America"; M.G.C. Edholm, "Traffic in White Girls."

38. "Chinese Slavery in America," p. 290; Edholm, "A Stain," p. 165.

39. Janney, *The White Slave Traffic in America*, p. 41.

40. "Chinese Slavery," p. 290.

41. See Hirata, "Free Workers," passim.

42. Roe, *Panders and Their Slaves*, p. 85.

43. Harriet Laidlaw, "Traffic in Women."

44. Harriet Laidlaw, "Suggested Introduction to Hattie Rose." Harriet Laidlaw, review of Elizabeth Robbins's *My Little Sister*, p. 20.

45. Harriet Laidlaw, "Scrapbook," clipping from a New York newspaper. Police are quoted as saying that 1,439 girls disappeared from New York homes in one year and that restlessness and rebellion were viewed as the primary reasons for the unusual runaway phenomenon. This is repeated by the well-known social worker and secretary of the New York Probation and Protection Association, Maude Miner, "The Community's Responsibility for Safeguarding Girls."

46. William Stead, *If Christ Came to Chicago*, p. 258.

47. U.S., Senate, *Reports of the Immigration Commission*, p. 67; Kneeland, *Commercialized Prostitution*, pp. 48, 86.

48. Ibid., p. 68.

49. Massachusetts, *Report*, p. 52.

50. "Presentment of the Rockefeller Grand Jury," June 29, 1910, reprinted in Niemoeller, *Sexual Slavery*, p. 245.

51. Ibid., p. 246.

52. "Rockefeller Report," p. 471; "Five 'White Slave' Trade Investigations," p. 346.

53. "Rockefeller Report," p. 471; Janney, *White Slave Traffic in America*, p. 714.

54. Massachusetts, *Report*, p. 23; Toronto, Social Survey Committee of Toronto, *Report of the*

Social Survey Committee, pp. 14, 15; Chicago, *Social Evil*, p. 178; Sims, "White Slave Trade Today," pp. 56–57.

55. U.S., Congress, House, Committee on Interstate and Foreign Commerce, *White Slave Traffic*, p. 12.

56. *New York Times*, February 22, 1913, p. 8. Also see U.S., Department of Commerce and Labor, Office of the Secretary, *Arrest and Deportation of Prostitutes and Procurers of Prostitutes*.

57. Stanley Finch, quoted in Laidlaw, "Review," p. 202.

58. Edholm, "White Girls," p. 830; Turner, "Daughters," p. 58; Roe, *White Slavery*, p. 239.

59. U.S., Senate, *Reports of the Immigration Commission*, p. 68; Miner, *Slavery of Prostitution*, p. 55; H. M. Lytle and John Dillon, *From Dance Hall to White Slavery*, p. 24; Laidlaw, "Scrapbook," clipping from *Evening Mall*, 1911.

60. Stead, *If Christ Came to Chicago*, p. 258.

61. Roe, *White Slavery*, p. 104; U.S., Senate, *Reports of the Immigration Commission*, p. 68; Janney, *White Slave Traffic in America*, pp. 23–24.

62. George Kneeland, *Commercialized Prostitution*, p. 86.

63. U.S., Senate, *Reports of the Immigration Commission*, p. 68; Kneeland, *Commercialized Prostitution*, p. 86; Janney, *White Slave Traffic in America*, p. 97; Law, *The Shame of a Great Nation*, p. 162.

64. Miner, *Slavery of Prostitution*, p. 96; U.S., Senate, *Reports of the Immigration Commission*, pp. 65–66.

65. Roe, *Panders and Their Slaves*, pp. 56–58.

66. "Rockefeller Report," p. 472.

67. In one recorded case, an Italian procurer promised a young Wisconsin woman a good position in Chicago. Upon her arrival there, however, she was taken to a house of prostitution and kept a virtual slave; U.S. Bureau of Immigration, *Report No. 540 12/201*.

68. Stanley Finch, "The White Slave Traffic."

69. "Rockefeller Report," p. 472.

70. See also Niemoeller, *Sexual Slavery in America*, p. 152; Chicago, *Social Evil*, p. 178; Seligman, *The Social Evil*, pp. 183, 184; Finch, "The White Slave Traffic," p. 5; Roe, *Panders and Their Slaves*, pp. 55, 216, 81, 39; Illinois, Senate Vice Committee, *Report of Senate Vice Committee*, pp. 140, 142, 427, 832.

71. *New York Times*, December 14, 1913, p. 1. Other examples include the following: Elizabeth Donnelly, while walking to visit her brother in a hospital, was stopped by a man who spilled powder on her wrist. He then proceeded to brush it off. After swelling had produced considerable discomfort, a physician's inspection concluded that three small marks on her wrist had produced the swelling. *New York Times*, December 27, 1913, p. 4. Again, in 1913, a Marion Brindle fell unconscious after walking home, waking up two hours later. A Dr. Schneider who treated her believed that it was a case of needle poisoning. He found needle marks in her arm. *New York Times*, December 13, 1913, p. 1.

72. *Regina Register*, November 14, 1909, quoted in James Gray, *Red Lights on the Prairies*, p. 62.

73. Jane Addams, *A New Conscience and an Ancient Evil*, p. 27.

74. Woolston, *Prostitution*, p. 167.

75. See Carol Green Wilson, *Chinatown Quest*.

76. These 1910 reports are unnumbered, in typescript form, in HLP folder 150. Laidlaw, as a prominent New York suffragist, was in touch with Hattie Rose, a prison missionary, and was promoting efforts to have her speak across the country about her discoveries and experiences with white slavery in Chinatown.

77. Ibid.

78. Ibid.

79. Stead, *If Christ Came to Chicago*, p. 246.

80. Roe, *Panders and Their Slaves*, p. 77.

81. U.S., Senate, *Reports of the Immigration Commission*, p. 76; Janney, *White Slave Traffic in America*, pp. 36–37.

82. U.S., Senate, *Reports of the Immigration Commission*, p. 75.

83. Ibid., p. 76.

84. Miner, *Slavery of Prostitution*, p. 14.

85. Ibid., p. 95; Niemoeller, *Sexual Slavery in America*, p. 165; Philadelphia, Vice Commission of Philadelphia, *Report of Existing Conditions, with Recommendations to the Honorable Rudolph Blankenburg, Mayor*, p. 7.

86. Maude Miner, "Two Weeks in the Night Court," p. 233.

87. HLP, folder 150.

88. Philadelphia, *Report*, pp. 16–17.

89. "Five 'White Slave' Trade Investigations," p. 347.

90. U.S., Senate, *Reports of the Immigration Commission*, p. 76.

91. Miner, *Slavery of Prostitution*, p. 38.

92. Barry, *Female Sexual Slavery*.

93. The concept of a subculture and its effects upon a new participant are discussed at length by Howard Saul Becker in *Outsiders*. The chapters, "Outsiders," "The Culture of a Deviant Group," and "Labeling Theory Reconsidered," formed the basis for my discussion of a subculture of prostitutes and the possible psychology of its participants. See also David Matza's discussion of labeling and signification in *Becoming Deviant* (Englewood Cliffs, N.J.: Prentice-Hall, 1969), p. 145.

94. Wisconsin, Wisconsin Legislative Committee, *Report and Recommendations of the Wisconsin Legislative Committee to Investigate the White Slave Traffic and Kindred Subjects*, p. 24.

95. Clayton Harrington, "White Slavery: 1912," *Transactions of the Commonwealth Club*, 1912, p. 6.

CHAPTER 8

1. First of all, most personal memoirs of prostitutes during the Progressive Era which I have encountered in my research are not, in my opinion, authentic memoirs. Like abolitionist narratives of slaves, the memoirs of some prostitutes were written by reformers anxious to point out the dangers that led young women to prostitution. Margaret Von Staden's "My Story: The History of a Prostitute's Life in San Francisco" (HLP), although written in a florid, moralistic manner, probably reflects the true story of a young woman whom a "Mrs. Hughes," the sister of Edgarten Parkens, befriended as Margaret lay ill from venereal disease. The original manuscript, however, has never been located and the typescript was circulated by suffragists.

Another memoir, Lydia Taylor's *From under the Lid, an Appeal to True Womanhood*, appears to be from the hand of a zealous reformer, who may or may not have based it on facts. It was published as a book.

The Maimie Papers (MP), a series of letters from a former prostitute to a female reformer in Boston, is undoubtedly an authentic series of handwritten letters.

Census records, unfortunately, rarely covered most prostitutes. Many women indicated other professions, and only brothel inmates, who also moved frequently, would have been covered.

One problem with the data collected by vice commissions is that the various reports and studies often differed widely in their reporting procedures. For this reason, the data from the different studies are not strictly comparable and have not been tabulated in aggregate form. The questions asked, the categories used, the differences in reporting procedures varied so widely that it has seemed preferable to let each study stand on its own merits. Another possibility, that of combining the data into the most frequently used categories, has been attempted to indicate the most commonly cited reasons which prostitutes listed for their entry into prostitution.

In addition, prostitutes were frequently permitted to select more than one response to a question (see Table 4).

2. Tessa L. Kelso, in *Clause 79*, p. 16, reported that wary and suspicious prostitutes sometimes asked, "Are you a reformer? Do you want to make us good girls?" Albert Elliot described his frustration with "rescuing" prostitutes. "I have positively entered at least two thousand and five hundred houses of ill repute and talked face to face with possibly fifteen thousand of these women," he asserted, "and I pledge you truthfully that I know them . . . and I do not hesitate to tell you that they are wedded to their ways and that they laugh and make fun of those who try to help them"; *Current Opinion*, November 1913, p. 348.

3. Benjamin Reitman, *The Second Oldest Profession*, p. 239; Kelso, *Clause 79*, p. 4.

4. In addition to the generalized trends that emerge from these data, there are other reasons to use these sources. Interestingly, the recommendations and conclusions that reformers drew from their data frequently contradict their own collected information. We can feel certain, then, that the data were not altered to conform to reformers' rather moralistic view of prostitutes and their experiences. Also, the data collected by urban vice commission reports, unlike census data, covered many women who formed the "proletariat" of prostitutes and who did not usually appear on census records.

5. This study of 647 prostitutes at the Bedford Reformatory, conducted by Katherine Davis in 1913, obtained occupations of prostitutes' fathers from 506 women. Most of these occupations were blue-collar, though 26 percent could be described as high or low white-collar; see Katharine Davis, "A Study of Prostitutes Committed from New York City to the State Reformatory for Women at Bedford Hills," p. 213. Pamela Kellogg compared the occupations of the Bedford fathers with occupational categories used by Steven Thernstrom in *The Other Bostonians* (Cambridge, Mass.: Harvard University Press, 1973), p. 50. Her results, compared with Thernstrom's study of the occupations of men in 1910 in Boston, resulted in the categories and figures given; see Pamela Parkinson Kellogg, "The Sporting Life."

6. William Chafe, *The American Woman*, p. 55; George Kneeland, *Commercialized Prostitution in New York*, p. 218.

7. The average size of prostitutes' families in the Bedford study was four children, about 1.3 higher than the New York City average in 1910; Kneeland, *Commercialized Prostitution*, pp. 217, 280.

8. For the foreign-born prostitute myth, see Clifford Roe, *The Great War on White Slavery*, p. 100; Ernest Bell, *Fighting the Traffic in Young Girls*; Albert Elliot, *The Cause of the Social Evil and Its Remedy*, pp. 87–88. For the "country girl" myth, see Jane Addams, *A New Conscience and an Ancient Evil*, p. 145; Maude Miner, *The Slavery of Prostitution*, p. 31.

9. For West Coast and southern prostitute populations, see Howard Woolston, *Prostitution in the United States prior to the Entrance of the United States into the World War*, p. 44; for Kansas prostitute population, see Fred Johnson, *The Social Evil in Kansas*, p. 4.

10. William Sanger, *The History of Prostitution*, p. 460. In her study of prostitution in New York City, Pamela Kellogg compared the prostitute population with the New York female population in general. The data was computed by comparing the statistics in Kneeland, *Commercialized Prostitution*, with census figures for the year 1911; Kellogg, "The Sporting Life," p. 54. See also Davis, "A Study," p. 54.

11. Davis, "A Study," p. 213.

12. Indices were computed by dividing the percentage of prostitutes from one kind of parentage by the percentage of New York City women of the same parentage. An index of one indicates proportional representation, less than one indicates underrepresented, and greater than one indicates overrepresentation; Kellogg, "The Sporting Life."

Austrian Jews, when compared with their population in New York City, had a low index of .59; Irish, .91; Russian Jews, .28; and Italians, .14. On the other hand, Canadian, English and French—all of whom were known to have looser family constellations—had an index of 1.4, or above their proportional representation in the general population.

When statistics are examined for first-generation women of foreign or mixed foreign native parentage, however, the indices change quite dramatically. With the exception of Canadian and

French women, all first-generation women were more likely to become prostitutes. With the exception of the French and Canadian women, first-generation women of mixed parentage had a higher representation among the prostitutes than did those of strictly foreign-born parentage. (First-generation English women of mixed parentage were as likely to become prostitutes as foreign-born English women, but first-generation English women of foreign parentage contributed less of their number.) All of the ethnic groups that had been underrepresented among the foreign-born women (with the exception of Russian women of mixed parentage) were now more likely to become prostitutes. The Irish index went from .4 for foreign-born women to 1.8 for those of mixed parentage. For Italians, the index went from .14 for foreign-born women to .23 for first-generation women of foreign-born parentage, to .60 for women of mixed parentage. Foreign-born Russian women were less likely to become prostitutes than first-generation Russian women of foreign parentage. There was no representation, however, of Russian women of mixed parentage. This study was done by Kellogg, "The Sporting Life," pp. 53, 54, 70–71; also, studies of Italian, Irish, and Jewish immigrants to the United States indicate that these groups attempted to re-create the patriarchal, close-knit, and community bonds of the villages and neighborhoods from which they came; see, for example, Herbert Gans, *The Urban Villagers*; Phyllis Williams, *South Italian Folkways in Europe and America*; Jerry Magione, *Mount Allegro* (Boston: Houghton Mifflin, 1943); William Shannon, *The American Irish*; Mark Zborouski and Elizabeth Herzog, *Life Is with People*. Further detailed research on the ethnic factors that may have influenced or prevented women from considering prostitution needs to be completed before we can be certain of Kellogg's results.

13. Other studies reinforce the impression that the majority of prostitutes were not foreign-born women but rather the native-born daughters of immigrant families, or native-born American women. One study of "wayward girls" found that, of 229 young women in several missions and homes in New York, 169 were native born. The Vice Commission of Philadelphia discovered that 83 percent of the city's prostitute population was born in the United States, whereas the Hartford Vice Commission found that 89 percent of its city's prostitutes were native born; 60 percent of the women came from Connecticut and 36 percent were born in Hartford itself. See Philadelphia results in Harriet Laidlaw, "Scrapbook"; see also Hartford, Hartford Vice Commission, *Report of the Hartford Vice Commission*, p. 44.

14. For Bedford, see Kneeland, *Commercialized Prostitution*, pp. 228–29; see Illinois, Senate Vice Committee, *Report of the Illinois Senate Vice Committee*, p. 292.

15. Of 447 women questioned in Kansas, 197 listed the Protestant faith and 89 claimed a Catholic background. No Jewish women were reported. This religious pattern reflected the predominant Anglo-Saxon Protestant background of the smaller cities of the Midwest. What is more interesting is that 161 out of 447 women stated that they had no religious affiliation whatsoever; Johnson, *Social Evil in Kansas*, p. 16. In New York, in contrast, 41.1 percent of the prostitutes in one survey claimed Catholic affiliation, 19.0 percent Jewish, and 39.9 percent Protestant; Kneeland, *Commercialized Prostitution*, p. 225.

16. U.S., Congress, Senate, *Report on the Condition of Women and Child Wage Earners in the United States, Relation between Occupation and Criminality in Women*, found that only one of thirty occasional prostitutes had reached the grammar grades (vol. 15, p. 98). In Kansas, interviewers similarly found that most prostitutes had finished only the fifth to eighth grades, and in Hartford one-third of the women were described as "barely literate"; Johnson, *Social Evil in Kansas*, p. 16; Hartford, *Report*, p. 49. Maude Miner further found that more than 50 percent of the one thousand prostitutes she studied in night court had already left grammar school and that only 5 percent had entered high school; Miner, *Slavery of Prostitution*, p. 36. Among prostitutes at the Bedford Reformatory, 45 percent had not finished the primary grades and another 40 percent had failed to complete the grammar grades. Half of the remaining 15 percent were illiterate in all languages; Davis, "A Study," p. 219.

17. Sanger, *History*, p. 539; Davis, "A Study," p. 182; Samir Khalaf similarly found that unstable family ties were an important factor in causing prostitution in Beirut in its emergent modernizing period; Samir Khalaf, *Prostitution in a Changing Society*.

18. Miner, *Slavery of Prostitution*, pp. 53–54.

19. U.S., Department of Labor, Bureau of Labor Statistics, *Summary of the Report on Conditions of Women and Child Wage Earners in the United States*, (hereafter referred to as the *Summary Report*), p. 169; the *Summary Report* does not, of course, represent a national sample of the incidence of broken homes, but rather the extent of family disruption among working women in these particular trades.

20. In Kansas, for example, 56 percent of the prostitutes said they had been married; Johnson, *Social Evil in Kansas*, p. 4. In Wisconsin, 50 percent were listed as married; Wisconsin, Wisconsin Legislative Committee, *Report and Recommendations of the Wisconsin Legislative Committee to Investigate the White Slave Traffic and Kindred Subjects*, p. 20. In Hartford, 26 children were counted among 66 married and unmarried prostitutes; Hartford, *Report*, p. 55. One-third of the prostitutes in a Philadelphia institution had borne children; a survey of prostitutes in Pittsburgh showed a somewhat lower percentage (152 out of 558 prostitutes). The data on the Massachusetts prostitutes is in Massachusetts, *Report of the Commission for the Investigation of the White Slave Traffic, So Called*, p. 39.

21. Only in Kansas was there a large percentage of prostitutes—48 percent—who stated that they had boarded alone before practicing their trade. Whether or not this difference was due to the greater influx from rural areas in the Midwest is uncertain; Johnson, *Social Evil in Kansas*, p. 13. The romanticized image of the young working girl starving alone in a boarding house room gave added political clout to reformers wishing to attack industrialists who paid such female workers subsistence wages; see Chicago, Vice Commission of Chicago, *The Social Evil in Chicago*, p. 43; also see Davis, "A Study," p. 223, and Hartford, *Report*, p. 55.

22. Massachusetts, *Report*, p. 35; Kneeland, *Commercialized Prostitution*, p. 247; Johnson, *Social Evil in Kansas*, p. 15; Hartford, *Report*, p. 49. It is interesting that in a study of 163 prostitutes, nearly 62 percent said that they had had sexual experience before practicing the trade; Louise de Koven Bowen, *The Road to Destruction Made Easy in Chicago*, p. 15; Hartford, *Report*, p. 51; Chicago, *Social Evil*, p. 169; Miner, *Slavery of Prostitution*, pp. 30–31; Davis, "A Study," p. 192; Hartford, *Report*, p. 52.

23. Pauline Tabor, *Memoirs of the Madam on Clay Street*, p. 23.

24. Hartford, *Report*, p. 51; Johnson, *Social Evil in Kansas*, p. 14; Chicago, *Social Evil*, p. 172. In smaller rescue homes, the girls' age tended to average between 15 and 22 years, with younger girls than at correctional institutions; *The Wayward Girl and The Church's Responsibility*, p. 18.

25. Tabor, *Memoirs*, passim; Sally Stanford, *The Lady of the House*, p. 117.

26. See Edwin Seligman, *The Social Evil, with Special Reference to Conditions Existing in the City of New York*, 2d ed. (New York: Putnam, 1912), p. 64; Hartford, *Report*, p. 51; Johnson, *Social Evil in Kansas*, p. 14; Chicago, *Social Evil*, p. 172; Al Rose, *Storyville, New Orleans*, p. 164.

27. U.S., Congress, Senate, *Report on Condition of Women and Child Wage Earners*, 15:93.

28. In Kansas, investigators found that 51 percent of prostitutes had earned less than six dollars a week in their former occupations, and in New York, Katherine Davis similarly found that the average minimum wage among prostitutes in their former occupation had been four dollars, whereas the maximum average wage had been near eight dollars. A Chicago study of thirty prostitutes revealed a weekly wage of five dollars for the majority of prostitutes in their former occupations; Johnson, *Social Evil in Kansas*, p. 5; Davis, "A Study," p. 187; Chicago, *Social Evil*, p. 170.

29. *Summary Report*, pp. 218–24; pp. 18–21.

30. Ibid., pp. 218–24; Illinois, *Report*, p. 238; "Wages and Sin," p. 623.

31. "Wages and Sin," p. 621; Elizabeth Beardsley Butler, *Women and the Trades*, p. 346; Illinois, *Report*, p. 34.

32. In Hartford, prostitutes earned an average weekly wage of $30; in Chicago, $50 to $400. In New York, Maude Miner stated that the average weekly wage of 197 prostitutes was $52, whereas Katherine Davis found that the average weekly wage ranged from a high of $71 to a low of $46. In Pennsylvania, investigators revealed that prostitutes averaged between $15 and $200 a week. Howard Woolston, in his early study of prostitutes before World War I, placed prostitutes' average weekly

wages between $30 and $50; see Wisconsin, *Report*, p. 23; Hartford, *Report*, p. 53; Miner, *Slavery of Prostitution*, p. 37; Davis, "A Study," p. 231; Woolston, *Prostitution*, p. 65; Philadelphia, Vice Commission of Philadelphia, *A Report on Existing Conditions, with Recommendations to the Honorable Rudolph Blankenburg, Mayor*, p. 15.

33. Chicago, *Social Evil*, p. 43; William Stead, *If Christ Came to Chicago*, p. 255.

34. Prostitute quoted in Maude Miner, "Two Weeks in the Night Court," p. 231.

35. Prostitute quoted in Kelso, *Clause 79*, p. 16.

36. *Summary Report*, pp. 84, 85. See also Kelso, *Clause 79*, p. 16.

37. *Summary Report*, pp. 19, 20.

38. Illinois, *Report*, p. 328.

39. Ibid., p. 815.

40. Elizabeth Goodnow, "Rosa," p. 16.

41. Illinois, *Report*, p. 820.

42. Ibid., p. 838.

43. Hartford, *Report*, p. 58.

44. Chicago, *Social Evil*, p. 79.

45. Ruth Rosen and Sue Davidson, *The Maimie Papers*, pp. 15–16, 20, 23, 32–33, 54.

46. Wisconsin, *Report*, p. 18; Illinois, *Report*, p. 930; Addams, *New Conscience*, p. 78; Davis, "A Study," p. 229.

47. Kelso, *Clause 79*, p. 7; Chicago, *Social Evil*, p. 186; Butler, *Women and the Trades*, p. 306; Illinois, *Report*, p. 818 (see p. 343 for other examples).

48. Illinois, *Report*, p. 818; Butler, *Women and the Trades*, pp. 306, 305.

49. Illinois, *Report*, p. 820.

50. Ibid., p. 819.

51. Tabor, *Memoirs*, p. 113; "Are Low Wages Responsible for Women's Immorality?"

52. Chicago, *Social Evil*, p. 195.

53. Rosen and Davidson, *Maimie Papers*, pp. 140–41.

54. Ibid., p. 154.

55. Ibid., p. 215.

56. U.S., Bureau of the Census, *American Census Taken from First Census of the United States*; Butler, *Women and the Trades*, p. 351.

57. Sue Ainslie Clark and Edith Wyatt, *Making Both Ends Meet*, p. 132.

58. Sadie Frowne, "The Story of a Sweatshop Girl," pp. 117–18.

59. Little Rock, Little Rock Vice Commission, *Report of the Little Rock Vice Commission and the Order of Mayor Chas. E. Taylor to Close All Resorts in Little Rock by August 25, 1913*, p. 22; Helen Campbell, *Prisoners of Poverty*, p. 226; Robert Smuts, *Women and Work in America*, p. 90.

60. The Bureau of Labor Statistics' study of female criminality (mostly sexual offenses) and women's occupations revealed that 57.4 percent of women criminals had formerly worked as domestic servants, 22 percent had had no means of gainful employment, and 12.6 percent had been employed as factory operatives. The next highest category, that of women in trade and transportation (mostly saleswomen) contributed 7 percent of female criminals, and .6 percent had been engaged in the "professional pursuits." Of 181 girls sent to the Illinois State Training School at Geneva, 63.55 percent had been in domestic service. The Bureau of Labor Statistics' report also indicated that 54 percent of all female juvenile delinquents had formerly been in domestic service; see *Summary Report*, pp. 379–80. Occupations deemed "dangerous" to women's morals by the Bureau of Labor Statistics after studying the relationship between female criminality and women's occupations included domestic service, hotel and restaurant workers, and "low grade factory trades;" *Summary Report*, pp. 282, 381; Illinois, *Report*, p. 39; Chicago, *Social Evil*, p. 268.

61. Illinois, *Report*, p. 914, quoting U.S. Census, 1900.

62. The report demonstrated that half of the 3,229 women criminals studied came from the traditional female pursuits such as domestic service and laundry work, as compared to the 40.4 percent of female workers employed in domestic service; *Summary Report*, p. 377.

63. Kellogg, "The Sporting Life," pp. 59, 60. In comparing New York prostitutes' former occupations at Bedford Reformatory, seven other institutions, and a study of streetwalkers, with the percentage of women in New York employed in various occupations, Kellogg found the following: saleswomen, office and errand girls and theatrical workers were overrepresented in all three groups of prostitutes; two skilled female occupations did not appear among the institutionalized prostitutes or the streetwalkers: dressmakers (10 percent of the New York female labor force) and bookkeepers (3 percent of the New York female labor force); stenographers and typists (both highly skilled and best paid female occupations) had no representation among the institutionalized groups, but were overrepresented among streetwalkers; teachers and nurses were underrepresented among the institutionalized cases, but had a higher representation among the streetwalkers (Kellogg suggests that this pattern indicates that for skilled workers, prostitution was more likely a temporary occupation, rather than a permanent vocation.) Kellogg's figures were obtained from the U.S., Bureau of the Census, *Occupations at the Twelfth Census*, pp. 638–40, and the Bedford study.

64. New York City, Committee of Fourteen, *Department Store Investigation Report of the Subcommittee.*

65. In the Chicago study of thirty "inmates," for example, there was one former governess and one former vaudeville actress, and in a Chicago study of forty prostitutes, there was one former stenographer; Chicago, *Social Evil*, p. 169. In the Kansas study of 386 prostitutes were thirteen former telephone operators; Johnson, *Social Evil in Kansas*, p. 14. Even if further study should demonstrate that these better paid workers (ten to sixteen dollars a week) were underrepresented in the prostitute population, it is nevertheless significant that women in higher paying jobs *did* practice prostitution—perhaps as a result of rising expectations gained in their work, or sudden unemployment.

66. Hartford, *Report*, p. 55; Chicago, *Social Evil*, p. 172.

67. George Bernard Shaw, *Plays Unpleasant*, p. 249.

68. Illinois, *Report*, p. 816.

69. Ibid., p. 818; Chicago, *Social Evil*, p. 133.

70. Illinois, *Report*, p. 820; Chicago, *Social Evil*, p. 204.

71. *Wayward Girl*, p. 12; Hartford, *Report*, p. 64; Chicago, *Social Evil*, p. 128.

72. Illinois, *Report*, pp. 165, 337.

73. Elizabeth Gurley Flynn, *The Rebel Girl*, p. 117.

74. Economic Opportunity Council of San Francisco, *Drugs in the Tenderloin* (San Francisco: The Council, 1967), p. 17; for a modern version of such an opinion, see Jeanne Cordelier, *"The Life,"* p. 351.

75. Many literary depictions of working-class women's lives include references to young working women describing upward mobility in terms of meeting young ambitious men; see, for example, Dorothy Richardson, *The Long Day*; Theodore Dreiser, *Sister Carrie*; Stephen Crane, *Maggie*. The "Cinderella" mystique was also widely upheld in women's magazines; see Donald Makosky, "The Portrayal of Women in Wide Circulation Magazines Short Stories, 1905–1955," Ph.D. dissertation, University of Pennsylvania, pp. 139–46.

76. The effect of such blocked mobility, according to Robert Merton, lies either in *innovation* (the invention of illegitimate ways of achieving socially acceptable goals) or *retreatism* (the withdrawal into alcohol or other self-destructive behavior). Merton further explains that "it is only when a system of cultural values extols virtually above all else, common sense goals for the population at large while the social structure rigorously restricts or completely closes access to approved modes of reaching these goals for a considerable part of the same population that deviant behavior ensues on a large scale"; Robert Merton, *Social Theory and Social Structure*, p. 146. Examples of "innovation" are particularly common in the United States since a variety of ethnic and racial groups have nearly always been denied equal access to material wealth and social status. Boxing, mafia, and wrestling are often cited as examples of ways in which such groups have achieved power and/or wealth through unconventional or illegitimate means.

77. Chicago, p. 189; New York City, *Department Store Investigation*, passim.

78. Chicago, *Social Evil*, pp. 190, 210; Illinois, *Report*, pp. 818, 820.

79. Miner, "Two Weeks," p. 231; *Wayward Girls*, pp. 12, 14.

80. Tabor, *Memoirs*, p. 105.

81. Illinois, *Report*, pp. 147, 669; Stanford, *Lady of the House*, passim. Stanford also became involved in local politics, much to the chagrin of some community leaders.

In her recent study of New York prostitutes, Gail Sheehy, too, described the aspirations of young prostitutes who wished to "chin up the social ladder toward a rich husband"; Gail Sheehy, *Hustling: Prostitution in Our Wide Open Society* (New York: Delacorte, 1973).

82. Rosen and Davidson, *Maimie Papers*, p. 3.

83. Ibid., p. 297.

84. Ibid., p. 219.

85. Ibid., p. 51.

86. Ibid., p. 113.

87. Ibid., pp. 156, 50

88. Illinois, *Report*, p. 817.

89. Chicago, *Social Evil*, pp. 175, 191.

90. Sheehy, *Hustling*, p. 223.

91. Illinois, *Report*, p. 819; Chicago, *Social Evil*, p. 228; Jean Weidensall, *The Mentality of the Criminal Woman*, passim; *Wayward Girl*, p. 30.

92. Hartford, *Report*, p. 61.

93. Miner, *Slavery of Prostitution*, p. 23; Portland, Portland Vice Commission, *Report of the Portland Vice Commission to the Mayor and City Council of the City of Portland*, p. 183; Crane, *Maggie*, passim.

94. *Wayward Girl*, pp. 29, 34; "Probation for Girls Who Err," p. 349; Bowen, *The Road*, p. 13; Sarah Cory Ripley, "The Case of Angeline," p. 252.

95. *Wayward Girl*, p. 34.

96. Rose, *Storyville*, p. 155; Illinois, *Report*, p. 328.

97. Hartford, *Report*, p. 59.

98. Ibid., pp. 58, 57.

99. *Wayward Girl*, pp. 19, 22–23, 30.

100. Rosen and Davidson, *Maimie Papers*, p. 270.

101. Ibid., p. 333.

102. Bridgeport, Bridgeport Vice Commission, *The Report and Recommendations of the Bridgeport Vice Commission*, p. 70; Chicago, *Social Evil*, p. 76 (for several other prostitutes from well-to-do families, see p. 172).

103. *New York Times*, June 17, 1914, clipping describing Kneeland's talk, in Laidlaw, "Scrapbook."

104. Sanger, *History*, p. 488.

105. See Tabor, *Memoirs*, p. 78; Stanford, passim.

106. Tabor, *Memoirs*, p. 78.

EPILOGUE

1. For a more detailed analysis of this interpretation, see David Rothman, "The State as Parent," in *From Doing Good: The Limits of Benevolence*, ed. Willard Gaylin, Ira Glasser, Steven Marcus, and David Rothman (New York: Pantheon, 1978).

2. Two books are helpful in reconstructing the history of twentieth-century prostitution: Charles Winick and Paul M. Kinsie, *The Lively Commerce*, and Gail Sheehy, *Hustling: Prostitution in Our Wide Open Society* (New York: Delacorte, 1973).

3. These similarities appear in Sheehy's description of contemporary prostitution, *Hustling*, p. 27, and Winick and Kinsie, *The Lively Commerce*, passim.

4. Sheehy, *Hustling*, p. 61, and Winick and Kinsie, *The Lively Commerce*, p. 114.

5. Kathleen Barry, *Female Sexual Slavery*.

6. Sheehy, *Hustling*, p. 103.

7. Fernando Henriques, *Prostitution and Society*, vol. 2, *Prostitution in Europe and the New World*, p. 353.

8. This seems to be the conclusion of a variety of researchers and is confirmed by oral interviews with four elderly prostitutes conducted by the author. These women, still peripherally involved in the trade, point to the newer emphasis on sadomasochism, oral sex, and "water sports" in the business. They also point out that much of prostitution now caters to sexual fetishes, whereas prostitution sixty years ago seemingly offered less variety of sexual practices.

9. Sheehy, *Hustling*, p. 50. For a particularly detailed portrait of the power of pimps see Jeanne Cordelier, *"The Life."*

10. See Sheehy, *Hustling*, and Cordelier, *"The Life."*

11. ABC, "Mission: Mind Control," July 10, 1979.

12. "A Shocking Glimpse at Cycle Gang Life," *San Francisco Chronicle*, October 12, 1979.

13. Oral interviews with eight student-prostitutes conducted in 1973, 1977, and 1979 by the author.

14. The following information came from an episode by Dan Rather on CBS, "60 Minutes," March 4, 1979, "Runaways, Throwaways."

15. The relationship between familial unrest and runaways and prostitution is extensively discussed in Sandra Butler, *Conspiracy of Silence, the Trauma of Incest* (New York: Bantam, 1979); CBS, "Runaways, Throwaways."

16. Ibid.

17. "The Teenage Prostitutes of S.F.'s Streets," *San Francisco Chronicle*, May 4, 1979.

18. For an extended analysis of pink-collar work, see Louise Kappe Howe, *Pink Collar Workers* (New York: Putnam, 1977).

19. Marilyn Neckes and Theresa Lynch, speaking at a conference on "Women and the Criminal Justice System," noted that, in San Francisco, "ten to twenty percent of the public defender's caseload in 1977 was burdened by prostitution cases; in 1977, 309 women and 105 men served sentences for prostitution averaging 54 days in the county jail at a total incarceration cost to San Franciscans at $433,000; and ten percent of all misdemeanor cases considered by the district attorney's office in 1977 were for prostitution." The two million dollars spent per year in San Francisco to enforce prostitution laws, they argue, "would be better spent if diverted into community service for such women." Strict law enforcement "does not decrease the extent of prostitution in San Francisco," and "the criminal justice process . . . does little to provide assistance to those persons wishing to change their lifestyles;" Marilyn Neckes and Theresa Lynch, quoted in *San Francisco Examiner*, January 19, 1979.

20. "Prostitution: It's a Taxing Proposition," *San Francisco Chronicle*, January 19, 1979.

21. Jennifer James, Jean Whithers, Marilyn Haft, and Sara Theiss, *The Politics of Prostitution* (Seattle: Social Research Associates, 1975). This excellent collection of essays and bibliographies on contemporary legal statutes, attitudes, and problems associated with prostitution can be ordered from 335 N.E. 53d St., Seattle, WA 98105. See also Robert Kent and Dennis Dingemans, "Prostitution and the Police: Patroling the Stroll in Sacramento," *Police Chief* 14, no. 9 (September 1977):66.

22. James et al., *Politics of Prostitution*, p. 65.

23. Kent and Dingemans, "Prostitution," p. 65.

24. "An Oakland March against Hookers," *San Francisco Chronicle*, June 12, 1979. See also a similar phenomenon in "Seeing Red: 5th and T Neighbors Claim Unfair Policing Practices," *Sacramento Bee*, May 30, 1977; "Fourth and T Used to Be a Nice Area," *Sacramento Union*, October 13, 1974.

25. Winick and Kinsie, *The Lively Commerce*, p. 66, discuss the issue of whether venereal disease is at all a function of contemporary prostitution.

26. Neckes and Bresler, "Women and the Criminal Justice System."

BIBLIOGRAPHY

Most unpublished sources cited are located in the Bancroft Library, University of California, Berkeley, or in the Schlesinger Library, Radcliffe College, Cambridge, Mass. A list of abbreviations of manuscript collections follows, listed by repository.

BANCROFT

Alfred Barstow Papers	ABP
Alfred Beasman Papers	ABeP
Cleintine Brainard Papers	CBP
Thomas Heath Papers	THP
John Nagy Papers	JNP
Sarah Royce Papers	SRP
Seth Smith Papers	SSP

SCHLESINGER

Mrs. Mark A. De Wolfe Howe Papers	MWHP
Ethel Sturges Dummer Paper	ESDP
Ellen Henrotin Papers	EHP
Harriet Laidlaw Papers	HLP
Leonora O'Reilly Papers	LOP
Maimie Papers	MP

PRIMARY SOURCES

Unpublished

American Social Hygiene Association. "A Confidential Statement Prepared for Mrs. James Lee Laidlaw by the American Social Hygiene Association." HLP. Folder 161.

Dummer, Ethel Sturges. "Comment on Wilfred Lay's Paper." 1920. ESDP.
_____. ESDP. Folders 240 and 385.
_____. "Feminism." Address given October 30, 1911, ESDP. Folder 132.
_____. Ethel Sturges Dummer to Bertha Lowell. July 26, 1919. ESDP. Folder 373.

————. "Material for Preface to Unadjusted Girl." 1923. ESDP. Folder 240.

————. "Miscellaneous Letters." ESDP. Folder 35.

————. "The Responsibility of the Home." ESDP. Folder 239.

————. "Some Thoughts on Love and Marriage." ESDP.

Finch, Stanley. "The Federal Campaign against White Slave Traffic." Address delivered December 13, 1912. HLP. Folder 161.

————. "Traffic in Women." HLP. Folder 147.

————. "The White Slave Traffic." April 14, 1913. HLP.

Gillespie, Mabel. Letter to Stella Frandel. March 3, 1913. Women's Trade Union League Papers, Library of Congress, Washington, D.C.

Henrotin, Ellen. "Position of the Prostitute in Society." EHP. Folder 18.

————. "The Psychology of the Prostitute." EHP. Folder 16.

————. "The Ravages of Prostitution." EHP. Folder 17.

————. "The Readjustment of Family Relations." EHP. Folder 22.

Laidlaw, Harriet. "The A.B.C. of the Question." HLP. Folder 149.

————. "Scrapbook." HLP.

————. "Letters from South Side Milwaukee, Wisconsin." HLP. Folder 156.

————. "New York State Suffrage Party Press Section, October 9, 1916." HLP. Folder 152.

————. "Suggested Introduction to Rose Livingston." HLP. Folder 152.

————. "Testimony and Addresses on Segregation and Commercialized Vice." November, 1912. HLP. Folder 163.

————. "White Slavery." HLP. Folder 149.

Miner, Maude. "The Community's Responsibility for Safeguarding Girls." Address given under the auspices of the Education Department of the Municipal Court of New York. February 6, 1920.

O'Reilly, Leonora. LOP. Folder 168.

Von Staden, Margaret. "My Story: The History of a Prostitute's Life in San Francisco." HLP. Box 10, Folder 162. Typescript.

Published

Abrams, Karl. "Manifestations of the Female Castration Complex." In his *Selected Papers*, translated by Douglas Bryan and Alix Strachey. London: Hogarth Press, 1942.

Acton, William. "Prostitution." *Transactions of the National Association for the Promotion of Social Sciences* 1 (1857): 605–8.

————. *Prostitution*. 1870. Reprint. Edited by Peter Fryer. New York: Praeger, 1968.

————. *Prostitution Considered in Its Moral, Social, and Sanitary Aspects in London and Other Large Cities, with Proposals for the Mitigation and Prevention of Its Attendant Evil.* London, 1857.

Addams, Jane. "A Challenge to the Contemporary Church." *Survey* 28 (1912): 195–98.

————. *A New Conscience and an Ancient Evil.* New York: Macmillan Co., 1912.

Adler, Felix. "Testimony." In his *The Tenement House Problem.* Vol. 2. London, 1903.

Adler, Polly. *A House Is Not a Home.* New York: Rinehart, 1953.

"Antivice Program of a Woman's Club." *Survey* 33 (1914): 81.

"Are Low Wages Responsible for Women's Immorality?" *Current Opinion* 54 (1913): 402.

Atlanta, Ga. Atlanta Vice Commission. *Report of the Vice Commission.* Atlanta: The Commission, 1912.

"Atlanta Vice Commission Reports." *Vigilance* 20, no. 11 (1912).

Baltimore. *The Evils of Adultery and Prostitution, with an Inquiry into the Causes of Their Present Alarming Increase and Some Means Recommended for Checking Their Process.* Baltimore, n.d.

Baltimore. Baltimore Vice Commission. "The Abolition of the Red-Light District." In *Baltimore Vice Report.* Baltimore, 1916.

Bell, Ernest A. *Fighting the Traffic in Young Girls.* Chicago: Illinois Vigilance Association, 1910.

Bierhoff, Frederick. "Concerning the Protest, by the Committee Representing Women's Clubs, against Paragraph 79 of the Bill Relating to the Procedures of the Lower Courts of the City of New York." *New York and Philadelphia Medical Journal* 92 (1910): 1107–12.

————. "The Problem of Prostitution and Venereal Diseases in New York City." *New York Medical Journal* 93 (1911): 560.

Bingham, Theodore. *The Girl That Disappears.* Boston: Gorham Press, 1911.

Blackwell, Elizabeth. *Purchase of Women: The Great Economic Blunder.* London: John Kensit, n.d.

————. *Rescue Work in Relation to Prostitution and Disease.* Pamphlet. n.d.

————. *Wrong and Right Methods of Dealing with the Social Evil.* New York: Brentano & Co., 1879.

Blackwell, Samuel. "The Lesson of Geneva." *Woman's Journal,* August 22, 1896.

Blake, Mabelle B. "The Defective Girl Who Is Immoral." *Boston Medical and Surgical Journal* 117 (1917): 492–94.

Bloch, Ivan. *The Sexual Life of Our Time.* London, 1909.

Bowen, Louise de Koven. "Dance Halls." In Roe, *The Great War on White Slavery.*

————. *The Road to Destruction Made Easy in Chicago.* Pamphlet. Chicago: Juvenile Protective Association, 1916.

————. *A Study of Bastardy Cases Taken from the Court of Domestic Relations in Chicago.* Chicago: Juvenile Protective Association, 1914.

————. "Women Police." *Survey* 30 (1913): 64–65.

Brewer, Isaac W. "The Incidence of Venereal Diseases among 6,806 Men Drafted into the Service Who Reported at Camp A. A. Humphreys, Virginia, between September 4 and September 18, 1918." *Boston Medical and Surgical Journal* 180 (1919): 122–24.

Bridgeport, Conn. Bridgeport Vice Commission. *The Report and Recommendations of the Bridgeport Vice Commission.* Bridgeport: The Commission, 1916.

Brooks, Virginia. *Little Lost Sister.* New York: Macauley Co., 1914.

———. *My Battles with Vice.* New York: Macaulay Co., 1915.

Bunting, M.H.L. "The White Slave Traffic Crusade." *Contemporary Review* 103 (1913): 49–52.

"The Bureau of Social Hygiene." *Outlook* 103 (1913): 287–88.

Butler, Elizabeth Beardsley. *Women and the Trades: The Pittsburgh Survey Findings in Six Volumes.* Edited by Paul V. Kellogg. 1909. Reprint. New York: Arno Press, 1969.

Cady, Vernon Mosher. "The Sex Hygiene Exhibit: A Reply." *Vigilance* 20, no. 11 (1912).

California Federation of Women's Clubs. "Report of Officers," 1914, and "President's Report," 1915.

"California Red-Light Law Still in Doubt." *Survey* 33 (1914): 167.

California. Senate. "The Social, Moral, and Political Effect of Chinese Immigration." Testimony. April 1876.

"California Women and the Vice Situation." *Survey* 30 (1913): 162–64.

Cameron, Donaldina. *Strange True Stories of Chinese Slave Girls.* San Francisco: Women's Occidental Board of Foreign Missions, n.d.

Caminetti v. United States. 242 U.S. 470 (1917).

"The Campaign against Vice." *Outlook* 66 (1900): 874–76.

Campbell, Helen. *Prisoners of Poverty.* Boston: Roberts Brothers, 1887.

"The Care of Vicious Women." *Outlook* 104 (1913): 101–2.

Carstens, C. C. "The Rural Community and Prostitution," p. 267. *Proceedings of the National Conference of Charities and Corrections.* May 12–19. Chicago: 1915.

Chesnut, Mary Boykin. *Diary from Dixie.* New York: Houghton & Mifflin, 1949.

Chicago. Chicago City Council. *Control of Vice Conditions in European Cities: Observations of Alderman O. Nance and Alderman Ellis Geiger, Embodied in a Report to Honorable Carter H. Harrison, Mayor.* Chicago, 1914.

Chicago. Vice Commission of Chicago. *The Social Evil in Chicago: A Study of Existing Conditions, with Recommendations.* Chicago: Gunthrop Warren, 1911.

"Chicago's 'Morals Court.' " *Literary Digest* 46 (1913): 1228–29.

"The Chicago Vice Commission." *Survey* 26 (1911): 215–18.

"Chinese Slavery in America." *North American Review* 165 (1897): 288–94.

Christian, Hilary. "The Social Evil from a Rational Standpoint." *Pennsylvania Medical Journal* 15 (1912): 788–91.

Clappe, Shirley. *The Shirley Letters from the California Mines.* New York: Knopf, 1949.

Clark, Sue Ainslie, and Wyatt, Edith. *Making Both Ends Meet: The Income and Outlay of New York Working Girls.* New York: Macmillan, 1911.

Clarke, Walter. "Prostitution and Alcohol." *Journal of Social Hygiene* 3 (1917–18): 75–90.

"Clause 79 of the Page Law." *Survey* 25 (1910): 276–80.

"Clause 79 of the Page Law: Symposium." *Survey* 25 (1910): 435–38.

Cleveland. Cleveland Baptist Brotherhood. *Report of the Vice Commission of the Cleveland Baptist Brotherhood.* Cleveland, 1911.

Cocks, Orrin. *The Social Evil and Methods of Treatment.* New York, 1912.

Coffee, Rudolph I. "Pittsburgh Clergy and the Social Evil." *Survey* 29 (1913): 815–16.

Collier, Robert Laird. *The Social Evil: An Address*. Chicago: Rand McNally, 1871.

Coolidge, Mary. "California Women and the Abatement Act." *Survey* 31 (1914): 739–40.

Cordelier, Jeanne. *"The Life": Memoirs of a French Hooker*. Translated by Harry Mathews. New York: Viking, 1978.

Cousins, Sheila [pseud.]. . . . *To Beg I Am Ashamed*. Paris: Obelisk Press, 1938.

Crane, Stephen. *Maggie: A Girl of the Streets* (1893). Greenwich, Conn.: Fawcett, 1960.

Creel, Herr Glessner. *Prostitution for Profit: A Police Reporter's View of the White Slave Traffic*. St. Louis: National Rip-Saw Publishing Co., 1911.

Creighton, Louise. *The Social Disease*. London, 1914.

Cunningham, Peter. *The Story of Nell Gwynne*. London: Lippincott, 1903.

Curtis, Mrs. T. P. *The Traffic in Women*. Boston: Woman Suffrage Party of Boston, n.d. HLP. Folder 163.

"A Danger Signal." *Outlook*, no. 94 (1910), pp. 426–27.

Davis, Katherine Bement. *Social Hygiene and the War: Woman's Part in the Campaign*. No. 159. New York: American Social Hygiene Association, 1918.

――――. "A Study of Prostitutes Committed from New York City to the State Reformatory for Women at Bedford Hills." In Kneeland, *Commercialized Prostitution in New York*.

"Dayton." *National Municipal Review* 4, no. 4 (October 1915): 689–90.

deForest, H. P. "Prostitution: Police Methods of Sanitary Supervision: Personal Observation of Police Methods of Dealing with Prostitution in Germany with Conclusions as to Their Sanitary Value." *New York State Journal of Medicine* 8 (1908): 516–35.

Deland, Margaret. "The Change in the Feminine Ideal." *Atlantic Monthly* 105 (1910): 290–91.

Dewson, Mary. *Conditions That Make Wayward Girls: A Study Based on Last Year's Commitments to the Massachusetts State Industrial School for Girls*. Lancaster, Mass., 1910.

Dorr, Rheta Childe. "Reclaiming the Wayward Girl." *Hampton's* 26 (1911): 67–78.

――――. *What Eight Million Women Want*. Boston: Small, Maynard, 1912.

Dreiser, Theodore. *Sister Carrie* (1900). New York: Modern Library, 1932.

Edholm, M.G.C. "A Stain on the Flag." *Californian*, February 1892.

――――. *Traffic in Girls: Personal Experiences in Rescue Work*. Social Welfare League, 1899.

――――. "Traffic in White Girls." *California Illustrated* 2 (1892): 825–38.

Editorial. *Mascot* (New Orleans). June 1892. Quoted in Rose, *Storyville, New Orleans*.

Editorial. *Vigilance* 20, no. 11 (1912).

Edson, Katherine Farwell. "Woman's Influence on State Legislation." *California Woman's Bulletin* 14, no. 24 (June 14, 1913): 7–8.

Ellington, George. *The Women of New York or the Underworld of the Great City*. New York, 1869.

Elliot, Albert. *The Cause of the Social Evil and Its Remedy*. Atlanta: Webb and Vary, 1914.

Ellis, Havelock. *Studies in the Psychology of Sex*. Vol. 6. Philadelphia: Davis, 1928.

――――. *The Task of Social Hygiene*. Boston, 1915.

Encyclopedia Britannica. 11th ed. S.v. "prostitution."

Engels, Frederick. *The Origins of the Family, Private Property, and the State in the Light of the Researches of Lewis H. Morgan.* New York: International, 1942.

Everett, Ray H. "The Cost of Venereal Disease to Industry." *Journal of Industrial Hygiene* 2 (1920/21): 178–81.

"Fighting Prostitution in Michigan." *Survey,* no. 41 (1918), pp. 70–71.

"Fighting Vice Segregation in Chicago." *Literary Digest* 45 (1912): 848.

Finch, Stanley. "The White Slave Traffic." *Senate Documents* 24, no. 982. 62d Cong., 1912–13.

"Five 'White Slave' Trade Investigations." *McClure's* 35 (1910): 346–48.

Flexner, Abraham. "Next Steps in Dealing with Prostitution." *Journal of Social Hygiene* 1 (1914): 529–38.

——. *Prostitution in Europe.* New York: Century, 1914.

Flower, B. O. "Prostitution within the Marriage Bond." *Arena* 13 (1895): 59.

Flynn, Elizabeth Gurley. *The Rebel Girl: An Autobiography.* New York: International, 1976.

Fournier, Professor. "Rapports préliminaires." Conférence Internationale, Brussels, 1899. In *The Social Evil, with Special Reference to Conditions Existing in the City of New York,* 2d ed., by Edwin Seligman. New York: Putnam, 1912.

Frank, Henrietta, and Jerome, Amalie. *Annals of the Chicago Women's Club for the Forty Years of Its Organization, 1876–1916.* Chicago: Chicago Women's Club, 1916.

Freud, Sigmund. "Contributions to the Psychology of Love: The Most Prevalent Form of Degradation in Erotic Life" (1912). In his *Collected Papers,* edited by Ernest Jones, translated by Joan Riviere, 4:203–17. New York: Basic Books, 1959.

Frowne, Sadie. "The Story of a Sweatshop Girl." In *Workers Speak,* edited by Leon Stein and Philip Taft. New York: Arno Press and the New York Times, 1971.

Furling, Mrs. W. H. "Do California Women Want Suffrage?" *Federation Courier* 11 (April 1911): 13.

"The Futility of the White Slave Agitation as Brand Whitlock Sees It." *Current Opinion,* no. 56 (1914), pp. 287–88.

Garrett, Laura. "Overemphasis on the Social Evil." *Vigilance* 20, no. 11 (1912).

Garrison, William Lloyd. "Relations of Poverty." In *Purity Congress Proceedings.* Baltimore, 1895.

Glasgow, Maude. "On the Regulation of Prostitution, with Special Reference to Paragraph 79 of the Page Bill," *New York and Philadelphia Medical Journal* 42 (1910).

Goldman, Emma. *Living My Life.* Vol. 1. New York: Dover, 1970.

——. "The Traffic in Women." In her *The Traffic in Women and Other Essays on Feminism.* 1917. Reprint. New York: Times Change Reprint, 1970.

Goodnow, Elizabeth. *The Market for Souls.* New York: 1910.

——. "Rosa: The True Story of a Sacrifice." *Harper's Weekly* 53 (September 4, 1909): 16–17.

Grand Rapids, Mich. Public Welfare Council. *Report on the Social Evil.* 1913.

Gregory, Maurice. *A Short Summary of the Parliamentary History of State-Regulated Vice in the United Kingdom.* London, 1900.

——. *The Suppression of the White Slave Traffic: Historical Sketch of the English Section of the Movement.* London, 1908.

Hall, Winfield Scott. *Sexual Knowledge*. Philadelphia: International Bible House, 1913.

Hallam, Wirt W. "The Reduction of Vice in Certain Western Cities through Law Enforcement." *Journal of Social Diseases*, April 1912.

Hancock, F. H. "Regulation of Prostitution in the City of Norfolk, Virginia." *Virginia Medical Semi-Monthly* 17 (1912/13): 559–61.

Harris, H. Wilson. *Human Merchandise*. London: Ernest Benn, 1928.

Hart, A. B. *The Southern South*. New York: Appleton, 1910.

Hartford, Conn. Hartford Vice Commission. *Report of the Hartford Vice Commission*. Hartford: Connecticut Woman Suffrage Association, 1913.

Healy, William. *The Individual Delinquent: A Textbook of Diagnosis and Prognosis for All Concerned in Understanding Offenders*. Boston: Little, Brown, 1915.

Henrotin, Ellen. "Address." *Vigilance* 11, no. 4 (November 1912).

Hepburn, Katherine Houghton. *Woman Suffrage and the Social Evil*. New York: National Woman Suffrage Publishing Co., n.d.

Hitchborn, Franklin. *Arguments Which Are Used against the California Redlight Abatement Act*. San Francisco: Barry, n.d.

———. "The Antivice Movement in California." *Social Hygiene* 6 (June 1920): 213–27.

Holmes, J. D. "Vice and Wages." *Survey*, no. 26 (1911), pp. 701–2.

Hooker, Isabella Beecher. *Womanhood: Its Sanctities and Fidelities*. Boston: Lee and Shepherd, 1974.

Hopwood, Eric C. "The Opinion of the Press as a Moral Educator." *Journal of Social Hygiene* 2 (1915/16): 21–36.

"How Atlanta Cleaned Up." *Literary Digest* 46 (1913): 1012–13.

Hurty, John. "The Sterilization of Criminals and Defectives." *Social Diseases* 3:1 (January 1913).

Illinois. General Assembly. Senate Vice Committee. *Report of the Senate Vice Committee*. Chicago: Allied Printing, 1916.

"Is White Slavery Nothing More than a Myth?" *Current Opinion*, no. 55 (1913), p. 348.

Jackson, Harry. *The New Chivalry*. New York: Hodder and Stoughton, 1914.

Janney, O. Edward. "A General Point of View." *Vigilance* 20, no. 11 (1912).

———. *The White Slave Traffic in America*. New York: National Vigilance Committee, 1911.

Johnson, Fred. *The Social Evil in Kansas*. Kansas City, Mo., 1911. [Kansas vice report]

Jones, W. R. "Prostitution in Seattle." *Northwest Medicine* 17 (1918): 239–42.

Kauffman, Reginald. *The Girl That Goes Wrong*. New York: Macaulay, 1911.

———. *The House of Bondage*. New York: Moffat, Yard, 1910.

Keller v. United States, Ullman v. United States. 213 U.S. 138 (1909).

Kelley, Florence. "Communications." *Survey*, no. 24 (1910), p. 646.

———. Review of Jane Addams's *A New Conscience and an Ancient Evil*. *American Journal of Sociology* 18 (1912): 271–72.

Kellogg, Paul V. "The Spread of the Survey Idea." *Proceedings of the Academy of Political Science* 2 (1912): 475–91.

Kelly, Howard. *The Double Shame of Baltimore: Her Unpublished Vice Report and Her Utter Indifference*. Baltimore: Society for the Prevention of Social Diseases, 1914.

————. *The Influence of Segregation upon Prostitution and upon the Public.* Philadelphia: Society for the Prevention of Social Diseases, 1912.

————. "Making Baltimore a Decent City." *Vigilance* 20, no. 11 (1912).

Kelso, Tessa L. *Clause 79: Report to the Woman's Municipal League of the City of New York.* Pamphlet, New York, 1911.

Kimball, Nell. *Her Life as an American Madam.* New York: Macmillan, 1970.

Kneeland, George. *Commercialized Prostitution in New York.* 1913. Reprint. Montclair, N.J.: Patterson-Smith, 1969.

Lafayette, Ind. Lafayette Vice Commission. *A Report on Vice Conditions.* 1913.

Laidlaw, Harriet. Review of Elizabeth Robbins's *My Little Sister. Survey* 30 (1913): 199–202.

Lancaster, Pa. Lancaster Vice Commission. *Report on Vice Conditions in the City of Lancaster.* Lancaster: American Vigilance Association, 1913.

————. *A Second Report on Vice Conditions in the City of Lancaster.* 1915.

Laughlin, Clara E. "Girls Who Go Wrong." *Pearson's,* no. 23 (1910), pp. 377–87.

————. "A Single Standard." *Pearson's,* no. 31 (1914), pp. 728–38.

Law, E. Norine. *The Shame of a Great Nation: The Story of the "White Slave Trade."* Harrisburg, Pa.: United Evangelical Publishing House, 1909.

Lecky, William Edward Hartpole. *History of European Morals.* 3d ed. Rev. London, 1877.

Letter to the *New York Evening Journal,* January 27, 1914. In "Scrapbook," HLP.

Lexington, Ky. Vice Commission of Lexington. *Report of the Vice Commission of Lexington.* 1915.

Lippman, Walter. *A Preface to Politics.* 1913. Reprint. Ann Arbor: University of Michigan Press, 1965.

Little Rock, Ark. Little Rock Vice Commission. *Report of the Little Rock Vice Commission and the Order of Mayor Chas. E. Taylor to Close All Resorts in Little Rock by August 25, 1913.* 1913.

Lombroso, Cesare, and Ferrero, G. *La donna deliquente, la prostituta, e la donna normale.* Turin, 1893.

Louisville, Ky. Louisville Vice Commission. *Report of the Vice Commission: Survey of Existing Conditions, with Recommendations to the Honorable John H. Buschmeyer, Mayor.* 1915.

Lytle, H. M. *Tragedies of the White Slave.* Chicago: Charles C. Thompson, 1909.

Lytle, H. M., and Dillon, John. *From Dance Hall to White Slavery.* Chicago: Stanton and Van Vuet, 1912.

McClure, S. S. "The Tammanyzing of a Civilization." *McClure's* 34 (November 1909): 117–28.

McCord, Clinton P. "One Hundred Female Offenders: A Study of the Mentality of Prostitutes and 'Wayward' Girls." *Journal of the American Institute of Criminal Law and Criminology* 6 (1915–16): 385–407.

Mackirdy, Mrs. Archibald, and Willis, W. N. *The White Slave Market.* London, 1912.

Madeleine: An Autobiography. With an Introduction by Judge Ben Lindsey. New York: Harper and Brothers, 1919.

Mandeville, Bernard. *A Modest Defense of Publick Stews.* London: A. Moore, 1726.

"Man's Commerce in Women." *McClure's* 41 (1913): 185.

Marchant, James. *The Master Problem.* London, 1917.

Massachusetts. *Report of the Commission for the Investigation of the White Slave Traffic, So Called.* H.D. No. 2281. Boston: Wright and Potter, 1914.

Mayer, Joseph. "The Passing of the Red-Light Districts." *Social Hygiene* 4: 199 (1918).

————. *The Regulation of Commercialized Vice: An Analysis of the Transition from Segregation to Repression in the United States.* New York: Klebold Press, 1922.

Merrill, Dora. "A Protection for Girls in Ohio." *Woman's Journal,* May 2, 1891, p. 142.

Mertz, Paul Allen. "Mental Deficiency of Prostitutes: A Study of Delinquent Women at an Army Post of Embarkten." *Journal of the American Medical Association* 72 (May 1919): 1597–99.

Miner, Maude. "The Problem of Wayward Girls and Delinquent Women." *Proceedings of the Academy of Political Science* 2 (1912): 604–12.

————. "Relation between Occupation and Criminality of Women." *Survey,* no. 30 (1913), pp. 731–32.

————. "Report of Commission on Social Hygiene." *Journal of Social Hygiene* 1 (1914): 81–92.

————. *The Slavery of Prostitution.* New York: Macmillan, 1916.

————. "Two Weeks in the Night Court." *Survey* 22 (1909): 229–34.

Minneapolis, Minn. Vice Commission of Minneapolis. *Report of the Vice Commission to His Honor James C. Haynes, Mayor.* 1911. Reprint. *The Prostitute and the Reformer,* edited by Rosenberg and Smith-Rosenberg.

Mitchell, Ellen. "A Plea for Fallen Women." In *Papers from the Second Congress of Women,* Chicago, 1874.

"The Moral Havoc Wrought by Moving Picture Shows." *Current Opinion* 56 (1914): 290.

Morris, Charles S. "The Terrible Tenderloin." *New York Age,* February 22, 1906.

Morrow, Prince. "A Plea for the Organization of a 'Society of Sanitary and Moral Prophylaxis.' " *Medical News* 84 (1904): 1073–77.

————. "The Relations of Social Diseases to the Family." *American Journal of Sociology* 14 (1909): 622–35.

————. "Venereal Diseases and Their Relation to Infant Mortality and Race Deterioration." *New York Medical Journal* 94 (1911): 1315–17.

Muhlenberg, W. A. *The Woman and Her Accusers: A Plea for the Midnight Mission.* New York: Pliny Smith, 1871.

New York City. Bureau of Social Hygiene. *Commercialized Prostitution in New York City: A Comparison between 1912, 1915, and 1916.* Pamphlet. New York: Century, November 1, 1916.

New York City. Committee of Fourteen. *Department Store Investigation Report of the Subcommittee.* 1915.

————. *A Summary of Vice Conditions in Harlem: Annual Report for 1928.* New York, 1929.

New York City. Research Committee of the Committee of Fourteen for the Suppression of "Raines Law Hotels" in New York City. *The Social Evil in New York City: A Study in Law Enforcement.* New York: Andrew H. Kellogg, 1910.

O'Higgins, H. J. "Case of Fanny." *Collier's* 48 (March 2, 1912): 11.

"Organized Vice as a Vested Interest." *Current Literature* 52 (March 1912): 292–94.

Ouida. "Love versus Avarice: The Causes Which Make for Social Evil." *Lippincott's* 83 (June 1909): 712–17.

Paducah, Ky. Paducah Vice Commission. *Report of the Paducah Vice Commission.* 1916.

Pappritz, Anna. *The Economic Causes of Prostitution.* Berlin, 1903.

Parent-Duchatelet, Alexandre Jean Baptiste. *De la prostitution dans la ville de Paris, considérée sous le rapport de l'hygiene publique, de la morale, et de l'administration.* Vol. 1. Paris, 1857.

Parkhurst, Charles. *Our Fight with Tammany.* New York, 1895.

Philadelphia, Pa. Vice Commission of Philadelphia. *A Report of Existing Conditions, with Recommendations to the Honorable Rudolph Blankenburg, Mayor.* 1913. Reprint. *The Prostitute and the Social Reformer,* edited by Rosenberg and Smith-Rosenberg.

Phillips, David Graham. *Susan Lennox: Her Fall and Rise.* 1915.

Pittsburgh, Pa. Morals Efficiency Commission. *Report and Recommendations of the Morals Efficiency Commission.* 1913.

"Popular Gullibility as Exhibited in the New White Slavery Hysteria." *Current Opinion* 56 (February 1914): 129.

Portland, Me. Citizen's Committee of Portland to Investigate the Social Evil. *First Report of the Citizen's Committee to Investigate the Social Evil.* 1914.

Portland, Ore. Portland Vice Commission. *Report of the Portland Vice Commission to the Mayor and City Council of the City of Portland.* 1913.

Powell, Aaron M., ed. *The National Purity Congress: Its Papers, Addresses, Portraits.* New York, 1896.

Powell, Adam Clayton, Sr. *Against the Tide.* New York: R. R. Smith, 1938.

"Prevent Crime to Reduce Poverty." *Survey* 25 (1911): 648–49.

"Probation for Girls Who Err." *Survey* 23 (1909): 349–50.

"Prostitution Banished in One New York Town." *Survey* 30 (1913): 158–59.

"Prostitution in Europe: Abraham Flexner's Study of Supply, Demand, Regulation." *Survey* 31 (1914): 471–73.

"Prostitution within the Marriage Bond." *Arena* 13 (1895).

"Protection of the Home." *Independent* 52 (1900): 2647.

Protest against the Clause 79 of the Inferior Courts Bill. Pamphlet. Signed by the Women's Prison Association, the National Women's Suffrage Association, the Women's Christian Temperance Union, the Hygiene Committee of the Woman's Medical Association, the Woman Suffrage Party of New York City, and others. January 20, 1911.

"The Punishment of a White Slave Trader." *Outlook* 98 (1911): 567–68.

Reckless, Walter. *Vice in Chicago.* 1933. Reprint. Montclair, N.J.: Patterson-Smith, 1969.

"Reminiscences of John T. Hetbrick." Oral History Research Office, Columbia University, 1949. In *The Making of Harlem: Negro New York, 1877–1920,* edited by Gilbert Osofsky. New York: Harper & Row, 1971.

"Report of Chicago Vice Commission." *Survey* 26 (1911): 99.

Richardson, Dorothy. *The Long Day: The Story of a Working Girl.* 1905. Reprinted in *Women at Work*, edited by William O'Neill. New York: Quadrangle, 1973.

Ripley, Sarah Cory. "The Case of Angeline." *Outlook*, no. 106 (1914), pp. 252–56.

Ritter, Mary. "The Social Evil and Its Prevention." *Federation Courier* 2, no. 1 (September 1910): 17.

Roberts, Florence. *Fifteen Years with the Outcast.* Anderson, Ind.: Gospel Trumpet Co., 1912.

Robins, Margaret Dreier. "One Aspect of the Menace of Low Wages." *Journal of Social Hygiene* 1 (1914): 358–63.

Rockefeller Grand Jury. "Presentment of the Rockefeller Grand Jury." June 29, 1910. Reprinted in Niemoeller, *Sexual Slavery in America.*

"The Rockefeller Grand Jury Report." *McClure's* 35 (1910): 471–73.

Rockland County, N.Y. Committee of Fifty. *Report of the Survey Made in Rockland County.* 1915.

Roe, Clifford G. *The Girl Who Disappeared.* Chicago: American Bureau of Moral Education, 1914.

———. *Panders and Their White Slaves.* New York: Fleming Revell, 1910.

———. *What Women Might Do with the Ballot: The Abolition of White Slave Traffic.* New York: National American Woman Suffrage Association, n.d.

———, ed. *The Great War on White Slavery.* New York, 1911.

Roosevelt, Theodore. "The Cause of Decency." *Outlook*, no. 98 (1911), pp. 569–71.

Rosen, Ruth, and Davidson, Sue, eds. *The Maimie Papers.* New York: Feminist Press, 1977.

Rosenberg, Charles, and Smith-Rosenberg, Carroll, eds. *The Prostitute and the Social Reformer.* New York: Arno, 1974.

Rosenstirn, Julius. *The Municipal Clinic of San Francisco.* New York: William Wood, 1913.

Royden, Maude. *Downward Paths: An Inquiry into the Causes Which Contribute to the Making of a Prostitute.* London: G. Beel and Sons, 1916.

———. *Woman and the Sovereign State.* London: Headley Brothers, 1917.

Sanger, William. *History of Prostitution: Its Extent, Causes, and Effect throughout the World.* New York, 1876.

"Sex O'Clock in America." *Current Opinion* 55 (1913): 113–14.

Shepherd, C. "Chinese Girl Slavery in America." *Missionary Review*, 1923, pp. 893–98.

Shreveport, La. Shreveport Vice Commission. *Brief and Recommendations.* 1915.

Sims, Edwin. "The White Slave Trade Today." In Bell, *Fighting the Traffic in Young Girls.*

Sinclair, Upton. *The Autobiography of Upton Sinclair.* London: W. H. Allen, 1963.

"The Slave Traffic in America." *Outlook* 93 (1909): 528–29.

"The Social Evil." *Medicine* 12 (1906): 614–17.

"The Social Evil." *Outlook*, no. 70 (1902), pp. 606–8.

"The Social Evil." *Outlook*, no. 101 (1912), pp. 245–48.

"Social Evil in a Smaller City." *Survey* 26 (1911): 212–13.

"The Social Evil in the American Army." *Current Opinion* 54 (1913): 273–74.

"The Social Evil: The Immediate Remedies." *Outlook*, no. 103 (1913), pp. 298–99.

Spencer, Anna Garlin. "The Age of Consent and Its Significance." *Forum* 49 (1913): 406–20.

———. "The Danger of Estimates." *Vigilance* 20, no. 11 (1912).

———. "Is the Page Bill All Right?" *Survey* 24 (1910): 354–55.

———. "Josephine Butler and the English Crusade." *Forum* 49 (1913): 703–16.

———. "Josephine Butler and the English Crusade, II." *Forum* 50 (1913): 77–81.

———. "The Scarlet Woman." *Forum* 49 (1913): 276–89.

———. "State Regulation of Vice and Its Meaning." *Forum* 49 (1913): 587–606.

———. "A Word More on the Page Bill." *Survey* 24 (1910): 514–15.

Spencer, Mrs. Dorcas James. *A History of the Women's Christian Temperance Union of Northern and Central California*. Oakland: West Coast Printing, 1911.

Stanford, Sally. *The Lady of the House: The Autobiography of Sally Stanford*. New York: G. P. Putnam, 1966.

Stanton, Elizabeth Cady; Anthony, Susan B.; and Gage, Mathilda Joceyln, eds. *History of Woman Suffrage*. 6 vols. n.p., 1889.

Starkweather, Mary. "Report of the Department of Women and Children." In the *Twelfth Biennial Report of the Bureau of Labor, Industries, and Commerce of the State of Minnesota*, pp. 619–20. 1909–10.

Sumner, Dean. "Address." *Vigilance* 20, no. 11 (1912).

Survey, no. 30 (May 3, 1913). HLP, Folder 149.

Swift, Morrison. *Prostitution—A Remedy: Bills and Petitions Presented to the Massachusetts Legislature in the Session of 1911–1912*. Pamphlet. Boston: Liberty Press, 1912.

Syracuse, N.Y. Committee of Eighteen, Morals Survey Committee. *The Social Evil in Syracuse*. 1913.

Szarkowski, John, ed. *E. J. Bellocq: Storyville Portraits—Photographs from the New Orleans Red Light District, circa 1912*. New York: Museum of Modern Art, 1970.

Tabor, Pauline. *Memoirs of the Madam on Clay Street*. Louisville, Ky.: Touchstone, 1972.

Tarbell, Ida M. "Good Will to Woman." *American* 75 (1913): 45–52.

Taylor, Graham. "Morals Commission and Police Morals." *Survey* 30 (1913): 62–64.

———. "Police Efficiency, the First Test of Vice Inquiries." *Survey* 29 (1912): 136–41.

———. "Routing the Segregationists in Chicago." *Survey* 29 (1912): 254–56.

———. "The War on Vice." *Survey* 29 (1913): 811–13.

Taylor, Lydia. *From under the Lid, an Appeal to True Womanhood*. N.p., 1913.

Terhune, Mary Virginia Hawes [Marion Harland]. "The Passing of the Home Daughter." *Independent* 71 (July 13, 1911).

Thomas, William I., and Znaniecki, Florian. *The Polish Peasant in Europe and America, 1918–1920*. Reprint. 2 vols. New York: Dover, 1958.

Toronto. Social Survey Committee of Toronto. *Report of the Social Survey Committee*. 1915.

Treadway, W. L. "A Psychiatric Study of Delinquent Women in Lansing, Kansas." *Public Health Reports* 35 (1920): 1197–1210.

Turner, George Kibbe. "The City of Chicago: A Study of the Great Immoralities." *McClure's* 28 (1907): 575–92.

————. "The Daughters of the Poor: A Plain Story of the Development of New York City as a Leading Center of the White Slave Trade of the World, under Tammany Hall." *McClure's* 34, no. 1 (November 1909): 45–61.

————. "The Strange Woman." *McClure's* 41 (1913): 25–33.

Union Signal. February 17, 1889.

U.S. Bureau of the Census. *American Census Taken from First Census of the United States*, by William R. Merriam. Washington, D.C.: Government Printing Office, 1904.

————. *Occupations at the Twelfth Census, 1900.* 1904.

————. *Report on Crime, Pauperism, and Benevolence: Eleventh Census of the United States*, 1890.

U.S. Bureau of Immigration. *Report No. 540 12/201.*

————. *Report No. 541 34/220.*

U.S. Commissioner of Labor. *Working Women in Large Cities: Fourth Annual Report.* 1888.

U.S. Congress. House. Committee on Interstate and Foreign Commerce. *White Slave Traffic.* H. Rept. 47, 61st Cong., 2d sess., 1909.

U.S. Congress. Senate. Committee on the District of Columbia. *Abatement on Houses of Ill Fame. Hearings before a sub-committee of Committee on the District of Columbia.* 62d Cong., 1912.

U.S. Congress. Senate. *Reports of the Immigration Commission.* 61st Cong., 3d sess., 1910. Vol. 19. *Importation and Harboring of Women for Immoral Purposes.*

————. *Importing Women for Immoral Purposes. A Partial Report from the Immigration Commission on the Importation and Harboring of Women for Immoral Purposes.* S. Doc. 196, 61st Cong., 2d sess., 1909.

————. *Report on the Condition of Women and Child Wage Earners in the United States.* S. Doc. 645, 61st Cong., 2d sess., 1911. Vol. 15. *Relation between Occupation and Criminality in Women.*

U.S. Department of Commerce and Labor, Office of the Secretary. *Arrest and Deportation of Prostitutes and Procurers of Prostitutes.* Department Circular #156. September 26, 1907.

U.S. Department of Justice. *Annual Report of the Attorney General of the United States.* 1913–20.

U.S. Department of Labor, Bureau of Labor Statistics. *Summary of the Report on Conditions of Women and Child Wage Earners in the United States.* 1916.

U.S. Public Health Service. *What Representative Citizens Think about Prostitution.* 1921. Pamphlet.

"The United States and the Importation of Vice." *Outlook* 92 (1909): 250–51.

Vecki, V. G. "Can We Abolish, Shall We Ignore, or Must We Regulate Prostitution?" *American Journal of Dermatology and Genito-Urinary Diseases* 14 (1910): 213–20.

"Vice Fought by the 'Golden Rule.' " *Literary Digest* 46 (1913): 234.

"Vice Investigation by the Illinois Senate." *Survey* 29 (1913): 897.

"The Vice Problem in Philadelphia." *Survey* 30 (1913): 259.

"The 'Vice Trust' in New York City." *Current Opinion* 54 (1913): 5–6.

Vilas, Martin. *The Barbary Coast of San Francisco*. San Francisco, 1915.
"Votes for Women and Votes to Table the Hartford Vice Report." *Survey* 31 (1913): 73.

"Wages and Sin." *Literary Digest* 46 (1913): 621–24.
Warren, John. *Thirty Years' Battle with Crime, or the Crying Shame of New York as Seen under the Broad Glare of an Old Detective's Lantern*. 1877. Reprint. Pough-keepsie, N.Y.: Arno, 1970.
Waterman, Willoughby Cyrus. *Prostitution and Its Repression in New York City, 1900–31*. New York: Columbia University Press, 1932.
"The Ways, Wages, and Wherefore of the Scarlet Woman." *Hearst's* 24 (1913): 147–49.
The Wayward Girl and the Church's Responsibility. Pamphlet. New York: Church Mission of Help, 1911.
"Wayward Girls." *Survey* 25 (1911): 690–91.
Weidensall, Jean. *The Mentality of the Criminal Woman: A Comparative Study of the Criminal Woman, the Working Girl, and the Efficient Working Woman in a Series of Mental and Physical Tests*. Baltimore: Warwick and York, 1916.
————. "Psychological Tests as Applied to Criminal Women." *Psychological Review* 21 (1914): 370–75.
"The White Slave Decision." *Literary Digest* 46 (1913): 500–2.
"The White Slave Films." *Outlook* 106 (1914): 120–22.
"The White Slave Films: A Review." *Outlook* 106 (1914): 345–50.
"White Slave Revelations." *Current Literature* 47 (December 1909): 594–98.
"White Slavers Routed." *Outlook* 103 (1913): 569–70.
"White Slaves." *Outlook* 94 (1910): 131–32.
"White Slaves and Immigration." *Outlook* 93 (1909): 881–83.
"The White Slaves and the Social Evil." *Chatauquan* 57 (1909/10): 331–33.
"The White Slave Trade." *Contemporary Review* 82 (1902): 735–40.
"White Slave Trade." *Missionary Review of the World* 26 (1903): 149.
"The White Slave Traffic." *Outlook* 95 (1910): 545–46.
"The White Slave Traffic before the Supreme Court." *Current Opinion* 54 (1913): 273.
Whitlock, Brand. "The White Slave." *Forum* 51 (1914): 193–216.
Williams, A. "The Antivenereal Campaign: Its Propaganda, Present Status, Future Possibilities." *Detroit Medical Journal* 9 (1909): 39–47.
Williams, Jessie. "The New Marriage." *Good Housekeeping* 52 (February 1914).
Wilson, Otto. *Fifty Years' Work with Girls, 1883–1933*. Alexandria, Va.: National Florence Crittendon Mission, 1933.
Wilson, Robert N. *The American Boy and the Social Evil: From a Physician's Standpoint*. Philadelphia: J. C. Winston, 1905.
————. "The Relation of the Medical Profession to the Social Evil." *Journal of the American Medical Association* 47 (1906): 29–32.
Wisconsin. Wisconsin Legislative Committee. *Report and Recommendations for the Wisconsin Legislative Committee to Investigate the White Slave Traffic and Kindred Subjects*. Madison, 1914.
"Wisconsin's Last Segregated District Closed." *Survey* 33 (1914): 328.
Woman's Journal 33 (December 6, 1902).
"Woman's Noblest Calling." *Federation Courier* 11:5 (April 1911): 12.

"Women Slavery on the Pacific Coast." *Woman's Journal*, March 26, 1892.

Wood, Mary. *The History of the General Federation of Women's Clubs*. New York: General Federation of Women's Clubs, 1912.

Woolston, Howard. *Prostitution in the United States prior to the Entrance of the United States into the World War*. 1921. Reprint. Montclair, N.J.: Patterson-Smith, 1969.

Zimmerman, Jean Turner. *America's Black Traffic in White Girls*, 8th ed. Chicago, 1912.

SECONDARY SOURCES

Ariès, Philippe. *Centuries of Childhood: A Social History of Family Life*. Translated by Robert Baldick. New York: Knopf, 1962.

Ashbury, Herbert. *The Barbary Coast: An Informal History of the San Francisco Underworld*. New York: Knopf, 1933.

Bacon, Alice. *Japanese Girls and Women*. Boston: Houghton Mifflin, 1919.

Bancroft, Frederick. *Slave Trading in the Old South*. Baltimore. J. H. Furst, 1931.

Banks, J. A., and Banks, Olive. *Feminism and Family Planning in Victorian England*. New York: Schocken, 1964.

Barker-Benfield, G. J. *The Horrors of the Half-Known Life: Male Attitudes toward Women and Sexuality in Nineteenth-Century America*. New York: Harper & Row, 1976.

———. "The Spermatic Economy: A Nineteenth-Century View." In *The American Family in Social-Historical Perspective*, edited by Michael Gordon. New York: St. Martin's, 1973.

Barnhart, Jacqueline Baker. "Working Women: Prostitution in San Francisco from the Gold Rush to 1900." Ph.D. dissertation, University of California, San Francisco, 1976.

Barry, Kathleen. *Female Sexual Slavery*. Englewood Cliffs, N.J.: Prentice-Hall, 1979.

Becker, Howard Saul. *Outsiders: Studies in the Sociology of Deviance*. New York: Free Press, 1963.

Bell, Daniel. "The Myth of Crime Waves." In his *The End of Ideology: On the Exhaustion of Political Ideas in the Fifties*. Glencoe, Ill.: Free Press, 1960.

Bendix, Rheinhard. "Compliant Behavior and Individual Personality." In *Personality and Social Systems*, edited by Neil J. Smelser and William T. Smelser. New York: Wiley, 1963.

Benjamin, H. "Prostitution." In *Encyclopedia of Sexual Behavior*, edited by A. Ellis and A. Arbanel. New York: Hawthorn, 1961.

Berg, Barbara. *The Remembered Gate: Origins of American Feminism—The Woman and the City, 1800–60*. New York: Oxford University Press, 1978.

Blum, Marjorie Christine. "Prostitution and the Progressive Vice Crusade." Master's thesis, University of Wisconsin, 1967.

Boyer, Paul S. *Purity in Print: The Vice Society Movement and Book Censorship in America*. New York: Scribner's, 1968.

———. *Urban Masses and Moral Order in America, 1820–1920*. Cambridge: Harvard University Press, 1978.

Breckinridge, Sophinisba P. *Women in the Twentieth Century: A Study of Their Political, Social, and Economic Activities*. New York: McGraw-Hill, 1933.

Briffault, Robert. *The Mothers*. 3 vols. London: Allen and Unwin, 1959.

Bristow, Edward. *Vice and Vigilance: Purity Movements in Britain since 1700*. Dublin: Gill & Macmillan, 1977.

Bryan, James. "Apprenticeships in Prostitution." In *Deviance: The Interactionist Perspective*, edited by Earl Rubington and Martin S. Weinberg. New York: Macmillan, 1973.

————. "Occupational Ideologies and Individual Attitudes of Call Girls." In *Deviance: The Interactionist Perspective*, edited by Earl Rubington and Martin S. Weinberg. New York: Macmillan, 1973.

Bullough, Vern L. *The History of Prostitution*. New Hyde Park, N.Y.: University Books, 1964.

————. "Problems and Methods for Research in Prostitution and the Behavioral Sciences." *Journal of History of the Behavioral Sciences* 1 (1965): 244–51.

Bullough, Vern L., and Bullough, Bonnie. *Prostitution: An Illustrated Social History*. New York: Crown, 1978.

————. *Sin, Sickness, and Sanity: A History of Sexual Attitudes*. New York: New American Library, 1977.

Bullough, Vern, and Voght, Martha. "Homosexuality and Its Confusion with the 'Secret Sin' in Pre-Freudian America." *Journal of the History of Medicine and Allied Sciences* 28 (1973): 143–55.

Burnham, John C. "American Historians and the Subject of Sex." *Societas: A Review of Social History* 1 (1972): 307–16.

————. "Medical Inspection of Prostitutes in America in the Nineteenth Century: The St. Louis Experiment and Its Sequel." *Bulletin of the History of Medicine* 45, no. 3 (1971): 203–18.

————. "Medical Specialists and Movements toward Social Control in the Progressive Era: Three Examples." In *Building the Organizational Society*, edited by Jerry Israel. New York: Free Press, 1972.

————. "The Progressive Era Revolution in American Attitudes toward Sex." *Journal of American History* 59 (March 1973): 885–908.

————. *Psychoanalysis and American Medicine, 1894–1918: Medicine, Science, and Culture*. New York: International Universities Press, 1967.

————. "The Social Evil Ordinance: A Social Experiment in Nineteenth-Century St. Louis." *Bulletin of the Missouri Historical Society* 27 (1971): 203–17.

Calhoun, Arthur. *Social History of the American Family*. 3 vols. Cleveland: Clark, 1919.

Chafe, William. *The American Woman: Her Changing Social, Economic, and Political Roles, 1920–70*. New York: Oxford University Press, 1972.

Clegg, Charles, and Clegg, Lucy. *The Legends of the Comstock Lode*. Oakland, Calif.: Grahame H. Arly, 1950.

Clinard, Marshall. *Sociology of Deviant Behavior*. New York, 1922.

————. "The Theoretical Implications of Anomie and Deviant Behavior." In *Anomie and Deviant Behavior*, edited by Marshall Clinard. New York: Free Press of Glencoe, 1964.

Cobble, Sue. "The Redeeming of the Prostitute: A Study in the Extension of Women's Morality, 1907–1917." Paper, Stanford University, 1975.

Coleman, Kate. "Carnal Knowledge: A Portrait of Four Hookers." *Ramparts* 10:6 (December 1971).

Cominos, Peter T. "Late Victorian Sexual Respectability and the Social System." *International Review of Social History* 8 (1963): 18–48.

Connelly, Mark Thomas. "Prostitution, Venereal Disease, and Married Women: Medical Opinion in the U.S., 1900–1920." Paper presented at the Berkshire Conference on the History of Women, Spring 1976.

———. *The Response to Prostitution in the Progressive Era.* Chapel Hill: University of North Carolina Press, 1980.

Davis, Henry. *Moral and Pastoral Theology.* Vol. 4. 7th ed., rev. and enl. London: Sheed, 1958.

Davis, Kingsley. "Sexual Behavior." In *Contemporary Social Problems*, edited by Robert K. Merton and Robert A. Nisbet. New York: Harcourt, Brace and World, 1961.

———. "The Sociology of Prostitution." *American Sociology Review* 2:5 (1937).

Degler, Carl. "What Ought to Be and What Was: Women's Sexuality in the Nineteenth Century." *American Historical Review* 79, no. 5 (December 1975): 1476–90.

Deutsch, Helene. *Psychology of Women.* Vol. 1. London: Grune and Stratton, 1940.

Ditzion, Sidney. *Marriage, Morals, and Sex in America.* New York: Bookman Associates, 1953.

Douglas, Mary. *Natural Symbols: Explorations in Cosmology.* New York: Pantheon, 1970.

———. *Purity and Danger: An Analysis of Concepts of Pollution and Taboo.* Baltimore: Penguin, 1970.

DuBois, W.E.B. *Black Reconstruction in America.* New York: Meridian, 1964.

Ellis, Albert. "Why Married Men Visit Prostitutes." *Sexology* 25 (1959): 344–47.

Escobar, Gayle. "The Protection of Virtue: Women as Citizens." Paper, University of California at Riverside, 1979.

Evans, Richard J. "Prostitution, State, and Society in Imperial Germany." *Past and Present* 70 (1976): 106–29.

Feinman, Clarice. "Separate Penal Institutions for Women: Who Benefited?" Paper, Trenton State College, 1975.

Feldman, Egal. "Prostitution, the Alien Woman, and the Progressive Imagination, 1910–1915." *American Quarterly* 30 (Summer 1967): 192–206.

Felt, Jeremy P. "Vice Reform as a Political Technique: The Committee of Fifteen in New York, 1900–1901." *New York History* 54 (1973): 24–51.

Flaherty, David. "Law and Enforcement of Morals in Early America." *Perspectives in American History* 5 (1971).

Foucault, Michel. *The History of Sexuality.* Vol. 1. *An Introduction.* Translated by R. Hurley. New York: Pantheon, 1978.

Friedman, Estelle. *Their Sisters' Keepers: Women's Prison Reform in America, 1830–1930.* Ann Arbor: University of Michigan Press, 1981.

Gans, Herbert. *The Urban Villagers*. New York: Free Press, 1962.

Gentry, Curt. *The Madams of San Francisco*. New York: Ballantine, 1964.

Gibbens, T.C.N. "Juvenile Prostitution." *British Journal of Delinquency* 8 (July 1957): 3–12.

Glover, Edward. "The Psychopathology of Prostitution." In *Roots of Crime*, edited by Franz Alexander and William Healy. London: Imago, 1960.

Glueck, Eleanor, and Glueck, Sheldon. *Five Hundred Delinquent Women*. New York: Knopf, 1954.

Goffman, Erving. *Asylums*. New York: Anchor, 1961.

———. *Stigma: Notes on the Management of Spoiled Identity*. Englewood Cliffs, N.J.: Prentice-Hall, 1963.

Gordon, Linda. "Voluntary Motherhood: The Beginnings of Feminist Birth Control Ideas in the United States." In Hartman and Banner, *Clio's Consciousness Raised: New Perspectives on the History of Women*.

———. *Woman's Body, Woman's Right: A Social History of Birth Control in America*. New York: Penguin, 1977.

Gorham, Deborah. "The 'Maiden Tribute of Modern Babylon' Re-Examined: Child Prostitution and the Idea of Childhood in Late Victorian England." *Victorian Studies* 21 (1978): 353–79.

Gray, James. *Red Lights on the Prairies*. Toronto: Macmillan, 1971.

Greenwald, Harold. *The Call Girl: A Social and Psychoanalytic Study*. New York: Ballantine, 1958.

Gusfield, Joseph. "Moral Passage: The Symbolic Process in Public Designations of Deviance." *Social Problems* 15, no. 12 (Fall 1967).

———. *Symbolic Crusade: Status Politics and the American Temperance Movement*. Urbana: University of Illinois Press, 1963.

Haber, Samuel. *Efficiency and Uplift: Management in the Progressive Era, 1890–1920*. Chicago: University of Chicago Press, 1964.

Haller, John S., Jr., and Haller, Robin M. *The Physician and Sexuality in Victorian America*. Urbana: University of Illinois Press, 1974.

Haller, M., and Haller, W. "The Puritan Art of Love." *Huntington Library Quarterly* 5, no. 2 (January 1942).

Haller, Mark H. *Eugenics: Hereditary Attitudes in American Thought*. New Brunswick, N.J.: Rutgers University Press, 1963.

———. "Historical Roots of Police Behavior: Chicago, 1890–1925." *Law and Society Review* 10, no. 2 (Winter 1976).

———. "Organized Crime in Urban Society: Chicago in the Twentieth Century." *Journal of Social History* 5, no. 2 (Winter 1971/72).

———. "Urban Crime and Criminal Justice: The Chicago Case." *Journal of American History* 57, no. 3 (December 1970).

———. "Urban Vice and Civic Reform: Chicago in the Early Twentieth Century." In *Cities in American History*, edited by Kenneth T. Jackson and Stanley K. Schultz. New York: Knopf, 1972.

Hartman, Mary S., and Banner, Lois W., eds. *Clio's Consciousness Raised: New Perspectives on the History of Women*. New York: Harper & Row, 1974.

Hass, Paul H. "Sin in Wisconsin: The Teasdale Vice Committee of 1913." *Wisconsin Magazine of History* 49 (1965): 138–51.

Hays, Samuel P. *The Response to Industrialism, 1885–1914.* Chicago: University of Chicago Press, 1957.

Hayward, C. *The Courtesan.* London, 1926.

Henriques, Fernando. *Prostitution and Society.* 3 vols. London: MacGibbon and Kee, 1962, 1963, 1968.

Higham, John. *Strangers in the Land: Patterns of American Nativism, 1860–1925.* New York: Atheneum, 1963.

Hirata, Lucy Cheng. "Free, Enslaved, and Indentured Workers in Nineteenth-Century Chinese Prostitution." *Signs* 5 (Fall 1979).

Hobson, Barbara. "Seduced and Abandoned: A Tale of a Wicked City—The Response to Prostitution in Boston, 1820–1860." Paper presented at the Fourth Berkshire Conference on the History of Women, August 1978.

Hofstadter, Richard. *The Age of Reform.* New York: Knopf, 1955.

———. *Anti-Intellectualism in American Life.* New York: Vintage, 1963.

———. *The Paranoid Style in American Politics and Other Essays.* New York: Vintage, 1967.

Hofstadter, Richard, and Wallace, Michael, eds. *American Violence: A Documentary History.* New York: Knopf, 1970.

Holmes, Kay Ann. "Reflections by Gaslight: Prostitution in Another Age." *Issues in Criminology* 7:1 (1972): 83–101.

Jackman, Norman R., and O'Toole, Richard. "The Self Image of the Prostitute." *Sociological Quarterly* 4:2 (1963).

James, Jennifer. *The History of Prostitution Laws.* Pamphlet. Social Sciences Research Associates, Seattle, 1975.

Jensen, Richard. "Family, Career, and Reform: Women Leaders of the Progressive Era." In *The Family in Social-Historical Perspective*, edited by Michael Gordon. New York: St. Martin's, 1973.

Johnson, Claudia D. "That Guilty Third Tier: Prostitution in Nineteenth-Century American Theaters." *American Quarterly* 27:5 (1975): 575–84.

Johnson, Robbie Davis. "Folklore and Women: A Social Interactionist Analysis of the Folklore of a Texas Madam." *Journal of American Folklore* 86:341 (July–September 1973): 211–25.

Kellogg, Pamela Parkinson. "The Sporting Life: Prostitution in America at the Turn of the Century." Senior thesis, Radcliffe College, 1974.

Kent, Robert, and Dingemans, Dennis. "Prostitution and the Police: Patroling the Stroll in Sacramento." *Police Chief* 14:9 (September 1977).

Khalaf, Samir. *Prostitution in a Changing Society: A Sociological Survey of Legal Prostitution in Beirut.* Beirut: Khayats, 1965.

Kinsey, A. C.; Pomeroy, W. B.; and Martin, C. E. *Sexual Behavior in the Human Male.* Philadelphia: W. B. Saunders, 1948.

Klein, Alice, and Roberts, Wayne. "Besieged Innocence: The 'Problem' and the Problems of Working Women—Toronto, 1896–1914." In *Women at Work: Ontario, 1850–*

1930, edited by Janice Acton, Penny Goldsmith, and Bonnie Shepard, pp. 211–60. Toronto: Canadian Women's Educational Press, 1974.

Kraditor, Aileen. *Ideas of the Women's Suffrage Movement*. New York: Columbia University Press, 1963.

Lemert, Edwin. "Social Structure, Social Control, and Deviation." In *Anomie and Deviant Behavior*, edited by Marshall Clinard. New York: Free Press of Glencoe, 1964.

Lubove, Roy. "The Progressives and the Prostitute." *Historian* 24 (1962): 308–30.

McBride, Teresa. *The Domestic Revolution: The Modernization of Household Services in England and France, 1820–1920*. New York: Holmes & Meier, 1976.

McGovern, James R. "The American Woman's Pre–World War I Freedom in Manners and Morals." *Journal of American History* 55 (1968): 315–33.

MacPhail, Elizabeth C. "When the Red Lights Went Out in San Diego: The Little Known Story of San Diego's 'Restricted' District." *Journal of San Diego History* 20 (1975): 1–28.

Marcus, Steven. *The Other Victorians: A Study of Sexuality and Pornography in Mid-Nineteenth-Century England*. New York: Basic, 1966.

Mauer, David. "Prostitutes and Criminal Argots." *American Journal of Sociology* 44:4 (January 1939).

Matza, David. *Becoming Deviant*. Englewood Cliffs, N.J.: Prentice-Hall, 1969.

May, Geoffrey. "Prostitution." *Encyclopedia of the Social Sciences*, vol. 12. New York: Macmillan, 1933.

May, Henry F. *The End of American Innocence: A Study of the First Years of Our Own Time, 1912–1917*. New York: Knopf, 1957.

Merton, Robert. *Social Theory and Social Structure*. New York: Free Press, 1968.

Millett, Kate. *The Prostitution Papers*. New York: Ballantine, 1976.

Millman, Marcia. "The History of the Sociology of Prostitution." Paper presented at the Second Berkshire Conference on the History of Women, October 1974.

Milner, Christina, and Milner, Richard. *Black Players*. Boston: Little, Brown, 1972.

Mohl, Raymond. *Poverty in New York, 1783–1825*. New York: Oxford University Press, 1971.

Murtagh, John M., and Harris, Sarah. *Cast the First Stone*. New York: McGraw-Hill, 1957.

Niemoeller, Adolph F. *Sexual Slavery in America*. New York: Panurge Press, 1935.

O'Neill, William. "Divorce in the Progressive Era." *American Quarterly* 17, no. 2, pt. 1 (Summer 1965):1.

———. *Divorce in the Progressive Era*. New Haven: Yale University Press, 1967.

———. *The Progressive Years: America Comes of Age*. New York: Dodd, Mead, 1975.

———, ed. *Echoes of Revolt: The Masses, 1911–1917*. Chicago: Quadrangle, 1966.

Perry, Mary Elizabeth. " 'Lost Women' in Early Modern Seville: The Politics of Prostitution." *Feminist Studies* 4, no. 1 (Feb. 1978): 195–215.

Phillips, Ulrich B. *Life and Labor in the Old South*. Boston: Little, Brown, 1929.

Pivar, David. "Cleansing the Nation: The War on Prostitution, 1917–21." Paper presented at the Southern California Meeting of the American Studies Association, Immaculate Heart College, Los Angeles, May 10, 1975.

―――. *Purity Crusade: Sexual Morality and Social Control, 1868–1900*. Westport, Conn.: Greenwood, 1973.

Quandt, Jean. *From the Small Town to the Great Community*. New Brunswick, N.J.: Rutgers University Press, 1970.

Reckless, Walter C. *Vice in Chicago*. 1933. Reprint. Montclair, N.J.: Patterson-Smith, 1969.

Reitman, Benjamin. *The Second Oldest Profession*. New York: Vanguard, 1931.

Reverby, Susan. "Sex O'Clock in America: Prostitution, White Slavery, the Progressives, and the Jews, 1900–1917." Paper, Cambridge, Mass.

Riegel, Robert E. "Changing American Attitudes towards Prostitution, 1800–1920." *Journal of the History of Ideas* 20 (1968): 437–52.

Roby, Pamela Ann. "Politics and Prostitution: A Case Study of the Formulation, Enforcement, and Judicial Administration of the New York State Penal Laws on Prostitution." Ph.D. dissertation, New York University, 1971.

Roche, Guy. "The Emergence of Militant Prostitution in America: Coyote, a 'Loose Woman's Organization.' " Master's thesis, San Diego State University, 1975.

Rosaldo, Michelle Zimbalist. "Women, Culture, and Society: A Theoretical Overview." Pp. 17–42. In *Women, Culture, and Society*, edited by Michelle Zimbalist Rosaldo and Louise Lamphere. Stanford: Stanford University Press, 1974.

Rose, Al. *Storyville, New Orleans: Being an Authentic, Illustrated Account of the Notorious Red Light District*. University: University of Alabama Press, 1974.

Rosen, Ruth. "Sexism in History." *Journal of Marriage and the Family* 33, no. 3 (August 1971).

―――. "Women in War: The Southern Lady, 1860–1865." Seminar paper, University of California, Berkeley, 1969.

Rosenberg, Charles. "And Heal the Sick: The Hospital and the Patient in Nineteenth-Century America." *Journal of Social History* 10 (1976/77): 428–47.

―――. "Sexuality, Class, and Role in Nineteenth-Century America." *American Quarterly* 24 (1973): 131–53.

―――. "The Therapeutic Revolution: Medicine, Meaning, and Social Change in Nineteenth-Century America." *Perspectives in Biology and Medicine* 20 (1977): 485–506.

Rosenkrantz, Barbara Gutmann. *Public Health and the State: Changing Views in Massachusetts, 1842–1936*. Cambridge: Harvard University Press, 1972.

Rothman, David. *The Discovery of the Asylum: Social Order and Disorder in the New Republic*. Boston: Little, Brown, 1971.

Rottenberg, Lori. "The Wayward Worker: Toronto's Prostitute at the Turn of the Century." In *Women at Work: Ontario, 1850–1930*, edited by Janice Acton, Penny Goldsmith, and Bonnie Shepard, pp. 37–70. Toronto: Canadian Women's Educational Press, 1974.

Ryan, Mary. "The Power of Women's Networks: A Case Study of Female Moral Reform in Antebellum America." *Feminist Studies* 5 (Spring 1979): 66–89.

———. *Womanhood in America from Colonial Times to the Present*. New York: New Viewpoints, 1975.

Sandos, James. "Social Problems of the Campaign: Prostitution, Liquor, Opium, and Cocaine with the U.S. Army in Mexico, 1916–1917." Paper. University of California, Berkeley.

Schlossman, Steven, and Wallach, Stephanie. "The Crime of Precocious Sexuality: Female Juvenile Delinquency in the Progressive Era." *Harvard Educational Review* 48:1 (1978).

Schneider, Eric. " 'A Fountain of Corruption': The Female Delinquent in Boston, 1870–1920." Paper presented at the Fourth Berkshire Conference on the History of Women, Mount Holyoke College, South Hadley, Mass., 1978.

Scott, Anne Firor. *The Southern Lady: From Pedestal to Politics, 1830–1930*. Chicago: University of Chicago Press, 1970.

Scott, George. *History of Prostitution*. London: T. Werner Laurie, 1936.

———. *Ladies of Vice: A History of Prostitution from Antiquity to the Present Day*. London: Tallis Press, 1968.

Scott, Joan, and Tilly, Louise. "Women's Work and the Family in Nineteenth-Century Europe." *Comparative Studies in Society and History* 17 (1978).

Shade, William G. " 'A Mental Passion': Female Sexuality in Victorian America." *International Journal of Women's Studies* (Canada) 1 (1978): 13–29.

Shannon, William. *The American Irish*. New York: Macmillan, 1964.

Shaw, George Bernard. *Plays Unpleasant: "Widowers' Houses," "The Philanderer," and "Mrs. Warren's Profession."* Baltimore: Penguin, 1961.

Sherwin, Robert. "Laws on Sex Crimes." *Encyclopedia of Sexual Behavior*, edited by Albert Ellis and Albert Abarbanel. New York: Hawthorn Books, 1961.

Showalter, Elaine. "The Great Scourge: *Fin de Siècle* Feminists and Venereal Disease." Paper presented at the Berkshire Conference on the History of Women, June 1976.

Shumsky, Neil Larry. "The Municipal Clinic of San Francisco: A Study in Medical Structure." *Bulletin of the History of Medicine* 52 (1978): 542–59.

———. "San Francisco's Municipal Clinic: A Re-examination of Prostitutes and Progressives." Dept. of History, Virginia Polytechnic Institute & State University.

Siegel, Nancy. "Prostitution on the Western Frontier, 1848–90." Seminar paper, University of California, Berkeley, 1973.

Sigsworth, E. M., and Wyke, T. J. "A Study of Victorian Prostitution and Venereal Disease." In *Suffer and Be Still: Women in the Victorian Age*, edited by Martha Vicinus. Bloomington: Indiana University Press, 1972.

Slovenko, Ralph. *Sexual Behavior and the Law*. Springfield, Ill.: Thomas, 1965.

Smith, Brian Sutton. *Child Psychology*. New York: Appleton-Croft, 1973.

Smith, Daniel Scott. "The Dating of the American Sexual Revolution: Evidence and Interpretation." In *The American Family in Social-Historical Perspective*, edited by Michael Gordon. New York: St. Martin's, 1973.

Smith-Rosenberg, Carroll. "Beauty, the Beast, and the Militant Woman: A Case Study in Sex Roles and Social Stress in Jacksonian America." *American Quarterly* 23 (1971): 562–84.

————. "Puberty to Menopause: The Cycle of Femininity in Nineteenth-Century America." In *Clio's Consciousness Raised: New Perspectives on the History of Women*, edited by Mary Hartman and Lois Banner.

————. *Religion and the Rise of the American City: The New York City Mission Movement, 1812–1870*. Ithaca: Cornell University Press, 1971.

Smith-Rosenberg, Carroll, and Rosenberg, Charles. "The Female Animal: Medical and Biological Views of Woman and Her Role in Nineteenth-Century America." *Journal of American History* 110 (1973): 332–56.

Smuts, Robert W. *Women and Work in America*. New York: Schocken, 1971.

Sochen, June. *The New Woman in Greenwich Village, 1910–20*. New York: Quadrangle, 1972.

Stage, Sarah J. "Out of the Attic: Studies of Victorian Sexuality." *American Quarterly* 27 (1975): 480–85.

Stead, William. *If Christ Came to Chicago*. New York: Living Books, 1964.

Swatos, William, and Kline, Judith. "The Lady Is Not a Whore." *International Journal of Women's Studies* 1:2 (March-April 1978).

Thomas, Keith. "The Double Standard." *Journal of the History of Ideas* 20 (1959): 195–216.

Trudgill, Eric. *Madonnas and Magdalens: The Origins and Development of Victorian Sexual Attitudes*. New York: Holmes & Meier, 1976.

Vicinus, Martha, ed. *A Widening Sphere: Changing Roles of Victorian Women*. Bloomington: Indiana University Press, 1977.

Wagner, Roland. "Virtue against Vice: A Study of Moral Reformers and Prostitutes in the Progressive Era." Ph.D. dissertation, University of Wisconsin, 1971.

Walkowitz, Judith K. "The Making of an Outcast Group." In *A Widening Sphere: Changing Roles of Victorian Women*, edited by Martha Vicinus.

————. *Prostitution and Victorian Society: Women, Class, and the State*. Cambridge: Cambridge University Press, 1980.

————. " 'We Are Not Beasts of the Field': Prostitution and the Campaign against the Contagious Diseases Acts, 1869–1886." In *Clio's Consciousness Raised: New Perspectives on the History of Women*, edited by Mary Hartman and Lois Banner.

Washburn, Charles. *Come into My Parlor: A Biography of the Aristocratic Everleigh Sisters of Chicago*. 1934. Reprint. New York: Arno, 1974.

Waterman, Willoughby Cyrus. *Prostitution and Its Repression in New York City, 1900–1931*. New York: Columbia University Press, 1932.

Weiner, Lynn. "Protecting the City from Sister Carrie: Women Transients and Travelers' Aid in Minneapolis, 1893–1935." Paper presented at the Fourth Berkshire Conference on the History of Women, Mount Holyoke College, South Hadley, Mass., August 1978.

Welter, Barbara. "The Cult of True Womanhood." *American Quarterly* 18 (1966): 151–74.

Whiteaker, Larry Howard. "Moral Reform and Prostitution in New York City, 1830–60." Ph.D. dissertation, Princeton University, 1977.

Wiebe, Robert. *The Search for Order, 1877–1920*. New York: Hill & Wang, 1968.

Williams, Phyllis. *South Italian Folkways in Europe and America*. New Haven: Yale University Press, 1938.

Wilson, Carol Green. *Chinatown Quest*. Stanford: Stanford University Press, 1950.

Wilson, R. Jackson. *In Quest of Community: Social Philosophy in the U.S., 1860–1920*. New York: Wiley, 1968.

Winick, Charles. "A Content Analysis of Orally Communicated Jokes of Prostitutes." *American Imago* 20 (1963): 271–91.

———. "Prostitutes' Clients' Perception of the Prostitutes and of Themselves." *International Journal of Social Psychiatry* 8 (1962): 289–97.

Winick, Charles, and Kinsie, Paul M. *The Lively Commerce: Prostitution in the United States*. Chicago: Quadrangle, 1971.

Wood, Ann Douglas. "The Fashionable Diseases: Women's Complaints and Their Treatment in Nineteenth-Century America." In *Clio's Consciousness Raised: New Perspectives on the History of Women*, edited by Mary Hartman and Lois Banner.

Wood, Stephen B. *Constitutional Politics in the Progressive Era: Child Labor and the Law*. Chicago: University of Chicago Press, 1968.

Wunsch, James L. "Prostitution and Public Policy: From Regulation to Suppression, 1858–1920." Ph.D. dissertation, University of Chicago, 1976.

Wynn, Marcia Rittenhouse. *Desert Bonanza: Story of Early Randsburg Mojave Desert Mining Camp*. Glendale, Calif.: Clark, 1963.

Yellis, Kenneth A. "Prosperity's Child: Some Thoughts on the Flapper." *American Quarterly* 21 (1969): 44–64.

Yinger, J. Walton. "Contra-Culture and Subculture." *American Sociological Review* 25 (October 1960).

Zborouski, Mark, and Herzog, Elizabeth. *Life Is with People*. New York: Schocken, 1967.

INDEX

THE JOHNS HOPKINS UNIVERSITY PRESS

THE LOST SISTERHOOD
Prostitution in
America, 1900–1918
This book was composed in Times Roman text and
Andover display type by The Oberlin Printing Company,
from a design by Susan P. Fillion. It was printed on S. D.
Warrens's 50-lb. Sebago Eggshell paper and bound in Holliston
Roxite A by Universal Lithographers, Inc.